About The Author

Joe Pettitt is a freelance high-performance automotive journalist, photographer, and car-fi guy. He's written hundreds of articles for the performance press including *Hot Rod, Sport Compact Car, Drag Racer, Car Craft, Circle Track*, and *Motor Trend*. His adventures as a high-performance journalist include piloting IROC cars around the famous ovals of Daytona and Talladega and strapping into the world's fastest open road race record holder vehicle as a journalist/passenger. This mind-warping experience offered 27 minutes of sheer terror at over 220 mph while making the 90-mile Silver State Challenge run from Ely to Lund, Nev., with an average speed of over 194 mph. As a car audio journalist he wrote for *Autotronics* magazine, where he indulged his passion for great cars and great music.

An avid do-it-yourselfer, Pettitt modified and tuned numerous sports cars, hot rods, and street machines, installing sound systems in all of them. His favorite was a '59 XK 150 Jag. "I didn't have the most expensive gear in that car," said Pettitt, "but I installed it right and it made wonderful music as it moved swiftly through the turns and twist of the canyons of Southern California. "Every time you build a car," says Pettitt, "you learn something new. You learn how to do it a little smarter and a little easier; you learn how to find the right people to answer your questions. Finding good information isn't easy; but once you have it, it makes your high-performance projects run much smoother."

That's why SA Design had Pettitt write this book — to help you cut through all the marketing hype and get to the truth of the subject. He knows how to find the best experts in the field and get the real high-performance story.

Pettitt currently lives in his own virtual reality in Southern California with wife Patricia, stepdaughter Vanessa, and their baby daughter, Jordan. In addition to this volume, Pettitt has written SA Design's *High Performance Honda Builder's Handbook Vol. 1, How To Install Nitrous Oxide Injection* and *How to Install High-Performance Car Stereos*.

By JOE PETTITT

Back Cover Captions:

Top:
One of the best ways to get more horsepower out of a sport compact's engine is to used forced induction – turbochargers or superchargers. This Greddy turbo system is installed on a 2002 Acura GSR Type S, and includes a TDO5H-18G turbo kit, a Type 31 intercooler, an E-Manage engine management system, a Pro-Fec B-spec electronic boost controller, an Evolution cat-back exhaust, and an Airinx air filter.

Bottom Left:
Done correctly, nitrous oxide is a relatively easy way to boost horsepower on small-displacement 4- and 6-cylinder sport compact engines. This system uses an AEM fuel rail with Nitrous Express nozzles plumbed directly into the intake on an Acura Integra.

Bottom Right:
It's not all about horsepower – most sport compacts can also be made to out-brake and out-corner the competition. This is a rear coil-over conversion and an aftermarket locator bar on a Honda Civic, set up for drag racing.

All text, photographs, drawings, and other artwork (hereafter referred to as information) contained in this publication is sold without any warranty as to its usability or performance. In all cases, original manufacturer's recommendations, procedures, and instructions supersede and take precedence over descriptions herein. Specific component design and mechanical procedures — and the qualifications of individual readers — are beyond the control of the publisher, therefore the publisher disclaims all liability, either expressed or implied, for use of the information in this publication. All risk for its use is entirely assumed by the purchaser/user. In no event will Cartech® Inc., or the author be liable for any indirect, special, or consequential damages, including but not limited to personal injury or any other damages, arising out of the use or misuse of any information in this publication.

This book is an independent publication, and the authors and/or publisher thereof are not in any way associated with, and are not authorized to act on behalf of any of the manufacturers included in this book. The publisher reserves the right to revise this publication or change its content from time to time without obligation to notify any persons of such revisions or changes.

SPORT COMPACT
Bolt-On Performance Guide

Volume I: Imports

By Joe Pettitt

Copyright © 2000 by Joe Pettitt. All rights reserved. All text, illustrations and photographs in this publication are the property of Joe Pettitt, unless otherwise noted or credited. It is unlawful to reproduce or copy in any way — resell, or redistribute this information without the expressed written permission of the author.

EDITED BY
MONICA DWYER ABRESS

Printed in China

PRODUCTION BY
TAMARA BAECHTEL

OVERSEAS DISTRIBUTION BY:

BROOKLANDS BOOKS LTD.
P.O. BOX 146, Cobham, Surrey, KT11 1LG, England
Telephone 01932 865051 • FAX 01932 868803

ISBN 1-884089-52-6
PART No. SA65

BROOKLANDS BOOKS AUSTRALIA
3/37-39 Green Street, Banksmeadow, NSW 2019, Australia
Telephone 2 9695 7055 • FAX 2 9695 7355

CARTECH® INC., 39966 GRAND AVENUE, NORTH BRANCH, MN 55056

CONTENTS

- CHAPTER 1: INTAKE COMPONENTS 4
- AIR FILTERS 4
- COOL AIR INTAKE SYSTEMS 7
- OVERSIZED THROTTLE BODY ASSEMBLIES 13
- INTAKE MANIFOLDS 18
- PORTED HEAD PACKAGES 20

- CHAPTER 2: CAMS, PULLEYS AND VALVETRAINS 24
- CAMS 24
- POWER PULLEYS 28
- TIMING GEARS 29
- VALVES, SPRINGS, RETAINERS 31

- CHAPTER 3: EXHAUST SYSTEM 34
- HEADERS 34
- CAT-BACK EXHAUST SYSTEMS 38
- MUFFLERS 45
- CATALYTIC CONVERTERS 49

- CHAPTER 4: ENGINE MANAGEMENT SYSTEMS AND COMPONENTS 50
- CHIPS, REPROGRAMMED ECUs AND TUNING ELECTRONICS 50
- PROGRAMMABLE ECU INTERFACE DEVICES 54
- STAND ALONE FUEL INJECTION SYSTEMS/COMPONENTS: 56
- AIR FLOW METERS 60
- FUEL INJECTORS 60
- AIR-TO-FUEL RATIO METERS 62
- FUEL INJECTION PUMPS & FUEL FILTERS 63
- VOLTAGE CONTROL UNITS 64
- FUEL INJECTION PRESSURE REGULATORS 64
- FUEL INJECTION SYSTEM INSTALLATION ACCESSORIES 66
- CARBURETORS 66
- FUEL LINES, RAILS, AND FITTINGS 68
- FUEL CELLS 69

- CHAPTER 5: IGNITION 70
- PROGRAMMABLE IGNITION CONTROL 70
- IGNITION AMPS 73
- HIGH PERFORMANCE CAP & COIL KITS 76
- IGNITION CABLES 77
- SPARK PLUGS 80

- CHAPTER 6: BOOSTED PERFORMANCE 82
- TYPES OF NITROUS OXIDE SYSTEMS 82
- SUPERCHARGERS 85
- TURBO KITS 85
- TURBO ASSEMBLIES 89
- WATER INJECTION 94
- TURBO MANIFOLDS 94
- TURBOCHARGER INSTALLATION ACCESSORIES 94
- DOWN PIPES 95
- INTERCOOLERS 96
- WASTEGATES 98
- BLOW-OFF, BY-PASS AND POP-OFF VALVES 99
- TURBO TIMERS 101
- BOOST CONTROLLERS 103
- ADDITIONAL INJECTOR CONTROL 105

- CHAPTER 7: ENGINE RELIABILITY COMPONENTS 106
- REMANUFACTURED ENGINES 106
- BOTTOM END, STROKER KITS 106
- BUILDING RELIABILITY 107
- HIGH PERFORMANCE ENGINE PACKAGES 108
- ENGINE SWAP KITS 109
- RODS 109
- CRANKSHAFTS 110
- PISTONS 110
- FASTENERS 112
- GASKETS 114
- SEALS 114
- LUBRICATION SYSTEM COMPONENTS 115
- OIL PANS 116
- LUBRICATION SYSTEM ACCESSORIES 117
- FLUID LINES, HOSES, AND FITTINGS 118
- VACUUM LINES AND FITTINGS 118
- COOLANT 119
- FANS AND ACCESSORIES 120

- CHAPTER 8: DRIVELINE 122
- SHIFTERS 122
- GEARS 125
- DIFFERENTIALS 125
- GEAR OIL & ADDITIVES 126
- CLUTCH AND PRESSURE PLATES 127
- FLYWHEELS 131
- CONVERTERS 133
- SAFETY-SCATTERSHIELDS, TRANS BLANKETS, ETC. 133
- MOTOR MOUNTS 133

- CHAPTER 9: BRAKES 134
- BRAKE SYSTEMS 134
- ROTORS 138
- BRAKE PADS 138
- BRAKE LINES 140
- ROLL CONTROL 141

- CHAPTER 10: SUSPENSION 142
- HANDLING KITS 142
- ANTI-SWAY BARS 143
- SHOCK TOWER BRACES 146
- LOWER TIE BARS 146
- CAMBER & CASTOR ADJUSTMENT COMPONENTS 147
- BUSHINGS 149
- SHOCKS 150
- STREET SPRINGS 155

- CHAPTER 11: WHEELS & TIRES 158
- DRAG RACING TIRES 158
- HIGH PERFORMANCE STREET TIRES 158
- WHEEL & TIRE ACCESSORIES 166

- CHAPTER 12: SOURCE GUIDE 168

Sport Compact Bolt-On Performance Guide Volume 1
Intake Components

AIR FILTERS

APEX INTEGRATION

The Apex Integration Super Intake is the premier air filter system using a dual funnel technology. The air filter is made of an unrestricted race quality element and has one funnel at the top of the filter and one funnel at the base.

Apex Integration engineers noticed in tests that when the vehicle sucked in air from the side, an area of wind turbulence occurred in the middle of the filter. To cure this problem, a funnel at the top of the filter was added to channel the air down to the base of the filter. A separate funnel at the base of the filter ensured the smooth transition of air from the atmosphere into the intake pipe.

Both funnels are constructed of a high-quality polished SUS 304 stainless steel and the craftsmanship found only in Apex Integration products.

Part #	Application
502-H005	1996-1999 Civic Coupe EX / Si
501-M001	1995-1998 Eclipse
502-H004	1994-1998 Integra, all except Type-R
502-Z001	1990-1993 Miata
502-Z002	1994-1997 Miata
501-T007	1991-1995 MR-2
501-Z001	1993-1995 RX-7
501-Z002	1986-1992 RX-7
501-T001	1986-1992 Supra
501-KN01	1995-1998 240 SX
500-A001	Universal (Filter Only)

AROSPEED

New Arospeed Monster Flow Filters, aka Heat Shield Filters, feature funnel technology which collects cold air and funnels it through the intake. This allows more air to flow into your engine, thus increasing horsepower. Plus, the heat shield keeps hot air from entering your intake pipe, giving you cooler air. Flow filters are available in red, yellow, black, and blue and come with brackets.

Arospeed Air Filters are available in silver, red, blue, gold, purple, yellow, and black.

Velocity stack filters are also available.

CHIKARA

Chikara by TD Performance renewable cotton filter elements are direct replacements for Chikara Air intakes. Made from natural cotton fibers and come pre-oiled. Simply wash and re-oil the filter according to the instructions and these filters will probably outlast your sport compact vehicle.

AROSPEED MONSTER FLOW FILTERS			
Part #	Description	Part #	Description
ARO102001	5" Open End — Black 3"	ARO103101	6" Velocity — Black 3" / 4.50"
ARO102002	5" Open End — Blue 3"	ARO103102	6" Velocity — Blue 3" / 4.50"
ARO102004	5" Open End — Purple 3"	ARO103014	6" Velocity — Purple 3" / 4.50"
ARO102005	5" Open End — Red 3"	ARO103105	6" Velocity — Red 3" / 4.50"
ARO102007	5" Open End — Yellow 3"	ARO103107	6" Velocity — Yellow 3" / 4.50"
ARO102013	5" Open End — Silver 3"	ARO104001	Heat Shield — Black 3"
ARO103001	5" Velocity — Black 3" / 4.50"	ARO104002	Heat Shield — Blue 3"
ARO103002	5" Velocity — Blue 3" / 4.50"	ARO104005	Heat Shield — Red 3"
ARO103004	5" Velocity — Purple 3" / 4.50"	ARO104007	Heat Shield — Yellow 3"
ARO103005	5" Velocity — Red 3" / 4.50"	ARO103501	7" closed-end opening Silver 3.5"
ARO103007	5" Velocity — Yellow 3" / 4.50"	ARO103502	9" closed-end opening Silver 3.5"
ARO103013	5" Velocity — Silver 3" / 4.50"		

GREDDY AIRINX Air Filter

Part #	Description
12500002	AIRINX AX-M Filter (Large)
12500001	AIRINX AX-S Filter (Small)
12900002	Replacement Filter Element AX-M
12900001	Replacement Filter Element AX-S
RX-7 T/T	Call Greddy for information

AIRINX Air Filter Kits

Part #	Application
12550103	1990-93 Acura Integra
12550108	1990-93 Honda Accord
12550109	1994-97 Honda Accord
12550105	1993-96 Honda Prelude, VTEC
12540101	1990-93 Mazda Miata 1.6 L
12540102	1994-96 Mazda Miata 1.8 L
12530304	1995-98 Mitsubishi Eclipse, turbo
12510319	1995-97 Toyota RAV-4

AIRINX Adapters

Part #	Application
525113	1994-98 Acura Integra GS-R
525353	1990-93 Acura Integra LS/RS
525356	1992-95 Honda Civic EX/Si/DX
12552005	1992-96 Honda Prelude, VTEC
12542101	1987-89 Mazda RX-7
12542102	1990-92 Mazda RX-7
12522109	1991-96 Nissan 300 ZX T/T
125121100	1990-96 Toyota MR-2, turbo
12512101	1987-92 Toyota Supra, turbo
12512113	1993-97 Toyota Supra, twin turbo
12500101	Universal Adapter 60mm
12500132	Universal Adapter 70mm
12500131	Universal Adapter 80mm
12500102	Universal Adapter 80mm
12500133	Universal Adapter 100mm

K&N FILTERCHARGER® REPLACEMENT AIR FILTER

CHIKARA AIR INTAKES

Part # Chrm	Red	Blue	Application
5750	5751	5752	1990-93 Acura Integra (3" neck)
5750	5751	5752	1994-98 Acura Integra RS / LS (3" neck)
5750	5751	5752	1994-98 Acura Integra GSR (3" neck)
5750	5751	5752	1995-98 Dodge NEON (3" neck)
5750	5751	5752	1990-93 Honda Accord (3" neck)
5750	5751	5752	1994-97 Honda Accord (3" neck)
5750	5751	5752	1988-91 Honda Civic (3" neck)
5750	5751	5752	1992-95 Honda Civic (3" neck)
5750	5751	5752	1996-98 Honda Civic EX (3" neck)
5750	5751	5752	1996-98 Honda Civic LX / DX / CX (3" neck)
5750	5751	5752	1992-96 Honda Prelude (3" neck)
5750	5751	5752	1997-98 Honda Prelude (3" neck)
5750	5751	5752	1995-98 Mitsubishi Eclipse, non-turbo (3" neck)
5753	5754	5755	1995-98 Mitsubishi Eclipse, turbo (114mm neck)

When it was first developed in 1962, the K&N Filtercharger® was a true design breakthrough in air filtration technology. Today, it still is because K&N's Filtercharger® can actually double air flow, which, in turn, adds extra horsepower.

The secret lies in the K&N Filtercharger®'s unique design. Conventional filters use paper or foam material permeated with millions of tiny, irregular passages, that screen dirt particles out of the air. Because the dirt particles are trapped inside the passages, they eventually clog. When this occurs, airflow restriction increases dramatically.

With the Filtercharger®, a special cotton fabric is sandwiched between the pleated aluminum screen wires. The pleated design provides five times more filtering surface over the element circumference. The cotton/screen wire filter media is then saturated with a formulated air filter oil.

Acting like a fluid curtain, this oil attracts particles of dirt and debris which build up on the outside of the filter. This buildup of dirt particles suspended in oil creates more and more irregular passages that actually create an additional filtering barrier with use. Not until very fine particles close this secondary "filter layer" does the filtercharger begin to clog.

In most cases, up to 1/8" of dust can cover a Filtercharger® before performance is significantly affected. On a street-driven vehicle, a Filtercharger® can last up to 50,000 miles before service is required. Then, because it's made of reusable materials, you can just clean it, apply fresh K&N Filter Oil, and re-install. Of course, K&N has developed biodegradable cleaning products designed to effectively clean the filter without harming the environment through the absence of fluorocarbons.

More air flow, increased horsepower, long-lasting performance — even after 35 years, the K&N Filtercharger® is still on the cutting edge of air filtration technology.

NEUSPEED® P-FLO

Snap-on factory type airpump hose connector for the new Beetle & Audi TT P-Flo.

Part #	Application
65.10.87	2000 Audi TT 1.8t
65.10.87	1999+ VW Beetle 1.8t

BLITZ BLACK POWER AIR FILTER

Blitz Black Power Air Filter is designed to fit inside the factory air box. This eliminates the hassle of removing your stock air box. Flow Bench tests show the Black Power Air Filter not only improves filtration and air flow, it minimizes pressure drop. The filter is made from a triple density foam element to assure the maximum filtration and air flow. The unit is washable and re-usable.

RACING SPORTS AKIMOTO AIR FILTER ACTIVATOR KIT WITH MRP ACTIVATION™

Racing Sports Akimoto utilizes a new oil technology. This filter care system utilizes "MRP Activation" to reportedly bond the filter oil to the filter element reducing the amount of oil necessary to achieve an even coat. MRP (Magnetic Resonance Pattern) Activation realigns the molecular structure of a specific product. It is said to take the positive and negative charges found in the atoms and cause them to flow in a more organized pattern. Because of the altered flow pattern, they attach themselves to the charges of the surfaces in a more uniform manner with fewer tendencies to clump or cluster. The oil is blended with special additives during the MRP Activation process resulting in a superior filter treatment. This system, although originally designed and tested on the Funnel Ram III kits, is now available for use on all washable and reusable filters. Now you can activate any reusable filter with the Air Filter Activator Kit.

Part # AFA991   Air Filter Activation Kit

JACKSON RACING'S DUAL-STAGE AIR FILTER

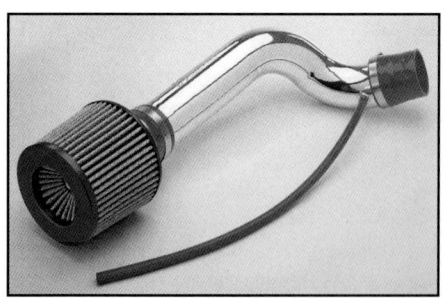

This filter is a direct replacement for the stock unit. It is made of two different types of pre-oiled foam. The unique design allows the engine to breathe through a flat panel of foam instead of the turbulent and restrictive wafered original-equipment style of air filter. It

TURBOCHARGER AIR FILTERSS

Part #	Connection Size	Power Rating	Length	D1	D2
30330	2", 2.25"	325 HP	6"	5.5"	4.63"
30330	Fits T2 / T25 / T3	325 HP	6"	5.5"	4.63"
30333-1	2.75", and 3"	400 HP	6"	6"	4.63"
30333-2	Fits TO4B / TO4E	625 HP	9"	6"	4.63"
30333-3		850 HP	12"	6"	4.63"
30334-1	4"	625 HP	9"	6"	4.63"
30334-2	Fits 60-1, 62-1, 68-1	850 HP	12"	6"	4.63"
30334-3	T-Series	1000 HP	14"	6"	4.63"

is easily cleaned and carries a lifetime warranty. You can expect a performance increase of 3 hp.

Part #	Description
901-975	1990-1997 Dual-Stage Filter
901-976	1999 Dual-Stage Filter

JACKSON FILTER CLEANING KIT

Keep your dual-stage air filter in top condition. Cleaning kits for cotton-gauze filters (like K&N) will not work with foam filters.

Part # 901-970   Foam Filter Cleaning Kit

JAMEX

The Jamex sports air filters ease the air flow "within" your car, resulting in an increase of both the horsepower and the torque. The washable filters also improve fuel economy and provide a sporty "sound." This is the most economical way to give your car more power!

Power sock sports filter from Jamex is the universal sports air filter for virtually all carburetors with inlet trumpets. A unique internal coil spring keeps the filter perfectly in place. The filter can be shortened, if necessary, and is easy to clean.

TURBOCHARGER AIR FILTERS

Turbonetics offers a select lineup of K&N air filters specifically intended for turbocharger applications. To protect your investment, K&N manufactures some of the highest-quality air filters available. These highly-efficient air filters can be cleaned and are backed by K&N's million-mile warranty, a perfect addition to your high performance engine.

WEAPON*R USA

V2 Hyper Filter
3" Mouth/ 5" Tall/ 6" Wide Base/ 5" Wide Top/ 4" Top Velocity Stack

Part#	Color
V2BL	BLACK
V2RD	RED
V2BU	BLUE
V2YL	YELLOW
V2PL	PURPLE
V2GR	GREEN
V2OR	ORANGE

V2 SHORTY FILTER

3" Mouth/ 4" Tall/ 6" Wide Base/ 5" Wide Top/ 4" Top Velocity Stack

Part#	Color
2BLS	BLACK
V2RDS	RED
V2BUS	BLUE
V2YLS	YELLOW
V2PLS	PURPLE
V2GRS	GREEN
V2ORS	ORANGE

V2 HYPER FILTER

4.25" Mouth/ 5" Tall/ 6" Wide Base/ 5" Wide Top/ 4" Top Velocity Stack

Part#	Color
V2ECBL	BLACK
V2ECRD	RED
V2ECBU	BLUE
V2ECYL	YELLOW

JIM WOLF TECHNOLOGY POP-CHARGER

1990-1995 300ZX POP-Charger

POP-Charger air filters are designed for maximum air flow by using a 6" diameter venturi surrounded by an oiled gauze filter element. The filter element is reusable after cleaning and reapplying filter oil. Horsepower increases from 4 hp on nonturbos to 18 hp on the 300ZXTT are typical. Available for most late-model Nissans.

POP-Charger aluminum venturis are made from lightweight cast aluminum and CNC machined to ensure a quality fit. Special bolt patterns can be requested.

DUAL POP-CHARGER

1990-1995 300ZX TT Dual POP-Charger System

This system is a must for cars intending to make 450 hp or more. By moving the Mass Air Flow (MAF) sensor to one side of the engine and adding a second POP-Charger, the precision of a MAF sensor is maintained and the air flow capacity is doubled! An added benefit is a quicker turbo spool-up due to the elimination of flow disturbance caused by the stock rubber t-hose. This system requires a special ECU program that is included (in exchange for your previous JWT EPROM).

LC ENGINEERING K&N FILTERCHARGER

K&N has built the best high-performance air filter for years. But the new K&N FilterCharger Injection Performance Kit takes performance to a new level. The FIPK replaces the restrictive factory air box with a free-flowing intake system that flows over 40% more air than the factory set-up. More air means more efficient combustion, and more power! Plus, the FIPK includes the famous K&N FilterCharger Air Filter, featuring a million-mile warranty.

Dyno proven to increase torque and horsepower. Offers easy, bolt-on installation and features the washable / reusable FilterCharger Air Filter. Kit includes cleaner and filter oil. Includes K&N's 10 year / million-mile warranty. Street Legal in 50 States.

Part # 16-579008 K&N FilterCharger Injection Performance Kit

OBX FILTERS

OBX PREMIUM FILTERS

Part #	Description
9980PSC	OBX Premium Filter 3.0" Opening Chrome
9980PSR	OBX Premium Filter 3.0" Opening Red
9980PSB	OBX Premium Filter 3.0" Opening Blue
9980PSY	OBX Premium Filter 3.0" Opening Yellow
867700C	OBX Premium Filter 4.5" Opening Chrome
867700R	OBX Premium Filter 4.5" Opening Red
867700B	OBX Premium Filter 4.5" Opening Blue
867700Y	OBX Premium Filter 4.5" Opening Yellow

OBX STAINLESS STEEL FILTER

Part #	Description
6280	OBX Super Charge Competition Stainless Filter 3.0"

OBX SUPER CHARGE COMPETITION FILTER

Part #	Description
6280SCC	Super Charge Competition Filter Chrome
6280SCR	Super Charge Competition Filter Red
6280SCB	Super Charge Competition Filter Blue
6280SCY	Super Charge Competition Filter Yellow

COOL AIR INTAKE SYSTEMS

AEM COLD AIR INTAKES

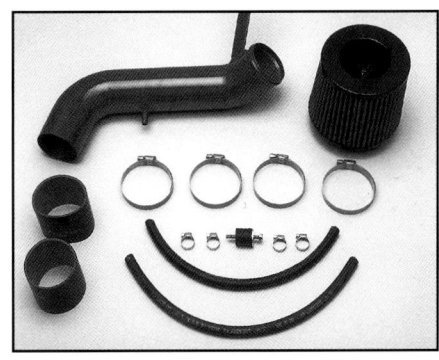

Air mass flow to the engine is increased due to reduced inlet temperature. Lower air temperature results in increased air density, creating more horsepower at the point of ignition. All AEM cold air systems are lightweight aluminum and powder coated for superior heat insulation. This extra process helps seal out engine compartment heat, preventing it from invading the air inlet flow.

AEM COLD AIR INTAKES

Application	Cold Air*	Short Ram**
ACURA		
1990-1993 Integra, all	21-402	22-402
1994-1999 Integra, non-VTEC	21-403	22-403
1994-1999 Integra, VTEC	21-404	22-404
1997-1998 Integra, Type R	21-412	N/A
HONDA		
1990-1993 Accord	21-407	22-407
1994-1997 Accord, 4 cyl.	21-408	22-408
1998-1999 Accord, 4 cyl.	21-415	22-415
1998-1999 Accord, V-6	21-416	22-416
1988-1991 Civic/CRX EX/Si	21-400	22-400
1992-1995 Civic EX, DX, Si	21-401	22-401
1996-1998 Civic EX	21-409	22-409
1996-1998 Civic DX	21-413	22-413
1999 Civic EX	21-414	22-414
1999 Civic Si DOHC	21-417	22-417
1993-1997 del Sol SOHC	21-401	22-401
1993-1997 del Sol DOHC	21-411	22-411
1992-1996 Prelude	21-405	22-405
1997-1999 Prelude	21-406	22-406
DODGE/PLYMOUTH		
Neon SOHC, 5-speed	21-421	N/A
Neon DOHC, 5-speed	21-420	N/A
MITSUBISHI		
1995-1999 Eclipse, non-turbo	21-430	22-430
1995-1999 Eclipse, turbo	21-431	22-431
VOLKSWAGEN/AUDI		
1997-99 Beetle 2.0L	21-460	22-460
1996-1998 Jetta, 4cyl.	21-462	22-462
Passat/A4 1.8L, turbo	21-461	22-461

*Available in Silver Powder Coating.
**When ordering, insert "B" for blue, "C" for clear, or "R" for red after part number to indicate color desired for Short Ram Intake System.

AMERICAN PRODUCTS COMPANY INTIMIDATOR INTAKE

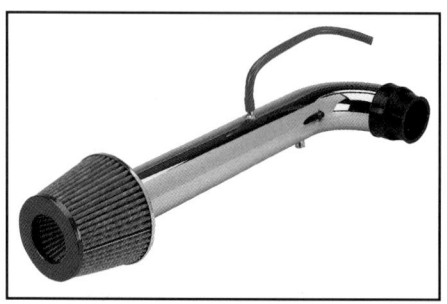

An APEX AIRDYNAMICS Direct Air Filter Kit replaces the standard air filter case. The larger effective surface of the AIRDYNAMICS sports air filter allows the engine to breath better and deeper. The result is improved performance, a perceptibly higher torque and a faster response to pressing the accelerator. Many AIRDYNAMICS Direct Air Filter Kits are supplied with a Cool Air Kit which directs oxygen-rich, cool external air to the engine. As the AIRDYNAMICS Direct Air Filter Kit is already impregnated with a special air filter oil during production, even the smallest dust particles are caught by the filter. AIRDYNAMICS Direct Air Filter Kits offer optimum protection against dirt. The AIRDYNAMICS Direct Air Filter Kit is simple to install, can be cleaned with the special APEX AIR FILTER OIL & CLEANER, and is therefore reusable. AIRDYNAMICS is supplied with a guaranteed service life of one-million kilometers. Available for almost all cars!

AROSPEED

Maintaining constant air flow to the engine is a key part of performance. That is why these intakes are designed around this basis, to allow more airflow than a stock filter and box. Used in combination with an Arospeed filter, they allow the engine to breathe easier, thus allowing the engine to perform better.

DC SPORTS

The DC Sports Direct Air Charger is a surefire way to improve your Honda or Acura with dyno-tested bolt-on performance. Because it takes more than just bending some tube to build a good intake, DC spends countless hours in the R&D department to ensure the parts work as claimed. The Direct Air Charger is constructed of three-inch mandrel bent aircraft quality aluminum tubing with 7-10 horsepower CNC-machined coupler. Exclusive DC Sports filter made by K&N. All hardware and instructions are included along with a two-year warranty.

DC SPORTS MAX AIR INTAKE

As its name implies, the Max Air intake provides your Honda and Acura with the maximum amount of air required by replacing the factory air box with the high flow DC Sports filter. Easy bolt-on installation; 5-6 Horsepower, exclusive DC Sports filter made by K&N. Available in black powder-coated finish with all hardware and instructions included. The Max Air Intake comes with a two-year warranty.

AROSPEED INTAKES

Part #	Application	Color
ACURA		
ARO113402	1990-1993 Integra	Blue
ARO113405	1990-1993 Integra	Red
ARO113406	1990-1993 Integra	Polish
ARO113102	1994+ Integra GSR	Blue
ARO113105	1994+ Integra GSR	Red
ARO113106	1994+ Integra GSR	Polish
ARO113702	1994+ Integra LS	Blue
ARO113705	1994+ Integra LS	Red
ARO113706	1994+ Integra LS	Polish
BMW		
ARO110306	1992-1997 318	Polish
DODGE		
ARO114002	1992-1997 Neon	Blue
ARO114005	1992-1997 Neon	Red
ARO114006	1992-1997 Neon	Polish
HONDA		
ARO110102	1990-1993 Accord	Blue
ARO110105	1990-1993 Accord	Red
ARO110106	1990-1993 Accord	Polish
ARO110402	1994-1997 Accord DX	Blue
ARO110405	1994-1997 Accord DX	Red
ARO110406	1994-1997 Accord DX	Polish
ARO110702	1994-1997 Accord EX	Blue
ARO110705	1994-1997 Accord EX	Red
ARO110706	1994-1997 Accord EX	Polish
ARO111002	1998+ Accord, V-6	Blue
ARO111005	1998+ Accord, V-6	Red
ARO111006	1998+ Accord, V-6	Polish
ARO111302	1988-1991 Civic/CRX	Blue
ARO111305	1988-1991 Civic/CRX	Red
ARO111306	1988-1991 Civic/CRX	Polish
ARO111602	1992-1995 Civic	Blue
ARO111605	1992-1995 Civic	Red
ARO111606	1992-1995 Civic	Polish
ARO111902	1996+ Civic DX	Blue
ARO111905	1996+ Civic DX	Red
ARO111906	1996+ Civic DX	Polish
ARO112202	1996+ Civic EX	Blue
ARO112205	1996+ Civic EX	Red
ARO112206	1996+ Civic EX	Polish
ARO112502	1993-1996 Corolla	Blue
ARO112505	1993-1996 Corolla	Red
ARO112506	1993-1996 Corolla	Polish
ARO112802	1995-1997 Eclipse, non-turbo	Blue
ARO112805	1995-1997 Eclipse, non-turbo	Red
ARO112806	1995-1997 Eclipse, non-turbo	Polish
ARO110606	1996+ Mirage	Polish
ARO114302	1992-1997 Prelude	Blue
ARO114305	1992-1997 Prelude	Red
ARO114306	1992-1997 Prelude	Polish
ARO110206	1997-1998 Prelude	Polish
ARO110506	1993+ Saturn	Polish
ARO114602	1996-1998 Tercel	Blue
ARO114605	1996-1998 Tercel	Red
ARO114606	1996-1998 Tercel	Polish

Arospeed Hi Flow intakes are designed for those who don't want to sacrifice low-end performance from adding an intake. The "chamber" stores cold air which is used at low RPM levels. This in turn increases low-end torque and acceleration, while still having higher horsepower output. It's a perfect application for your everyday driver. There are applications for Acura, Honda, Mitsubishi, and others.

Part #	Application	Color
ARO130106	1990-1993 Accord	Polish
ARO130406	1994-1997 Accord	Polish
ARO131306	1988-1991 Civic/CRX	Polish
ARO131606	1992-1995 Civic	Polish
ARO131906	1996+ Civic DX	Polish
ARO132206	1996+ Civic EX/HX	Polish
ARO133406	1990-1993 Integra	Polish
ARO133106	1994+ Integra GSR	Polish

GREDDY AIRINX II

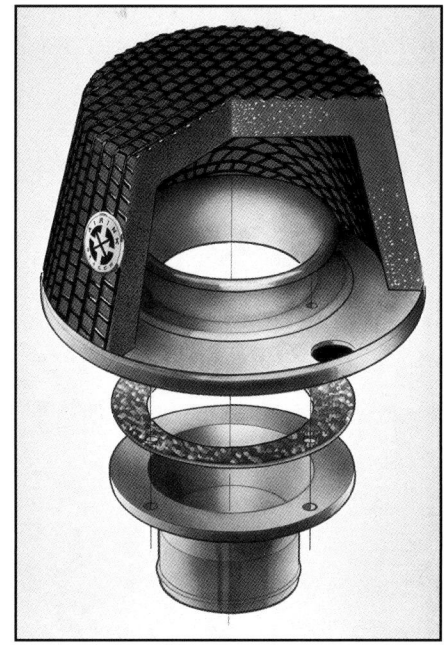

Greddy intake systems are superbly engineered and tastefully designed.

Part #	Application	
12550001	HN-1	Honda/Acura
12550002	HN-2	Honda/Acura
12550003	HN-3	Honda/Acura
12550004	HN-4	Honda/Acura
12550005	HN-5	Honda/Acura
12540001	MZ-1	Mazda
12540002	MZ-2	Mazda
12540003	MZ-3	Mazda
12530001	MT-1	Mitsubishi
12530002	MT-2	Mitsubishi
12530003	MT-3	Mitsubishi
12530005	MT-5	Mitsubishi
12520001	NS-1	Nissan, Infinity, Subaru
12510001	TY-1	Toyota/Lexus
12510003	TY-3	Toyota/Lexus
12510005	TY-5	Toyota/Lexus

HOTSHOT INTAKES

Hotshot Systems intakes not only provide you with added horsepower, but add show-quality polished-chrome finish looks to your engine compartment. Genuine K&N filters top off every intake made by Hotshot. Included with each intake are 3-inch diameter mandrel bent tubing and all necessary couplers and hoses, made of high-grade Silicon.

ELP MAX-FLOW INTAKE FILTER SYSTEMS

The stock air filter's performance is restricted by the shape of its

ELP MAX-FLOW INTAKE FILTER SYSTEMS	
Part #	Application
ACURA	
IS031	1990-1993 Integra
IS017	1994+ Integra
IS003	1994+ Integra GSR
IS3502	1991-1994 NSX
BMW	
IS4038	1984-1985 318I
IS0120	1992-1996 318i/is
IS4049	1995+ 318ti/Z3 1.9 liter
IS4043	1982-1985 325/528e 2.7 liter
IS4031	1986-1991 325i/is/528e
IS4042	1992-1995 325/M3 E-36
IS4047	1996+ 328/M3 E-36
IS4032	1983-1988 533/535I
IS4050	1989-1995 535I
IS4032	1984-1987 633/635
IS4050	1988-1989 635
IS4050	1988-1994 735
IS4040	1987-1991 M3 E-30
IS4048	1987-1989 M6
IS4051	1997+ Z3 2.8 liter
DODGE	
IS1500	1992-1995 Stealth
FORD	
IS2500	1991-1995 Escort GT
HONDA	
IS019	1990-1993 Accord
IS018	1994+ Accord
IS195	1995+ Accord, V-6
IS004	1986-1987 Civic/CRX Si
IS006	1988-1991 Civic/CRX
IS001	1992-1995 Civic/del Sol
IS296	1996+ Civic/del Sol
IS392	1992+ Prelude
MAZDA	
IS5001	1990-1993 Miata 1.6 liter
IS5009	1994+ Miata 1.8 liter
IS2507	1993-1995 MX-6 2.5 liter, V-6
IS5006	1986-1988 RX-7
IS5003	1989-1992 RX-7
IS5930	1993-1995 RX-7, twin turbo
MITSUBISHI	
IS0100	1995+ Eclipse/Talon, turbo
IS1500	1992-1996 3000GT
NISSAN	
IS6000	1989-1993 240SX
IS2800	1975-1983 280Z/280ZX
IS6002	1984-1989 300ZX
IS6001	1990-1995 300ZX
IS2950	1991+ Maxima
IS2910	1991-1993 NX-2000
IS2910	1991+ Sentra SER
SATURN	
IS016	1992+ Twin Cam Engines
TOYOTA	
IS9000	1985-1987 Corolla GTS
IS9010	1985-1989 MR2
IS9001	1990-1995 MR2, inc. turbo
IS9005	1986-1992 Supra
IS9004	1986-1992 Supra, turbo
IS9300	1993+ Supra, twin turbo
VOLKSWAGEN	
IS1056	1990-1992 Corrado G-60
IS1055	1992+ Corrado VR6
IS1057	1993+ Golf/Jetta 111 2.0L
IS1059	1993+ Golf/Jetta 111 VR6
IS1054	1993+ Passat VR6

housing and the filter media itself. The Max-Flow Intake Filter Systems eliminate the factory air box with a semi-conical velocity stack-like filter allowing maximum effective air flow to enter the engine. By allowing the engine to ingest a much larger volume of air, the net result is quicker throttle response and more power through the entire RPM range. Dyno results show a healthy 4-10 horsepower gain depending on make of vehicle. If your engine is supercharged or turbocharged, the power gains can be even greater. These engines are very sensitive to intake air flow.

Each Max-Flow Intake System is designed to exactly replace the OEM factory air box. All necessary mounting hardware, including bolts, hoses, brackets, screws, and nuts are supplied. These systems are true bolt-on do-it-yourself systems.

NOTE: For applications not listed, custom intake systems are available. Contact ELP Motorsport for your year, make, and model of vehicle.

HKS

HKS High Performance Air Filter Systems offer the ultimate in both air filtration and air flow for maximum engine performance. HKS now offers purple replacement filters in addition to chrome and gold Super Mega Flow Cages. The perfect combination of show and GO!

LIGHTSPEED RACING HI-PER FLO INDUCTION

Provide a substantial improvement in air flow for a 4-7 horsepower increase. Finished in bright yellow powdercoat with red throttle sleeve to insulate the air. CARB EO # D-377-8.

Part #	Application
HO3042	1992-1995 Civic
HO3044	1990-1993 Integra
HO3045	1994-1998 Integra
HO3046	1995-1998 Integra, GSR
HO3124	1996-1998 Civic, EX
HO3195	1998-1998 Civic, HX/LX/DX coupe, 4-door hatchback
HO3041	1988-1991 CRX/Civic SI

ICEMAN COOL AIR SYSTEM

From the time it was first introduced, the Iceman Cool Air System has generated a lot of interest both here and abroad, and much discussion relative to its merits. It's one of the most aerodynamically designed systems allowing more air into your engine. Plus its insulated intake increases the mass flow delivered for more power. California Air Resources Board has approved Iceman Cool Air Systems for the following vehicles:

Acura	1990-1996 Integra
Honda	1994-1996 Accord
	1988-1997 Civic
	1993-1995 del Sol
	1992-1995 Prelude
Eagle	1995-1996 Talon
Mitsubishi	1995-1996 Eclipse
Saturn	1995-1999 SOHC
Saturn	1991-1999 DOHC

All other vehicles pending CARB approval:

Honda	1994-1997 Accord
	1994-1997 Accord Street
	1998-1999 Accord I4
	1992-1995 Civic
	1988-1991 Civic SI
	1996-1999 Civic CX DX LX
	1996-1998 Civic EX HX
	1999 Civic EX HX
	1988-1991 CRX
	1993-1995 del Sol
	1996-1997 del Sol
	1997 del Sol Sir
	1992-1996 Prelude
	1992-1996 Prelude Street
	1997-1999 Prelude

KNIGHT ENGINEERING

Iceman Cool Air System

Reportedly good for 3-tenths of a second off of your 1/4-mile times with this incredible ram air system! Knight Engineering, makers of Iceman intakes has developed the Air Force ram air system for the serious competitor. It uses the high air pressure of the headlight area to force more air into your engine. Available for these applications:

ACURA
  1994-1999 GSR
  1994-1999 Integra
  1990-1993 Integra (non-ABS)
CHEVROLET
  1996-1998 Cavalier
DODGE
  1995-1997 Avenger I4
  1995-1999 Neon (manual tran.)
EAGLE
  1995-1997 Talon 2.0 I4
FORD
  1988-1993 Mustang S/C
  1988-1993 Mustang GT
HONDA
  1992-1995 Civic
MITSUBISHI
  1995-1997 Eclipse
PONTIAC
  1996-1998 Grand Am
  1996-1998 Sunfire
SATURN
  1995-1999 Saturn (SOHC)
  1991-1999 Saturn (DOHC)
TOYOTA
  1991-1993 Celica GT
  1996-1998 Tacoma

V-RACING

Big Bang Air Induction System

Big Bang is the latest Air Induction System from V-Racing. Made of heat-dissipating composite material, the Big Bang's Funnel Air design forces cold air in your engine while allowing for better breathing. Complete with performance air filter and mounting hardware, available in red or blue.

Big Bang Funnel Ram Air Induction System

Part #	Application
WS55101B	1992-1995 Honda Civic
WS55101R	1992-1995 Honda Civic
WS55102B	1992-1995 Honda Civic VTEC
WS55102R	1992-1995 Honda Civic VTEC
WS55300B	1996-1998 Honda Civic
WS55300R	1996-1998 Honda Civic Blue

RS AKIMOTO FUNNEL RAM III

The Ultra Light Funnel Ram III is a new design exclusive to Racing Sports Akimoto. The Funnel Ram III filter is the next stage in washable cotton gauze filter. Its metal construction inhibits corrosion, increases strength, and provides greater sound resonance. The attributes mentioned above combine to give the user the most durable and best sounding intake system on the market.

The aluminum top and base are resistant to deterioration and tearing. The aluminum base is spun into a velocity stack radius to provide improved airflow. The aluminum is not susceptible to heat cracking. It is also resistant to damage in a backfire condition. The aluminum will promote the harmonics and provide a more aggressive intake tone. The aluminum is lighter than rubber, yet the bonding agent is over 100% stronger than rubber.

Not only have we eliminated the rubber from our filter design, but we have also taken the element to the next level. We use a stainless steel wire mesh for added rigidity as well as its improved corrosion resistance relative to the epoxy-coated steel used by other manufacturers. Extra deep pleats improve flow through the filter as well as providing improved filtration by increasing the filter surface area. Our medical grade cotton gauze has a more consistent weave than standard gauze and is capable of greater longevity.

JACKSON RACING MAZDA MIATA COLD AIR INDUCTION

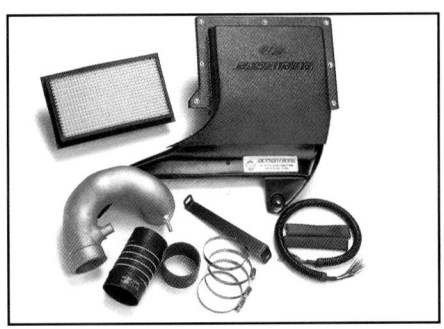

This system gets its air supply from the nose piece of the car and brings in nice, cool, pressurized air (at speed) to the engine instead of all that hot air from around the exhaust system. The result is a very happy Miata with much greater power and fuel economy! You can expect an increase of 14 horsepower from the cooler air and an additional horsepower gain as your Miata starts pressurizing (ramming) air into the cold air induction air filter box. This kit is simply the best way yet to get cold air to your engine. Smog Legal in all 50 States!

Part #	Application
901-985	1990-1993 Miata
901-980	1994-1997 Miata
901-987	Replacement Air Filter

KONIG PRODUCTS

Air Force One Aluminum Air Intake Systems are available in blue, red, purple, and polished.

Part #	Application
ACURA	
WS45100B	1988-1992 Integra
WS45100P	1988-1992 Integra
WS45100R	1988-1992 Integra
WS45101B	1993-1997 Integra
WS45101L	1993-1997 Integra
WS45101P	1993-1997 Integra
WS45101R	1993-1997 Integra
HONDA	
WS44111B	1994-1997 Accord
WS44111L	1994-1997 Accord
WS44111P	1994-1997 Accord
WS44111R	1994-1997 Accord
WS44100B	1988-1991 Civic
WS44100P	1988-1991 Civic
WS44100R	1988-1991 Civic
WS44101B	1992-1995 Civic
WS44101L	1992-1995 Civic
WS44101P	1992-1995 Civic
WS44101R	1992-1995 Civic
WS44102B	1992-1995 Civic VTEC
WS44102L	1992-1995 Civic VTEC
WS44102P	1992-1995 Civic VTEC
WS44102R	1992-1995 Civic VTEC
WS44300B	1996-1998 Civic
WS44300L	1996-1998 Civic
WS44300P	1996-1998 Civic
WS44300R	1996-1998 Civic

KONIG REPLACEMENT ACCESSORIES

Part #	Application
WS5000B	Air Filter Blue
WS5000C	Air Filter Chrome
WS5000R	Air Filter Red
WS500100	Oil Air Breather Filter Honda (Small Filter)

KONIG REAL CARBON FIBER AIR INTAKE

Part #	Application
WS669402	1994-1997 Honda Accord
WS669201	1992-1995 Honda Civic
WS669601	1996-1997 Honda Civic
WS669001	1990-1993 Honda Integra
WS669401	1994-1997 Honda Integra Ls/Rs
WS669403	1994-1997 Honda Integra Gsr
WS669203	1992-1996 Honda Prelude
WS669703	1997+ Honda Prelude
WS669501	1995-1997 Mitsubishi Eclipse (X-turbo)

ABD RACING VW QUICK FLOW

The factory air box robs throttle response as well as genuine horsepower; ABD Racing's answer is the Quick Flow Air Filter System. These units require the removal of the original air box followed by a simple installation of an aggressive-looking red anodized aluminum bracket. These kits utilize the largest K&N filter element available per application with more surface area than most competitors' systems. This results in more air inducted directly into the mass air sensor and throughout the intake system providing greater efficiency, a great sound when on the gas, and a horsepower gain you can feel.

ABD Racing now has a virtually indestructible billet aluminum Mass Air Sensor adapter for the 70;40 Digifant injection cars. CARB approval number applies to model years of 1988-1995 per EXO# D-416.

Part #	Application
70;Q80	Beetle 2.0L
70;Q81	Beetle 1.8T
70;Q10	Corrado G60
70;Q70	Corrado VR6
70;Q40	1988-1992 Golf/Jetta II 8V (Digifant Inj.)
70;Q20	Golf/Jetta III, 4 cyl.
70;Q30	Golf/Jetta III VR6
70;Q80	Golf/Jetta IV 2.0L, 4 cyl. (requires use of Big Bore #70;940)
70;Q90	Golf/Jetta IV VR6

K & N AIR PUMP FILTER

A snug fitting filter to cover the input of the air pump when removing the O.E. hose for Quick Flow installation. Required on all VR6 cars from 1993 and on 4-cyl. cars from 1997 on up.

Part #	Description
RC;2540	K & N Air Pump Filter
99;5000	K & N Filter care kit

AIR BATH FORCED INDUCTION SYSTEM

By placing a large diameter flexible hose in the front of your car, your Quick Flow can now breathe undisturbed fresh air. Air Bath kits come complete with all necessary hardware including an intake scoop for a clean installation into the front spoiler, flexible intake hose to connect the scoop to the intake system, and finally the Air Bath shroud, an open-top unit that fits nicely around the Quick Flow Filter.

Part #	Application
70;A10	Golf
70;A20	Jetta III, 4 cyl.
70;ALOC	Charcoal canister hose relocation kit required on most cars

AIR INTAKE SYSTEMS IMPORTS

Chikara by TD Performance Air Intake Systems radically improves air flow to increase horsepower. Better performance can be installed onto your sport compact in just minutes. Manufactured from anodized aluminum. All kits come complete with a cotton filter and all hardware.

JIM WOLF TECHNOLOGY

POP-Chargers are available for many different vehicles. Call your local dealer for price and availability.

Ford, Toyota, Nissan, Honda, Mitsubishi.

AIV Breather Filter, CARB Exemption on some models.

CHIKARA BY TD PERFORMANCE AIR INTAKE SYSTEMS

Part # / Color			Application
Chrome	Red	Blue	
5700	5701	5702	1990-1993 Acura Integra
5703	5704	5705	1994-1998 Acura Integra RS / LS
5706	5707	5708	1994-1998 Acura Integra GSR
5709	5710	5711	1995-1998 Dodge Neon
5712	5713	5714	1990-1993 Honda Accord
5715	5716	5717	1994-1997 Honda Accord
5718	5719	5720	1988-1991 Honda Civic
5721	5722	5723	1992-1995 Honda Civic
5724	5725	5726	1996-1998 Honda Civic EX
5727	5728	5729	1996-1998 Honda Civic LX / DX / CX
5730	5731	5732	1992-1996 Honda Prelude
5733	5734	5735	1997-1998 Honda Prelude
5736	5737	5738	1995-1998 Mitsubishi Eclipse, non-turbo
5739	5740	5741	1995-1998 Mitsubishi Eclipse, turbo

Air Intake Kit, Comptech Sport (GSR 94-99). Polished intake with filter.
For Years 1994-1999

Air Intake Kit, Comptech Sport (RS, GS, LS 94-99). Polished intake with filter.
For Years 1994-1999

Air Intake Kit, Comptech Sport (Type R 97-00). Polished intake with filter.
For Years 1997-2000

Intake — polished aluminum (Civic Si 99). Intake -- polished aluminum.
For Year 1999 Civic Si

WEAPON*R F1 RACING SPEC INTAKES

Part #	Application
ACURA	
WRC98CL	1997+ CL 2.2L
WRC97CL	1997+ CL V-6
WRC90AI	1990-1993 Integra
WRC94AI	1994+ Integra
WRC94GR	1994+ Integra GSR
WRC97TR	1997+ Integra Type-R
WRC90LG	1986-1990 Legend
WRF92LG	1991-1996 Legend w/oTCCS
HONDA	
WRC88AC	1986-1989 Accord LXI
WRC90AC	1990-1993 Accord
WRC94AC	1994-1997 Accord
WRC98AC	1998+ Accord
WRC96CV	1994+ Accord V-6
WRC91CV	1988-1991 Civic / CRX SI
WRC90CV	1988-1991 Civic / CRX DX
WRC92CV	1992-1995 Civic
WRC96EX	1996+ Civic EX / HX
WRC96DX	1996+ Civic DX / CX
WRC97CR	1997+ CRV
WRC95OD	1995+ Odyssey
WRC91PR	1986-1991 Prelude SI
WRC92PR	1992-1996 Prelude
WRC97PR	1997+ Prelude
MITSUBISHI	
WRC95EC	1995+ Eclipse, non-turbo
TOYOTA	
WRC92CA	1992-1997 Camry 2.2L
WRC92CE	1990-1997 Celica
WRC92CO	1990-1997 Corolla 1.6L & 1.
WRC92TO	1990-1995 MR2, non-turbo
WRC97RV	1997-2000 RAV4

WEAPON*R F1 RACING SPEC INTAKES

Polished intakes standard, add $10.00 for colors: red / blue / yellow / purple (see chart).

Part #	Application
ACURA	
WRF98CL	1997+ CL 2.2L
WRF89AI	1986-1989 Integra
WRF90AI	1990-1993 Integra
WRF94AI	1994+ Integra non-VTEC
WRF94GR	1994+ Integra VTEC
WRF90LG	1987-1990 Legend
WRF92LG	1991-1996 Legend, w/o TCCS
WRF93LG	1991-1996 Legend, w/ TCCS
WRF99TL	1999+ TL 3.2L
FORD	
WRF96PB	1996-1998 Probe
WRF97PB	1996-1998 Probe
WRF98ZT	1998-1999 ZX-2 ZTEC
HONDA	
WRF90AC	1990-1993 Accord
WRF94AC	1994-1997 Accord
WRF98AC	1998+ Accord
WRF96CV	1994+ Accord V-6
WRF88AC	1986-1989 Accord LXI
WRF91CV	1988-1991 Civic 1.6L
WRF92CV	1992-1995 Civic
WRF96EX	1996+ Civic EX / HX / Si
WRF96CD	1996+ Civic DX / LX / CX
WRF97CR	1997 CRV
WRF92PR	1992-96 Prelude
WRF97PR	1997+ Prelude
WRF91PR	1986-1991 Prelude SI
MAZDA	
WRF92MA	1992+ Miata 1.8L
WRF92MV	1992-1993 MX3 V-6
WRF96PB	1996-1998 MX6, 4 cyl.
WRF97PB	1996-1998 MX6 V-6
WRF90RX	1989-1992 RX-7
WRF93RX	1993-1997 RX-7, twin turbo (dual filter)

Part #	Application
MERCURY	
WRF98CG	1998-1999 Cougar
MITSUBISHI	
WRF96EC	1995+ Avenger, 4 cyl. & 6 cyl.
WRF91EC	1989-1994 Eclipse 1.8L & 2.0L, non-turbo
WRF95EC	1995+ Eclipse 2.0L, non-turbo
WRF99GA	1998-1999 Galant 4 cyl. & 6 cyl.
WRF91MI	1989-1992 Mirage 1.6L
WRF98MI	1997-1999 Mirage 1.5L
NISSAN	
WRF94AL	1995-1998 Altima
WRF98MX	1995-1999 Maxima
WRF90SE	1990-1994 Sentra 1.6L
WRF94SR	1994+ Sentra SE-R
WRF96SE	1995-1999 200SX 1.6L
SATURN	
WRF95SA	1995+ Saturn DOHC
TOYOTA	
WRF92CA	1992-1997 Camry 2.2L
WRF90CE	1986-1989 Celica 2.0L
WRF92CE	1990-1997 Celica
WRF98TO	1998-2000 Corolla
WRF92CO	1990-1997 Corolla 1.6L & 1.8L
WRF92TO	1990-1995 MR2, non-turbo
WRF92PA	1992-1999 Paseo
WRF97RV	1997-2000 RAV4
WRF92TE	1991-1994 Tercel
VOLKSWAGEN	
D2A3C	1993-1999 Jetta 8V

PLACE RACING

Cold Air Intake Systems have been Vericom tested, dyno tested, and track tested to be one of the best performance upgrades for your car. Place Racing is well-known for its custom intake systems which can be designed to fit just about any car. Place Racing offers systems for Civics, Integras, Accords, Preludes, Nissan Sentras, 200SXs, 240s, Maxima, and Infiniti I30s just to name a few.

Cold Air Intake for 1990-1993 System Acura Integra: Integra systems feature 3" diameter mandrel-bent systems, as do all of Place Racing's systems.

Cold Air Intake System for 1988-1991 Honda Civic: All Cold Air Intakes come in Chrome, Red, Blue, or Yellow. Custom colors are available.

Cold Air Intake System for 1992-1995 Honda Civic: Setups can include a second joint for the ability to change from wet to dry setups. Dry setups protect your engine from possible water damage by allowing you to place the filter in the engine bay instead of under the bumper.

Cold Air Intake System for 1992-1995 Honda Civic: Cold Air Intakes are manufactured for stock as well as motor-swapped engines.

Cold Air Intake System for 1991-1994 Nissan Sentra SE-R, 94 and up 200SX SE-R: This system has been dyno tested by Sport Compact Car on its Project 200SX SE-R and made 8 hp mid range and 3 hp peak over what a standard air filter upgrade made.

OBX INTAKE SYSTEMS & ACCESSORIES

See charts next page.

OVERSIZED THROTTLE BODY ASSEMBLIES

ELP MOTORSPORT HOT BODY

ELP Motorsport modifies the stock throttle body so it can supply the air flow your engine demands. ELP starts by boring a stock throttle body utilizing the latest in CNC equipment technology to accept a larger precision-machined and fitted throttle plate, usually 2mm - 5mm larger depending on your model of car.

The Hot Body can wake up your car's performance in conjunction with appropriate fuel and air flow tuning measures, offering a noticeable improvement in the mid-range and top end power. You will also realize an improvement in throttle response. These units have been flow tested and offer an 8% - 22% flow increase over stock depending on model of vehicle. The Hot Body has an easy bolt-on installation, is a perfect addition for daily street vehicles, and is a necessity for modified vehicles and club racers.

NOTE: All Hot Bodies feature a lifetime warranty against defects to the original purchaser. All Hot Bodies are sold on an exchange basis. For outright purchases please contact ELP Motorsport for core charge. For nonstocked or special-order models, you must ship your stock throttle body for ELP Motorsport to modify. Please allow five (5) to fourteen (14) business days. ELP Motorsport Hot Bodies are pending 50 state smog

OBX PRODUCTS

OBX RACING SPORTS INTAKE SYSTEM

Part #	Application
ACURA	
OB8889	1988-1989 Integra RS/LS/GS
OB9093	1990-1993 Integra
OB9497	1994-1998 Integra RS/LS/GS
OB9499	1994-1999 Integra GSR
OB0022	1997-1998 2.2CL
OB0024	1997-1999 3.0CL BMW
OB9297E	1992-1998 E-36 3 25is/M3/325i, w/ air sensor
OB9298E	1992-1998 E-36 325, w/o air sensor
DODGE	
OB0094	1994 + Neon SOHC
HONDA	
OB9093A	1990-1993 Accord
OB9495A	1994-1997 Accord, 4 cyl.
OB9495B	1996-1997 Accord, 6 cyl.
OB9899A	1998-2000 Accord, 4 cyl.
OB9899B	1998-2000 Accord, 6 cyl.
OB9295	1992-1995 Civic
OB8891L	1988-1991 Civic/CRX DX/LX/HF
OB8891C	1988-1991 Civic/CRX Si
OB9697D	1996-1999 Civic DX/LX/CX
OB9697H	1996-1999 Civic EX/HX/Si/SiR
OB9701	1997-2000 CRV
OB9295	1993-1997 del Sol
OB9296P	1992-1996 Prelude
OB9198P	1997-1999 Prelude
MITSUBISHI	
OB9597	1995-1999 Eclipse RS/GS, non-turbo
OB9597T	1995-1999 Eclipse Turbo/Spider
OB007M	1997+ Galant
OB003M	1997-1999 Mirage
NISSAN	
OB9798N	1995+ Altima
OB9599N	1995+ Maxima
OB9093N	1990-1993 Sentra
OB9498	1994-1998 Sentra/200SX
OB9598	1995-1999 240SX (12V)
OB89941	1989-1994 240SX (12V)
OB89942	1989-1994 240SX (16V)
SATURN	
OB9199	1991-1999 SL1/SL2
SUBARU	
OB0197S	1997+ Impreza
TOYOTA	
OB9296T	1992-1996 Camry 2.2L
OB9397	1993-1997 Corolla 1.6L/1.8L
OB9800	1998-2000 Corolla 1.6L/1.8L
OB9711	1996-1999 RAV-4
OB9396	1993-1996 Tacoma, 4 cyl.
OB8994	1989-1994 Tercel
OB9500	1995-2000 Tercel
VOLKSWAGEN	
OB9398	1993-1998 Golf/Jetta iii 2.0L

OBX COMBAT INTAKE SYSTEMS

Part #	Application
ACURA	
CD9093	1990-1993 Integra
CD9497	1994-1998 Integra RS/LS
CB9499	1994-1998 Integra GSR
CB0022	1997-1998 2.2CL
CB0024	1997-1998 3.0CL
BMW	
CB9297M	1992-1998 E-36, w/ air flow sensor
CB9298	1992-1998 E-36, w/o air flow sensor
DODGE	
CB0094	1994 + Neon SOHC
HONDA	
CB9093A	1990-1993 Accord
CB9495A	1994-1997 Accord, 4 cyl.
CB9495B	1994-1997 Accord, 6 cyl.
CB9899A	1998-2000 Accord DX/LX, 4 cyl.
CB9896A	1998-2000 Accord, all 6 cyl.
CB8891C	1988-1991 Civic/CRX (Si)
CB9295	1992-1995 Civic
CB9697D	1996-1999 Civic DX/LX/CX
CB9697H	1996-1999 Civic EX/HX/Si/Si-R
CB9701	1997-1999 CRV
CB9295	1993-1997 del Sol
CB9296P	1992-1996 Prelude
CB9798P	1997-1998 Prelude
MITSUBISHI	
CB9597	1995-1999 Eclipse, non-turbo GSR
CB003M	1997-1999 Mirage
TOYOTA	
CB9397	1993-1997 Corolla
CB9800	1998-1999 Corolla
CB9500	1995-1999 Tercel
CB9711	1996-1999 Rav-4

OBX COLD AIR EXTENSION KIT

Part #	Application
OB9298	1992-1998 Honda Civic
OB9497	1994-1997 Honda Accord

OBX PURE SILICONE REDUCER & COUPLER

Part #	Description
R001R	3.0" to 2.5" Reducer Red
R001Y	3.0" to 2.5" Reducer Yellow
R001B	3.0" to 2.5" Reducer Blue
R002R	3.0" to 3.0" Coupler Red
R002Y	3.0" to 3.0" Coupler Yellow
R002B	3.0" to 3.0" Coupler Blue

OBX PRODUCTS (CONT.)

OBX CARBON FIBER INTAKE SYSTEMS

Part #	Application
ACURA	
FB8889	1988-1989 Integra RS/LS/GS
FB9093	1990-1993 Integra
FB9497	1994-1999 Integra RS/LS/GS
FB9497G	1994-1999 Integra GSR
FB0022	1997-1998 2.2CL
FB0024	1997-1998 3.0CL
BMW	
FB9297E	1992-1997 E-36 325is
DODGE	
FB0094	1994+ Neon SOHC
HONDA	
FB9093A	1990-1993 Accord
FB9495A	1994-1997 Accord, 4 cyl.
FB9894A	1998-1999 Accord, 4 cyl.
FB9896A	1998-1999 Accord, 6 cyl.
FB9295	1992-1995 Civic
FB8891C	1988-1991 Civic/CRX Si
FB9697D	1996-1999 Civic DX/LX/CX
FB9697H	1996-1999 Civic EX/HX/Si
FB9296P	1992-1996 Prelude
FB9798P	1997-1999 Prelude
MITSUBISHI	
FB9597	1995-1998 Eclipse, non-turbo

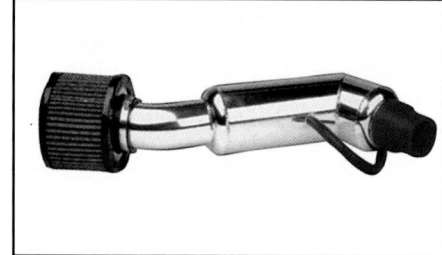

OBX COMBAT INTAKE SYSTEMS

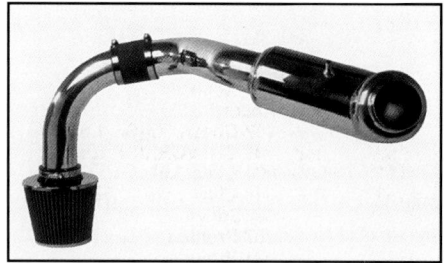

OBX COMBAT COLD AIR SYSTEMS

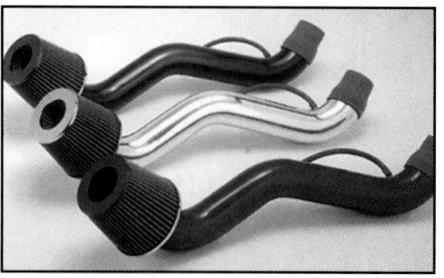

OBX RACING SPORTS INTAKE SYSTEMS

ELP MOTORSPORT HOT BODY THROTTLE BODIES

Part #	Application	Stage 1	Stage 2
ACURA			
4004*	1986-1989 Integra 1.6L	3.0mm	4.5mm
4010*	1990-1993 Integra 1.8L	3.0mm	4.5mm
4005*	1992-1993 Integra 1.7L VTEC	3.0mm	5.0mm
4020*	1994+ Integra 1.8L	3.0mm	4.5mm
4021*	1994+ Integra 1.8L VTEC	3.0mm	5.0mm
4009	1986-1990 Legend 2.5/2.7L	2.0mm	3.5mm
4014	1991+ Legend 3.0L	3.0mm	4.5mm
4025	1991-1994 NSX 3.0L	3.0mm	4.5mm
4015	1991-1994 Vigor 2.5L	3.0mm	-----
AUDI			
1507	1988-1991 80 (Type 89), 4 cyl.	3.0mm	-----
1508	1988-1992 80/90 (Type 89), 5 cyl.	3.0mm	-----
1529	1992+ 100 S4/C4	3.5mm	-----
1502	1984-1987 4000	3.0mm	-----
1506	1983-1990 5000	3.0mm	-----
BMW			
2001	1977-1979 320I 2.0L	3.0mm	-----
2002	1980-1983 320I 1.8L	3.0mm	-----
2003	1984-1985 318i (E-30) 1.8L	3.0mm	-----
2004	1990-1991 318is (E-30) 1.8L	3.0mm	-----
2010	1995+ 318ti/Z3 1.8/1.9L	3.0mm	-----
2012	1992-1993 318is (E-36) 1.8L	3.0mm	-----
2014	1994-1996 318i-is (E-36) 1.8L	3.0mm	-----
2005e	1985-1991 325/528e 2.7L	3.0mm	4.5mm
2005i	1986-1991 325/525I 2.5L	3.0mm	4.5mm
2033	1992-1995 325i/525/M-3 2.5L/3.0L	3.0mm	-----
2038	1996+ 328/528I 2.8L	3.0mm	-----
2008	1982-1984 533/633 3.3L	3.0mm	4.5mm
2007	1985-1989 535/635/735 3.5L	3.0mm	4.5mm
2009	1989+ 535/735I 3.5L	3.0mm	4.5mm
2017	1987-1991 M-3 2.3L	2.0mm	4.0mm
2040	1987-1988 M-5/M-6 3.5L	2.0mm	4.0mm
2040	1989-1991 M-5 3.5L	2.0mm	4.0mm
2012	1996+ Z3/M3 2.8/3.2L	2.5mm	-----
DODGE			
2811	1991-1994 Stealth RT 3.0L, turbo	3.0mm	4.5mm
2813	1991-1994 Stealth ES 3.0L, non-turbo	3.0mm	4.5mm
FORD			
3512	1985-1990 Escort 1.9L	3.0mm	5.0mm
3526	1991-1994 Escort1.8L	3.0mm	4.5mm
5511	1988-1992 Probe 2.2L	3.0mm	4.5mm
5527	1993+ Probe, 4 cyl.	3.0mm	4.5mm
5522*	1993+ Probe 2.5L	4.0mm	6.0mm
3528	1989+ Taurus SHO 3.0/3.2L	3.0mm	4.5mm
HONDA			
4105	1986-1989 Accord LXI 1.8L	3.0mm	4.5mm
4111*	1990-1993 Accord 2.2L	3.0mm	4.5mm
4122*	1994+ Accord 2.2L	3.0mm	4.5mm
4103	1986-1987 Civic/CRX(Si) 1.6L	3.0mm	4.5mm
4107*	1988-1991 Civic/CRX(Si) 1.6L	3.0mm	4.5mm
4117*	1992-1994 Civic 1.6L	3.0mm	4.5mm
4133*	1992-1994 Civic VTEC 1.6L (si/ex)	3.0mm	4.5mm
4131*	1993+ del Sol VTEC 1.6L	3.0mm	4.5mm
4101	1985-1987 Prelude si 1.8L	3.0mm	4.5mm
4118*	1988-1991 Prelude si 2.0L	3.0mm	4.5mm
4116*	1992+ Prelude 2.3L	3.0mm	4.5mm
4127*	1992+ Prelude VTEC 2.3L	3.0mm	4.5mm
MAZDA			
5503	1986-1989 323 1.6L	3.0mm	4.0mm
5511	1988-1991 626/MX-6 2.2L	3.0mm	4.5mm
5522*	1992+ 626 2.5L	4.0mm	6.0mm
5515*	1989-1994 Miata 1.6L	3.0mm	4.5mm
5521*	1992+ MX-3 1.8L, V-6	4.0mm	5.5mm
5527	1993+ MX-6, 4 cyl.	3.0mm	4.5mm
5530	1986-1991 RX-7	13B	2.5mm
5532	1993-1995 RX-7	13B	2.5mm

Part #	Application	Stage 1	Stage 2
MITSUBISHI			
2811	1991-1994 3000GT VR43.0L, turbo	3.0mm	4.5mm
2813	1991-1994 3000GT SL 3.0L, non-turbo	3.0mm	4.5mm
6011	1989-1994 Eclipse 2.0L, turbo	3.0mm	4.5mm
6010	1989-1994 Eclipse 2.0L, non-turbo	3.0mm	4.5mm
6003	1983-1989 Starion 2.6L, turbo	3.0mm	4.5mm
NISSAN			
6355	1986-1988 200SX 2.0L	3.0mm	4.5mm
6310	1989-1990 240SX 2.4L, 12 valve	3.0mm	4.5mm
6310	1991-1994 240SX 2.4L, 16 valve	3.0mm	4.5mm
6302	1975-1983 280Z/ZX 2.8L	3.0mm	4.5mm
6301	1984-1989 300ZX 3.0L	3.0mm	4.5mm
6319	1990-1994 300ZX 3.0L	3.0mm	4.5mm
6320	1990-1994 300ZX, turbo 3.0L	3.0mm	4.5mm
6307	1993+ Altima 2.4L	3.0mm	4.5mm
6354	1985-1988 Maxima 3.0L	3.0mm	4.5mm
6311	1989-1994 Maxima 3.0L	3.0mm	4.5mm
6324	1991-1994 NX/Sentra 1.6L	3.0mm	4.5mm
6316	1991-1994 NX/-2000/SER 2.0L	3.0mm	4.5mm
PLYMOUTH			
6010	1989-1992 Laser 2.0L, non-turbo	3.0mm	4.5mm
PONTIAC			
3822	1984-1987 Fiero 2.5L	3.0mm	-----
3802	1985-1987 Fiero 2.8L	3.0mm	4.5mm
PORSCHE			
7580	944 2.5L	3.0mm	-----
7584	944S, turbo 2.5L	3.0mm	-----
7585	944S2 3.0L	3.0mm	-----
7581	1984-1988 911 3.2L	3.0mm	-----
7586	1989-1990 911 C2/C4 3.6L	3.0mm	-----
7582	1991-1994 911 C2/C4 3.6L	3.0mm	-----
7592	1992-1995 968 3.0L	3.0mm	-----
7593	1995+ 993 3.6L	3.0mm	-----
7599	1996-1997 993 3.6L	1.5mm	-----
SATURN			
8150	1991-1994 Coupe/Sedan, 4 cyl.	3.5mm	-----
TOYOTA			
8248	987-1991 Camry 2.2L	3.0mm	-----
8216	1992-1994 Camry V-6	4.0mm	-----
8204	1982-1985 Celica GTS 2.4L	3.0mm	5.0mm
8212	1986-1989 Celica 2.2L	3.0mm	4.5mm
8207	1990-1993 Celica 2.2L	3.0mm	4.5mm
8227	1990-1993 Celica, all trac, 2.2L, turbo	3.0mm	4.5mm
8203	1985-1987 Corolla GTS 1.6L	3.0mm	4.5mm
8224	1988-1990 Corolla GTS 1.6L	3.0mm	4.5mm
8208	1992- Corolla 4 cyl.	3.0mm	4.5mm
8210	1985-1990 MR-2 1.6L	3.0mm	4.5mm
8215*	1991-1994 MR-2 2.2L	3.0mm	5.0mm
8245	1991-1994 MR-2, turbo 2.2L	3.0mm	4.5mm
8250	1991-1993 Paseo, 4 cyl.	3.5mm	-----
8221	1982-1985 Supra 2.8L	3.0mm	4.5mm
8211	1986-1993 Supra, non-turbo 3.0L	4.0mm	6.0mm
8229	1986-1993 Supra, turbo 3.0L	3.0mm	5.0mm
8234	1993.5+ Supra, non-turbo 3.0L	3.0mm	4.5mm
8222	1993.5+ Supra, turbo 3.0L	3.0mm	5.0mm
8254	1986-1993 PU/4runner 2.4L	3.0mm	5.0mm
8228	1988-1993 PU/4runner 3.0L	3.0mm	4.5mm
VOLKSWAGEN			
8513	1990-1993 Corrado (G-60) 1.8L	3.0mm	-----
8503	1992-1994 Corrado (VR-6) 2.8L	3.5mm	-----
8519	1987-1993 Golf II (16v) 1.8/2.0L	3.5mm	-----
8530	1993.5+ Golf III 2.0L	3.0mm	-----
8531	1993.5+ Golf III (VR-6) 2.8L	3.5mm	-----
8519	1987-1993 Jetta II (16v) 1.8/2.0L	3.5mm	-----
8531	1993.5+ Jetta III (VR-6) 2.8L	3.5mm	-----
8531	1993+ Passat (VR-6) 2.8L	3.5mm	-----
8519	1986-1989 Scirocco 1.8L	3.0mm	-----

(*) Denotes special Stage III Race Hot Body available. To order add R to end of Part #.

Sport Compact Bolt-On Performance Guide, Volume 1 - Imports

ELP BMW THROTTLE BODY

ELP HONDA/ACURA THROTTLE BODY

ELP MITSUBISHI THROTTLE BODY

legal certification. Legal in CA only for racing vehicles which may never be used on a highway.

Contact ELP Motorsport for other applications or for models not listed.

JG ENGINE DYNAMICS

Offers a line of enhanced throttle bodies for Honda/Acura applications.

GUDE

Bullfrog Throttle Bodies are bored to micro tolerances, and a new purple anodized butterfly is machined and hand-fitted to provide the best idle possible. The velocity stack is tapered to induce high velocity air flow into the intake manifold resulting in super throttle response, increased midrange, and big top end.

Part #	Application
AITB01	1986-1989 1.6 DOHC
AITB02	1990-1992 1.8 DOHC
AITB03	1993-1995 1.8 DOHC
AITB04	1996-1997 1.8 DOHC
AITB05	1992-1993 GSR VTEC DOHC
AITB06	1994-1995 GSR VTEC DOHC
AITB07	1996-1997 GSR VTEC DOHC
	1990-1994 Eagle Talon, turbo
	1990-1994 Eagle Talon, non-turbo
	1995-1997 Eagle Talon, turbo
	1995-1997 Eagle Talon, non-turbo

HOLLEY HONDA CIVIC 68MM THROTTLE BODY

Holley Performance Products has a billet aluminum 68mm throttle body for 1992-1995 Honda Civic 1.6L engines. Flowing 650cfm (tested 28" of water), this enlarged throttle body offers enough flow for even the most radical engine combinations. Not only do these Holley billet throttle bodies flow more air, they provide a high-tech custom appearance. Available in five anodized colors, clear (part #112-511), red (part #112-511-1), blue (part #112-511-2), green (part #112-511-3), and purple (part #112-511-4), they match Holley's new anodized high-flow fuel rails.

Holley's 68mm Honda Civic throttle bodies fit the stock manifold plenum flange and have provisions for the fast-idle valve, MAP sensor, TPS, and EAC valve. All throttle bodies feature a red-billet throttle plate, with an optional stainless-steel throttle plate kit available for supercharged and turbocharged applications.

ABD RACING BIG BORE INTAKES

Quality is always the main concern when creating ABD Racing products and the Big Bore Intake program is another example of a perfect part that shines with excellence in craftsmanship. Originally, cars are equipped with an undersized plastic or flexible rubber intake tube. ABD Racing Big Bore intakes are constructed from oversized 3" stainless steel tubing that is mandrel bent and then powder coated bright silver to perfection. Theoretically, more air equals better performance, and this is the case with the ABD Racing replacement intake system. As mentioned previously, all parts are mandrel bent to ensure a non-disturbed flow of air that cut & welded parts cannot match. Kits come complete with all necessary hardware for a proper installation. (Not legal for use on public roads. Race use only.)

Part #	Applications
70;900	Rabbit/Cabriolet/ Scirocco 8V/Jetta I, fuel injected only
70;910	1985-1987 Golf / Jetta II 6v
70;911	1988-1992 Golf / Jetta II 8v
70;920	1987-1989 Golf / Jetta II 16V
70;921	1990-1992 Golf / Jetta II 16V
70;930	1993-1998 Golf / Jetta III 8V

(1998 MODELS W/O SENSOR ON INTAKE TUBE/96 NEWER CARS CAN EITHER HAVE A 2.5" OR A 3" INTAKE ON THROTTLE BODY)

70;931	1994-1998 Golf / Jetta III VR6
70;940	Golf / Jetta IV 2.0L
70;940	Beetle 2.0L
70;941	Golf / Jetta IV VR6

Note: Some models must have a sensor removed from O.E. part and attached into new intake.

LC ENGINEERING

A Big Bore Throttle Body should be included on your list of performance improvements for your EFI 4-cyl. Toyota. LC Engineering starts with a factory throttle body, then bores and hones to 3.5mm overstock size. Next it is taper bored to 4.0mm on the back side. A custom CNC-machined throttle plate and new shaft seals are then installed. This modification will increase air flow CFM by over 12%. Sold with a core charge to eliminate your vehicle down time, the Big Bore Throttle Body can be shipped immediately. After installing your new throttle body, simply return the old housing and your core charge will be refunded.

Remember you have to increase the air flow to gain maximum output. Combine the Big Bore Throttle Body with LC Engineering's Header Kit, EFI Camshaft, and K&N Filter Charger Kit for best results. This combination will result in over 25 hp increase from stock.

16-100 — EFI Big Bore Throttle Body

TMW INDUCTION SINGLE-BARREL THROTTLE BODY

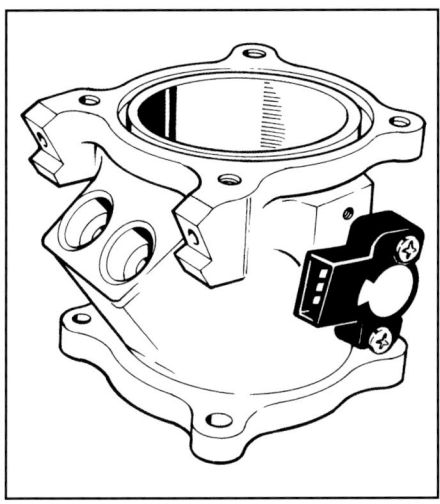

2805 Series (formerly 3005 series) is available in stock sizes of 65mm, 70mm, and 80mm. This unit has provision for two injectors side by side, both of which can be plugged if not used. Created to satisfy demand for a large single-barrel throttle body, these units will fill the need for "air door" type throttles for plenum or tunnel ram manifolds, where the injector facility can be used for high speed or turbo enrichment. They also can be ganged together, to provide "straight shot" individual runner injection for a variety of large V-8 engine layouts. There are integral mounts for the fuel rail which is supplied with the unit. AN-6 threads are in each end of the rail for which a specific fitting, part #2900-9206, is available. In standard form, these units cannot be mounted at less than 110mm centers.

Dimensions: in/mm
Height: 3.86/98
Width: 4.65/118
Bottom flange PCD:
4.17/106 4 x 8mm
Top flange PCD:
4.17/106 4 x 6mm

These units are designated "front, center, and rear" to distinguish their respective linkage layouts. The front unit incorporates a shaft with a single 5/16" D drive and mounting pad for TWM and other throttle position sensors. The center unit has interconnect linkage on both ends of the shaft and the rear unit has an interconnect which interfaces with the center units. A typical part number would be 2805-6502/F where 2805 is the series number, 6502 indicates a 65mm bore with two injectors, and F indicates a TPS drive.

TMW INDUCTION DCOE STYLE THROTTLE BODIES

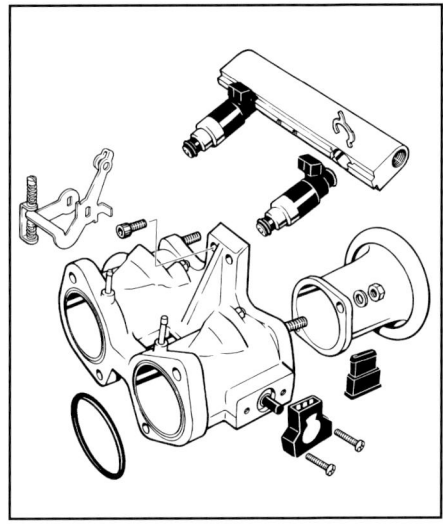

TWM 2900 Series throttle bodies are a direct replacement for the following sidedraft carburetors: Dellorto DHLA, Mikuni PHH, SK Racing, Solex ADDH, Weber DCO and DCOE, all available in the following sizes: 40mm, 42mm, 45mm, 48mm, 50mm, and 55mm to special order. TWM DCO type throttle bodies are supplied with a center compensating linkage which connects the two throttle shafts allowing adjustment for balance. Where the center-to-center distance between the barrels of cylinders 2 and 3 (on a 4 cyl. engine) is less than 97mm, use left-hand unit 2910 series. A fuel rail kit, adjustable for different manifold layouts, attaches to integral mounting points. Each barrel has a by-pass screw, for idle speed and air flow adjustment. The left-hand unit, incorporates a 5/16" "D" drive and mounting bosses for TWM and other throttle position sensors. "O" rings are supplied for the manifold / throttle body interface. Ports are provided, in each barrel, for connection to a MAP sensor.

TWM 2910 Series throttle bodies are engineered for today's smaller engines where space is limited between the units. Available only in left-hand configuration these throttle bodies are used in conjunction with a righthand 2900 Series to make up a dual installation. When selecting suitable units for a particular installation the manifold runner spacing should be measured. 2910 series throttle bodies are available in 40mm, 42mm, and 45mm bore sizes. By reducing the throttle shafts and nuts, a center-to-center dimension of 83mm can be achieved.

TWM throttle bodies are equipped with pockets for standard Bosch, Lucas, Rochester, or Weber injectors, using an "O" ring, top and bottom. 48mm and 50mm units may be ordered with two injectors per barrel. In the sidedraft configuration, the additional injectors mount on the bottom of the throttle body. Dimensions in/mm: height 3.46/88, bore C-to-C 3.54/90.

A typical DCOE type throttle body would have a part number like 2900-4502. Where 2900 is the DCOE series, 45 is the bore size in mm, and 02 represents two injectors per unit or one per barrel. 2910 series are available in 40mm, 42mm, and 45mm sizes.

TWM air horns are manufactured from 6061 alloy spinnings, machined for accuracy and combined with 6061 T6 billet flanges. The full radius design is accepted by the performance industry as the best for maximum air flow. Air horns should be selected by the inside diameter which should correspond to the throttle plate

TMW INDUCTION AIR HORNS FOR THROTTLE BODIES					
Part #	SERIES	A	B	C	H
2000-4835	2000	48	35	88	69
2000-4850	2000	48	50	88	69
2000-4875	2000	48	75	88	69
2000-5050	2000	50	50	88	69
2700-4535	2700	45	35	84	
2700-4550	2700	45	50	84	
2710-4550	2710	45	50	84	
2900-4050	2900				
	2930				
	3003	40	50	80	65
2900-4075	2900				
	2930				
	3003	40	75	80	65
2900-40100	2900				
	2930				
	3003	40	00	80	65
2900-4250	2900	42	60	80	65
2900-4275	2900	42	75	80	65
2900-42100	2900	42	100	80	65
2900-4450	3003	44	50	87	65
2900-4550	2900				
	2930	45	50	84	65
2900-4575	2900				
	2930	45	75	88	65
2900-4835	2900				
	2930				
	3000				
	3003	48	35	88	65
2900-4850	2900				
	2930				
	3000				
	3003	48	50	88	65
2900-4875	2900				
	2930				
	3000				
	3003	48	75	88	65
2900-4890	2900				
	2930				
	3000				
	3003	48	90	88	65
2900-48100	2900				
	2930				
	3000				
	3003	48	100	88	65
2900-48115	2900				
	2930				
	3000				
	3003	48	115	88	65
2900-5050	2900				
	2930				
	3000				
	3002				
	3003	50	50	88	65
2900-5560	2900				
	3000	55	65	95	69
3000-5075	3000				
	3002				
	3003	50	75	110	69
3000-50100	3000				
	3002	50	100	110	69
3003-4650	3003	46	50	87	65
3004-4050	3004	50			
3004-4450	3004	50			
3004-4650	3004	50			
3006-4675	3006	46	75	110	69
3006-4875	3006	48	75	110	69
3006-5075	3006	50	75	110	69
3006-5275	3006	52	75	110	69
3006-5475	3006	54	75	110	69
3006-5675	3006	56	75	110	69

diameter of the throttle body, then by the required length.

Part #	Bore size
2950-4000	40mm
2950-4200	42mm
2950-4500	45mm
2950-4800	48mm
2950-5000	50mm

TMW INDUCTION EXTENSIONS FOR THROTTLE BODIES

Use these extensions to provide a mounting surface for an air filter baseplate, beyond the fuel rails on 2900, 2930, and 3000 series throttle bodies. These components can also be used to extend the effective length of an air horn during dyno testing. Not required if you are using the TWM air box 2900-1575.

AIR HORNS FOR THROTTLE BODIES

TMW Induction designs and manufactures air horns for various car and engine manufacturers. This design service is available to produce one-off, prototype, and production horns at reasonable prices.

Air horns should be selected by the inside diameter (Dimension A), which should correspond to the throttle plate diameter of the throttle body, then by the required length. Dimension H is the dimension between the stud hole centers (see chart at left).

INTAKE MANIFOLDS

OBX HIGH POWER INTAKE MANIFOLD

OBX's High Power Air Intake Manifold Systems are designed for maximum air intake flow. The flow increase is reported to be good for around 10 to 15 hp with appropriate fuel and exhaust tuning. Made from T-6061 aluminum. Bolts to the engine without modifications.

Part #	Application
MF001	1988-1999 Civic/CRX/ del Sol/EX/Si/HX

STR AIRMAXX PRO DRAG MANIFOLD

Headers, intakes, exhaust systems, and throttle bodies can improve your power by helping the car inhale air and exhale air easier. Since intake air travels into the intake manifold after the throttle body, your stock intake manifold can become a performance bottleneck and may not allow your car to "breath" properly.

The solution is the STR Speedlab Intake Manifold which has been dyno tested and track proven to increase the flow of intake air into your engine. The easier your car can breath, the easier it can make POWER. It features a CNC Machined Flange (Custom Design). Lets you bolt-on 30% more flow. Is available for most Honda, Acura, and Eclipse.

Part #	Application
ACURA	
IM0104	1990-1998 Integra B18A (DOHC)
IM0103	1992-1993 Integra B17A (DOHC)
IM0105	1994-1998 Integra B18C (DOHC)
HONDA	
IM0100	1988-1991 Civic Si & CRX D16A (SOHC)
IM0100	1992-1995 Civic Si & EX B16A (SOHC)
IM0102	1992-1995 del Sol B16A (DOHC)
IM0107	1988-1997 Prelude (H23A1)
IMO108	1992-1997 Prelude (H22A1)
MITSUBISHI	
IM0106	1989-1998 Eclipse Turbo (1st Generation)
IMO109	1992-1997 Eclipse Turbo (2nd Generation)

TMW INDUCTION 2000 SERIES

Designed with the serious motorsport enthusiast in mind, the 2000 series brings the advantages of individual runner performance potential, to many of today's high-output small engines, including Acura (B18C), Honda (B16A), Mazda Miata 1600 and 1800, and the Series 3 VW (water cooled) engine. Each runner is a straight shot to the cylinder head, where it joins the port at the optimum angle, for maximum air flow. Available in 48mm or 50mm throttles. Two alternative injector positions enable engine builders to tune for power band requirements and, if necessary run eight injectors. Can be CNC ported to non-stock port sizes, at extra cost. See section on air horn selection.

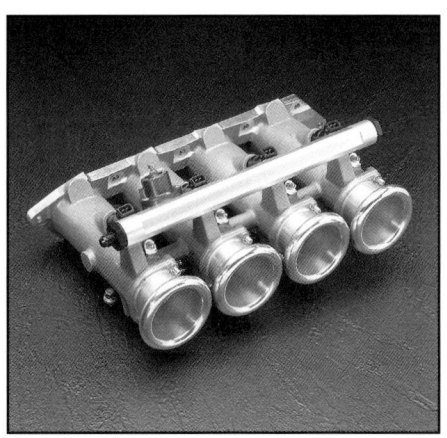

Engines with B18 C cylinder heads (Acura GS R etc.)
2000-0111/48
2000-0111/50

Engines with B16 A cylinder heads (del Sol & Acura Type R)
2000-0122/48
2000-0122/50

Available soon for:
Honda H22, Mazda Miata 1600 and Miata 1800, Volkswagen Series 3.
Weight: including 4 injectors, air horns and linkage 2.8 kg / 6.2 lbs.

Length, overall including 50 mm air horns: 250 mm/9.84 in.

TMW INDUCTION INTAKE MANIFOLDS

All manifolds are, in most cases, suitable for TWM Fi throttle bodies and Weber or Mikuni carburetors. Manifolds are supplied with linkage, fuel fittings, and antivibration mounts for Weber DCOE carburetors (Part #1); or, for other carburetor makes and TWM fuel injection throttle bodies, they are supplied with studs and nuts only (Part # 2).

The components parts listed in this section are those which, primarily, have a carburetor application. For Fi components, air horns and velocity stacks, and competition air filters, see the appropriate section of this guide.

TMW Inductions Intake Manifolds Dimension A is the center-to-center dimension of a dual sidedraft manifold. This is useful for planning engine bay layouts and air filter installations, such as the TMW air box. Dimension B is that of the cylinder head flange to the carburetor flange, taken at the center line of the casting. Dimension C is the offset of the center line, if any.

In addition to those components listed and shown, TMW Induction also has extensive applications for Toyota, Nissan, VW, and Mitsubishi.

INTEGRA

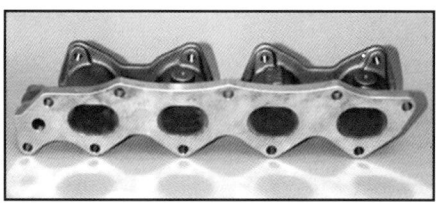

Integra B16 C: A 93 B 70 C –
Cyls/Cap 4/1600 Pt No 1 0109
Cam/Valves DOHC/4 Pt No 2 8-0109
TB's or carbs 2 X DCOE

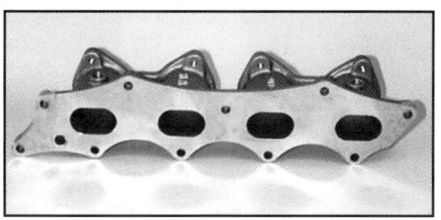

Integra B18 A: A 93 B 70 C –
Cyls/Cap 4/1800 Pt No 1 0110
Cam/Valves DOHC/4 Pt No 2 8-0110
TB's or carbs 2 X DCOE

Integra B18 C: Cyls/Cap 4/1800
Cam/Valves DOHC/4
Note: Fuel injection only.

BMW

BMW 1602 & 2002: A 93 B 70 C –
Cyls/Cap 4/1600-2000 Pt No 1 0044
Cam/Valves SOHC/2 Pt No 2 8-0044
TB's or carbs 2 X DCOE
Note: For Fi applications use 0116

BMW 318i & 320i: A 110 B 70 C –
Cyls/Cap 4/1800-2000 Pt No 1 0116
Cam/Valves SOHC/2 Pt No 2 8-0116
TB's or carbs 2 X DCOE

MAZDA

MX 5 MIATA: A – B – C – Cyls/Cap
6/4200 Pt No 1   2038 Cam/Valves
DOHC/2 Pt No 2 8-2038 TB's or carbs
3 X DCOE

HONDA

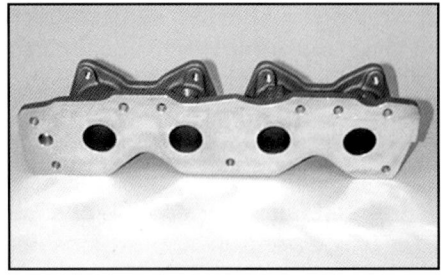

CRX: A 93 B 73 C – Cyls/Cap 4/1600
Pt No 1 0099/i Cam/Valves SOHC/3 Pt
No 2 8-0099/i TB's or carbs 2 X DCOE
Note: Fi cylinder heads only

CRX V-Tec: A 93 B 73 C – Cyls/Cap
4/1600 Pt No 1 0102 Cam/Valves
DOHC/4 Pt No 2 8-0102 TB's or carbs
2 X DCOE

CRX: A 93 B 73 C – Cyls/Cap 4/1600
Pt No 1 0102 Cam/Valves SOHC/4 Pt
No 2 8-0102 TB's or carbs 2 X DCOE

del Sol B 16 A: A – B – C – Cyls/Cap
4/1600 Cam/Valves DOHC/4 Note: see
2000 series throttle body

Prelude H 22 A: A – B – C – Note: See
2000 series throttle body.

Prelude (ET Engine): A 97 B 98 C 22
Cyls/Cap 4/1600 Pt No 1 0047
Cam/Valves SOHC/4 Pt No 2 8-0047
TB's or carbs 2 X DCOE
Note: Imported

Prelude (ES Engine): A 82 B 83 C 22
Cyls/Cap 4/1600 Pt No 1 3132
Cam/Valves SOHC/4 Pt No 2 8-3132
TB's or carbs 2 X DCOE

A 93 B 66 C Mazda – Engine type 13
B Cyls/Cap 2 rotor/ 4 port Pt No 1
0049 Cam/Valves – Pt No 2 8-0049
TB's or carbs 2 X DCOE

VENOM

Venom offers a line of high-performance intake manifolds for Cavalier, Civic, del Sol, Eclipse, Integra, and Saturn. Call for details.

PORTED HEAD PACKAGES

ELP MOTORSPORT

ELP MOTORSPORT offers Ultra Performance Cylinder Heads in various stages depending on your budget, class rules, and horsepower needs. These Pro-Street Heads are the result of years and hundreds of hours of computerized flow bench development, as well as dyno, street, and track testing. These heads don't lose low-end response while still improving upper mid-range and top-end power only. ELP heads match, and in most cases, improve velocity (or air speed) through the port at all valve lift points, while substantially increasing cylinder head flow.

ELP specializes in 4-valve technology and developed custom larger racing valves and valve train components for most import and exotic European performance machines. ELP can custom make larger racing valves in both stainless steel and titanium for most vehicles and specialize in air flow development. They welcome custom one off racing projects. Contact ELP MOTORSPORT to discuss details.

STAGE 1

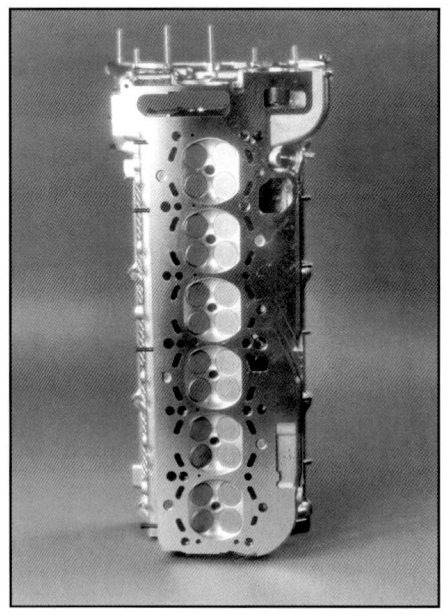

This package offers excellent reliability with a noticeable flow increase over stock. This is the perfect head for showroom stock and street drivers who want more performance from their stock vehicles. It features a competition multi-angle valve job on Serdi 100, SCCA legal port match work, surface/milled head, and backcut & polished valves as well as being magnafluxed and cleaned, blueprinted and assembled.

STAGE 2

This package is excellent for hot street and club racers who require a noticeable power gain but are on a budget. This head works well with improved induction systems and sport cam(s), however a free flow exhaust system is a must. Adds Pro-Street full port & polish, port match intake manifold, and backcut and polished valves.

STAGE 3

This package is the maximum head recommended for daily ultra hot street use. This head offers the same modifications as the Stage 2 head but includes big stainless-steel, swirl-polished racing valves. The porting is also more aggressive in the valve pocket and runner area due to the larger valves. This head also includes hi-rev performance valve springs. This is an excellent budget racer's head. With proper cam(s), induction, exhaust system, and fuel management large amounts of horsepower and upper RPM torque can be achieved.

STAGE 4 - 6

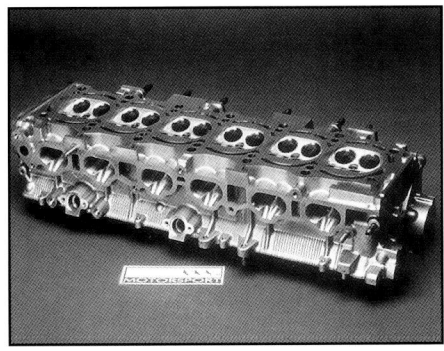

Special Racing Cylinder Heads. Call ELP Motorsport to discuss your specific class of racing and horsepower needs.

NOTE: All Stage 3 thru 6 Ultra Performance Cylinder Heads come with computerized flow sheets documenting before and after velocity and flow results. Sport and racing cam(s) are available to extract maximum horsepower from ELP Motorsport Ultra Performance Cylinder Heads. With Stage 2 and above ultra performance cylinder heads installed on turbocharged vehicles, ELP says the stock turbo is the flow and performance limiter. For maximum results contact ELP Motorsport for recommendations on hi-flow sport and racing turbos. For those in search of even more power and reliability beyond the Ultra Performance Cylinder Heads, ELP Motorsport has Sport Engine packages.

EXTRUDE HONE

Primary applications are engine cylinder heads and intake manifolds. By smoothing and streamlining cast-intake passages in automatic engines, Extrude Hone can dramatically enhance air induction and combustion chamber "swirl" velocity. The increased air volume and improved fuel/air mixture result in a cleaner burning, more powerful, and more fuel-efficient engine. The Extrude Hone processing of intake manifolds and cylinder head intake ports already has met the challenge for viability, reliability, and cost effectiveness. Its value was proven in a four-year, $8 million effort supported by Ford, GM, and the Advanced Technology Program of the National Institute for Standards and Technology.

The Abrasive Flow Machining (AFM) process is applied to intake and exhaust manifolds, as well as cylinder heads, to remove rough-cast surfaces that restrict horsepower efficiency. AFM enlarges and uniformly polishes air and fluid passages to maximize the flow velocity through the component. All polishing is performed parallel to the air/fluid flow. The result is a surface finish "grain" achieved in the same direction.

Superior results are reflected in the widespread use of Extrude Hone AFM by professional race teams in NASCAR, NHRA, IRL, CART, and SCCA. Production vehicles, such as the Ford Contour SVT, rely on Extrude Hone to produce the increased airflow required for the 2.5L V-6 to achieve 195 hp.

Extrude Hone processes the intake manifolds and cylinder heads of more than 5000 engines annually at its headquarters facility in Irwin, PA, located 30 miles east of Pittsburgh. In addition to meeting the rigid requirements of professional race teams and production automotive manufacturers, AFM is an effective process for the performance enthusiast as well. Mustangs, Corvettes, muscle cars, and high-performance imports offer many excellent performance enhancing opportunities for Extrude Hone.

Increased custom airflow can be tailored specifically for an AFM application. Results have demonstrated that such increases can exceed 30 percent on aluminum intake manifolds and 25 percent on cylinder heads.

Another popular AFM application is strengthening a component. The process eliminates stress risers, such as burrs, from edges and surfaces where a crack can occur. Gears and brake rotors are commonly processed by Extrude Hone to provide a uniform edge that significantly improves the dependability and life of highly stressed components.

GUDE PORTED AND POLISHED CYLINDER HEADS

Part #	Application
ETRH01	1990-1994 Eagle Talon, turbo
ETRH02	1990-1994 Eagle Talon, non-turbo
ETRH03	1995-1997 Eagle Talon, turbo
ETRH04	1995-1997 Eagle Talon, non-turbo

PERFORMANCE RESEARCH

The more air your engine flows, the greater amount of fuel will be burned in a given time period. The result is higher torque and horsepower levels to move you down the road or race track.

Performance Research's cylinder head 'template' was fully race prepared and flow benched to move the greatest amount of air and fuel possible from a stock casting, while maintaining high-flow velocity. Because most import heads are symmetrical, a five-axis CNC machine can be utilized to exactly duplicate the porting process for each cylinder. The end result is the highest flowing cylinder head possible, with the ability to maintain flow velocity. In addition, all ports are exactly matched to size and shape. Because the porting process is CNC computer controlled, the potential for human error during hand porting is eliminated.

Special CNC patterned combustion chambers increase flow during low valve lift, increasing low and midrange horsepower. Intake runner surface textures are controlled to minimize boundary layer losses.

Performance Research offers different packages to save you money. You can perform the disassembly and assembly work yourself, or Performance Research can do it all.

First, If you're certain you have the mechanical skill, remove the cylinder head from your car, wash it with engine cleaner, and decide which price/package best fits your needs. If you're unsure of your mechanical skills, find a competent import mechanic to do the work. You'll be happier in the long run. If you're in central Florida, Performance Research recommends G-Force Engines & Chassis at (407) 321-8881. For technical questions regarding Performance Research products, e-mail: support@perfresearch.com

STAGE I PACKAGE

Send your disassembled cylinder head to Performance Research. Make sure to remove and keep the valves, springs, retainers, and all other components. The 'bare' casting is the only part required. Performance Research will pressure check the head for cracks and perform a custom porting job on a five-axis CNC machine. Performance Research will also check for worn valve guides. If any are found, a Performance Research representative will call you for permission to change them out. Changing valve guides is not included in the $499 package price. Performance Research will ship your head back to you by UPS. Shipping costs are in addition to the Stage 1 package price.

When you reassemble your CNC-ported cylinder head, Performance Research recommends using new high-performance springs and having a multi-angle valve job performed. Performance Research also carries titanium retainers, keepers, and high-performance stainless-steel valves.

STAGE II PACKAGE

Send Performance Research your cylinder head assembly. The company will disassemble, pressure check for cracks, deck the head, CNC port, perform a multi-angle valve job, and reassemble with your stock valves, valve springs, retainers, and keepers.

Performance Research will call for permission to change any worn valve guides at additional charge. The company recommends installing new high-performance valve springs, titanium retainers, and stainless-steel valves for ultimate performance gains. Performance Research then ships your head back to you by UPS, ready to bolt on.

STAGE III PACKAGE
(16 VALVE HEAD)*

Send Performance Research your cylinder head assembly. The service department will disassemble, pressure check for cracks, deck and mill the head for higher compression, CNC port, install stainless-steel intake and exhaust valves, install high-performance valve springs and titanium retainers.

Performance Research will also change out any worn valve guides at additional charge and ship your head back to you by UPS, ready to bolt on.

* Higher charge for 16 Valve Head with 32 Inner/Outer Valve Springs & Titanium Retainers.

Options for all Packages
Intake Manifold Porting, except GSR
Intake Manifold Porting, GSR
Titanium Valve Spring Retainers
Stainless-Steel Valves,
standard sized
Stainless-Steel Valves,
1mm oversized
Machining for Oversized Valves
Valve Springs, inner or outer
(25% stiffer)
Valve Guides Replacement

TOYOTA HI-PO HEADS FROM
LC ENGINEERING (LCE)

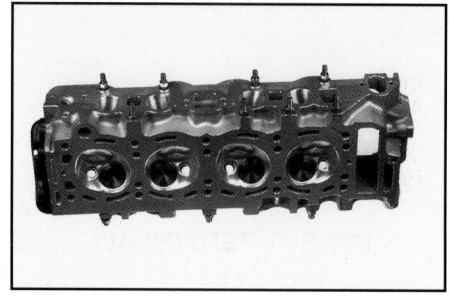

LCE uses a Flow Data computerized flow bench and a Depac Engine Dyno to develop cylinder heads that achieve the most power possible from the Toyota engine. All complete cylinder heads include a new camshaft specified for the valve diameter, porting, and chamber of that cylinder head.

LC Engineering uses only the highest quality materials. All cylinder heads include new Manganese Bronze Pro Valve Guides, new LC Engineering valve springs, new one-piece stainless-steel chrome stem swirl polished valves, and three-angle valve job. Each head is carefully assembled by trained technicians then goes through a complete 10-Step quality control inspection.

All complete cylinder heads include: Pressure-tested core. Full deburring of casting. Head deck surfaced and lapped. Intake manifold deck surfaced. Exhaust manifold deck surfaced. New valve guides. Viton® valve seals. Stainless-steel valves. Three-angle valve preparation. New exhaust and intake studs. Valves unshrouded for enhanced air flow. Valve springs shimmed for proper valve seat pressures. Valve height set for proper rocker arm geometry.

STREET PERFORMER
HEAD 20R

The 20R Street Performer head can be configured for a 20R engine as well as both early and late 22R blocks. An excellent choice for stock replacement and performance carbureted apps.

Valve Seats fully machined for oversize valves. Street Performer single valve springs and camshaft. Polished ports.

Intake Valve:
44mm stainless steel
Exhaust Valve:
36mm stainless steel
Part # 13-101

STREET PERFORMER HEAD 81-84 22R

The 22R Street Performer head is available for both the late- and early-model 22R engines. Free-flow stainless valves and all new components add up to a performance head that will give you years of trouble-free service. Valve seats fully machined for oversize valves. Street Performer single valve springs, carburetor, and camshaft. Polished ports.

Intake Valve:
45.5mm stainless steel
Exhaust Valve:
37.5mm stainless steel
Part # 13-8184

LATE/EFI PRO HEAD 85-95 22R/22RE

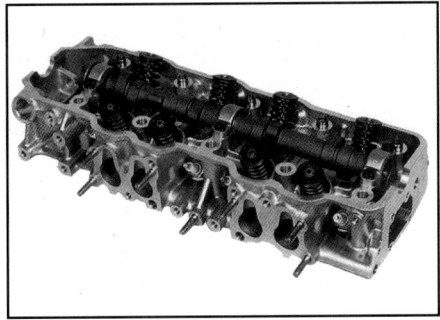

This is a new cylinder head not a rebuild! LC Engineering is now producing a NEW Replacement Performance Cylinder head for the 85-95 Toyota 22R/22RE engine. Modeled after the successful Street Performer Cylinder Head, it includes oversized stainless-steel valves, LC Street Performer valve springs, performance ported and polished for increased horsepower and torque.

Intake Valve:
45.5mm stainless steel
Exhaust Valve:
37.5mm stainless steel
Part # 13-100,
Part # 13-100NC (no cam)

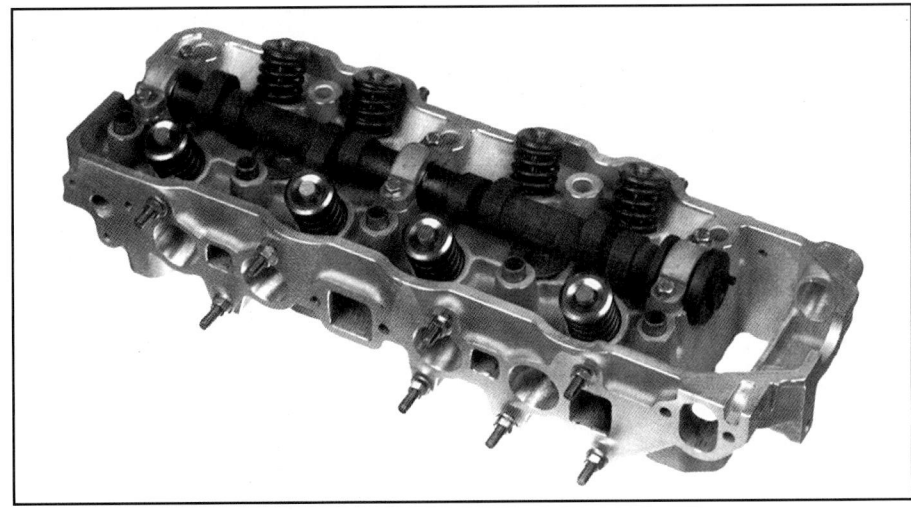

LC Engineering Pro Cylinder Heads are available for a variety of applications.

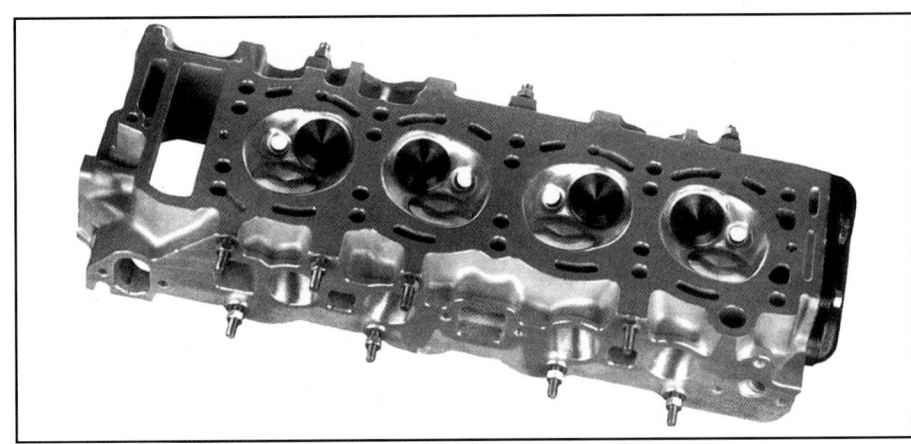

STAGE 2 PRO HEAD

The Stage 2 heads can be assembled for both the 20R or 22R. They include more extensive port work, LC Pro Dual Valve Springs, and Titanium Retainers. Excellent torque and low-end performance. A driveable cam profile great for hot 2WD street engines. Can be configured for both late- and early-block engines.

Intake Valve:
44mm stainless steel
Exhaust Valve:
36mm stainless steel
Part # 13-2101

STAGE 3 PRO HEAD

The Stage 3 head produces torque and horsepower in the 5800-6800 rpm range. This combination is excellent for smaller 1/8 to 3/8. Outstanding performance in both mud bog and off-road racing. Can be configured for both late- and early-block engines.

Intake Valve:
45.5mm stainless steel
Exhaust Valve:
37.5mm stainless steel
Part # 13-3101

STAGE 5 PRO HEAD

Each Stage 5 head is designed for the customer's specific application. Port volume, compression ratio, and camshaft design are all chosen to get maximum performance for each customer. Whether drag-race turbo, circle-track sand rail, hill climb, off-road, or street, an LC Stage 5 Pro Head offers the most powerful out-of-the-box performance your money can buy! Titanium retainers. Stellite Pro valve seats. CC combustion chambers. Stage 5 porting and polishing. Flow-bench tested.

Intake Valve:
48mm stainless steel
Exhaust Valve:
40mm stainless steel.
Part # 13-5101

Sport Compact Bolt-On Performance Guide Volume 1
Cams, Pulleys, and Valvetrains

CAMSHAFTS

ACURA B18A AND B18B CAMSHAFTS

Crower has its all new line of chilled cast cores for the Acura B18A and B18B GS/LS/RS (non-VTEC). These are not regrinds of stock cores. These are fully-round cores specifically made for Crower that exceed factory specs for hardness and compatibility. No more base circle problems typical with stock regrinds. Crower has developed several performance grinds from stock replacement, high performance street/strip, to full race (drag or road). Custom, proprietary race grinds also available. See below for dyno results on Crower cam #62403 vs stock cam (8% more HP), #62404 vs stock cam (16% more HP) and #62404 vs the hottest regrind (10% more HP).

Part #	Description	Duration @ 1mm (at valve)	Gross Lift 1.75 Intake	Gross Lift 1.75 Exhaust	RPM Range
Stock	Factory O.E.M. specs (96-up)	205 / 208	09.95mm	09.64mm	Idle to 6800
#62400	Stock replacement, automatic	207 / 210	10.22mm	09.78mm	Idle to 7000
#62401	Stock idle, 8-10 hp, OK to run w/stock springs	220 / 216	10.05mm	9.80mm	2000 to 7500
#62402	Stock idle, turbo, Crower spring kit req.	230 / 230	10.50mm	10.20mm	2500 to 8000+
#62403	Stock idle, 15-20 hp, Crower spring kit req.	238 / 237	10.80mm	10.50mm	2500 to 8000
#62404	Lope @ idle, 18-25 hp, port job recommended	243 / 241	11.30mm	11.10mm	2750 to 8500+
#62405	Rough idle, race only, perf built heads	255 / 255	12.40mm	12.40mm	3500 to 9000+
#00062	Custom ground, proprietary cams available, contact factory for specs. Add $50 to total.				
#68181	Crower spring kit				

VTEC CAM CORES

Crower has new DOHC VTEC cam cores available for the Honda B16A and the Integra B18C. Crower, with over 50 years of camshaft experience, offers a wide variety of designs, from stock replacement to road race to fully-prepared, all-out drag race. These are premium Crower cores, not regrinds. Custom, proprietary grinds also available. For details, contact Crower Tech or call 619-422-1191.

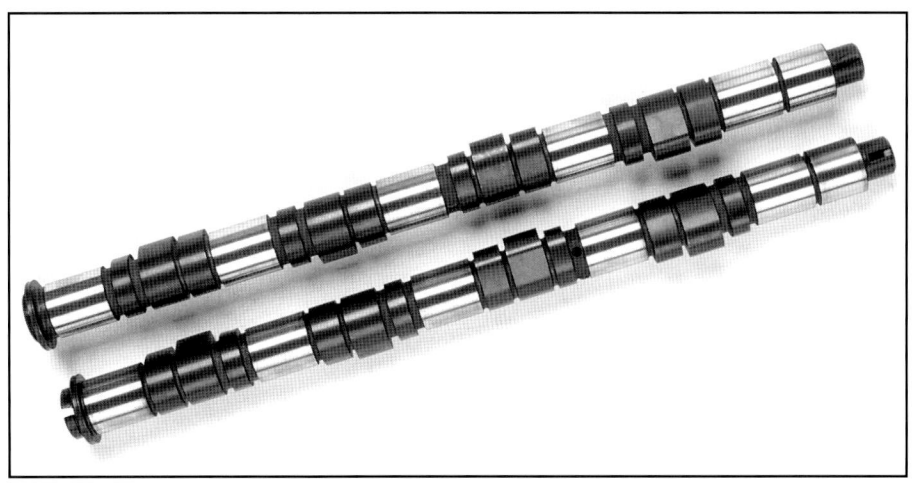

Part #	Description	Duration @ 1mm (at valve)	Gross Lift 1.55 Intake	Gross Lift 1.55 Exhaust	HP/RPM Range
#63400	Stock replacement, similar to ITR spec	Int-257 mid Exh-245 mid	Int-10.82 mid	Exh-09.72 mid	5-7 hp / 9200 rpm
#63401	Street/Strip, similar to CTR (JDM) spec	Int-259 mid Exh-251 mid	Int-11.37 mid	Exh-10.69 mid	8-10 hp / 9500 rpm
#63402	Road/Rally race, mild drag race	Int-265 mid Exh-260 mid	Int-11.37 mid	Exh-11.37 mid	10-15 hp / 9700+ rpm
#63403	Top end drag profile, perf built heads	Int-274 mid Exh-268 mid	Int-11.98 mid	Exh-11.40 mid	15-25 hp / 9900+ rpm
#00063	Custom ground, contact factory for specs				

CAMSHAFT HARDFACING AND REGRINDS

When you supply Crower your stock cam core, the company draws on 50 years of camshaft experience to grind the exact profile required for your application. Whether it's cruising (lope at idle) or full race with full NOS shot, Crower has the profile you need.

Option 1: Hardfacing. Welding up stock lobes (if VTEC, mid only) to allow unlimited spec while maintaining stock base circle. Cost $20 per lobe plus $100 per cam for the grinding. VTEC weld is only on mid lobe (8 lobes + grinding = $360 total). You supply stock cores. VTEC specs listed above are available on hardfaced cores. Full drag race, road race, turbo, or nitrous. No wear or compatibility issues.

Option 2: Straight regrind. Reduced base circle allows more lobe lift. Limited spec, emphasis on top end power. Typical specs are .005" to .010" more lift, 5 to 10 degrees more duration at .050" and about 5-10 more HP depending on engine mods. $100 per cam for the grinding. You supply stock cores.

Part #	Description
65000	SOHC — Custom ground, any make, contact factory for specs
65014	DOHC — Custom ground, any make, contact factory for specs
65020	VTEC (DOHC) — Custom ground, contact factory for specs

ELP PERFORMANCE CAMSHAFTS

Stock cams are great for non-spirited, general-purpose driving; but for serious street performance, club racing, drivers schools, and time trials, ELP offers enthusiasts a performance alternative.

Stage 1 camshafts retain excellent idle characteristics while increasing output by 6 - 14 horsepower. The Stage 1 camshafts also extend the usable power range by 500 - 700 rpm. Perfect for dual purpose vehicles.

Stage 2 camshafts are suited more toward the hot street and track enthusiasts, since idle quality suffers slightly. Stage 2 camshafts increase output by 14 - 22 horsepower depending on application, while allowing the engine to pull hard to maximum RPM. When matched with ELP's ultra performance spring and retainer package, Stage 2 camshafts extend usable RPM range 800 - 1000 rpm. Professional installation required.

ELP offers wilder camshaft profiles for those using their vehicles for serious club and drag racing events. Contact ELP Motorsport for your specific application.

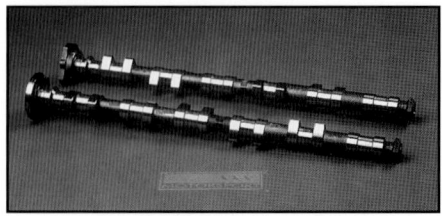

BMW SPORT CAMSHAFTS

Through street and racing involvement with the BMW line, including working with several well-known US and European tuners, several dyno-proven profiles have been developed for the BMW line. The Stage 1 cams for the M50-powered 95 M3 retains excellent idle and driveability characteristics while offering a dyno proven 12 - 14 hp increase. ELP also offers special billet and re-profiled 95 M3 exhaust cams for turbo and supercharged applications. Performance camshafts are available for the M42 16-valve 1.8L & 1.9L 318is/ti, including the Z3. ELP offers several other BMW performance applications for the early 325is, M3, M5, and M6 models. Contact ELP Motorsport for your specific application.

GUDE

Gude Bullfrog Camshafts are designed and engineered by Mr. Roy Gude (Bill) of Gude Performance. Mr. Gude is a state-of-the-art engineer whose designs have supported some of the world's best performance aircraft and world record holding racing boats. One of the most effective ways to increase the performance of any four-stroke engine is to optimize the valve lift and timing of the camshaft. Bullfrog Camshafts are designed for the performance enthusiast who wants top-end power, or more torque through the midrange.

Mr. Gude has developed the most effective camshafts for drag race, road race, and solo I or solo II cars. Every Bullfrog Camshaft is constructed from a factory core, tested, and proven to the highest racing standards. Camshafts and valve-train components are available for imported engines 4- and 6-cylinder: BLMC, Triumph, Jaguar, Nissan, Toyota, and English Ford.

GUDE ACURA INTEGRA CAMSHAFTS

1986-1989 ACURA INTEGRA 1.6L DOHC

2222 — Part # AICS01
DESCRIPTION: Strong midrange and top end power.
POWER BAND: 3500 rpm to 7200 rpm
IDLE: (Good) Around 750 rpm
SPECIFICATIONS: Intake LIFT - 0.407 DURATION - 224
Exhaust LIFT - 0.407 DURATION - 224

2352325F — Part # AICS02
DESCRIPTION: For racing only! Strong top end. Good for NOS!
POWER BAND: 4000 rpm to 7500 rpm
IDLE: (Fair) Around 900 rpm
SPECIFICATIONS: Intake LIFT - 0.418 DURATION - 228
Exhaust LIFT - 0.418 DURATION - 228

2020G — Part # AICS03
DESCRIPTION: For all out racing. Recommended for carburetors or NOS!
POWER BAND: 5000 rpm to 8000 rpm
IDLE: (Poor) Around 1000 rpm
SPECIFICATIONS: Intake LIFT - 0.418 DURATION - 242
Exhaust LIFT - 0.418 DURATION - 242

2222T — Part # AICS04
DESCRIPTION: Special grind for turbo charged engines.
IDLE: (Fair) Around 800 rpm
SPECIFICATIONS: Intake LIFT - 0.418 DURATION - 226
Exhaust LIFT - 0.418 DURATION - 226

1990-1996 ACURA INTEGRA 1.8L DOHC

235235F — Part # AICS05
DESCRIPTION: Good midrange torque and good top end.
POWER BAND: 3600 rpm to 7500 rpm
IDLE: (Good) Around 750 rpm
SPECIFICATIONS: Intake LIFT - 0.41 DURATION - 228
Exhaust LIFT - 0.41 DURATION - 228

245245F — Part # AICS06
DESCRIPTION: Aggressive! Includes valve spring kit.
POWER BAND: 4800 rpm to 7800 rpm
IDLE: (Fair) Around 900 rpm
SPECIFICATIONS: Intake LIFT - 0.431 DURATION - 236
Exhaust LIFT - 0.431 DURATION - 236

241R — Part # AICS07
DESCRIPTION: For all out racing. Recommended for carburetors or NOS!
POWER BAND: 5000 rpm to 8200 rpm
IDLE: Fair
SPECIFICATIONS: Intake LIFT - 0.412 DURATION - 264
Exhaust LIFT - 0.412 DURATION - 264

228228TE — Part # AICS08
DESCRIPTION: Special grind for turbo charged engines.
POWER BAND: 4000 rpm TO 7800 rpm
IDLE: (Good) Around 750 rpm
SPECIFICATIONS: Intake LIFT - 0.410 DURATION - 236
Exhaust LIFT - 0.410 DURATION - 236

92-96 ACURA INTEGRA 1.7/1.8L DOHC VTEC

30527P — Part # AICS09
DESCRIPTION: Strong midrange torque. Pulls hard to redline.
POWER BAND: 5000 rpm to 8500 rpm
IDLE: (Good)
SPECIFICATIONS: Intake LIFT - 0.425 DURATION - 264
Exhaust LIFT - 0.405 DURATION - 258

30527T — Part # AICS10
DESCRIPTION: For turbo charged engines.
SPECIFICATIONS: Intake LIFT - 0.434 DURATION - 264
Exhaust LIFT - 0.405 DURATION - 258

EAGLE TALON CAMSHAFTS

1990-1996 TALON

235F — Part # ET0001, turbo ET0003
DESCRIPTION: Pulls hard 2800 all the way up.
POWER BAND: 2000 rpm to 7800 rpm
IDLE: (Good)
SPECIFICATIONS: Intake LIFT - 0.387 DURATION - 228
Exhaust LIFT - 0.387 DURATION - 228

TRD CAMS

COROLLA GTS, 1988-1991

Exhaust Cam — Duration: 272°
Exhaust Cam — Duration: 288°
Exhaust Cam — Duration: 304°
Intake Cam — Duration: 272°
Intake Cam — Duration: 288°
Intake Cam — Duration: 304°

ZEX INNOVATION

Zex Innovation (a division of COMP Cams) is proud to announce import camshafts from the same team of designers that produces the industry's leading cams for Winston Cup, NHRA, and others. These aren't ordinary stock replacements. They are only for those who can handle extreme power and in-your-face performance. Call for availability.

PERFORMANCE RESEARCH CAMS

Performance Research starts with original equipment manufacturer (OEM) cast camshaft cores from Honda, Acura, Mitsubishi, Nissan, and BMW. Performance Research Vice President of Engineering and resident 'Rocket Scientist' Rob DeBardeleben develops custom lift and duration specifications for each application and the cores are then ground accordingly.

Because Performance Research camshaft cores come from the manufacturer, their specifications and tolerances are perfect. When ground to specific lift and duration figures, the cams work like they were designed to, without having the tolerance problems that regrinds create. Performance Research also has the capability to perform custom grinding for your application. Please call with your specifications.

JG ENGINE DYNAMICS

JG Engine Dynamics has a variety of high performance cam profiles for Honda/Acura engines. Call for specs and custom applications.

JIM WOLF TECHNOLOGY

Camshafts for Nissan

STAGE I — STREET

APPLICATION:
Naturally aspired. Good idle quality. Works well with header and cylinder head porting. High performance valve springs and retainers recommended. Includes both intake and exhaust camshafts.

Part # 1010-010

MAX TORQUE:
118 ft./lbs. @ 5,200 rpm (at wheels)

MAX POWER:
127 hp @ 6,200 rpm (at wheels)

MANIFOLD VACUUM AT IDLE (NO LOAD): 17.5"

STAGE II — STREET/STRIP/NITROUS

APPLICATION:
Naturally aspired or nitrous injected. Good idle quality. Works well with header and cylinder head porting. High-performance valve springs and titanium retainers recommended. Includes both intake and exhaust camshafts.

Part # 1010-020

MAX TORQUE:
128 ft./lbs. @ 3,700 rpm; w/nitrous: 192 ft./lbs. @ 3,750 rpm (at wheels)

MAX POWER:
133 hp @ 5,500 rpm; w/nitrous: 181 hp @ 5,700 rpm (at wheels)

MANIFOLD VACUUM AT IDLE (NO LOAD): 17"

STAGE III — STREET/STRIP/NITROUS

APPLICATION:
Naturally aspired or nitrous injected. Fair idle quality. Works well with header and cylinder head porting. High performance valve springs and titanium retainers highly recommended. Includes both intake and exhaust camshafts.

Part # 1010-030

MAX TORQUE:
134 ft./lbs. @ 3,400 rpm; w/nitrous: 210 ft./lbs. @ 3,000 rpm (at wheels)

MAX POWER:
139 hp @ 6,500 rpm; w/nitrous: 194 hp @ 6,700 rpm (at wheels)

MANIFOLD VACUUM AT IDLE (NO LOAD): 16"

240SX Cams
KA24 Billet Autocross Cam

Fits 1989-1990 240SX and 1990+ 4-cyl. trucks. Power increase from 3600-6000 rpm.

300ZX TT High Boost Billet Cams

This set is designed specifically to work with high-flow turbos like the Sport 600 and 650. These cams are ground from new billets to insure that the critical overlap event is kept short while allowing rapid opening and closing of the valves, thus producing exceptional flow at moderate valve lift. Base circle radius is kept large to insure compatibility with stock hydraulic lash adjusters. 1993 and later require use of early intake sprockets.

AZ320-T00R4 — Cam Set
AZ320 — Spring

This mildly reground profile increases air flow from 3800 rpm on up. Good idle and driveability; does not require springs.

AZ320-000S1 — Cam Set, 1990+ 300ZX, non-turbo

LC ENGINEERING CAMSHAFTS FOR TOYOTA

LC Engineering is constantly striving to improve both the quality and performance of its products. LCE has recently finished extensive camshaft testing on the street and race track. The results are an improved line of camshafts that offer a broader selection of grinds, increased horsepower, and higher quality.

When comparing camshaft profiles, always reference the duration @ .050 valve lift. LCE also stocks Circle Track "Limited Class" camshafts and can custom grind to your specifications.

Choosing the correct camshaft and matching valvetrain components is critical for the maximum performance and reliability. LC Engineering offers a full selection of valvetrain components. Use the Pro Camshaft Kit (Part # 13-200) for all high-lift, high-RPM applications.

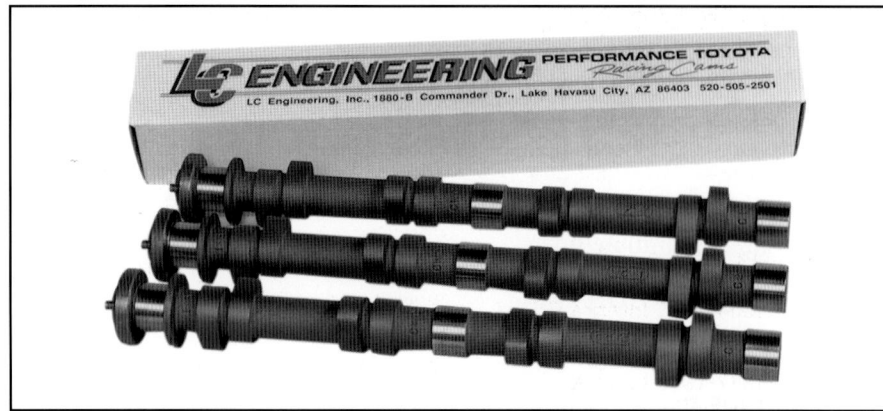

Part #	Description	Max Lift Int/Exh.	Duration @ .050"	Application
18-100	Mild Street Performer	430/430	270/210	Carb/EFI 1000-4000 rpm Smooth Idle, Stock Replacement
18-101	Street Performer	440/440	280/230	Carb. 1200-5000 rpm Smooth Idle, Torque Improvement
18-101E	EFI Pro	440/440	280/230	Smooth Idle, 1200-5000 rpm Header, T-Body, Filter Charger
18-102	Stage 2 (Off-Road)	460/460	290/240	Hot Street 1500-5500 rpm Modified Carb & 1 1/2" Header
18-103	Stage 3	475/475	295/255	Hot Street/Circle Track 2500-6500 rpm Side Drafts, Holley 2 Barrel, 1 5/8" Header
18-104	Stage 4	490/490	310/264	Circle Track/Drag Race 2500-7200 rpm Side Drafts, Holley 2 Barrel, 1 5/8" Header
18-105	Stage 5	510/510	320/270	Circle Track/Drag Race 3000-7500 rpm Side Drafts, Holley 2 Barrel, 1 5/8" Header
18-092	Outlaw	527/527	325/274	Circle Track/Drag Race 3000-8000 rpm Pro Fuel Injection, Side Drafts, Stage 5+
18-106S	Turbo/S-Charged	Custom	Custom	Call the Tech Line for a Camshaft Recommendation

POWER PULLEYS

AEM HIGH-PERFORMANCE PULLEY KITS

These high-performance pulley kits are made with the same level of commitment to performance as AEM's Tru-Time cam gears. Made from 6061-T6 billet aluminum, each is CNC machined for perfect balance, lightweight and precise function. Tru-Power Pulley Kits come complete and ready to install with correctly engineered performance belts. AEM Tru-Power pulleys are made from CNC machined 6061-T6 billet aluminum to increase horsepower and engine response without the need to remove the torsional vibration damper or emission control devices. AEM Tru-Power Pulleys are lighter in weight and larger in diameter slowing down the power steering and alternator, reducing the amount of energy needed to drive them.

Significant horsepower gains can be realized with this simple to install package with no recorded effect on emission levels. Each application includes both power steering and alternator pulleys and high-performance custom-fitted belts. Available in anodized red, blue, or silver. Tru-Power Pulleys can be matched with Tru-Time Cam Gears and Short Ram air intake.

Note: Removing the torsional vibration damper has been proven to be highly detrimental to the engine. This practice should never be encouraged as the torsional vibration damper helps eliminate the crankshaft's torsional vibration. To improve power, larger pulleys can be used to slow down the power steering and alternator. Power steering pulleys should not be increased in size over the factory components as much as the alternator pulley. Power steering systems run considerably slower than alternators and have a bypass system that reroutes the fluid at higher speeds.

AEM HIGH-PERFORMANCE PULLEY KITS

Part #	Description
ACURA	
23-7005	1990-1991 Integra
23-7006	1992-1993 Integra RS, LS, GS
23-7007	1992-1993 Integra GS-R
23-7008	1994-1998 Integra RS, LS, GS
23-7013	1994-1998 Integra GS-R
23-7014	1997-1998 Integra TYPE-R
HONDA	
23-7015	1990-1993 Accord DX, w/o AC
23-7016	1990-1993 Accord
23-7017	1994 Accord, w/o AC
23-7018	1994-1999 Accord, 4 cyl.
23-7019	1998-1999 Accord, V-6
23-7012	1988 Civic/CRX Si/DX, w/Mitsu Alt.
23-7011	1988 Civic/CRX Si/DX, w/ND Alt.
23-7011	1989-1991 Civic/CRX, Si/DX w/Mitsu Alt.
23-7009	1988-1991 Civic/CRX
23-7024	1989-1991 Civic/CRX Si/DX, w/o PS
23-7002	1992-1995 Civic DX, w/Mitsu Alt.
23-7001	1992-1995 Civic Si/EX
23-7000	1996-1999 Civic SOHC
23-7004	1999 Civic Si DOHC
23-7002	1993-1995 del Sol S SOHC
23-7001	1993-1995 del Sol Si SOHC
23-7003	1994-1995 del Sol Si DOHC
23-7010	1996-1997 del Sol SOHC
23-7004	1996-1997 del Sol DOHC
23-7020	1992-1994 Prelude S, w/o AC
23-7021	1992-1996 Prelude S/Si, non-VTEC
23-7022	1992-1996 Prelude Si VTEC
23-7022	1997-1998 Prelude
VOLKSWAGEN/AUDI	
23-7030	1998-1999 Beetle/Golf 2.0L NA
23-7031	1997-1999 Passat/A4 1.8L, turbo

*When ordering, insert "B" for blue, "C" for clear, or "R" for red at the end of the part number to indicate color desired.

GREDDY PULLEY KITS

13542101
1993-1996 Mazda RX-7, twin turbo

13512102
1993-1997 Toyota Supra, twin turbo

LC ENGINEERING

6" Water Pump Pulley

The 6" Underdrive Pulley reduces water pump RPM. This improves cooling and increases horsepower. These pulleys are CNC machined from billet 6061-T6 aluminum bar stock, cut with performance lightening holes to reduce weight and polished to a high-luster finish. The 6" Underdrive Pulley fits any 20R/22R/22RE engine and looks great!

Part # 18-406   6" Underdrive Pulley

7" Water Pump Pulley

The 7" Underdrive Pulley works with LC's Crank Power Pulley to reduce water pump RPM. For racing applications, the slower water speed improves cooling and increases horsepower for quicker lap times. LC Engineering's pulleys are CNC machined from billet 6061-T6 aluminum bar stock, cut with performance lightening holes and hard-anodized for durability. The 7" Underdrive Pulley fits any 20R/22R/22RE engine and looks great!

Part # 18-407   7" Underdrive Pulley

Timing Tag (Toyota

Set your ignition timing exactly with the new adjustable Timing Tag. Designed to work with 4" crank pulleys, set the tag one time at TDC and then time your motor with 100% accuracy. No guess work.

Part # 18-125   Timing Tag

UNDERDRIVE PULLEY KIT

Underdrive Kit for race applications includes a 4" crank power pulley, 7" water pump pulley, adjustable Timing Tag, and belt. Excellent for all circle track, drag racing, and other high-RPM applications.

Part # 18-410   Underdrive Pulley Kit

UNORTHODOX RACING'S ALUMINUM PULLEYS

Gain horsepower without major modifications. The smaller pulley size reduces belt speed and the horsepower loss associated with driving the waterpump, air conditioner, and alternator. The material used is "6061" CNC machined to ensure that the pulleys are true and perfectly balanced. The anodizing protects the pulley from long-term elements of weather. There is no long-term maintenance associated with this part, just regular belt wear and tear with normal daily driving.

ULTRA Series Lightened Underdrive Pulleys

Unorthodox Racing, Inc. Ultra Race. Single-belt race pulley. Only drives alternator and water pump (if applicable).

Unorthodox Racing, Inc. Ultra Street For street and track use. Drives all accessories.

Unorthodox Racing, Inc. Ultra Street Set For street and track use. Kits contain all pulleys except A/C.

Unorthodox Racing Ultra Series Lightened Underdrive Pulleys can yield up to 40 hp and 50 ft./lbs. gain at the wheels. Increased fuel efficiency. Low cost-per-hp gain. Lowers stress on accessories, extending service life. Computer designed to .001-inch tolerances and CNC machined from lightweight 6061-T6 aluminum billet. Available in a variety of anodized maintenance-free colors adding a custom or factory look. Includes all necessary hardware for easy installation.

TIMING GEARS

AEM TRU-TIME CAM GEARS

Tru-Time cam gears are unique in the way they look and the way they work. The belt surface is hard anodized for lasting durability. Laser-etched markings are designed for precise one-degree increment adjustments. Each is made from 6061-T6 billet aluminum and is CNC machined to aerospace standards. New to the Tru-Time line is a reduction in weight. The new gears feature the same strength and durability as the original Tru-Time gears, but are engineered to be 45% lighter.

Timing is everything. AEM Adjustable Cam Gears provide sig-

AEM TRU-TIME CAM GEARS

Part #	Applications
ACURA	
23-603	1997-1998 CL, 4 cyl.
23-603	1986-1989 Integra
23-602	1990-1999 Integra
DODGE	
23-651	Neon 2.0 L SOHC
23-650	Neon 2.0 L DOHC
HONDA	
23-603	1990-1999 Accord, 4 cyl.
23-603	1985-1987 Civic/CRX
23-600	1988-1995 Civic/CRX
23-604	1996-1999 Civic SOHC
23-602	1999 Civic Si DOHC
23-600	1993-1995 del Sol SOHC
23-604	1996-1997 del Sol SOHC
23-602	1993-1997 del Sol DOHC
23-602	1988-1991 Prelude B20-21
23-602	1992-1996 Prelude H23A1
23-603	1992-1996 Prelude F22A1
23-601	1992-1998 Prelude H22A1
MAZDA	
23-620	Miata 1.6L & 1.8L Int.
23-621	Miata 1.6L & 1.8L Ex.
MITSUBISHI	
23-630	1989-1998 Eclipse, turbo
23-630	1989-1994 Eclipse, non-turbo
23-650	1995-1998 Eclipse 2.0L, non-turbo
TOYOTA	
23-614	1993-1998 2JZGTE
23-612	1990-1995 3SGTE
23-611	1985-1987 4AG/E
23-614	1981-1985 5MG Round Tooth
23-613	1986-1992 7MGTE
VOLKSWAGEN/AUDI	
23-680	2.0L, non-turbo SOHC
23-681	1.8L, turbo

*When ordering, insert "B" for blue, "C" for clear, or "R" for red at the end of the part number to indicate color desired.
*The above applications are legal in California for racing vehicles only which may never be used on public highways.

nificant performance gains by allowing precise camshaft adjustments. Designed with laser-etched calibrated markings in exact one-degree increments, timing adjustments can be quickly and easily made from 10-degrees advance to 10-degrees retard. Tru-Time cam gears can be matched with Tru-Power Pulleys and Short Ram intakes.

In applications where aftermarket or reground performance cams have been installed, adjustable cam gears are required to realize optimum performance gains. This is also true for engines in which the cylinder head has been milled. Recorded gains when using AEM Cam Timing Gears can easily reach 10-15 horsepower.

Available in blue, red, or silver — all with hard black anodized belt surfaces for increased durability.

LIGHTSPEED RACING ADJUSTABLE CAM GEARS

HO3271	1990-1997 Accord
HO3257	1988-1997 Civic
HO3270	1993-1997 Civic del Sol VTEC DOHC
HO3270	1990-1997 Integra

GUDE ADJUSTABLE CAM SPROCKETS

HONDA/ACURA

AIAS01	1986-1989 1.6 DOHC
AIAS02	1990-1996 1.8 DOHC

JG ENGINE DYNAMICS

Adjustable timing gears are available for Honda/Acura applications. Call for details.

NEUSPEED VW ADJUSTABLE CAM GEAR

The main gear is 7075-T6 aluminum (an alloy stronger than steel), and then it's black hard-anodized for even longer wear and appearance. The hub is 6061-T6 aluminum which features locking stainless-steel threaded inserts that will never wear out or pull out with repeated adjustments, and finished in red anodizing. All hex head allen bolts and washers are stainless steel. All adjustment points are precision-laser engraved with up to a usable seven degrees of advance or retard. A hex allen wrench is included.

Adjust the power band exactly where you want it for the most efficient use of camshaft, provide more power at low- or high-RPM range, dial in camshaft for precision tuning. Fits all Volkswagen 4-cylinder, 8V engines 1975+ except new Beetle, Golf IV, and Jetta IV.

STR PRO GEARS

STR gears are CNC machined from 6061-T6 billet aluminum. Three windows are cut for lighter weight and balance, and holes are drilled through the teeth for lighter weight as well as cooling properties. All load-bearing edges are radiused for maximum strength. The mating surface tolerance is only .0002. To maintain balance while rotation takes place the lateral and radial runout are kept at .002 TIR (total indicator reading). In addition, 10mm 12-point grade A steel bolts are used for the highest torque ability. These steps have been taken to prevent slippage or breakage so you can keep the horsepower you've dialed in. To make timing adjustment user friendly, the degree markings are made flush on the inner and outer hub for visual ease. Indexed in 1° increments, +/- 10°.

When ordering STR products available in colors, please add a letter to the end of the part number to designate your desired color, ie: R= red / B= blue / P= purple / Y= yellow. With no letter it will be shipped with a polished finish.

UNORTHODOX RACING, INC. ULTRA TIME

Adjustable cam timing sprockets to maximize performance. Indexed in 1° increments, +/- 10°. Lighter than OEM because they are CNC machined from lightweight 6061-T6 aluminum billet. Super-hard anodized timing belt ring. Five-bolt locking pattern fastened with stainless-steel hardware.

IMPORTS	DOMESTICS
Acura	Chrysler
Honda	Dodge
Hyundai	Eagle
Lexus	
Mazda	
Mitsubishi	
Toyota	
Volkswagen	

VALVES, SPRINGS, RETAINERS

CROWER

Honda/Acura Premium Valve Springs

Crower's spring and retainer kits are available for the VTEC (B16A / B18C) as well as the LS / RS (B18A/B). Premium Crower dual spring with Crower titanium retainers are intended for use up to 10,000+ rpm for VTEC. Designed for high-lift, high-RPM camshafts. Works well with stock valves and keepers. Drop-in installation; no machine work required. See table below.

ELP MOTORSPORT

Performance Spring/Retainer Packages

These Ultra Performance Valve Spring/Retainer Packages ensure valvetrain stability street and race enthusiasts demand. These packages prevent valve float and bent valve problems associated with stock components while using an engine's upper RPM range and experiencing the occasional missed shift. These packages are a must for hi-lift, long-duration sport and racing cams. These packages have been used in some hi-revving 10,000 plus RPM Formula Atlantic engines without a single failure. Depending on application and usage, these packages are available with single or dual springs, and 4340 chromoly or titanium valve retainers. Contact ELP Motorsport for your specific application and vehicle usage.

Hi-Flow Sport/Racing Valves

For the enthusiast who's looking for the ultimate in cylinder head flow, ELP offers big, hi-flow, swirl-polished stainless-steel and titanium racing valves. These are the same valves used in ELP's street and race-proven Stage 3 through Stage 6 cylinder heads. These valves offer improved durability over standard replacement valves. Perfect for nitrous, turbo, and supercharger applications. Contact ELP Motorsport for your specific application.

JG ENGINE DYNAMICS

Stainless steel valves for Honda/Acura and Mitsubishi Eclipse. The valves are stock size replacements featuring harden tips, chrome stems, and swirl-polished finish.

LC ENGINEERING

Stainless-Steel Valves

When it comes to power, step up to LCE's Pro Stainless-Steel Valves. Increased air flow on any engine means more power and torque! These "big" valves are larger for more air flow and are available for all 20R, 22R, and 22RE engines. Made from temperature-resistant stainless steel, these valves are swirl-polished for max air flow. They are lighter than factory steel valves and have hardened tips for longer valve life. May be used with factory valve guides & seats. These are sold in sets of 4 and offer many trick features over factory valves.

Pro Camshaft Kits

For all Pro Camshafts this matching is a sure deal! 99% of all cam problems are caused from mismatched valve springs and related components. This kit will provide you with all of the necessary valvetrain components for use with high-lift performance cams. Kit includes: 8 Pro valve guides, 8 Pro dual valve springs, 8 Pro valve spring shims, 8 titanium retainers, 8 Viton® valve seals, and 16 valve keepers.

Part # 13-200 Pro Camshaft Kit

Street Springs

When you install a new camshaft or rebuild an engine, it's a good idea to

STR PRO GEARS

Part #	Application
	ACURA
DC0200	1990-1998 Integra
	DODGE
DC0206	Neon 2.0L DOHC
	HONDA
SC0100	1990-1997 Accord
SC0100	1988-1997 Civic
SC0100	1988-1991 CRX
SC0100	1993-1997 del Sol (SOHC)
DC0200	1993-1997 del Sol (DOHC)
DC0201	1988-1997 Prelude (H23A1)
DC0201	1992-1998 Prelude (H22A1)
	MAZDA
DC0102	1995 Miata 1.6L & 1.8L
	MITSUBISHI
DC0203	1989-1998 Eclipse, turbo
DC0204	1989-1998 Eclipse 2.0, non-turbo
DC0105	1990-1997 Galant, non-turbo
	TOYOTA
DC0110	2JZGTE, round
DC0108	3SGTE
DC0107	4AG
DC0109	7MGTE

TRD ADJUSTABLE CAM GEARS

1988-1993 Celica, turbo
1990-1995 MR2, turbo
1988-1992 Corolla GTS
1985-1988 Corolla GTS
1985-1989 MR2 (4AGELC engine)
1988-1989 MR2 (4AGZE engine)
1986-1992 Supra
1993-1998 Supra, non-turbo and twin turbo

CROWER HONDA/ACURA PREMIUM VALVE SPRINGS

Part #	Description	O.D./I.D.	(Seat Pressure)	(Open Pressure)	Coil Bind	Wire Dia.
68180	Single Spring (B18A/B)	1.081/0.805	(1.320=77#; 1.425=65#)	(0.954=123#; 1.079=106#)	.810	.134
68181	Dual Spring (B18A/B)	1.105/0.815/.630	(1.320=66#; 1.425=42#)	(0.908=153#; 1.010=136#)	.710	.141 / .086
68185	New VTEC Dual Spring	1.175/0.890/.628	(1.400=37#; 1.300=60#)	(1.000=138#; 0.900=170#)	.830	.146 / .097

NEW CROWER TITANIUM RETAINERS		
Part #	Description	Weight
87080	Aluminum Retainers for B18A/B18B fits #68180 spring	5.5 grams
87092	Titanium Retainers for B18A/B18B fits #68181 spring	6.0 grams
87091	Titanium Retainers for B18C/B16A fits Type R spring	6.0 grams
87093	Titanium Retainers for B18C/B16A fits #68185 spring	5.5 grams
87095	Titanium Retainers for Mits/DSM 2.0L fits stock spring	8.0 grams
Note: Stock Honda/Acura retainers weigh 11.5 grams.		

LC ENGINEERING STAINLESS-STEEL VALVES		
Part #	Description	Application
13-036	36mm Exhaust Valve	20R Head w/ Stock Valves Seats
13-044	44mm Intake Valve	20R Head w/ Stock Valves Seats
13-375	37.5mm Exhaust Valve	20R Head w/ #13-375S Valve Seats 22R Head w/ Stock Valves Seats
13-455	45.5mm Intake Valve	20R Head w/ #13-455S Valve Seats 22R Head w/ Stock Valves Seats
13-040	40mm Exhaust Valve	20R/22R w/ #13-040S Valve Seats
13-048	48mm Intake Valve	20R/22R w/ #13-048S Valve Seats

replace your stock valve springs with new ones. LCE's Street Performer Springs fit in the stock spring pockets and install with all of the stock valve-train components. The Street Performer Springs will control your valves up to 5500 rpm, with a valve lift of .475. For high-lift cams, LCE recommends using harden valve keepers (Part #13-016).

Part # 13-110   Street Performer Springs

Dual Springs

LCE's Pro Dual Valve Springs will control your valves up to 8,500 rpm, with .550 of valve lift. You must use Pro Titanium Retainers with these springs. For high-lift cams, LCE recommends using harden valve keepers (Part #13-016).

13-108P   Dual Valve Springs

Titanium Retainers

Pro Titanium Retainers are less than half the weight and ten times stronger than factory steel. These retainers allow you to use high-lift camshafts without the chance of retainer failure. Use only with Pro Dual Valve Springs.

13-111T   Titanium Retainers

Hardened Valve Keepers

Hardened Valve Keepers fit all 8mm valves using Toyota retainers and Pro Titanium Retainers. A must for all high-RPM applications.

13-016   Hardened Valve Keepers

Valve Guides

Pro Valve Guides are made of the highest quality manganese bronze material available. Providing additional clearance between the retainer and seal for increased valve lift, Pro Valve Guides provide excellent stability so they can be run with less clearance between the valve guide and the valve, thus preventing engine oil from entering the chamber.

Combined with Viton® Valve Seals, you'll have the finest valve guide and seal combination available. Sold as a set of eight.

13-107P   Pro Valve Guides

Viton® Valve Seals

Viton® Valve Seals are the latest in valve seal material, surpassing Teflon! Heat resistant to 440 degrees, they eliminate oil consumption through the valve guide, and provide smoother engine idling by stopping manifold air and oil leakage past the seal. Sold as a complete set, they insure a perfect seal for maximum performance.

13-70816   Pro Guide
13-72869   Stock Guide

Aluminum Rocker Arms & Rocker Assembly

When installing an LC Engineering camshaft, you are encouraged to replace rocker arms to prevent premature camshaft failure. Rockers are available separately or in complete assemblies including rockers, adjuster, nuts, pro shafts, and stands.

18-107   Rocker Arms
18-110   Rocker Assembly

Pro Rocker Shafts

The stock Toyota rocker shafts have 2 oiling holes on the top of the shafts, and very shallow oiling grooves. LCE Pro Rocker Shafts are hard chromed with 4 oiling holes for improved oil delivery to the rockers. A must for high-RPM applications. Sold in sets for all 20R, 22R, and 22RE applications.

18-108   Pro Rocker Shafts

PERFORMANCE RESEARCH

Performance Research offers custom valvetrain packages to increase performance and eliminate valve 'float' at high RPM. Performance Valve Springs, Titanium Retainers, and Stainless Steel Valves are custom manufactured to stringent specifications, providing you with the highest-quality products available.

TRD

TRD has high-performance valve springs available for the 4AGE engine. These springs, appropriate for both street and off-road use, have proven to be very reliable for high-RPM engines. They work especially well with TRD camshafts. Set includes 16 valve springs.

00643-90501-000 — Spring Set

TITANIUM RETAINERS

For use in conjunction with TRD's High-Performance valve springs, they will result in quicker revs and better valve control at higher-RPM operation.

VALVE SPRINGS

Currently under development — a TRD exclusive design — to maximize valve control in applications where other high-RPM cam designs are used.*

SI VALVES

SI Valves is pleased to announce the arrival of its 80-page, fully-revamped 2000 catalog. Over 17 years of manufacturing high-quality valves is brought to you for nearly every application, from Indian Motorcycles to International Harvesters, from Chevrolets to BMWs, from Jaguars to Fords.

SI Valves' 2000 catalog also features all the top-quality performance products that have made SI a big name in durable, affordable racing valves and valve components, such as the ever-popular Claimer Series used in Claimer race classes. All SI valves feature one-piece, stainless-steel construction; hardened tips; and chromed stems. They're fully swirl polished and undercut for better flow.

SI's new Silver Line valves — ideal for the most extreme racing conditions — are made from premium-grade EV8 stainless steel, fully swirl polished, have chrome stems for better guide wear as well as stellite tips for improved reliability, and are available with undercut stems.

MALVERN RACING

Malvern carries custom-built roller-tipped aluminum rockers for Nissan R-16, A-12 through A-15 engines, and Triumph Spitfire/GT-6/TR-6 engines. All are available in four different ratios 1.5 through 1.65.

Malvern also has steel heat-treated lightweight lifters for R-16 and A-series Nissan engines designed for race camshaft use.

For racing applications, Malvern offers custom steel and titanium valves in metric stem sizes.

PERFORMANCE RESEARCH VALVETRAIN PACKAGES

Part #	Description	Quantity
ACURA INTEGRA GS-R (1994+), INTEGRA TYPE-R (all), HONDA DEL·SOL VTEC (all)		
1001-010	Valve Spring, Outer	16
1001-020	Valve Spring, Inner	16
1002-010	Valve Retainer	16
1009-010	Valve, Intake (std)	8
1009-020	Valve, Exhaust (std)	8
1009-015	Valve, Intake (+.5mm)	8
1009-025	Valve, Exhaust (+.5mm)	8
ACURA INTEGRA (1988-1993 1.6-L DOHC)		
1001-030	Valve Spring	16
1007-010	Valve Retainer	16
1009-130	Valve, Intake (std)	8
1009-140	Valve, Exhaust (std)	8
1009-135	Valve, Intake (+1mm)	8
1009-145	Valve, Exhaust (+1mm)	8
HONDA CIVIC EX (VTEC)		
1002-010	Valve Retainer	16
1009-090	Valve, Intake	8
1009-100	Valve, Exhaust	8
HONDA CIVIC/CRX Si (1988-1991)		
1009-150	Valve, Intake	8
1009-160	Valve, Exhaust	8
HONDA PRELUDE VTEC (1993+)		
1001-040	Valve Spring, Outer	16
1001-050	Valve Spring, Inner	16
1002-010	Valve Retainer	16
HONDA PRELUDE Si (1992+)		
1001-090	Valve Spring	16
1003-010	Valve Retainer	16
1009-030	Valve, Intake	8
1009-040	Valve, Exhaust	8
HONDA PRELUDE 2.0 (up to 1991)		
1009-110	Valve, Intake	8
1009-120	Valve, Exhaust	8
MITSUBISHI ECLIPSE (TALON, LASER), GALANT (1990-1994 w/4G63 engine)		
1001-100	Valve Spring	16
1006-010	Valve Retainer	16
1009-070	Valve, Intake	8
1009-080	Valve, Exhaust	8
NISSAN SENTRA, NX2000, ETC. (all w/SR20DE engine)		
1001-110	Valve Spring	16
1004-010	Valve Retainer	16
1010-011	Camshafts, Street	2
1010-012	Camshafts, Mild Race	2
1010-013	Camshafts, Full Race	2
TOYOTA MR-2, COROLLA, ETC. (all w/4AGE engine)		
1001-120	Valve Spring	16
1005-010	Valve Retainer	16
1009-050	Valve, Intake	8
1009-060	Valve, Exhaust	8
TOYOTA SUPRA TURBO (1990)		
1001-120	Valve Spring	24

Sport Compact Bolt-On Performance Guide, Volume 1 - Imports

HEADERS

COMPTECH

Comptech Sport — s/s (Civic Si 99)
stainless-steel header 4-2-1
For Years: 1999

Comptech Sport — s/s (GSR 2000)
stainless-steel header 4-2-1
For Years: 2000 GSR

Comptech — s/s (V-6 Accord 98-00)
header and downpipe
For Years: 1998-1999 V-6 Accord

Comptech — s/s (GSR 2000)
MIG welded stainless-steel header
For years: 2000 GSR

Comptech — s/s (GSR 94-99)
MIG welded stainless-steel header
For years: 1994-1999 GSR

Comptech — s/s (Type R 97-00)
MIG welded stainless-steel header
For years: 1997-2000 Type R

DC SPORTS

Designed and tested on DC's in-house Dynamic Test Systems engine dyno. Some of DC's models will be changed to a new single-piece design. This header not only offers great looks, it also offers the durability of T-304 stainless steel. Mandrel-bent tubing, CNC machined flanges, and hand-welded construction assures you that you're getting the best header available. The new single-piece design is said to offer more power (1 - 2 hp over the two-piece model) and is lighter. Not all the models can be changed to the new design because of installation difficulties. Hardware and instructions included. Original equipment style harness included. Dyno tested with a two-year warranty.

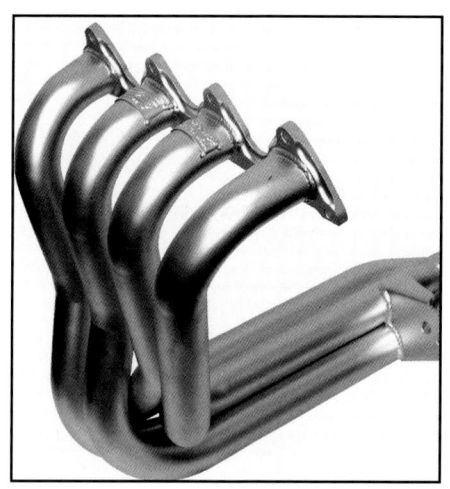

4-1 Header
Designed to optimize top-end performance. This 4-1 header features dyno-tested equal-length header tubes to provide the most power of any 4-1 header. Lightweight CNC machined flanges. High-flow merge style collectors are used to help evacuate exhaust gasses and increase horsepower. Comes with two-year warranty.

Turbo Header
A great starting point for your turbo kit or the perfect upgrade to an existing system. All the quality you have come to expect from DC Sports such as mandrel-bent T-304 stainless-steel tubing, CNC machined flanges, and hand-welded construction. Designed to fit a T-3 Turbo.

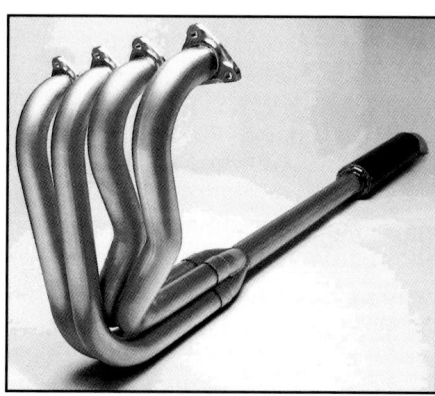

Racing 4-1 Header
Designed to be used at the track. 4-1 design with large diameter primaries to make maximum top-end power coupled to a lightweight straight-through race muffler. Designed to be run without the catalytic converter. Available in ceramic-coated mild steel, polished stainless steel, and lightweight titanium.

ELP PERFORMANCE

Performance headers are designed to optimize engine exhaust flow and increase engine output levels 6 - 14 horsepower depending on model and modifications done. These units feature high-quality CNC machined, and MIG welded flanges ensuring durable protection against vibration fatigue and exhaust leaks. All units are mandrel bent ensuring the most efficient exhaust flow. Offered in ceramic coated or stainless steel depending on model. Perfect bolt-on power modification for club racers as well as street drivers looking to win those stoplight battles.

FLOWTECH

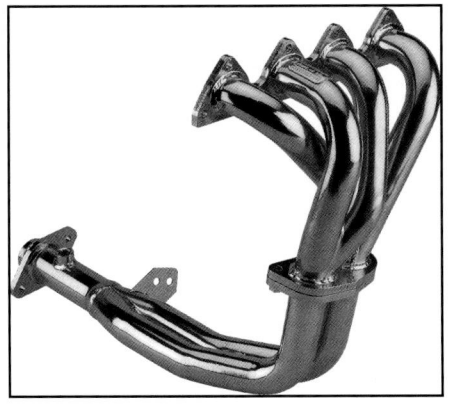

AIRMASS Pro Racing Headers represent an important performance improvement for four-cylinder Honda and Acura applications. AIRMASS Headers feature a bifurcated design that allows the tube to flow together as one without added restriction or back pressure. This allows the exhaust velocity to remain uninterrupted throughout the RPM range for maximum flow. Made of 100% heli-arc welded 16-gauge tubing, the mandrel-bent AIRMASS headers are finished with premium JET-HOT exterior coating PLUS an internal FloCote ceramic finish that increases flow. Special pulse-welding and thick CNC billet o-ringed A to B flanges provide a perfect seal without warping.

Available in your choice of JET-HOT® CompBlu™ or Sterling ShoCrom™ finishes, AIRMASS Pro-Racing Headers carry CARB. E.O. D-465 and are emissions-legal in all 50 states.

GREDDY

50-state legal headers.

Part #	Application
ACURA	
10551010	1994-1998 Integra GSR *CARB EO #D-397-4
HONDA	
10551030	1994-1997 Accord EX
10551000	1992-1998 Civic EX Coupe
10551000	1992-1995 Civic Si Hatchback
10551000	1992-1995 Civic DX
10551020	1993-1996 Prelude Si

FLOWTECH AIRMASS HEADERS

COMPBLU™	SHOCROM™	Application
ACURA		
80000	80500	1990-1991 Integra hatchback
80002	80502	1992-1993 Integra GSR
80004	80504	1994-1998 Integra non-GSR
80006	80506	1994-1998 Integra GSR
80008	80508**	1997-1998 Integra Type "R"
HONDA		
80034	80534	1998 Accord SOHC VTEC
80020	80520	1990-1993 Accord
80026	80526	1994-1995 Accord
80032	80532	1996-1997 Accord VTEC Only
80022	80522	1988-1991 Civic CRX
80024	80524	1992-1995 Civic
80028	80528	1996-1998 Civic EX
80040	80540	1994-1997 del Sol DOHC VTEC
80056	80506	1988-1989 Prelude SI
80054	80554	1990-1991 Prelude SI
80050	80550	1992-1996 Prelude SI
80052	80552	1992-1996 Prelude VTEC
80057	80557	1997-1998 Prelude SH
80058	80558	1997-1998 Prelude non-SH

**Four into one design. Does not have E.O.

GUDE RACING HEADERS

Bullfrog Headers are fine tuned and match ported to the high flowing Bullfrog ported and polished cylinder head. This unique 4-into-1 design allows for excellent torque in the midrange and monstrous top end.

Part #	Application
HONDA/ACURA	
AIHD01	1986-1989 1.6 DOHC
AIHD02	1990-1996 1.8 DOHC
AIHD03	1992-1996 GSR VTEC-DOHC

HOTSHOT

HotShot Systems Headers provide over 30 years of design and manufacturing experience. Mandrel-bent heavy-walled tubing, 3/8" thick machined flanges, and all required smog fittings. Ceramic Coating is standard on all headers. HotShot reports its Nissan Sentra SE-R header has consistently proven on the dyno to deliver 12 horsepower to the wheels on stock SE-Rs. And these race headers for the Honda and Acura have shown the way for many to break into the 12 and 11 second all motor classes.

All HotShot headers feature minimum 3/8-inch machined flanges and show-quality ceramic coating. All smog fittings remain intact in stock locations. Designed for easy installation.

RSR

RSR has headers for most popular import cars.

JACKSON RACING

Jackson Racing Performance Miata Headers

JR's newest header design is now 50 state legal! Meticulously built from 14-gauge mandrel-bent tubing, these headers incorporate wide, soft radius bends and merged collectors for maximum flow. All flanges are CNC machined, not flame cut, from high grade 1018 steel. Each header is then coated with aircraft quality ceramic coating which will not burn off or peel. This ceramic coating, combined with 14-gauge steel tubing keeps heat where it belongs — in the header, not in your engine compartment. Smog legal in all 50 States!

Part #	Application
903-110	1990-1993 Tuned Header
903-120	1994-1997 Tuned Header
903-115	1990-1993 Polished stainless-steel header

LIGHT SPEED HEADERS

HO3029	1992-1993 Integra
HO3030	1994-1998 Integra RS/LS
HO3034	1994-1998 Integra GSR
HO3119	1996-1998 Civic HX/LX/DX (with free-flo converter) not CARB legal
HO3120	1988-1998 CRX/Civic SI/EX/DX/LX
HO3120S	1988-1998 CRX/Civic SI/EX/DX/LX, 100% stainless-steel

NEUSPEED

N2 Header

An all-out, no compromises header. Four-coat ceramic finish on the outside for a great appearance, one coat on the inside for more efficient airflow. Includes splatter-free welds, flat-ground CNC flanges, 3-year limited warranty, and more.

PACESETTER PERFORMANCE PRODUCTS

Tubular header for 1995-1997 2.0 liter DOHC Dodge/Plymouth Neon, uses thick 3/8" steel for the flange and 1-1/2" diameter, mandrel-bent steel tubing. The flange is also ground flat on the head side for a better seal. It is designed to hook up to the stock catalytic converter and accept factory smog and sensing equipment. Like all headers manufactured by PaceSetter, the Neon unit receives a standard black-painted finish, but is also available with Armor*Coat metallic ceramic coating. Each header comes complete with hardware, gaskets, and illustrated instructions.

PaceSetter Honda Headers

Pacesetter Performance Products has significantly expanded its line of headers for Honda Accord, Prelude, and Civic applications. Designs were thoroughly tested before tooling was developed and manufacturing begun. These PaceSetter headers feature thick-steel flanges, ground-

PACE SETTER HEADERS FOR HONDA

Standard Part #	Coated Part #	Application	Tubing Diameter	Collector Diameter	Gasket	Notes
70-1053	72C1053	1976-1983 Accord 1.8L/2-Port	1-1/2"	2"		1, 4, 6
70-1250	72C1250	1986-1989 Accord 2.0L	1-5/8"	2"		1, 3, 6
70-1251	72C1251	1990-1993 Accord 2.2L	1-5/8"	2"		1, 3, 6
70-1252	72C1252	1994-1995 Accord 2.2L, non-Vtec	1-5/8"	2"	G7252	1, 3, 6
70-1254	72C1254	1998-1999 Accord 2.3L	1-5/8"	2"	G7252	1, 3, 6
70-1139	72C1139	1984-1987 Civic CRX Si 1.5L, fuel injection only	1-3/8"	2"	G7139	1, 3, 5
70-1139	72C1139	1984-1987 Civic Si 1.5L, fuel injection only	1-3/8"	2"	G7139	1, 3, 5
70-1144	72C1144	1988-1991 Civic Si/DX/LX 1.6L/1.5L	1-1/2"	2"	G7146	1, 3, 6
70-1160	72C1160	1992-1997 Civic Si/EX 1.6L SOHC VTEC	1-5/8"	2"	G7146	1, 3, 6
70-1149	72C1149	1992-1995 Civic 1.6L, non-VTEC	1-1/2"	2"	G7146	1, 3, 6
70-1265	72C1265	1999-2000 Civic Si 1.6L DOHC VTEC	1 5/8"	2.5"	G7146	1, 3, 6
70-1250	72C1250	1985-1987 Prelude Si 2.0L	1 5/8"	2"	G7250	1, 3, 6
70-1241	72C1241	1988-1989 Prelude Si 2.0L	1-5/8"	2"	G7241	1, 3, 6
70-1242	72C1242	1990-1991 Prelude Si 2.0L	1-5/8"	2"	G7241	1, 3, 6
70-1243	72C1243	1992-1995 Prelude Si 2.2L	1-5/8"	2"	G7240	1, 3, 6
70-1244	72C1244	1992-1995 Prelude Si 2.3L	1-3/4"	2"	G7244	1, 3, 6
70-1247	72C1247	1997-1999 Prelude 2.2L VTEC	1-3/4"	2"	G7243	1, 3, 6

NOTES
1. Flanged collector.
2. Slip-fit connector.
3. Hook-ups for smog and engine management sensors.
4. No smog or engine management sensors.
5. Comes with collector reducer. Fabrication required to hook to exhaust system.
6. Comes with header extension to connect to stock system. Fabrication may be required.
7. Fits cylinder heads with evenly-spaced exhaust ports.
8. Fits cylinder heads with paired exhaust ports.
9. Catalytic converter must be relocated.
10. Fits vehicles with 14-1/2" catalytic converter.
11. 50 States legal.

PACE SETTER MAZDA/FORD PROBE HEADERS

Part #	Application	Tubing Diameter	Collector Diameter	Gasket	Notes
MAZDA					
70-1161	1993-1994 MX6 3.0L V-6	1-1/2"	2"	7161	2, 3, 6
70-1152	1984-1992 RX-7 1.3L/13B	2"	2-1/2"	7152	1, 4, 6
70-1070	1979-1985 RX-7 1.2L/12A	2"	2-1/2"	7070	1, 4, 6

gasket surfaces, mandrel-bent tubing, and reinforced gasket material in critical locations. They are designed to bolt-in with minimal or no modifications and include hook-ups for all emission control fittings and engine management sensors. The efficient "tri-Y" design gives the best combination of gains in horsepower and torque.

Applications are available for many Civics from 1984-95, including the CRX Si and late-model Civic coupe, Accord from 1988-95, and the popular Prelude from 1988-95. All PaceSetter headers come with a black paint finish as standard and PaceSetter's three-year limited warranty. Armor*Coat metallic ceramic "C" finish is also available. 50-States Certification Pending!

PaceSetter Mazda/Ford Probe Headers

PaceSetter Performance Products has recently introduced a header for the 1993-95 Mazda MX6 with the 2.5L V-6. Manufactured using thick steel flanges and mandrel-bent mild steel tubing, this header, which also fits the Ford Probe 2.5L V-6 of the same years, was carefully designed to minimize installation problems while retaining the advantages of a tubular header system. The header comes with upgraded flanges, gaskets, installation fasteners, and all smog and engine management sensor fittings.

PaceSetter designers were very careful to route the primary header tubes so that the desired swirl pattern is created in the preformed collector. This design feature insures maximum cylinder scavenging at the tuned RPM. Increased engine efficiency at low- and mid-range RPMs and better high-RPM power output will be the result.

This header is available with black painted or the NEW Armor*Coat metallic-ceramic finish.

TRD

Exhaust Headers
Corolla GTS, 1985-1987.
MR2, Normally Aspirated, 1985-1989.
MR2, Supercharged, 1987-1989.

LC ENGINEERING

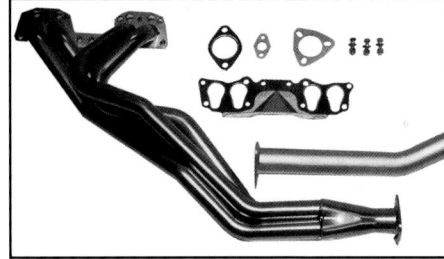

LC Engineering manufactured its own line of headers under strict quality controls. They carry replacement free-flow catalytic converters, header tube kits, header flanges, merge collectors, exhaust systems, and more!

All LC Engineering header systems are made with 16-gauge mandrel-bent tubing with a 3/8" thick header flange and fully ceramic coated. These headers are designed to use with the factory exhaust manifold gasket (included with kit).

LC Engineering has aggressively attacked the problem of header corrosion. A specially-developed corrosion resistant ceramic coating is used that will withstand temperatures to 1,600 degrees. It's well known that a chrome header just doesn't last, especially in cold, wet climates. Ceramic coating is the best protection available. Each kit includes 1-5/8" 16-gauge steel tubing, 3/8" header flange, 4 into 1 true merge collector, fully ceramic coated, OEM-style header gasket.

Part # 14-6158P   1-5/8" Pro Headers for early Celica.

Pro Flow 2 1/4" Muffler

The Pro Flow Performance Muffler is the same one used in Pro Flow Exhaust Systems. The fully-welded 2-1/4" muffler features a chamber design with no packing to burnout. The Pro Flow muffler delivers optimum back pressure for more power with a deep, throaty sound.

Part # 14-86310   Pro Flow 2 1/4" Muffler

Header Tubing Kit

This header tubing kit is a "fabricate yourself" kit for racers with custom tube chassis that require a large tube competition header. Each kit includes 1-5/8" header flange, merge collector, four 1-5/8" J Bends, six 1-5/8" straight tubes, two 3-bolt flanges, exhaust gasket.

Part # 14-1158TK   Header Tubing Kit

20R, 22R header flanges are available in 1-5/8" port size for custom exhaust fabrications.

Part # 14-158   Header Flange

Performance engines require improved exhaust flow. This 1-5/8" true merge collector installed on your custom header will improve exhaust flow, resulting in more horsepower.

Part # 14-141   Pro Merge Collector

RPS PERFORMANCE PRODUCTS

Turbo Toyota Supra Header

Header (equal-length stainless-steel header)
Applications:
2JZ80 and 7MGTE engines.

OBX

Ceramic-Coated Headers

Product#	Application
ACURA	
H9091	1990-1991 Integra
H9293	1992-1993 Integra
H9498L	1994-1999 Integra RS/LS/GS
H9498G	1994-1999 Integra GSR
HONDA	
H9093	1990-1993 Accord
H9497	1994-1997 Accord
H9804	1998-2000 Accord 4 cyl.
H8891	1988-1991 Civic/CRX/Si
H8892	1988-1991 Civic/CRX HF/DX/LX
H9297	1992-1999 Civic HX/EX/Si
H9296	1992-1996 Prelude Si
H9297	1992-1997 Prelude VTEC
H9700	1997-1999 Prelude
MITSUBISHI	
H9599	1995-1999 Eclipse, non-turbo
H9798	1997-1998 Mirage 1.8L
NISSAN	
H9598	1995-1998 Sentra/200SX 2.0L SE-R
TOYOTA	
H9397	1993-1997 Corolla 1.8L

CAT-BACK EXHAUST SYSTEMS

TRI-FLO PERFORMANCE

Installation of the cat-back alone shows a gain in power to the wheels of 13 ft./lb. and 11 hp over stock as proven on a DynoJet chassis dyno. The complete kit with the factory catalytic converters in place for our test brought power up to 15 ft./lb. and 15 hp over stock. With the complete exhaust system installed, throttle response is more linear and power is appreciably improved across the entire power band.

If sheer performance isn't enough for you, then the unmistakable sound of a Tri-Flo exhaust will demand your attention. The Tri-Flo system has a rich, high-performance sound designed for the street so it isn't too loud and emits very little resonance.

Meticulously fabricated by hand, the Tri-Flo system is constructed entirely of high-grade T-304 stainless steel offering great looks and a lifetime of performance. Even the flanges are solid stainless-steel billets precisely machined on a CNC mill for accurate fit and seal. Primary header tubes are 1.75-inch diameter and are soft radius, mandrel bent throughout. Merging of the primary tubes is carried out through a long collector which gives more top-end performance than shorter collectors, without sacrificing bottom-end power. Coming off of the collector is a high-strength slip joint to relieve stress from the headers due to engine torquing. Exit diameter of the header/collector is 2.5-inches.

The cat-back muffler for the NSX is state-of-the-art as well, offering a rich performance note that is not overly loud. Each is hand-built using polished T-304 stainless steel with mandrel bent 2.5-inch inlet pipes and 3-inch outlet pipes. Inlet and outlet pipes are gusset reinforced for added strength.

APEX INTEGRATION INC.

All APEX exhaust systems are manufactured in Japan and feature trademark ROBOTIC TIG WELDS and flawless design. It is important to understand that welding alone does not produce quality exhaust. It is the

APEX INTEGRATION INC.			
Part#	Application	Pipe Size (mm)	Tip Size (mm)
MAZDA			
163-Z002	1993-1995 RX-7	65	290
163-Z001	1986-1991 RX-7 (1 muffler per side/ 1 tip per side)	60-65	290
NISSAN			
163-N004	1995-1998 240SX	60-65	290
163-N003	1989-1993 240SX	60-65	290

database of information regarding exhaust pulse, engine characteristics, and silencing techniques that sets Apex exhaust systems apart.

Every product has an intended concept to it, a purpose that it is designed for. In tuning, every gain usually sacrifices another aspect of performance. Some sacrifices may be low-end power in exchange for a high-end punch. Drag racing exhaust systems make power on the top end while a road racer would want plenty of midrange torque to propel out of the corners.

The most apparent difference in Apex exhaust systems is the cosmetics. Apex uses robotic TIG welds and are mandrel bent to prevent any loss of efficiency. The Apex factory also boasts one of the only 95mm pipe bending machines for high HP applications. All canisters use aircraft quality SUS 304 stainless steel and have a titanium particle-based high-temperature paint to protect the pipes.

The N-1 Dual is a variant of the smash hit N-1 single. The Dual N-1 splits into two small-diameter pipes that flow into two 120mm canisters with two 90mm tips at the end. The dual pipe configuration starts right after the catalytic converter with computer-aided pipe bends and clearance adjustments. The Dual N-1 achieves greater power than the single N-1 because federal regulations prevent the single N-1 piping diameter from being excessively big. This means that the dual pipe design of the Dual N-1 flows more volume of exhaust than a single pipe could while retaining more midrange torque at the same peak HP. As with the single N-1 the Dual N-1 canisters and tip are constructed of a SUS 304 polished stainless steel while piping is treated to a titanium particle-based high-temperature paint.

DUNK

THE DUNK 115 SERIES

Intimidating looks, and dyno-proven HP gains, good mid- to high-end power. The DUNK 115 Series was designed especially for U.S. spec vehicles that differed from their Japanese counterparts in engine design and catalytic converter placement. The DUNK 115 Series are all made to U.S. market demands with full 60mm piping and a straight-through canister design. The 200mm SUS 304 stainless-steel canister also allows for ample ground clearance. The tip is also constructed of a polished SUS 304 stainless steel. Piping is treated in a high temperature titanium particle-based paint. All of the DUNK 115s have a 115mm tip size which allows the use of the SUPER SILENCER for an extra 7 dB of sound deadening. All exhaust systems conform to the 95dB limit and do not modify any emissions equipment.

APEX

Apex was the first to produce an angled muffler and has continued to pioneer new and more efficient ways of making exhaust systems. Engineered from feedback data of an N-1 series race car, the N-1 stands as the second benchmark exhaust system from Apex.

In an N-1 Endurance Race, efficiency is everything. That is why all of the N-1 exhaust pipes aim for the straightest possible line with the least number of pipe bends. This allows exhaust gases to pass smoothly through the piping. The exhaust system canister is made of a rugged SUS 304 stainless steel and features a 115 mm tail. The canister projects from the car at an

DUNK 115 SERIES

Part#	Application	Pipe Size (mm)	Tip Size (mm)
HONDA			
152-KH07	1994-1997 Accord	60	115
152-KH08	1990-1993 Accord	60	115
152-KH01	1992-1999 Civic Coupe EX/Si	60	115
152-KH01	1992-1995 Civic DX	60	115
152-KH02	1992-1995 Civic H/B	60	115
152-KH09	1996-1999 Civic H/B	60	115
152-KH03	1994-1996 Integra GSR	60	115
152-KH04	1994-1999 Integra, non-VTEC	60	115
152-KH0R	1997-1998 Integra Type-R	60	115
152-KH06	1993-1996 Prelude	60	115
152-KH10	1997-1998 Prelude, except Type SH	60	115
152-KH11	1997-1998 Prelude SH	60	115
MITSUBISHI			
151-KM01	1995+ Eclipse GSX	85	115
151-KM02	1995+ Eclipse GST	85	115
152-KM01	1995+ Eclipse GS	60	115

RS EXHAUST

Part#	Application	Pipe Size (mm)	Tip Size (mm)
ACURA			
112-KH03	1994-1998 Integra GSR	60	95-105 oval
112-KH04	1994-1998 Integra, non-VTEC	60	95-105 oval
112-KH0R	1997-1998 Integra Type-R	60	95-105 oval
HONDA			
112-KH07	1994-1997 Accord	60	105-115 oval
112-KH08	1990-1993 Accord	60	105-115 oval
112-KH12	1998+ Accord Coupe V-6	60x2	105-115 oval
112-KH13	1998+ Accord Coupe V-6	60	105-115 oval
112-KH14	1998+ Accord Coupe 4 cyl.	60	105-115 oval
112-KH01	1992-1998 Civic 2dr/4dr EX	60	95-105 oval
	1992-1995 Civic DX	60	95-105 oval
112-KH02	1992-1995 Civic H/B	60	95-105 oval
112-KH09	1996-1998 Civic H/B	60	95-105 oval
112-KH06	1993-1996 Prelude	60	105-115 oval
112-KH10	1997-1998 Prelude	60	105-115 oval
112-KH11	1997-1998 Prelude SH	60	105-115 oval
MAZDA			
112-Z001	1990-1993 Miata	50-60	105
111-Z001	1993-1995 RX-7	70-85	120
111-Z002	1986-1992 RX-7	75-85	120
MITSUBISHI			
111-KM01	1995-1998 Eclipse GSX	85	110-120 oval
111-KM02	1995-1998 Eclipse GS-T	70-85	110-120 oval
112-KM01	1995-1998 Eclipse GS	60	110-120 oval
NISSAN			
111-N006	1995-1998 240 SX	75-85	90-120
111-N004	1989-1994 240 SX	75-85	90-120
112-N007	1988-1993 240 SX	54-60	80-115
TOYOTA			
111-T005	1991-1995 MR-2	75-85	90-120
111-T003	1993-1998 Supra	85-95	100-120

angle which also contributes to smooth flowing exhaust. Because all of the exhausts are straight-through design, throttle response and horsepower levels are improved. The N-1 Series Exhaust is available for both NA (normally aspirated) and turbocharged vehicles.

RS

The RS Exhaust is designed to achieve high-end power while preventing excessive noise levels commonly associated with similar exhaust systems. The canister and tip are constructed out of a polished SUS 304 stainless steel. Tip sizes differ according to engine specification and are available in 105mm for NA cars and 120mm for turbo cars.

APPLIED TECHNOLOGIES & RESEARCH, INC.

Makers of T304 3-inch mandrel bent exhaust systems with 4-inch polished stainless tips. Applications for most popular import and high-tech domestics.

AROSPEED

Arospeed bolt-on rear sections are made with the same quality as Arospeed mufflers, but include mandrel-bent, stainless-steel piping that is also polished to a mirror-like finish. These rear sections bolt right on to the stock piping and do not require any welding or modifications.

Part #	Application
ARO915002	1994-1999 Acura Integra GSR
ARO915004	1994-1997 Honda Accord
ARO915000	1992-1999 Honda Civic
ARO915001	1992-1999 Honda Civic Hatchback
ARO915006	1988-1991 Honda Civic 4-door
ARO915006	Mitsubishi Mirage

BORLA

Stainless-steel cat-back exhaust systems. See table next page.

COMPTECH

Cat-back exhaust - Stainless/Tig
For Years: 1999 Civic Si

Power Pro
Cat-back stainless exhaust system
(GSR, 2dr) For Years: 2000

Power Pro
Cat-back stainless exhaust system
(GSR Coupe, 2dr) For Years: 1994+

Power Pro
Cat-back stainless exhaust system
(GSR Sedan, 4dr)
For Years: 1994-1999

Power Pro
Cat-back stainless exhaust system
(RS, LS, GS, 2dr) For Years: 1994+

Power Pro
Cat-back stainless exhaust system
(Type R) For Years: 1997-2000

Street Pro
Aluminized steel cat-back exhaust
(GSR Coupe, 2dr)
For Years: 1994-1999

Street Pro
Aluminized steel cat-back exhaust
(LS, RS, GS Coupe) For Years: 1994+

BORLA EXHAUST

Part #	Application	Tip Description	Tip Exit
ACURA			
11662	1996-1997 Integra RS, 4 cyl.	S RD AC IC	R
14855 new	1996-1999 Integra, 4 cyl., 2dr	S RD RL AC PH	R
HONDA			
14715 (discont.)	1996 Accord Wagon	S RD RL	R
11730	1998 Accord EX/LX	S RD RL	R
11503	1994-1997 Civic EX/LX Sedan, Coupe	S RD RL	R
11727	1992-1995 Civic Si	S RD RL	R
11779	1997-1998 Prelude VTEC	S RL RD	R
14877 new	2000 S2000 2.0L	S RD RL	SR
LEXUS			
11729	1998 GS400 V-8	S CF	SR
11733 new	1998 GS300/400	S RL OV	SR
11401	1992-1998 SC300/SC400 V-6, V-8	S RD AC IC	SR
11689	1996-1998 LS400 V-8	S RD AC IC	SR
14760 discont.	1995-1997 LX450, 6 cyl.	D SQ AC IC	R
14814 new	1998-1999 LX470 V-8	S RD AC	R
MAZDA			
14411	1990-1997 Miata, 4 cyl.	S RD AC IC	R
11732	1999 Miata, 4 cyl.	S RED CF	R
14192	1986-1992 RX-7	S RD AC IC	SR
15175	1986-1992 RX-7 turbo	S RD AC IC	SR
15433	1993-1994 RX-7 turbo	S RD AC IC	R
14429	1993-1994 MX6 V-6	D RD IC	R
MITSUBISHI			
14508	1991-1996 3000GT V-6	S RD AC IC	SR
15443	1991-1996 3000GT VR-4 V-6, twin turbo	S RD AC IC	SR
14804	1995-1999 Eclipse RS, GS	S RD RL	R
NISSAN			
15320	1990-1995 300ZX V-6, turbo w/H-PIPE	D RD IC	SR
TOYOTA			
15725	1993-1995 Supra, twin turbo	S RD AC	R
VOLKSWAGEN			
14792	1998-1999 Beetle 2.0L	D RD RL AC IC	R
14859 new	1999 Beetle 1.8L, turbo	D DTM	R

TIPS DESCRIPTIONS		TIP EXITS	
AC	Angle Cut	R	Rear
CF	Carbon Fiber	S	Side
D	Dual Tips	SR	Split Rear
IC	Intercooled	SS	Split Side
PH	Phantom		
RD	Round		
RE	Rectangular		
RL	Rolled		
S	Single Tip		
SQ	Square		
TD	Turndown		
TO	Turnout		

DINAN FREE FLOW EXHAUST

3 Series E46
3 Series E36
3 Series E30
328i (E46) 1999
323i (E46) 1999
M3 (E36) 1996-1999
M3 (E36) 1995
328i (E36) 1996-1999
325i, iC (E36) 1992-1995
323i (E36) 1998-1999
318i (E36) 1996-1998
318i (E36) 1992-1995
318ti (E36) 1996-1999
318ti (E36) 1995
M3 (E30) 1987-1991
325i, ix, Convertible (E30) 1987-1991
325, 325e (E30) 1984-1988
318i (E30) 1990-1993
318i (E30) 1983-1985
323i (E30) 1983-1991

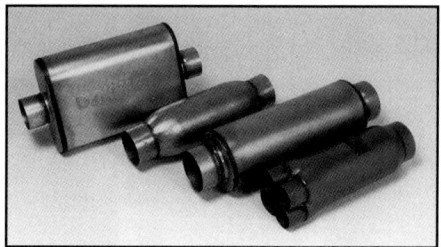

DYNOMAX

DynoMax now has state-of-the-art systems for most popular late-model import vehicles. The new systems cover applications for Acura, Honda, Mitsubishi, and VW. These feature T304 stainless-steel pipes, a straight-through stainless-steel Ultra Flow muffler with a highly polished mirror-like finish and all new roll-formed stainless exhaust tips.

Dynomax Ultraflo muffler features all stainless-steel materials for optimum appearance, corrosion resistance, and longer life. Withstands the heat of competition with durability up to 1500° F. Includes high chromium content stainless-steel mesh for high temperature durability and long life, high-luster T-304 cover and heads. Exclusive CRF (continuous roving fiberglass) for deep, powerful true performance sound. Continuous perf tube design maximizes sound absorption and minimizes turbulence.

Super Turbo has exclusive patented flow directors which channel exhaust flow and eliminate turbulence. All-aluminized materials for sharper appearance and longer life. Super Turbo mufflers are arc-welded for reduced high-temperature fatigue and longer life.

DC SPORTS CAT BACK EXHAUST

Performance and great looks built into one system -- that's what you get from the DC Sports Cat-Back Exhaust. The DC Sports exhaust system includes everything from the catalytic convertor back including a factory style resonator and a performance muffler finished off with a 4" laser engraved tip. Made of T-304 polished stainless-steel construction. An increase of 6-8 horsepower is possible. 4" Laser Engraved Tip. Mandrel-bent tubing. Hardware and instructions included. Two-year warranty.

DINAN 3-SERIES BMW FREE FLOW EXHAUST SYSTEM

This exhaust system does it all. It creates additional power by reducing back pressure, it's lightweight, and sounds terrific. Made from stainless steel for long life. Complete with polished exhaust tips to give your 3 Series a sportier look.

Withstands temperatures up to 1100° F. Large diameter internal tubes for maximum flow. Fiberglass matting delivers a mello true performance sound. Now available with 3-inch internal flow tubes for some applications.

Pipes are critical to winning performance. DynoMax pipes feature mandrel bends for better flow versus stock. All-aluminized materials give them a longer-lasting, sharper appearance. Thanks to OE design expertise of DynoMax engineers, DynoMax pipes follow OE routing precisely so they fit right the first time. They're the optimum match to your engine's specific performance needs.

The improved flow that comes from mandrel bent pipe makes DynoMax pipes, systems, and headers superior. The mandrel bending process maintains a constant inside diameter, even through pipe bends. Flow area remains consistent, increasing flow more than 35% compared to stock, serrated bent pipes.

ELP PERFORMANCE EXHAUST SYSTEMS

These cat-back bolt-on smog legal systems are designed to increase horsepower output by decreasing restrictive back pressure. These systems feature larger than stock mandrel bent tubing with hi-flow sport muffler(s). These systems give an authoritative deep exhaust note as you roll into the throttle and experience a noticeable HP increase. Engine output is increased 7 - 15 hp on aspirated cars and as much as 30 hp on turbo cars depending on application. Contact ELP Motorsport for specific year, make, and model.

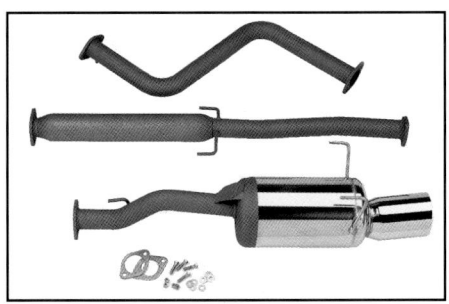

FLOWTECH

AIRMASS Extreme Exhaust Systems are second to none. Two different styles are available: WARLOCK

GREDDY EXHAUST SYSTEMS

Part #	Application	Pipe	Tip	Type
ACURA				
10155550	1990-1991 Integra LS/RS	50	100 X 110	SP
11050102	1992-1993 Integra Extension adapter	50	NA	--
10155560	1994-1998 Integra LS/RS	60	100 X 110	SP
10155562	1994-1998 Integra LS/RS	60	100 X 110	SP
10155561	1994-1998 Integra GS-R	60	100 X 110	SP
10156010	1994-1998 Integra GS-R	60-70	101	PE
10155563	1994-1998 Integra GS-R	60	100 X 110	SP
10155690	1991-1995 Legend, 2dr	60	120 X 130	SP
HONDA				
10155602	1998+ Accord V-6 2dr	60	115	MX
10155604	1998+ Accord Dual Option	60	115	MX
10155603	1998+ Accord 4 cyl., 4dr	60	130	SP
10155605	1998+ Accord 4 cyl., 2dr	60	130	SP
10155590	1990-1993 Accord EX/LX	60	100x110	SP
10155600	1994-1995 Accord EX/LX	60	100x110	SP
10155600	1996-1997 Accord EX	60	100x110	SP
10156011	1994-1995 Accord EX/LX	60-70	101	PE
10156011	1996-1997 Accord EX	60-70	101	PE
10155601	1995-1997 Accord EX V-6	60	100x110	SP
10155500	1989-1991 Civic Si/DX	50	100x110	SP
10155512	1992-1995 Civic Si/DX	60	100x110	SP
10155520	1996-1997 Civic DX	60	100x110	SP
10155510	1992-1995 Civic EX/DX Coupe	60	100x110	SP
101569001	1992-1995 Civic Hatchback	60-70	101	PE
10155510	1996-1997 Civic EX Coupe	60	100x110	SP
10156000	1992-1995 Civic EX/DX Coupe	60-70	101	PE
10156000	1996-1997 Civic EX Coupe	60-70	101	PE
10156001	1992-1995 Civic Si/DX	60	101	PE
10155660	1988-1991 CRX Si	60	100x110	SP
10155700	1997+ CR-V	60	110	SP
10155670	1992-1996 del Sol	60	100x110	SP
10155641	1997+ Prelude	60	130	SP
10155640	1992-1996 Prelude	60	100x110	SP
10156020	1992-1996 Prelude	60-70	101	PE
10156021	1997+ Prelude	60-70	101	PE
INFINITY				
10125531	1996-1997 I-30	60	100 X 110	SP
10121540	1991-1997 G-20	60	101	MX
LEXUS				
10111550	1992-1997 GS300	60	115	MX
10111541	1992-1997 SC300	60	115	MX
10116020	1998-1999 GS300/GS400	70	115	PE
MAZDA / FORD				
10145510	1991-1997 MIATA 1.6L/ 1.8L	50	102	SP
10145511	1998-1999 MIATA 1.8L	60	100x110	SP
10146000	1991-1997 MIATA 1.6L/ 1.8L	50-70	101	PE
10141520	1987-1992 RX-7, turbo/ NA	70	102	MX
10140010	1987-1992 RX-7, turbo/ NA	60-80	101	PE
10140502	1993-1996 RX-7, twin turbo	80	120x130	SP
10146010	1993-1996 RX-7, twin turbo	80-94	115	PE
10145500	1993-1996 Probe GT	60	120x130	SP
MITSUBISHI				
10135520	1989-1991 Eclipse 2WD, turbo	60	120x130	SP
10135521	1989-1994 Eclipse AWD, turbo	60	120x130	SP
10135530	1995-1997 Eclipse 2WD, turbo	60	120x130	SP
10136000	1995-1997 Eclipse 2WD, turbo	60-70	115	PE
10135532	1995-1997 Eclipse 2WD N/A	50	120x130	SP
10135531	1995-1997 Eclipse AWD, turbo	60	120x130	SP
10136001	1995-1997 Eclipse AWD, turbo	60-80	115	PE
10135550	1991-1996 3000GT VR-4, twin turbo	80	120x130	SP
NISSAN				
10125570	1992-1997 Altima GXE	60	100x110	SP
10125530	1989-1994 Maxima SE	60	100x110	SP
10125531	1995-1996 Maxima SE	60	100x110	SP
10125532	1997+ Maxima SE	60	100x110	SP
10125510	1991-1994 Sentra SE/SE-R	50	100x110	SP
10125550	1995-1997 200SX SE-R	60	110	SP
10121551	1998-1999 200 SX SER	60	120x130	SP
10125500	1989-1994 240 SX	60	120x130	SP
10120584	1995-1997 240 SX	60	120x130	SP
10126000	1995-1997 240 SX	60-70	115	PE
10121541	1995-1998 240 SX	60	115	MX
10125520	1990-1995 300 ZX Cpe.T/T & NA	60	120x130	SP
10126010	1990-1995 300 ZX Cpe.T/T & NA	60-70	115	PE
10121500	1990-1995 300 ZX 2+2 na	60	115	MX
10125521	1990-1995 300 ZX 2+2 na	60	120x130	SP
TOYOTA				
10116000	1997-1998 Camry	60-70	115	PE
10115500	1994-1996 Celica GT	60	94	SP
10110000	1985-1997 Corolla GT-S	50-70	101	PE
10010630	1990-1996 MR-2, turbo	70	115	PE
10115511	1990-1996 MR-2, turbo	60	100x110	SP
10115510	1990-1996 MR-2 N/A	60	100x110	SP
10115530	1995-1997 RAV-4	60	100x110	SP
10115540	1987-1992 Supra, turbo	80	120x130	SP
10115550	1993-1997 Supra, twin turbo	80	120x130	SP
10116010	1993-1997 Supra, twin turbo	80-94	130	PE
10110561	1993-1997 Supra N/A	80-60	130	MX
10115560	1997-1998 4-Runner	70	130	SP

MX (Maximum & Extreme) Power Extreme SP (Street Performance)
50-State Legal Headers

GREDDY 50-STATE LEGAL HEADERS		
Part #	Application	
10551000	1992-1998 Honda Civic EX Coupe	4-2-1
10551000	1992-1995 Honda Civic Si Hatchback	4-2-1
10551000	1992-1995 Honda Civic DX	4-2-1

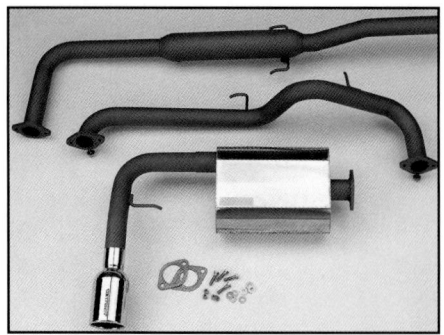

and THUNDERMUFF. Both systems feature show-polished 304 stainless, fully-welded mufflers and tips. The pipes are constructed from specially selected lengths of aluminized tubing to prevent rust and corrosion. Call for applications.

GIBSON

Gibson Headers High Performance Exhaust System includes: stainless-steel headpipe, stainless-steel muffler, and stainless-steel tip. Bolts directly onto the OEM system. Systems are designed with a fully-polished 304 stainless muffler for a show-quality look. Systems are designed for maximum flow. Welded-on 4" rolled polished stainless tips. It's backed by a limited lifetime warranty.

Part #	Application
125-10	1994-1998 Acura Integra, 2dr, 4 cyl.
125-20	1996-1998 Honda Civic EX, 2dr, 4 cyl.
125-21	1995-1997 Honda Accord, 4dr, 4 cyl.
125-22	1998-1999 Honda Accord, 2dr & 4dr, 4 cyl.
125-30	1995-1998 Mitsubishi Eclipse 2.0, 2dr, non-turbo
125-40	1998-1999 Volkswagen Beetle 2.0, dual 3" tip
125-41	1996 Volkswagen Jetta GL, 4dr, 4 cyl.

JACKSON RACING MIATA SPORT EXHAUST SYSTEM

Jackson Racing's sport exhaust system for the Miata has been engineered to optimize exhaust flow, integrate with JR's cold air induction system, and give a pleasant exhaust note. The exhaust system features include rust-proof 304 stainless-steel construction, a high-flow single-pass muffler, and a large diameter oval tip for that European performance look. JR is the only aftermarket system which incorporates a center resonator like the factory system. This helps keep the exhaust quiet and eliminates the tinny sound heard in other replacement systems. Smog Legal in all 50 States!

Part # 900-495   1990-1997 Sport Exhaust

Polished Sport Exhaust System

JR started with the fine stainless-steel sport exhaust system and took the muffler portion on a trip to the polishers. The result: a jewel in which you can actually see your reflection! If you pride yourself on the immaculate condition of your Miata, this is the exhaust system for you. Smog Legal in all 50 States!

Part # 903-000   1990-1997 Sport Exhaust System

LIGHTSPEED

Megaflo Sport Exhaust System

Unique Lightspeed design features, free-flow muffler that produces 4-7 horsepower through the entire RPM range -- dyno tested (Super Street magazine June 1997). The ultimate in horsepower and lasting great looks. No other system compares.

Part #	Application
HO3219	1996-1998 Civic 2 & 4dr HX/LX/DX
HO3247	1996-1998 Civic hatch back DX/LX/CX
HO3221	1992-1995 Civic 2 & 4dr EX/DX/LX/
HO3221	1996-1998 Civic 2 & 4dr EX
HO3162	1988-1991 CRX SI/DX
HO3163	1988-1991 Civic SI/DX

PACESETTER PERFORMANCE PRODUCTS

MONZA Performance Exhaust Systems

The exhaust flow of an engine has a direct effect on its performance. MONZA Performance Exhaust Systems for the 1992-1995 Honda Civic Coupe utilize the right combination of larger than stock, 16-gauge, mandrel-bent tubing and a low back-pressure, high-flow performance muffler for cooler, smoother operation and increased performance.

Each MONZA Performance Exhaust System for the Honda Civic uses 2-1/2" diameter mandrel-bent steel tubing, a corrosion-resistant aluminized steel muffler, and features the popular 4" diameter MONZA BIG BORE Exhaust Tip with Resonator pre-welded to each muffler. The finish is a durable black paint. Necessary hardware and instructions are included.

The MONZA Performance Exhaust System for the Honda Civic is designed to replace the original equipment muffler system and attach to the stock catalytic converter ("cat-back"). Each carries a limited three-year warranty.

MONZA Performance Exhaust Systems for Mazda

Each MONZA Performance Exhaust System for the Mazda Miata uses 2-1/4" diameter mandrel-bent steel tubing, corrosion-resistant aluminized-steel muffler, and the popular 3" diameter MONZA BIG BORE Exhaust Tip with Resonator pre-welded to each muffler. The finish is a durable black paint. Necessary hardware and instructions are included.

The MONZA Performance Exhaust System for the Mazda Miata is designed to replace the original equipment muffler system and attach to the stock catalytic converter ("cat-back"). Each carries a limited three-year warranty.

MONZA Performance Exhaust Systems are also available for Mazda MX5 and MX6, as well as other popular makes.

MONZA Performance Exhaust Systems for Dodge and Plymouth Neon

MONZA Performance Exhaust Systems for the 1995-1997 Dodge and Plymouth Neon utilize the right combination of 2-1/2" diameter, 16-gauge, mandrel-bent tubing, and a low back-pressure, high-flow performance muffler with a tailpipe exiting on each side of the car (a true dual exhaust) for cooler, smoother operation and increased performance.

Each MONZA Performance Exhaust System for the Neon (#88-1430) uses mandrel-bent steel tubing for maximum flow, a corrosion-resistant aluminized-steel muffler, and larger than stock polished and chrome-plated MONZA BIG BORE Exhaust Tips pre-welded to each of the dual tailpipes for a custom, high-performance look. The system is finished with a durable black paint. Necessary hardware and instructions are included.

The MONZA Performance Exhaust System for the Neon is designed to replace the original equipment muffler system and attach to the stock catalytic converter ("cat-back"). Each carries a limited three-year warranty. A four-tube header is also available (#70-1210).

MONZA Performance Exhaust Systems Available for Toyotas

MONZA Performance Exhaust Systems for Toyotas utilize the right combination of larger-than-stock, 16-gauge, mandrel-bent tubing, and low back-pressure, high-flow performance mufflers for cooler, smoother operation and increased performance.

Each MONZA Performance Exhaust System uses mandrel-bent steel tubing for maximum flow and corrosion-resistant Galvalume steel mufflers with the popular MONZA exhaust tips with resonators pre-welded to each. The finish is a durable black paint. Necessary hardware and instructions are included.

These MONZA Performance Exhaust Systems for Toyotas are designed to replace the original equipment muffler system and attach to the stock catalytic converter, where applicable. Each carries a limited three-year warranty.

MONZA Performance Exhaust Systems are available for Toyota Celica, Supra, Corolla, MR2, and even the Tercel (as well as many other makes).

RSR EXHAUST SYSTEMS

RSR and Racing Beat have combined efforts to bring the import market one of the highest quality performance exhaust systems available today. RSR exhaust systems yield proven horsepower gains and an improved, aggressive exhaust tone. All RSR Exhaust Systems are 50-state emissions legal and are sound certified to meet strict noise limits imposed by many law enforcement agencies.

MONZA PERFORMANCE EXHAUST SYSTEMS FOR HONDAS

Part #	Application	Engine Code	Tubing Diameter	MONZA Tips Style/Diameter
88-1280	1976-1978 Accord 3dr 1.8L	R	1-5/8"	DA/2-1/2"
88-1386	1982-1983 Accord 3dr 1.8L	R	1-3/4"	DA/2-1/2"
88-1345	1984-1986 Accord 3dr 1.8L	R	1-3/4"	DA/2-1/2"
88-1416	1986-1989 Accord DX, LX, LXi, 2 & 4dr Sedan 2.0L	C	2-1/4"	SP/4"
88-1270	1976-1979 Civic CVCC 1488	R	1-5/8"	DA/2-1/2"
88-1376	1984-1987 Civic CRX 1.3L, 1.5L	C	1-3/4"	DA/2-1/2"
88-1377	1985-1987 Civic CRX Si (Dual Twin Tips) 1.5L F.I. Only	R	1-3/4" (2)	DA/2-1/2"
88-1385	1985-1987 Civic CRX Si (Single Twin Tips) 1.5L F.I. Only	R	2"	DA/2-1/2"
88-1405	1988-1991 Civic CRX Si 1.6L	C	2"	SP/4"
88-1420	1992-1995 Civic 2dr Sedan 1.6L	C	2-1/2"	SP/4"
88-1417	1985-1987 Prelude Si 2.0L F.I.	C	2-1/4"	DA-2-1/2"
88-1346	1988-1991 Prelude S, Si 2.0L	C	2-1/4"	DA/2-1/2"
88-1418	1992-1993 Prelude S, Si 2.2, 2.3L	C	2-1/2"	DA/2-1/2"

Tips Style: D = Dual; S = Single; A = Angle Cut; P = Straight Cut, Rolled End

MONZA PERFORMANCE EXHAUST SYSTEMS FOR MAZDA

Part #	Application	Engine Code	Tubing Diameter	MONZA Tips Style/Diameter
88-1342	1980-1985 GLC 1.2, 1.4L	R	2"	DA/2-1/4"
88-1315	1979-1982 626 2.0L	R	2"	DA/2-1/4"
88-1278	1992-1993 MX3 Coupe GS 1.6L, 1.8L DOHC V-6	C	2-1/4"	DA/2-1/2"
88-1316	1990-1993 MX5 Miata 1.6L	C	2-1/4"	SP/3
88-1328	1988-1992 MX6 2.2L	C	2-1/2"	DA/2-1/2"
88-1378	1978-1980 RX7 12A	R	2"	DA/3"
88-1319	1981-1982 RX7 12A	R	1-1/2" (2)	DA/2-1/2"
88-1379	1983-1985 RX7 12A, 13B	R	2"	DA/2-1/2"
88-1390	1986-1992 RX7 14A	C	2" (2)	DA/2-1/2"

RSR exhaust systems are offered in your choice of polished 304 stainless steel or Midnight Black 409. Available for most popular models including: Nissan 240SX, 300ZX; Honda Accord, Civic, CRX, del Sol, Prelude, NSX; Mitsubishi 3000GT, Eclipse; Acura Integra, Legend; Mazda Miata, RX-7; Toyota Celica, MR2, Supra.

STILLEN

Stainless-Steel Exhaust System

STILLEN has completed testing, development, and production of its newest performance exhaust, the twin turbo 300ZX. Featuring T-304 stainless-steel inner and outer construction, the 300ZX system is designed to be the most powerful version available. By synchronizing exhaust gas flow, the intermediate pipe allows for quicker boost and improves horsepower. Mufflers feature ceramic-blanket baffling and 4" tips. Testing shows quicker spool up, higher boost, and more power than competitive systems.

Quality construction includes heli-arc welding and ceramic blanket packing material. It has been "ear-tuned" (by Steve Millen himself) for an ideal exhaust note. Four-inch polished stainless-steel tips feature STILLEN logo with smooth bull nose ends.

Mitsubishi Eclipse Exhaust

STILLEN has completed testing, development, and production of its newest performance exhaust, the Mitsubishi Eclipse Exhaust. The rear section is a simple bolt-on, with a reasonable horsepower gain. You receive a dual tip for an aggressive look. The Mistu Eclipse system was designed to be the most powerful version available.

HKS EXHAUST SYSTEMS

Each HKS exhaust system is vehicle specific, designed for only a particular engine/vehicle configuration. Using extensive computer-controlled flow analysis, dyno testing, and precision fitment design, HKS produces maximum horsepower without dramatically depleting low-end torque. Each HKS exhaust system is flanged and comes with all gaskets and hardware to provide the easiest direct bolt-on installation possible. Additionally, HKS exhaust systems utilize factory mounting points and hanger locations and are 50 state emissions and sound legal. Available in the following configurations: Turbo Exhaust, Drager Exhaust, Sport Exhaust, and Hiper Exhaust.

Hiper Exhaust

Inspired by and designed from the N-1 Endurance Race series in Japan, HKS has developed its Hiper Exhaust systems for both turbocharged and normally-aspirated vehicle applications. Like the Super Drager systems, each Hiper system is constructed using an unchambered (SUS 304) stainless-steel muffler assembly, high-quality computerized welds, and large-diameter ceramic-coated steel piping. However, unlike the Drager systems, the Hiper muffler and tip feature a unique offset flow and mounting design. Two stainless exhaust tip configurations are currently available: 120mm and 96mm.

NEUSPEED AUDI TT EXHAUST SYSTEM

The NEUSPEED Audi TT exhaust is 9 lbs. lighter than stock, and features T-304 stainless steel 2.25" mandrel-bent pipes, cat back with polished-end muffler and 4-inch diameter tip with a custom billet 6061T6 aluminum tip cap designed exactly like the interior trim -- another NEUSPEED innovation and first! Available for FWD & AWD.

NEUSPEED S2000 Exhaust System

The NEUSPEED S2000 exhaust is 15 lbs. lighter than stock. Made of T-304 stainless steel 2.25" cat-back mandrel-bent tubes, polished-end mufflers, and 4-inch diameter tip with custom billet 6061T6 aluminum tip caps for a vastly different custom look.

THERMAL R&D MUFFLERS CUSTOM EXHAUST SYSTEMS

Part #	Application
ACURA	
B111-C108	1990-1991 Integra 3dr
B110-C108	1992-1993 Integra 3dr
B112-C110	1994-1998 Integra 3dr LS & RS models
B113-C110	1994-1998 Integra 3dr VTEC model
B108-C111	1992-1993 Integra 4dr
B105-C105	1994-1995 Integra 4dr VTEC
M150	1991-1994 NSX
ACURA -- Turbo 3"	
B138-C138	1990-1993 Integra 3dr
B130-C130	1994-1998 Integra 3dr
B131-C131	1994-1998 Integra 4dr
DODGE/PLYMOUTH	
M501	1994-1999 Neon
HONDA	
B120L-C120R	1998 6 cyl.
B101-C101	1993-1998 Civic 2dr (all, except 1996-1998 DX)
A101-B101-C101	1996-1998 Civic 2dr DX model
B104-C104	1988-1991 Civic 3dr
B103-C103	1992-1993 Civic 3dr (all, except 1993 California models)
B112-C103	1993-1995 Civic 3dr (all, except 1993 California models)
A101-B106-C106	1996-1998 Civic 3dr
B104-C109	1988-1991 Civic 4dr
B101-C101	1992-1998 Civic 4dr (all, except 1996-1998 LX)
A101-B101-C101	1996-1998 Civic 4dr LX model
B107-C107	1988-1991 CRX
B114-C114	1988-1991 Prelude
B102-C102	1992-1993 Prelude (all, except VTEC models)
HONDA -- Turbo 3"	
B131-C131	1992-1998 Civic 2 & 4dr
B134-C134	1988-1991 Civic 3dr
B133-C133	1992-1996 Civic 3dr
B137-C137	1988-1991 CRX
MAZDA	
B402-C402	1990-1998 Miata
M401	1993-1996 RX7
MITSUBISHI	
B303-C303	1989-1994 Eclipse AWD
B304-C304	1989-1991 Eclipse FWD
B304-C305	1992-1994 Eclipse FWD
B302-C302	1995-1998 Eclipse GST
B301-C301	1995-1998 Eclipse GSX
TOYOTA	
M202	1991-1996 MR2, turbo
M201	1993-1997 Supra, twin turbo

OBX T-304 Stainless Steel Cat-Back Bolt On Exhaust Systems

Part #	Application
ACURA	
EX9093A	1990-1993 Integra 2dr
EX94982	1994-1999 Integra 2dr RS/LS/GS
EX94984	1994-1999 Integra 4dr RS/LS/LS/GS
EX9498G	1994-1999 Integra 2dr GSR
HONDA	
EX9093	1990-1993 Accord 2&4dr
EX9497	1994-1997 Accord 2&4dr, non-V-6
EX9806	1998-2000 Accord 2&4dr, V-6
EX9804	1998-2000 Accord 2&4dr, V-4
EX8891C	1988-1991 Civic 3dr hatchback
EX8892C	1988-1991 Civic 4dr
EX92974	1992-1999 Civic 2&4dr HX/EX/Si
EX9699L	1996-1999 Civic hatchback 2&4dr DX/HX/LX
EX92973	1992-1999 Civic hatchback
EX8891X	1988-1991 CRX
EX9296	1992-1996 Prelude
EX9798	1997-1999 Prelude
MITSUBISHI	
EX9597	1995-1999 Eclipse/Talon RS/GS
EX9597X	1995-1999 Eclipse/Talon GSX/Spyder
EX9597T	1995-1999 Eclipse/Talon GST
EX97004	1997-1999 Mirage 4dr
EX97002	1997-1999 Mirage 2dr
NISSAN	
EX9292	1995-1999 240SX
EX9599R	1995-1999 Sentra/200SX
TOYOTA	
EX9397	1993-1997 Corolla

OBXT-304 Stainless Steel Bolt On (Rear Section Only) Exhaust Systems

Part #	Application
ACURA	
EX9093AR	1990-1993 Integra 2dr&4dr
EX9498AR	1994-1999 Integra 2dr RS/LS/GS
EX9498GR	1994-1999 Integra GSR
EX9494R	1994-1999 Integra RS/LS/GS 4dr
BMW	
EX92986R	1992-1998 325/325is/328is/M3
EX92984R	1994-1998 318/318is/318ia
DODGE/PLYMOUTH	
EX9198R	1994-1998 Neon 2&4dr
HONDA	
EX8891CR	1988-1991 Civic 3dr hatchback
EX8892CR	1988-1991 Civic 4dr
EX8891XR	1988-1991 CRX
EX92974AR	1992-1999 Civic 2&4dr
EX92973R	1992-1999 Civic 3dr hatchback
EX9093R	1990-1993 Accord 2&4dr
EX9497R	1994-1997 Accord, 4cyl.
EX9296R	1992-1996 Prelude
EX9798R	1997-1999 Prelude
MAZDA	
EX9299R	1994-1998 RX-7
EX9200R	1992-1999 Miata
MITSUBISHI	
EX9597R	1995-1999 Eclipse/Talon RS/GS
EX9598R	1995-1999 Eclipse/Talon GST
EX9599R	1995-1999 Eclipse/Talon GSX/Spyder, AWD
EX9700R	1997-2000 Mirage 2&4dr
NISSAN	
EX9292R	1992-1998 240SX (S-14)
EX9599R	1995-1999 Sentra/200SX 2&4dr
TOYOTA	
EX9397R	1993-1997 Corolla 1.6L/1.8L
VOLKSWAGEN	
EX9298R	1992-1998 Golf III

JWT 300ZX EXHAUSTS

JWT carries top-quality 2.5" mandrel-bent, cat-back, oval-tip exhausts for the 300ZX and 300ZX twin turbo. These systems are fully stainless steel including a special stainless packing material that won't burn, rust, or pack to the rear of the muffler. This exhaust will allow enough air flow to 600 hp. It sounds slightly deeper than stock with only a small db increase overall.

High-powered turbo cars produce a lot of water in the exhaust system.

That water sits inside the mufflers and resonators, destroying the system from the inside in a short period of time. Stainless steel is a must to protect the system from heat and moisture. You should think of it as a required upgrade not only for the added horsepower but for longevity.

MUFFLERS

BOSAL BROSPEED PROSPORT MUFFLERS

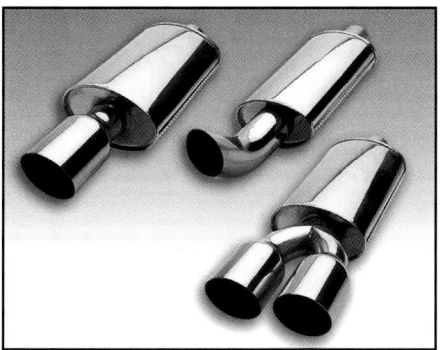

Bosal USA, Inc., one of the world's leading manufacturers and marketers of exhaust systems and related components, has just introduced a new line of Bosal Brospeed Prosport Mufflers for universal applications. The new mufflers use a free-flow design for an aggressive, high-performance tone. Each muffler is TIG welded from 16-gauge T-304 stainless steel and features a mirror-polished finish and a polished stainless-steel tip. Designed for universal applications, Prosport Mufflers feature three different tip configurations: a single, straight large-diameter outlet (#247 210); a straight dual outlet (#247 211), and a single, curved outlet (#247 212). They are available with 2 1/4" diameter inlets and can be welded or clamped on for an easy installation. Each Bosal Brospeed muffler comes with a five-year, unlimited-mileage warranty.

DYNOMAX HIGH PERFORMANCE

DynoMax high performance muffler line offers maximum flow, seriously cool engine note, and a product sure to fit the street tuner's needs for power, performance, and style.

AROSPEED DUAL MONSTER AKA "TWIN BULLET TUBES"

Part #	Description	Tip Size	Size
ARO911001	Muffler Round, AMG	4"	2.5 inch
ARO911002	Muffler Round, Round Angle Cut	4.5"	2.5 inch
ARO911003	Muffler Round, Round	4"	2.5 inch
ARO911004	Muffler Round, Round	4.5"	2.5 inch
ARO911005	Muffler Round, Round Beveled	4.5"	2.5 inch
ARO911006	Muffler Round, Oval Beveled Angle Cut	4.5"	2.5 inch
ARO911007	Muffler Round, Round with 3.5 Angle Insert	4.5"	2.5 inch
ARO911102	Muffler Round, Round Angle Cut	4.5" - 3" Inlet	3 inch
ARO912001	Muffler Small Round	4" x 7" Long Angle	2.5 inch
ARO912002	Muffler Small Round	3.5" Angle Cut	2.5 inch
ARO912003	Muffler Small Round	4" Angle Cut	2.5 inch
ARO912004	Muffler Small Round	Apex Style	2.5 inch
ARO913001	Muffler Offset In, Center Out	2.5"	2.5 inch
ARO913002	Muffler Center In, Dual Out	2.5"	2.5 inch
ARO913003	Muffler Center In, Center Out	2.5"	2.5 inch
ARO913004	Muffler Center In, Center Out	3"	2.5 inch
ARO913005	Muffler Round Center In, Center Out	3"	3 inch
ARO914001	Muffler Oval, Rectangle	3.5"	2.5 inch
ARO914002	Muffler Oval, Dual Rectangle Angle	3.5"	2.5 inch
ARO914003	Muffler Oval, Dual AMG	3.5"	2.5 inch
ARO914004	Muffler Oval, Dual DTM	3"	2.5 inch
ARO914005	Muffler Oval, Dual DTM Square	3"	2.5 inch
ARO914006	Muffler Oval, Angle Cut	4"	2.5 inch
ARO914007	Muffler Oval, AMG	4"	2.5 inch
ARO914008	Muffler Oval, Round Angle Cut	4.5"	2.5 inch
ARO914009	Muffler Oval DTM	3.5"	2.5 inch
ARO914010	Muffler Oval DTM	4.5"	2.5 inch
ARO914011	Muffler Oval Round	4"	2.5 inch
ARO914012	Muffler Oval Round	5.25"	2.5 inch
ARO914013	Muffler Oval Round	4.5"	2.5 inch
ARO914014	Muffler Oval Round Angle Cut	4.5"	2.5 inch
ARO914015	Muffler Oval Angle Cut	4.5"	2.5 inch
ARO914016	Muffler Oval 5-Zigen	4.5"	2.5 inch
ARO914017	Muffler Oval Dual Euro Style DTM	3"	2.5 inch
ARO914018	Muffler Oval Dual Octagon	3"	2.5 inch
ARO916000	Muffler Twin Bullet Tubes, Angle	4"	2.5 inch
ARO912101	Muffler, Cannon Style Angle Cut w/Rivets		2.5 inch
ARO912102	Muffler, Cannon Style Round Tip w/Rivets		2.5 inch
ARO912103	Muffler, Cannon Style Apex w/Rivets		2.5 inch

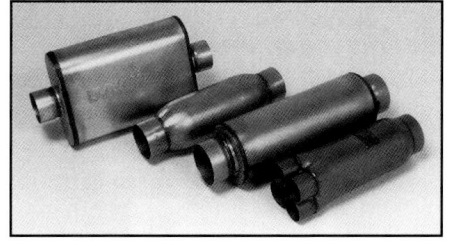

DynoMax Race Mufflers
DynoMax offers a full line of racing venue-specific exhaust technology products.

AROSPEED DUAL MONSTER AKA "TWIN BULLET TUBES"

These are new mufflers that feature a double canister design. It has a 2.5" inlet and two 3.5" outlets. It gives your car a unique look that is rarely seen on street cars, but quite common to high performance race cars. This shotgun-style muffler offers a deep throaty growl and is made from aircraft quality stainless steel.

Arospeed offers a wide variety of muffler canisters and tip styles to accommodate your needs. Canister styles include round, oval, and racing style canisters. Each provides a low throaty tone that is quiet, yet sporty. Arospeed exhausts compliment any car with good looks and deep sound. Arospeed mufflers can be welded onto any vehicle, as they are designed to be universal. Why settle for a 1-inch

CONE ENGINEERING UNIVERSAL APP MUFFLERS

Part #	Description
7" ROUND MUFFLERS	
BM 725	2.25" in/out, 7" x 20" overall length
BM 750	2.5" in/out, 7" x 20" overall length
BM 730	3" in/out, 7" x 20" overall length
BM 718	2.25" in/out, 7" x 26" overall length
6" X 9" OVAL MUFFLERS	
BO 725	2.25" in/out, 20" overall length
BO 750	2.5" in/out, 20" overall length
BO 730	3" in/out, 20" overall length
BO 718	2.25" in/out, 26" overall length
4" ROUND PRE MUFFLERS	
BP 422	2.25" in/out, 12" can length
BP 452	2.5" in/out, 12" can length
BP 426	2.25" in/out, 16" can length
BP 456	2.5" in/out, 16" can length

FLOWMASTER MUFFLERS

Part #		Application
ACURA		
1986-1989 Integra		
9420402	9420502	2.00" In/ Dual 2.00" Out
9424402	9424502	2.25" In/ Dual 2.00" Out
1990-1993 Integra		
942043	942053	2.00"
942443	942453	2.25"
1994-1998 Integra		
942041	942051	2.00"
942441	942451	2.25"
HONDA		
1986-1989 Accord		
942041	942051	2.00"
942441	942451	2.25"
1990-1997 Accord		
942043	942053	2.00"
942443	942453	2.25"
9420402	9420502	2.00" In/ Dual 2.00" Out
9424402	9424502	2.25" In/ Dual 2.00" Out
1986-1991 Civic/CRX		
942043	942053	2.00"
942443	942453	2.25"
9420402	942052	2.00" In/ Dual 2.00" Out
9424402	9424502	2.25" In/ Dual 2.00" Out
1992-1995 Civic/CRX		
942043	942053	2.00"
942443	942453	2.25"
1995-1998 Civic/CRX		
942041	942051	2.00"
942441	942451	2.25"
1988-1991 Prelude		
942041	942051	2.00"
942441	942451	2.25"
9420412	9420512	2.00" In/ Dual 2.00" Out
9424412	9424512	2.25" In/ Dual 2.00" Out
1992-1995 Prelude		
9420412	9420512	2.00" In/ Dual 2.00" Out
9424412	9424512	2.25" In/ Dual 2.00" Out
MITSUBISHI		
1990-1994 Eclipse/Eagle Talon		
942441	942451	2.25"
9424412	9424512	2.25" In/ Dual 2.00" Out
1995-1998 Eclipse/Eagle Talon		
942441	942451	2.25"
9424412	9424512	2.25" In/ Dual 2.00" Out
NISSAN		
1989-1997 240 SX		
9420402	9420502	2.00" In/ Dual 2.00" Out
9424402	9424502	2.25" In/ Dual 2.00" Out
1990-1996 300ZX, turbo		
9420402	9420502	
9424402	9424502	2.25" In/ Dual 2.00" Out
TOYOTA		
1984-1992 Supra, turbo		
9420412	9420512	2.00" In/ Dual 2.00" Out
9424412	9424512	2.25" In/ Dual 2.00" Out
1993-1996 Supra, turbo		
942441	942451	2.25"
942541	942551	2.50"
VOLKSWAGEN		
1985-1997 Golf/GTI/Jetta/GLI		
942042	942052	2.00"
942442	942452	2.25"
9420402	9420502	2.00" In/ Dual 2.00" Out
9424402	9424502	2.25" In/ Dual 2.00" Out

muffler tip and dull muffler canister when you can have a stainless steel muffler canister with a tip ranging from 3 to 5 inches?

FLOWTECH

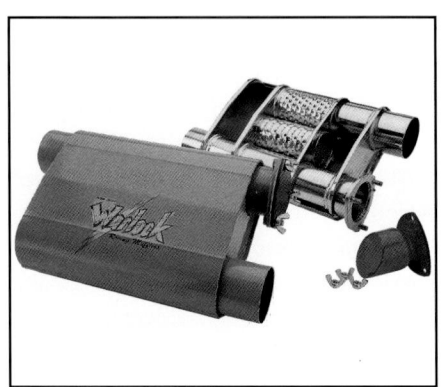

Warlock Racing Muffler

The high-flow, low-restriction patented triple pass-tube design provides lots of horsepower with an awesome throaty sound. But the best feature is that when you're ready to battle the titans at the track, the Warlock lets you go from street legal to race ready with the turn of three wing nuts. The result is unrestricted, straight-through flow. All case sizes are 5" x 10" x 13".

FLOWTECH Afterburner

These mufflers are your very best bet for optimum performance and awesome sound. All Afterburners are made with an aluminized case for miles and miles of rust and corrosion protection. Their fully-welded construction offers stronger seams to prevent blowout under extreme conditions. Large pass tubes provide increased horsepower, while the sound-tuned chambers provide unbelievable sound without the resonation that the competition is famous for. The Afterburner is designed for maximum flow in either direction. Reduces backpressure, increases horsepower.

Thick steel construction. Designed to flow in either direction. Limited lifetime warranty. All case sizes are 4" x 10" x 14".

FLOWTECH Raptor Turbo Performance Muffler

The Raptor features a unique sound rib-case design and aluminized, lock-seal construction. It offers gigantic, high-output flow tubes to provide more horsepower, better mileage, and a sound of pure performance! These universal performance mufflers have case sizes of 4-1/2" x 10" x 13".

XTEC

Unitec mufflers all utilize a straight-through core design, which is constructed of stainless steel and then wrapped with a stainless-steel sound-dampening material. This combination provides minimal back-pressure, an aggressive, deep sporty exhaust tone, and has been proven to last in high-performance, high-heat situations.

To enclose the stainless internals, a stainless-steel outer casing is used for durability, and it is fully polished for a brilliant appearance. Each muffler is equipped with a large 4" diameter, polished stainless-steel exhaust tip with the logo etched into each side for an aggressive race-ready appearance. All Unitec mufflers are fully rebuildable with removal of the endcaps. The endcaps are die stamped from stainless steel and then polished to match the other components of the muffler, and all welding on the muffler is done internally for a very clean outside appearance.

The rebuildable option allows the enthusiast more versatility. If any component of the muffler is damaged in action it can be replaced inexpensively, core diameters can be changed to larger size, etc. The only component that is not stainless is the center canister, which is aluminized and high-temperature painted silver. For the discriminating enthusiast, the choice is clear.

Pressuretec tunable exhaust tip inserts are available for all XTEC mufflers. Pressuretec inserts have proven to be a valuable tuning tool, especially for naturally-aspirated cars. These inserts allow the user to adjust the backpressure to tune the exhaust system for his/her individual driving environment (i.e. drag, autocross, etc.) and extract the greatest amount of usable horsepower.

Adjustment of the Pressuretec is done easily trackside without the use of any tool — simply reach inside the tip, turn the adjustment knob, and continue. A Pressuretec-equipped muffler also has the ability to quiet the sound output levels of the exhaust system for street use and everyday driving.

FLOWTECH WARLOCK "BY-PASS SERIES" RACING MUFFLERS w/ 2-1/2" Bypass Plate

Part #	Inlet Size	Inlet Location	Outlet Size	Outlet Location
50522	2-1/2"	Centered	2-1/2"	Offset
50551	2-1/4"	Offset	2-1/4"	Offset
50522	2-1/2"	Offset	2-1/2"	Offset
50560	3"	Offset	3"	Offset

FLOWTECH WARLOCK "BYPASS SERIES" 3" HEADER MUFFLER w/ 3" Bypass Plate

Part #	Inlet Size	Inlet Location	Outlet Size	Outlet Location
50580	3"	Offset	3"	Offset

FLOWTECH Afterburner

Part #	Inlet Size	Inlet Location	Outlet Size	Outlet Location
50320	2"	Centered	2"	Offset
50321	2-1/4"	Centered	2-1/4"	Offset
50322	2-1/2"	Centered	2-1/2"	Offset
50330	3"	Centered	3"	Offset

FLOWTECH RAPTOR TURBO PERFORMANCE MUFFLER

Part #	Inlet Size	Outlet Size
50050	2"	2"
50051	2-1/4"	2-1/4"
50052	2-1/2"	2-1/2"

FLOWTECH Afterburner Muffler

FLOWTECH Raptor Turbo Performance Muffler

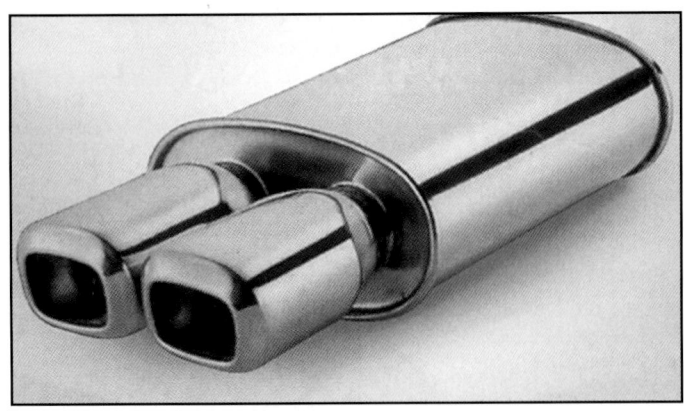
OBX Stainless Steel T-304 Universal Muffler - MV3023

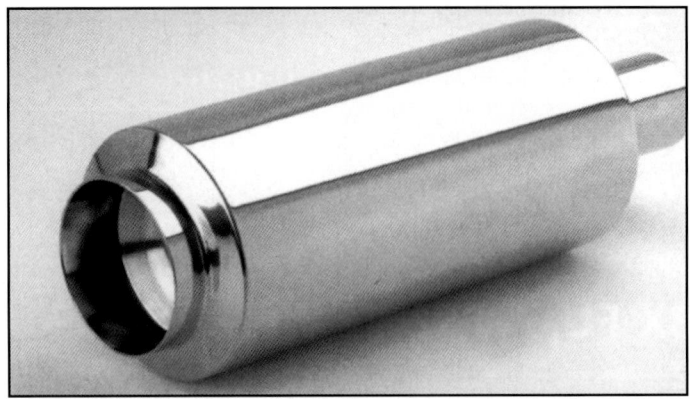
OBX Stainless Steel T-304 Seamless Hyper-Flow Muffler - HF01

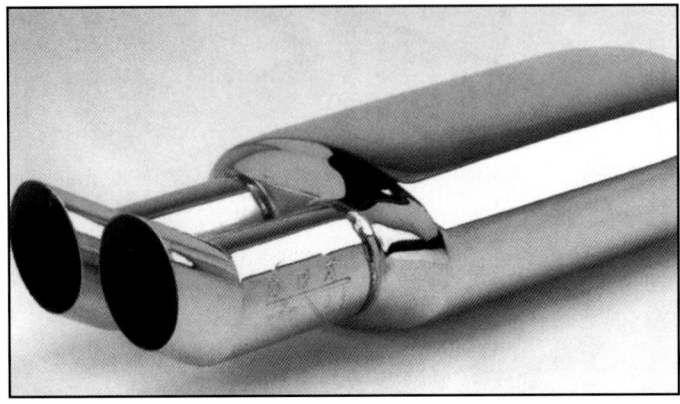
OBX Stainless Steel T-304 Muffler Tuner Type II - SV002

OBX Stainless Steel T-304 Dual Bazooka Muffler - DB002

OBX
OBX Stainless-Steel T-304 Universal Muffler

Product#	Description	Dia.
KV1013	Muffler w/o tip center in center out	2-1/2"
KV3013	Muffler w/o tip center in dual out	2-1/2"
KV2013	Muffler w/o tip side in center out	2-1/2"
KV5014	Muffler w/o tip dual in dual out	2-1/2"
KV6610	Muffler oval seamless center to center	2-1/2"
KV6210	Muffler round seamless center to center	2-1/2"
MV1013	Muffler with Tanabe style tip center to center	2-1/2"
MV1015	Muffler with RSR-style tip center to center	2-1/2"
MV1016	Muffler with Tanabe V-2 tip center to center	2-1/2"
MV1017	Muffler with HKS-style tip center to center	2-1/2"
MV3013	Muffler with DTM-style tip center to dual	2-1/2"
MV3015	Muffler with HKS-style tip center to dual	2-1/2"
MV3023	Muffler with Mercedes-style tip center to dual	2-1/2"
MV3089	Muffler dual round tip center	2-1/2"
MV6212	Muffler round with 5" slant cut tip	2-1/2"

OBX Stainless-Steel T-304 Muffler Tuner Type II

Product#	Description	Dia.
SV001	Seamless oval type II with slash cut tip	2-1/2"
SV002	Seamless oval type II with dual DTM tip	2-1/2"
SV003	Seamless oval type II with RSR-style tip	2-1/2"
SV004	Seamless oval type II with 5 Zigen-style tip	2-1/2"
SV005	Seamless round type II with slash cut tip	2-1/2"
SV006	Seamless round type II with Tanabe-style tip	2-1/2"
SV007	Seamless round type II with straight cut tip	2-1/2"

OBX Stainless-Steel T-304 Dual Bazooka Muffler

Product#	Description	Dia.
DB001	Muffler with slash cut tips	2-1/2"
DB002	Muffler with flare tips	2-1/2"
DB003	Muffler with rolled out tips	2-1/2"
DB004	Muffler with DTM tips	2-1/2"

OBX Stainless-Steel T-304 Seamless Hyper-Flow Universal Muffler

Product#	Description
HF01	Hyper-flow oval with dual round double edge tips
HF02	Hyper-flow oval with dual DTM tips
HF03	Hyper-flow oval with dual square tips
HF04	Hyper-flow oval with double lip tip
HF05	Hyper-flow oval with slant cut tip
HF06	Hyper-flow oval with cone tip
HF07	Hyper-flow oval with oval-round tip

COMPTECH

Power Pro — 3.5" tip
(GSR, RS, GS, LS 94-00, 2dr)
Axle-Back Stainless Exhaust System (coupe) For Years: 1994-2000

Power Pro — 3.5" tip
(GSR, RS, GS, LS 94-00, 4dr)
Axle-Back Stainless Exhaust System (GSR, GS, LS, RS Sedans)
For Years: 1994-2000

Power Pro — 3.5" tip
(Type R 97-00)
Axle-Back Stainless Exhaust System (coupe) For Years: 1997-2000

Power Pro — DTM tip
(All 2dr Integra 1994-2000)
Axle-Back Stainless Exhaust System
(coupe) For Years: 1994+

Street Pro — (Type R 97-00)
Axle-Back aluminized Exhaust
System (coupe)
For Years: 1997 - 2000

CATALYTIC CONVERTERS

BOSAL USA

One of the world's leading manufacturers and marketers of import exhaust systems and related components now offers a complete line of catalytic converters for import and domestic vehicles. Bosal's new product line includes a wide range of direct-fit catalytic converters, O.E. oxygen sensors, air tubes, and air pumps. The line also features a comprehensive selection of universal catalytic converters. Bosal's catalytic converter line meets federal warranty standards with a 2-year, unlimited mileage emissions warranty and a 5-year, 50,000-mile outer shell rust-through warranty.

JACKSON RACING

Miata High Flow Catalytic Converter

If your car has over 50,000 miles and you are looking for a higher flowing catalytic converter for your performance Miata, this is the one! Built in Jackson Racing's own facility, this cat-

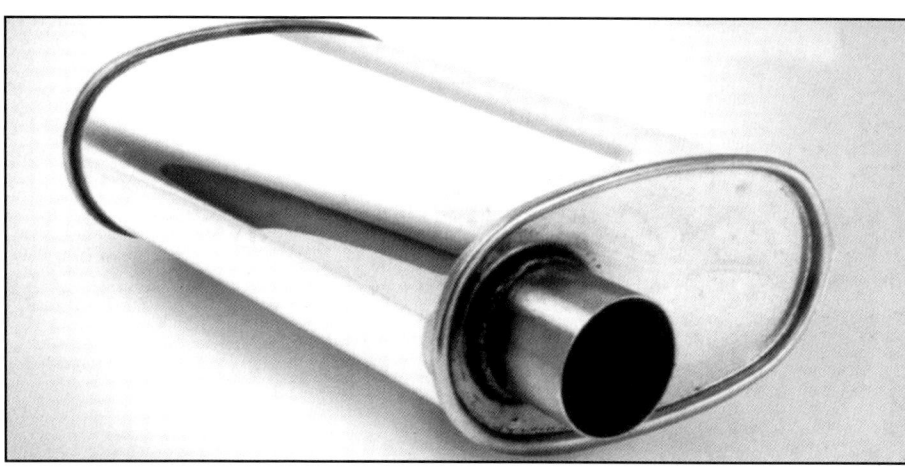

OBX Stainless Steel T-304 Universal Muffler - KV2013

alytic converter features computer-machined flanges for an accurate fit and ceramic coating to protect it from the elements. The perfect compliment to a header and performance exhaust system and it helps clean the air. Smog Legal in all 50 States!

Part #	Application
900-390	1990-1993 Catalytic Converter
900-395	1994-1997 Catalytic Converter

LC ENGINEERING

Free Flow stainless-steel catalytic converter fits OEM or aftermarket exhaust systems.

Part # 14-862386 Performance Catalytic Converter

RANDOM TECHNOLOGIES

These high-performance catalytic converters are available for most late-model vehicles. These cats feature a direct-line free flowing honeycomb design. In addition, the compact cats fit in small spaces with their 4-inch O.D. Offered in 2-, and 3-inch inlet and outlet sizes, these units are perfect for single- or dual-converter systems.

COMPTECH

High Flow Replacement Catalytic Converter (Type R 97-98)
For Years: 1997-1998

JacksonRacing Miata High Flow Catalytic Converter

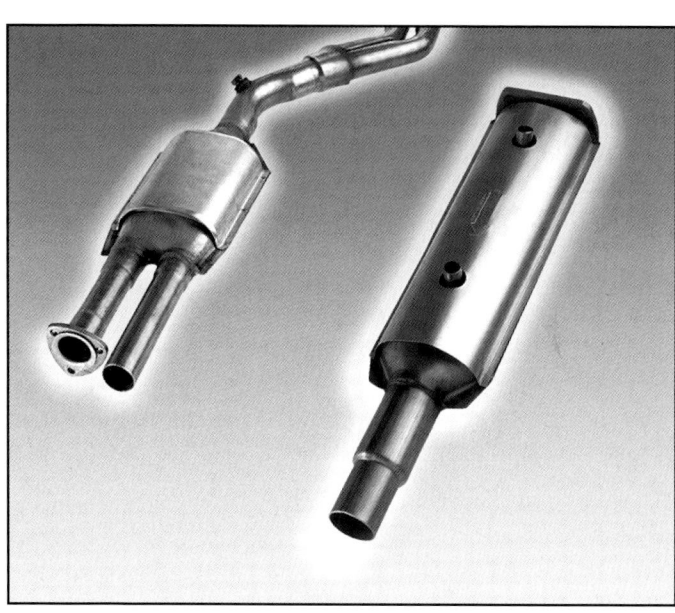

Bosal USA Catalytic Converter

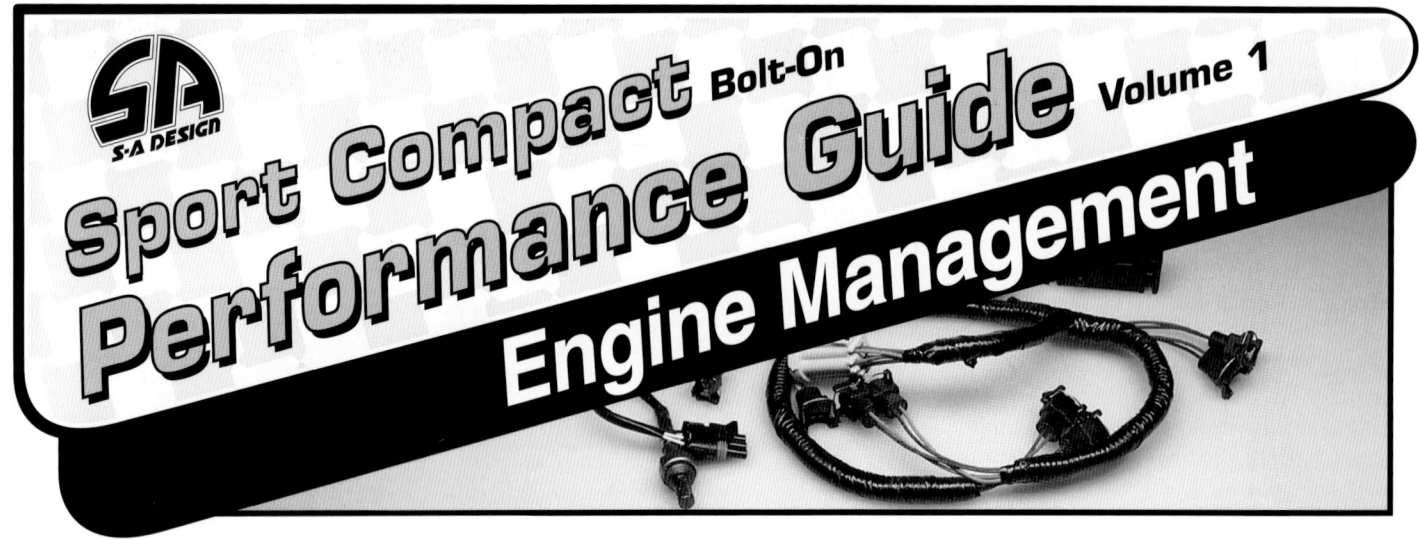

Sport Compact Bolt-On Performance Guide Volume 1
Engine Management

CHIPS, REPROGRAMMED ECUs, AND TUNING ELECTRONICS

COMPTECH SPORT

ECU w/modified chip (GSR)
For Years: 1996-1999
CORE CHARGE $450

ECU w/modified chip (Type R 97-98)
For Years: 1997-1998
CORE CHARGE $450

To save the core charge and have the modifications performed to your ECU, send it to Comptech, they will modify it and ship it back Next Day Air (with the shipping cost included in the price of the ECU).

DINAN

BMW 3-SERIES CHIP

Performance software is the first step to increased power in today's advanced engines. It takes full advantage of 91+ octane fuel by a reprogrammed combination of fuel mixture and ignition timing. Your stock rev limit is raised, producing a broader power band and greater road speed in each gear. During part throttle or "cruise" conditions, fuel economy is actually improved. The top speed governor is also removed. Granted, you probably wouldn't take your BMW over 130 mph, but now you can.

BMW AUTOMATIC TRANSMISSION SOFTWARE

Sporty acceleration is no longer the sole domain of those who like to shift gears. Automatic transmission software raises your shift points for quicker acceleration and greater speed in each gear, taking full advantage of the extra power created by Performance Engine Software. Available for these models:

3 Series E46
3 Series E36
3 Series E30
M3 (E30) 1987-1991
M3 (E36) 1995-1999
318i (E30) 1983-1985
318i (E30) 1990-1993
318i (E36) 1992-1998
318ti (E36) 1995-1999
323i (E30) 1983-1991
323i (E36) 1998-1999
323i (E46) 1999
325, 325e (E30) 1984-1988
325i, ix, Convertible (E30) 1987-1991
325i, iC (E36) 1992-1995
328i (E36) 1996-1999
328i (E46) 1999

ELP MOTORSPORTS SPORT COMPUTER SOFTWARE

Most late-model engines use an integrated computer system which controls the fuel and ignition engine functions to meet the multiple goals of performance, emissions, and fuel economy. Manufacturers must make compromises to meet the average driver's needs that do not optimize the performance potential of the motor. Since ELP's customers are far more performance oriented, ELP has researched and modified the internal "maps" within the EPROM (chip) that control the computer to improve the performance of your vehicle. Getting extra performance is accomplished the same way hot rodders have gotten power for decades; more ignition advance and a better fuel flow curve. ELP's chips also increase the engine redline 300 - 600 rpm. Due to increased spark advance or higher boost on turbocharged vehicles, it is necessary to run supreme unleaded fuel 91 Octane or higher. This is the perfect addition to ELP's Big Bore Throttle Bodies.

Application	HP Increase
ACURA	
Integra LS/GS/RS*	16
Integra GSR, VTEC*	20
Legend*	15
NSX*	23
NSX-R*	28
AUDI	
5000 turbo*	45
Quattro turbo*	65
S2 & S4 Quattro*	50
BMW	
M-3 E30	18
M-3 E30 club racer	28
M-3 E36	12
M-5/M-6	30
318/318is/ti/Z3	12
325/528e	20
325/525I	12
328/528I	---
535/635/735	20
540/740/840	23
750/850	30
DIAMOND STAR	
Eclipse/Talon/Laser turbo*	55
Stealth/3000GT VR4*	70
Conquest/Starion*	30
Galant VR4*	55

FORD
Probe turbo*	30
Probe V-6*	20
SHO 3.0/3.2L	15

HONDA
Accord*	12
Civic/CRX*	15
del Sol VTEC	12
Prelude S/SI	14
Prelude VTEC	18

MAZDA
626/MX-6 turbo*	30
MX-3 V-6*	15
MX-6 V-6*	20
Miata 1.6L*	10
Miata 1.8L*	12
RX-7 non-turbo*	16
RX-7 turbo*	50
RX-7 twin turbo*	40

NISSAN
240SX*	15
300ZX turbo	50
300ZX 1990-1995*	22
300ZX twin turbo*	70
Maxima 1989-1996*	18
Sentra SER/NX2000*	12

TOYOTA
Celica All Trac turbo*	50
Corolla GTS*	12
Supra turbo*	55
Supra twin turbo*	60
MR2 1985-1989*	12
MR2 Supercharged*	18
MR2 turbo*	50

VOLKSWAGEN
2.0L 16 valve	15
Corrado G60 (includes chip and supercharger pulley)	25
Corrado/Jetta/Passat VR6	15

*Stock ECU has non-removable chips on these models. The ECU must be sent to ELP Motorsport to have program installed. Custom programs are available for vehicles with extensive bolt-on and internal modifications.

GUDE

Bullfrog Computer Chips are matched to the specific Bullfrog Camshaft. Each ECU fine tunes ignition timing, fuel curve, and rev limiter to provide the optimum performance available.

Part #	Application
AIECU1	1990-1992 1.8 DOHC
AIECU2	1993 1.8 DOHC
AIECU3	1994-1995 1.8 DOHC

SUPERCHIP

Available for these vehicles:

ACURA	Integra
	Integra 1995-1997
HONDA	Accord
	Civic & CRX
	Civic & CRX 1995-1997
	Prelude
HYUNDAI	Scoupe turbo
INFINITI	G20 & Q45

G-FORCE ENGINEERING REPROGRAMMED ECUS

Part #	Application	Engine	Features
ACURA			
DCR256	1992-1995 Integra	B18	F, T, R
DCM66	1996+ Integra	B18	F, T, R, V
CHRYSLER			
A175BTR64	1988-1989 Conquest	G54BT	F
DODGE			
Z16BT8401G	1991-1995 Stealth turbo 5MT	6G72BT	F, T, B, S, R
Z15B8401G	1991-1995 Stealth	6G72B	F, T, S, R
Z16BT8401F	1993-1995 Stealth turbo 6MT	6G72BT	F, T, B, S, R
Call Manufacturer	1996-1998 Stealth turbo 6MT	6G72BT	F, T, B, S, R
Call Manufacturer	1996-1998 Stealth	6G72B	F, T, S, R
FORD			
GD2TR256	1988-1992 Probe	F2T	F, T, B
GE5ER256	1993-1995 Probe	KLZE	F, T
HONDA			
CDR256	1994-1995 Accord	H22	F, T, R, S
Call Manufacturer	1996+ Accord		TBA
EGR256	1993-1995 Civic	B16	F, T, R
EGM66	1996+ Civic	B16	F, T, R, V, S
EGR256	1993-1995 del Sol	B16	F, T, R
EGM66	1996+ del Sol	B16	F, T, R, V, S
NA1R256	1991-1994 NSX	C30A	F, T, R
NA1H8536	1995-1996 NSX	C30A	F, T, R
Call Manufacturer	1997+ NSX	C32A	TBA
BBR256	1992-1995 Prelude	H22	F, T, R
Call Manufacturer	1996- Prelude	1422	TBA
INFINITI			
HP10DE377A	1990-1994 G20	SR20DE	F, T, R, S
G50DER256 495	1990-1994 Q45	VH45DE	F, T
LEXUS			
Call Manufacturer	1998 GS400	2UZ-FE	TBA
	1993-1997 GS300	2JZ-GE	
JZS147GE64AV42ASF	Full Version		F, T, R
JZS147GE64AVSF	Single Version (F)		F, R
JZS147GE42AST	Single Version (T)		T
Call Manufacturer	1998 SC400	1UZ-FE	TBA
	1995-1997 SC400	1UZ-FE	
UZZ30FE68A2SF	Full Version		F, T, R
UZZ30FE68ASF	Single Version (F)		F, R
UZZ30FE68AST	Single Version (T)		T
	1991-1994 SC400	1UZ-FE	
UZZ30FE64AV2SF	Full Version		F, T, R
UZZ30FE64AVSF	Single Version (F)		F, R
UZZ30FE64AVST	Single Version (T)		T
Call Manufacturer	1998 SC300	2JZ-GE	TBA
	1992-1997 SC300	2JZ-GE	
JZZ31GE64AV42ASF	Full Version		F, T, R
JZZ31GE64AVSF	Single Version (F)		F, R
JZZ31GE42AST	Single Version (T)		T
MAZDA			
FC3BTR64	1987-1988 RX-7 turbo	13BT	F, T, B
FC3BTR256	1989-1991 RX-7 turbo	13BT	F, T, B, C
FD3BRW9705	1993-1995 RX-7 twin turbo	13B-REW	F, T, B, R, C
FC3BR64	1987-1988 RX-7 NA	13B	F, T
FC3BR256	1989-1991 RX-7 NA	13B	F, T
NA6E05M	1990-1993 Miata MX-5	B6ZE	F, T
NA8ER512	1994-1995 Miata MX-5	BPZE	F, T, R
Call Manufacturer	1996-1998 Miata MX-5	BPZE	TBA
Call Manufacturer	1999+ New Miata MX-5	BPZE	TBA
GD2TR256	1988-1992 MX-6	F2T	F, T, B
GE5ER256	1993-1995 MX-6	KLZE	F, T
BF6TR64	1988-1989 323GTX	B6T	F, T, R
MITSUBISHI			
Z16BT8401F	1993-1995 3000GTVR-4 6MT	6G72BT	F, T, B, S, R
Call Manufacturer	1996-1998 3000GTVR-4 6MT	6G72BT	F, T, B, S, R
Z16BT8401G	1991-1995 3000GTVR-4 5MT	6G72BT	F, T, B, S, R
Z15B8401G	1991-1995 3000GT NA	6G72B	F, T, S, R
Call Manufacturer	1996-1998 3000GT NA	6G72B	F, T, S, R
D27BT6111B	1989-1994 Eclipse GSX	4G63BT	F, T, B, S, R
D33BTR512	1995 Eclipse GSX	4G63BT	F, T, B, S, R
D33BT6371B	1996-1997 Eclipse GSX	4G63BT	F, T, B, S, R
Call Manufacturer	1998+ Eclipse GSX	4G63BT	TBA
D26BT6111B	1989-1994 Eclipse GS-T	4G63BT	F, T, B, S, R
D32BTR512	1995 Eclipse GS-T	4G63BT	F, T, B, S, R
D32BT6371B	1996-1997 Eclipse GS-T	4G63BT	F, T, B, S, R
Call Manufacturer	1998+ Eclipse GS-T	4G63BT	TBA
D26B6111B	1989-1994 Eclipse GS	4G63	F, T, S, R
E33BT6111B	1991-1992 Galant VR-4	4G63BT	F, T, B, S, R
A175BTR64	1988-1989 Starion	G54BT	F

Sport Compact Bolt-On Performance Guide, Volume 1 - Imports

G-FORCE ENGINEERING REPROGRAMMED ECUS (CONT.)

Part #	Application	Engine	Features
NISSAN			
Z32TTR256	1990-1995 300ZX twin turbo	VG30DETT	F, T, B
Z32E377S4	1990-1995 300ZX NA	VG30DE	F, T
S13ER256	1989-1990 240SX	KA24E	F, T, R, S
S13DE377A	1991-1994 240SX	KA24DE	F, T, R, S
S14DE377M1	1995+ 240SX	KA24DE	F, T
B14DE377S4	1995+ 200SX SE-R	SR20DE	F, T
KB13DE377A	1991-1993 NX2000	SR20DE	F, T, R, S
Call Manufacturer	1995-1996 Maxima	VQ30DE	F, T
B13DE377A	1991-1994 Sentra SE-R	SR20DE	F, T, R, S
Call Manufacturer	No Years Sentra SE	GA16E	F, T
PLYMOUTH			
D26BT6111B	1989-1994 Laser	4G63BT	F, T, B, S, R
D32BTR512	1995 Laser	4G63BT	F, T, B, S, R
D32BT6371B	1996-1997 Laser	4G63BT	F, T, B, S, R
Call Manufacturer	1998+ Laser	4G63BT	TBA
TOYOTA			
VCV10ZFE64AV	1991-1993 Camry	3VZ-FE	F, T
SXV10FE42A	1991-1993 Camry	5S-FE	F, T, R
ST165GE42A	1986-1989 Celica GT-S	3S-GE	F, T, R
ST165GT64AV	1988-1989 Celica All Trac turbo	3S-GTE	F, T, B, R
ST185GT64AV	1990-1993 Celica All Trac turbo	3S-GTE	F, T, B, R
AE86GE05A	1985-1988 Corolla GT-S	4A-GE	F, T, R
AE92GE42A	1989-1991 Corolla GT-S	4A-GE	F, T, R
AW11GE05A	1985-1990 MR-2 NA	4A-GE	F, T, R
AW11GZ64AV	1988-1990 MR-2 Supercharged	4A-GZE	F, T, B, R
SW20FE42A	No Years MR-2 NA	5S-FE	F, T, R
SW20GT64A	1991-1996 MR-2 Turbo	3S-GTE	F, T, B, R
EL44FE42A	1992-1995 Paseo	5E-FE	F, T, R
	1993-1995 Supra twin turbo	No #	
JZ80GT68AF	Full Version		F, T, B, R, S (MT only), C
JZ80GT68ASF	Single Version (F)		F, B, R, S (MT only)
JZ80GT68AST	Single Version (T)		T
	1993-1995 Supra NA	2JZ-GE	
JZ80GE64AV42AF	Full Version		F, T, R
JZ80GE64AVSF	Single Version (F)		F, R
JZ80GE42AST	Single Version (T)		T
MA70GT64A	1987-1992 Supra turbo	7M-GTE	F, T, B, R
MA70GE64AV	No Years Supra NA	7M-GE	F, T, R
	1996+ Supra twin turbo	2JZ-GTE	
Call Manufacturer	Full Version		F, T, B, R, S (MT only), C
JZ80GT268ASF	Single Version (F)		F, B, R, S (MT only)
Call Manufacturer	Single Version (T)		T

FEATURE KEY

F	Fuel Map	B	Boost Limiter	C	Boost Control	R	Rev Limiter
T	Ignition Timing Map	S	Speed Limiter	V	VTEC Point		

ISUZU	Amigo
	Impulse turbo
	Pickup
	Rodeo
	Trooper
LEXUS	GS300\400
	SC300\400
MAZDA	323 & 626
	Miata
	MX3 & MX6
	RX7 & RX7 turbo
MITSUBISHI	3000GT
	Eclipse
NISSAN	240 SX 12v
	300 ZX non-turbo
	300 ZX turbo
	300 ZX twin turbo
	Maxima
	Sentra
SUZUKI	Swift
TOYOTA	Camry
	Celica All-Trac
	Corolla
	MR2 & MR2 turbo
	Paseo
	Supra & Supra turbo

JET PERFORMANCE PRODUCTS

Custom computer upgrade packages are available for Acura, Honda, Audi, Mazda, Mitsubishi, VW, and other popular sport compact cars. Each package includes step-by-step instructions, shipping instructions, shipping carton, packing materials, preaddressed shipping form, computer location chart, horsepower specification chart, and warranty information. Return shipping is included in the price.

JIM WOLF TECHNOLOGY

300ZX ECU Upgrades

JWT's engine control units (ECUs) are used worldwide in all forms of competition. Specializing in Nissan/Infinity ECUs, JWT's Performance Optimized Programming (POP) has earned a reputation for meticulous and complete tuning. An ECU contains much more than just the parameters for a single maximum-horsepower point. Tuning only in this single dimension — without regard for other attributes like throttle response, thermal control, or torque — simply is not optimized tuning! JWT's winning experience in off-road, rally, and road racing is present in every fully-optimized ECU we offer. JWT engine control units are sold on an exchange basis and can be upgraded using your stock unit or JWT can send a finished unit on an exchange basis.

300 ZX Twin Turbo POP Power Package

Rev limiter raised 200 rpm. Cam timing control optimized. Eliminates top speed limiter and boost limiter at computer level. Throttle response code optimized. Control maps "resized" for control at high RPM and power. Air/fuel ratios corrected for higher power levels. Ignition timing corrected for optimum torque and cylinder temperature. Boost increased to 12.5 psi (13.5 psi flash boost). Computer-controlled safety boost level maintained. Performance EPROM is socketed to allow stock chip replacement (8 bit only). Each package includes: engine control unit upgrades and boost calibration jets. Optional POP-Charger air filter system is available. Street legal (1990-1992 twin turbo, Emission E.O. # D-244). Easily installed in 25 minutes. No adjustments needed.

300 ZX Non Turbo POP Power Package

Rev limiter raised 200 rpm. Cam timing control optimized. Eliminates top speed limiter at computer level. Throttle response code optimized. Control maps "resized" for control at high RPM and power. Air/fuel ratios corrected for higher power levels. Ignition timing corrected for optimum torque and cylinder temperature. Performance EPROM is socketed to allow stock chip replacement (8 bit only). Each package includes: engine control unit upgrades and POP-Charger air filter. Easily installed in 25 minutes. No adjustments needed.

The JWT ECU upgrade has been heavily tested for years and has proven itself with real world HP gains and extreme reliability. Clark Steppler is the man behind the ECCS ECU modifications. He is one of the few people in the world with enough knowledge about this and all Nissan ECUs to give you maximum power and flexibility. If you really want to know how good someone is at programming Nissan code, ask a few questions like: "Can you provide me with a program for bigger injectors?" "Can you change Mass Air Flow sensors when I need more power?" "Are power gains only at wide-open throttle or are there increases in daily driveability?" "Can I add ECU controlled nitrous?" Jim Wolf Technology answers YES to every one of these questions. Due to the amount of Nissan ECUs JWT can modify, please call for specific details and customization features. Jim Wolf Technology has applications for many Nissan vehicles.

JWT 396 Twin Turbo Upgrade Kit

396 street legal horsepower! The package includes: POP engine control unit (exchange); boost calibration orifices (not shown); POP-Charger hi-flow air filter system; JWT stainless exhaust system (oval tip); installation instructions.

JWT 252 Non-turbo Upgrade Kit

252 street legal horsepower! The package includes: POP engine control unit (exchange); POP-Charger hi-flow air filter system; JWT stainless exhaust system (oval tip); installation instructions.

HKS

PFC F-CON (Programmed Fuel Computer System)

As boost pressure increases, the PFC F-CON can help maintain the proper air-fuel mixture for optimum performance. Harnesses and accessories available.

GCC (Graphic Control Computer)

The GCC is an additional electronic tuning component designed to add flexibility to the VPC and PFC F-CON. The GCC simply plugs into either the VPC or PFC F-Con harness and allows the user to adjust the fuel pulse duration at specific RPM intervals.

HKS Injection Pulse Monitor

This device interfaces with the PFC F-CON and will display the difference between the stock and upgraded pulse.

HKS AFR (Air Fuel Ratio Regulator)

The AFR is designed for lightly-tuned vehicles (filter, exhaust) to allow for mild adjustments in the mixtures through sensors. The AFR allows up to 1 A/R point rich or lean for the best possible power gains.

SPLIT SECOND

The Split Second GPM1 (Gauge Pressure Meter) operates with a MAP sensor to provide a calibrated bar graph display. The display begins to operate at a half-scale input. Therefore, with a turbocharged engine using a two-bar MAP sensor, the GPM1 indicates the amount of boost and goes blank when the engine is operating in the vacuum region.

The Split Second ESC1 (EGO Sensor Conditioner) alters the signal from the EGO sensors under boost conditions. It may be used in either single- or dual-EGO sensor applications. Under vacuum conditions it outputs a signal which is identical to the EGO signals that appear at the input. Under boost, it outputs an internally generated signal to allow open loop operation.

The Split Second FC1 (Frequency Clamp) is designed to condition the output of frequency-based air flow meters such as those used on late-model GM cars and Karman Vortex. Under normal operating conditions, the FC1 outputs a signal that is identical to the flow signal present at its input. When the frequency of the flow signal reaches the internally set clamp level, the FC1 maintains a constant output frequency at clamp level as the input frequency rises. The FC1 is especially useful for forced induction conversions where a supercharger or turbocharger is fitted to an engine which is normally naturally aspirated.

The Split Second FCC1 (Frequency Calibrator and Clamp) is designed to condition the output of frequency-based air flow meters such as those used on late-model GM cars and Karman Vortex. The FCC1 is especially useful for re-calibrating modified engines. The alteration or addition of turbochargers, superchargers, fuel injectors, or MAF sensors can alter air/fuel ratio. A secondary feature of the FCC1 is that it will clamp the output at a designated frequency. The FCC1 provides a way to set the air/fuel ratio for rich, lean, or stoichiometric operation over the entire RPM and load range. The FCC1 is intended for use in kits for specific applications and may be ordered with fixed calibration. No user adjustment is provided.

The Split Second ARC1 (Air/fuel Ratio Calibrator) provides precise adjustment of air/fuel ratio over the

entire operating range of an internal combustion engine. It is especially useful for re-calibration of modified engines that have ECU (Engine Control Units) designed for MAP or MAF (Mass Air Flow) sensors, also compatible with GM and Karman Vortex applications. The ARC1 features low- and high-load adjustments and provides a means to adjust air/fuel ratio for desired performance while driving. Does not include MAP or MAF sensor.

The Split Second ARC2 (Air/fuel Ratio Calibrator) provides additional features over the ARC1. These features make it possible to fit an MAF sensor to engines that were designed to operate with vane-type air flow meters. It is especially useful for re-calibration of modified engines that have ECU (Engine Control Units) designed for MAP or MAF (Mass Air Flow) sensors, also compatible with GM and Karman Vortex applications. In addition to the low- and high-load adjustments of the ARC1, the ARC2 also provides adjustments for mid-load and acceleration boost. Does not include MAP or MAF sensor.

Split Second TSC1 (Temperature Signal Conditioner) is designed to work with engines that have modified cooling systems. Engine performance can be optimized by changing operating temperature. Cooler engine temperatures are better for forced induction applications, while warmer temperatures can work better on normally aspirated engines. When an engine cooling system is altered during warm-up and normal operation, the TSC1 conditions the output of the coolant temperature sensor so that the input to the ECU is kept within the range of the stock operation.

Manifold Absolute Pressure Sensors

Split Second is your source for multiple bar Manifold Absolute Pressure (MAP) sensors. Split Second offers one-, two-, and three-bar sensors. A one-bar sensor would be used on a naturally aspirated engine. Two- and three-bar sensors are used on a turbo or supercharged engine. For questions on which sensor is best for your application please contact a Split Second technician.

Manifold Absolute Pressure (Boost) Pressure Sensor Monitor Range

1 bar	vac-0 psi
2 bar	vac-14.7 psi
3 bar	vac-29.4 psi

Cable and Connector

MAP-con   Connector

PROGRAMMABLE ECU INTERFACE DEVICES

APEX INTEGRATION

Second Generation Super AFC

The Second Generation Super AFC follows the highly successful Super AFC in an upgraded package. The SUPER AFC is a vehicle-specific fuel computer that modifies the air flow meter signal/pressure sensor signal and allows the user to either richen or lean the fuel mixture. Adjustment ranges from +/- 50%. The Super AFC boasts an 8-point adjustable fuel curve with 500 rpm increment setting points. The Super AFC also allows the user to adjust fuel enrichment according to either LO/HI throttle positions. The AFC also cures the erratic idle problems associated with open atmosphere blowoff valves on hot-wire air flow meter-equipped vehicles. Monitor mode displays analog meter faces, Y graph display, and numerical display. Other displays include Peak Hold, Replay Mode, 1 point/10 point, and ghost map tracing. All correction factors are also displayed in percentages. All values and graphs are displayed through the exclusive VFD (Vacuum Fluorescent Display) screen.

Part # 401-A007 Super AFC (Digital)

Power FC

The Power FC allows access to every parameter of tuning within the ECU. Installation of the unit is the easiest on the market. Simply switching out the factory ECU and plugging in the Power FC transforms the factory ECU into a fine tuning instrument capable of growing with the tuning menu. The Power FC comes complete with base programs for exhaust, air filter, upgraded air flow meters, and upgraded boost (with the optional boost control kit). All base programs are currently calibrated for 100 octane fuel used in Japan. Our US engineers are in the process of calibrating the Power FC for US spec fuels. The programs are also tested under four-seasons testing and high-and low-altitude testing. Each new model takes approximately 4 - 6 months to develop due to the rigorous standards and responsibilities that come with selling a fuel computer. Apex Integration purchases a test vehicle exclusively for Power FC development.

Tuning parameters include: ignition timing map, air flow meter signal adjustment, injector pulse timing adjustment, boost control, acceleration enrichment compensation, fuel/ignition test, ignition cranking fuel adjustment, water temperature correction, rev-limiter control. All parameters of the vehicle including water temp, oil temp, oil pressure can be monitored from the display. The optional Power FC Commander allows complete tuning of the vehicle with an easy to use keypad. The commander can also be substituted for a laptop computer with our exclusive software to have complete control over every aspect of the engine. The Power FC is one of the most technologically advanced fuel management systems for today's racecar.

HYPERTECH

Shogun Power Tuner™ is user-friendly and allows the operator to optimize the ignition timing and air/fuel ratio, over the entire RPM range, for stock or modified Japanese imports...at the touch of a button. Easy to follow instructions allow maximum power tuning for any combination of modifications and readjustment of the factory rev-limiter.

Tuning is simple! From the driver's seat, select the tuning point RPM on the Shogun™ Controller, select TIMING and scroll up or down to the desired spark setting, select FUEL and scroll up or down to the change in air/fuel ratio desired, and make a run. Spark tuning is adjustable in 1-degree increments, air/fuel ratio is adjustable as a percentage (+/-%) of baseline settings, and the factory rev limiter is adjustable in 500 rpm increments. At the track, on a dyno, or by the seat of your pants, if necessary, you find the best tuning...period! Follow the instructions, and no one, anywhere, and any price can tune it better!

Installation is quick and easy...no cutting into the wiring harness. Just plug the Shogun™ adapter between the stock computer and the stock wiring harness, snap the cable into the Controller, and you are ready to tune. The engine starts and runs as it always did, but now, you can build your custom tuning program for maximum performance. And when tuning is complete, the Shogun™ Controller displays real time RPM, ignition timing, and fuel settings. The Controller can be permanently mounted, or removed and stored after tuning is complete.

Maximum power gains from typical bolt-on parts (including turbochargers, nitrous, headers, cam-shaft timing sprockets, cams, cat-back systems, throttle bodies, cold-air packages and other popular bolt-on equipment) require custom- tailored ignition timing and air/fuel calibrations. For your car, the Hypertech Shogun™ Power Tuner™ is the only custom-tuning, emissions legal, programming product available for popular import engines.

VENOM 400™ PERFORMANCE CONTROL MODULE

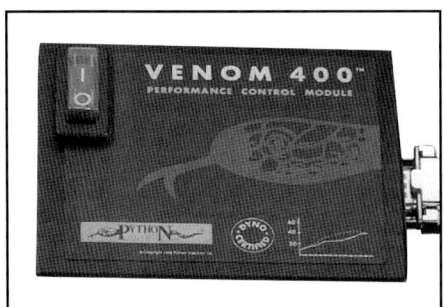

The VENOM 400™ Performance Control Module is an add-on control unit that features its own micro-controller. This module is connected to the vehicle's sensors and increases engine performance by monitoring the sensors' output characteristics and modifying the input to the existing vehicle's computer.

The VENOM 400™ improves horsepower by as much as 25% through the range of approximately 1,000 to 5,000 rpm. The VENOM 400™ is OBD II compatible. Besides a substantial increase of torque, the VENOM 400™ reduces flat spots or delay time during sudden acceleration. It incorporates an 8-bit micro-controller that is capable of monitoring the various sensor inputs and modifying their output at more than 40 times per second.

If you have already installed a performance prom, the VENOM 400™ will enhance the vehicle's performance beyond the parameters set by the performance prom.

The VENOM 400™ is only active when peak performance is required. During normal driving, the VENOM 400™ remains passive until the microcomputer determines that engine airflow and throttle position warrants increased performance. Normal fuel economy prevails while under normal load.

The VENOM 400™ enhances the performance gains achieved by installing an upgraded chip. Whatever the gains are as specified within the chip, they will be magnified through the use of the VENOM 400™. The VENOM 400™ has an off switch so smog certification is achieved when not racing. The VENOM 400™ will not trigger the emission safeguards of today's vehicles.

Easy installation in 20-30 minutes with basic hand tools requiring only four electrical connections.

Red cockpit LED indicating VENOM 400™ activation.

RACER'S GROUP

Over the years, the coming of the computer did marvels for the automotive industry. Unfortunately workshops lost all control over the tuning of these vehicles. Even the slightest idling problem cannot be cured by the non-franchised workshop. In most cases, even the authorized dealers cannot cure these problems. In short, the tuning of computerized vehicles became nearly impossible.

The PROgram gives the properly trained technician full control over the timing and mixture functions of most electronically controlled vehicles. Not only can mixtures and timing be set, but they can also be set under various load and RPM conditions. This gives one the ability to optimize the vehicle for economy under light-load conditions and set it up for optimum performance under full-throttle conditions as well.

The PROgram is much more than just a "chip." In fact, it is a fully-functioning computer which is added to the vehicle's existing engine control unit (ECU). Apart from controlling general timing and mixtures it can do idling control, drive extra injectors, take full control over timing functions, eliminate speed governors, etc. It can be more accurately described as a "Piggyback" computer.

The PROgram gets wired into the existing ECU wiring harness. If it is removed from the vehicle it returns back to the standard ECU settings. If the PROgram is specifically programmed with zeros the vehicle will be standard. Only areas which need additional tuning need to be altered. Many of the aftermarket components that many of you have already installed on your car can now be used to their fullest.

The factories program their ECUs to operate under the worse conditions possible. They have to assume that customers will be travelling from state to state, using different types of fuel, encountering altitude changes, temperature variations, etc. ALL engines are a little different (more than you would think) and people drive and maintain their cars differently. When the factories offer a "bonus" of not having to service your new vehicle for an extended period of time, it definitely comes at a "price." They have to factor in so many variables and assure the general public that their shiny new car will start every time and under all conditions that they are forced to simply "neuter" the tuning. The ECU is set up for the lowest common denominator otherwise it will not function correctly. With the PROgram, everything changes and each car can now perform to its optimum. Remember: YOUR car gets mapped, not some other car of the same model, so the performance of YOUR vehicle, with whatever modifications are in place, is optimized! The gains can be significant.

If within three months you are not fully satisfied with the PROgram, the company will promptly remove the unit and refund the full amount including installation and mapping fee.

EFI SYSTEMS

Programmable Management System

The Programmable Management System from EFI Systems is a state-of-the-art microprocessor-controlled engine control system. The PMS reads the stock fuel injection and spark timing signals from the engine's control unit, then changes them to the settings that you specify via terminal or PC laptop entry. This allows different fuel and timing adjustments to be made for situations of idle, part throttle, and wide open throttle.

The PMS includes specialized functions for maximizing the performance of turbocharged, supercharged, and nitrous-oxide fuel-injected engines, including turbo boost control, for engines that are equipped for it. There are also two user-programmable switches that allow the PMS to activate power adders like nitrous oxide, with two stages that need to be activated at different times. The non-volatile storage area of the PMS allows you to create and store three different performance programs for different operating conditions. For example, you may define one program for the everyday street use, one for the track, and one for maximum highway performance. The PMS even gives you the ability to change individual settings or programs instantly, even while driving.

The PMS can monitor your stock engine control unit and give you the ability to control the engine's timing and fuel curves. It controls the timing in one-degree increments and the fuel in two-percent increments.

With the release of the optional InterACQ PC Software, you can capture, log, and play back performance data on a notebook PC. With the release of the optional Windows InterACQ PC Software, you can also make changes to your program sets right from the PC.

Installation manuals and supporting documentation for Ford, GM, Honda, Mazda, Mitsubishi, and Porsche versions of the PMS are available as PDF files for viewing or download. You need the free Adobe Acrobat Reader to view or print the manuals. Available for these models:

1988-1999 Honda/Acura, 4 cyl.
1993-1996 Mazda RX/7
1990-1999 Mitsubishi, 4 cyl. turbo
1990-1994 Mitsubishi MAF Kit
1990-1996 Porsche 3.2

Systems Secondary Injector Driver

The EFI Systems Secondary Injector Driver will support from 1 to 8 high impedance (10 to 15 ohm) injectors and is used to provide extra fuel for supercharged, turbocharged, or other high-performance engine applications. The Secondary Injector Drivers are available for 4-, 6-, or 8-cylinder engines, and for the following calibrations: -25 to 0 vacuum; 1 to 15 psi; and 1 to 30 psi.

Easy 5 wire installation. Complete with wiring harness and map sensor. RPM on adjustment, with LED monitor. Boost on adjustment, with LED monitor. Aux. input for remote control. Start fuel adjustments from 1 to 15 msec. End fuel adjustments at max. psi setting. Pot adjustments (no software adjustments). 12 MHZ microprocessor for precise control. Six-month warranty. Technical support.

The INTERACQ system is a data-logging and retrieval system that enhances the Programmable Management System by adding a monitoring capability using a laptop PC. Because it is difficult to monitor the PMS in real time using the hand-held terminal, the INTERACQ system was developed to enable users to record a run at the drag strip or a lap around a road course, then stop and play back the recorded data to view how the car reacted to the changes made by the PMS system. This provides a baseline for future changes.

The INTERACQ system is comprised of three components: an EPROM chip for the hand-held terminal, an EPROM chip for the PMS controller, and a diskette with the INTERACQ software for the laptop PC.

The user must furnish the laptop PC, with the following minimum requirements: a 286 processor, MS-DOS 4.0 or higher operating system, serial port, 3.5 floppy disk drive, and at least one megabyte of RAM. Faster processors (486 or better), additional memory (8MB or more), and a hard drive will greatly improve the performance of the INTERACQ system. A color screen will enhance the viewing of data as it is replayed.

The new enhanced WINDOWS INTERACQ system will also allow you to make all changes from the notebook PC by uploading and downloading data sets to the PMS. You can modify data sets on screen, every 500 rpm beginning at 2000 rpm, which makes programming the PMS even easier and more user-friendly. This software requires a 486/100 processor, or better, and 16 Mbytes of RAM.

STAND ALONE FUEL INJECTION SYSTEMS/COMPONENTS

ACCEL

Closed Loop System

The Closed Loop System includes ECU, main harness, injector harness, one-bar MAP sensor, and heated water sensor. Two- and three-bar MAP Sensors are also available at extra cost for turbocharged and supercharged applications.

Part # 74040-A   Universal 4, 6, 8 cyl.

Inductive Pickup Modification

The 74043-I modification needs to be ordered with an ACCEL Control

System if timing control is to be utilized when using an aftermarket crank trigger or aftermarket magnetic pickup distributor without a mechanical or vacuum advance. This modification requires the use of an aftermarket ignition enhancer box, like the ACCEL 300+ system.

Part # 74043-I   Inductive Pickup Modification

Heated Oxygen Sensor

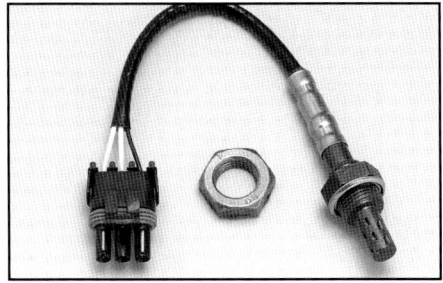

This sensor measures the amount of oxygen in the exhaust gases in order to tell the fuel injection ECU how much fuel to inject for optimum air-fuel mixture. ACCEL's gas-tight ceramic body uses zirconium dioxide stabilized with zirconium oxide for high durability and accurate measurement. Platinum electrodes ensure positive catalytic reaction.

Part # 74761   Heated Oxygen Sensor

Throttle Position Sensor (TPS)

The TPS Sensor attaches to the throttle body telling the ECU the amount of throttle opening. ACCEL's TPS sensor uses high-conductivity plastic resistance material with extra-light wiper arm for accurate throttle angle measurement and long service life.

Part # 74763   Throttle Position Sensor-SuperRam Systems
Part # 74781   Throttle Position Sensor-TBI Systems

Manifold Absolute Pressure Sensor (MAP)

This sensor monitors manifold vacuum, varying output voltage to the ECU as a function of load placed on the engine, providing necessary data to control fuel enrichment.

Part #	Description
74764	One-bar MAP Sensor
74776	Two-bar MAP Sensor
74777	Three-bar MAP Sensor

Coolant Temperature Sensor (CLT)

ACCEL's Coolant Temperature Sensor employs a thermistor to obtain accurate measurement of engine temperature. As the engine warms, thermistor resistance decreases, letting the ECU know that it can reduce fuel enrichment.

Part # 74765   Coolant Temperature Sensor

Air Temperature Sensor

ACCEL electronic fuel injection systems monitor inlet air temperature to provide the ECU with more accurate status of engine operating conditions. This air temperature sensor is a replacement for the unit supplied with ACCEL SuperRam™ EFI System. It helps determine the proper amount of fuel to inject.

Part # 74773   SuperRam EFI System

CALMAP Program Engine Management Controls for Special Applications

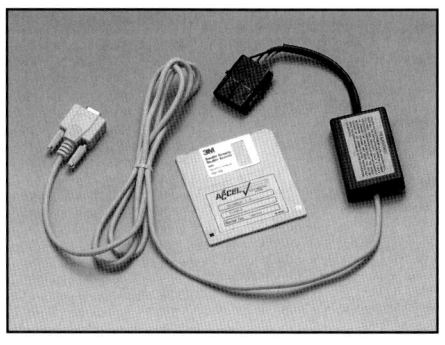

A user-friendly calibration tool that allows anyone with a basic understanding of engine tuning to recalibrate ACCEL SuperRam Fuel Injection Systems, or ACCEL EFM (Electronic Fuel Management) Systems for specific engine component combinations. With CALMAP, you can access and change any table within ACCEL ECUs. Calibration can be performed on engine dyno or "on the fly" (in the vehicle under actual driving conditions). Calibrations may be saved in computer files to be stored, or changed and reused as often as desired. No PROMs to burn in order to change fuel delivery and spark timing calibration. The digital ACCEL ECUs allow CALMAP direct user interface of fuel injection and ignition-system controls to accommodate virtually any engine components selected. CALMAP can be used with PC or laptop computer with the following features: DOS (version 2.11 minimum), E-232 serial port, 3 1/2" disc drive, minimum CPU speed 8MHz, 200 x 640 pixel display capability. CALMAP software package includes: 3 1/2" floppy disks, serial interface cable, CALMAP instruction booklet.

Part #	Description
74990-L	CALMAP software with 25 ft. cable
74990-S	CALMAP software with 5 ft. cable
74990-N	CALMAP software only, V-6.32

TWM

Honda Billet Check Valve

Check02	Check01
1994+ Accord	1988-1993 Accord
1992+ Civic	1988-1991 Civic
1994+ Integra	1988-1993 Integra
1997+ Prelude	1988-1996 Prelude

TWM Oxygen Sensor

This 4-wire sensor provides a very accurate output voltage which is directly related to air/fuel ratio. It has an internal heater to assure accurate readings soon after startup, and a signal ground. Connections: 2 wires for the internal heater, 1 wire for the output signal, and 1 wire for the signal ground.

ELECTROMOTIVE

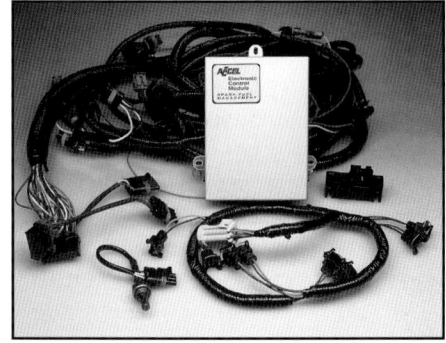

Innovation and hard work were used to create product lines of ignition and engine management systems, and these are backed up by continuing research and development. To maximize the utility of these units, Electromotive also carries a broad range of related products, both individually and packaged as complete systems.

Total Engine Control

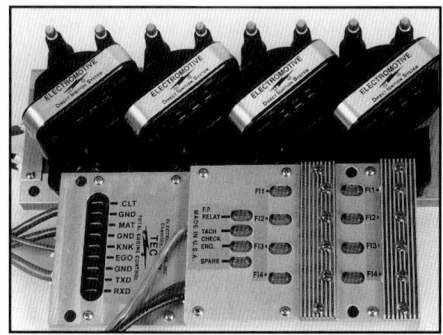

The TEC combines state-of-the-art fuel injection with the industry leading Direct Ignition System, replacing the existing carburetor or fuel injection system, ignition, distributor, and coil. The use of advanced, digital computer-based technology offers the absolute best power delivery, smoothest drive-ability, and lowest emissions possible. All these features, along with the high energy coils, packaged in one easy-to-install unit, can be mounted conveniently in the engine compartment.

Unlike any other fuel control system, TEC needs only two inputs to establish the base fuel curve. Where other systems rely on huge tables that must be filled with individual pulse width values, TEC is based on thermodynamically linear fuel delivery. TEC Configurations: 4 cyl.; 6 cyl. dual plug; 8 cyl., 8 injector drivers; 12 cyl. and 3 rotor rotary. Contact Electromotive for details on four cylinder, odd-fire, two-stroke, and other unusual engine configurations.

Calibration Software

Electromotive offers calibration software to suit any engine. Super and Super*Blend are designed for simple, straightforward operation of an engine with closed loop and idle speed control. Both PAFZ and Super*Blend accommodate both speed density (manifold pressure) or mass air flow configurations. Super*Blend and PAF*Blend (our newest software package), blend throttle position signal with manifold pressure inputs in programmable steps for smooth, stable running in all ranges, even with the most radical engine configurations. Both PAFZ and PAF*Blend offer advanced closed-loop operation, so that more than one air to ratio can be targeted with the same calibration. Graphical data logging is available to make tuning and troubleshooting easy.

Engine Management System Hardware

Electromotive's goal is to make available to customers the sensors, components, tools, and information required to make engine management system installation a success. Technical support staff can help with selecting the components which will best meet your needs.

TEC Options:

Super	standard speed density software
SUPER*B	super with mass air flow capabilities and blend routines
PAFZ	proportional air/fuel control with mass air flow capabilities
PAF*Blend	proportional air/fuel control with blend routines
"G"	graphical data logging option for Super and PAFZ

NOTE: Calibration Software is not included in these TEC hardware options and must be ordered separately.

Power Requirements:

Battery voltage:
10 to 16 vdc clean
Ground:
Direct to engine block

Average Current:

4 Cylinder: 3 amps @ 6000 rpm
6 Cylinder: 4.5 amps @ 6000 rpm
8 Cylinder: 6 amps @ 6000 rpm

Performance:

Spark energy output:
120mJ at the plug
Spark burn time:
1200 millisec. avg.
Timing resolution:
+/- 1/4 crankshaft degree
RPM range:
40 to 12,000 rpm

HALTECH

The E6K is a powerful "real-time" programmable fuel injection and ignition system computer designed to control most ignition type engines. Whether 1-6, 8, 10, or 12 cylinders, 1-2 rotors, naturally aspirated, turbocharged or supercharged, the HALTECH E6K can control it. The E6K uses all of the functionality included with the E6S family plus the E6K adds the following: doubled microprocessor speed; an internal barometric pressure sensor; dedicated PWM outputs (4) to control numerous solenoids, valves, shiftlights, and other devices; and an "intelligent" on-board reluctor adapter to cater for all types of trigger inputs. Immediate software updates via your PC.

The E6K is capable of controlling up to 8 low-impedance or 16 high-impedance injectors. If necessary an additional driver box can be added for more injector outputs. The E6K System optimizes engine performance through the following capabilities: ignition timing control, fuel control, idle speed control, barometric pressure compensation, closed loop O2 control, and on-board reluctor adapter.

The E6K is much more than a programmable fuel injection computer — it provides logging of engine data and allows access in real time to maximize performance and troubleshoot problems in a vehicle while running. Typical Applications: conversion from carburetion to fuel injection; control of fuel injection on modified engines; race and rally applications of all description; design and development purposes.

The patented HALTECH system of programming virtually eliminates the input of numbers. You simply manipulate graphics in the form of bar graphs and by pressing arrows you increase or decrease the amount of fuel or ignition delivered at that particular load point.

E6K Kit Contents:

Electronic Control Unit (ECU)
Main Wiring Loom (Flying)
Injector Wiring Loom
2 x Power Relays
Air Temperature Sensor
Coolant Temperature Sensor
Throttle Position Sensor
Communication Cable
Programming Software
Instruction Manual
MAP Sensor (Extra Cost)
Ignition Module (Extra Cost)

System Features:

Number of Cylinders:
1-6, 8, 10, 12 and 1-2 Rotors
Max Operating RPM: 16000 rpm
RPM Range increments:
500/1000 rpm
Max. Range: 10500/16000 rpm
Number of Fuel Maps: 22/17
Number of Ignition Maps: 22/17
Number of Bars per Map: 32

Fuel Correction Maps:

Coolant Temperature
Air Temperature
Battery Voltage
Cold Prime
Zero Throttle
Full Throttle
Injector Phasing
Throttle Pump
Injector Trim (Seq. only)

Ignition Correction Maps:

Coolant Temperature
Air Temperature

Trigger Signal Type:

Inductive Magnetic
(Internal Signal Conditioning)
Ignition Crank
Hall Effect Sensor
Optical Sensor

Trigger Pattern:

Twin Trigger:
Single pulse per cycle
Multi-Tooth:
Bosch Motronic (60t-2)

Ignition Configuration:

Twin Distributor
Twin Rotor (Dist. or DF)
Single Distributor
Direct Fire (1-4) & 6, 8
Cylinder Waste Spark

Injector Firing Mode:

Throttle Body (Batch) Multi-Point
Sequential (up to 4 banks) Staged

ECU Inputs:

MAP Sensor
Throttle Position
Internal Barometric Sensor
Coolant Temp
Air Temp
Primary Trigger
Secondary Trigger
Oxygen Sensor
Spec Purpose Digital
Gen. Purpose Analog

ECU Outputs:

Injector Drivers (8)
Fuel Pump Relay Control
Idle Air Control (IAC)
Ignition Output
Dedicated PWM Outputs (4)
Spec. Purpose Digital (0-2)

Accessories:

Idle Air Control Motor
Fuel/Ignition Trim Module
RPM Limit
Deceleration Fuel Cut-Off
Oxygen Sensor

Engine Data:

US or Metric Units
Map Storage and Retrieval
Data Logging

The HALTECH E6S is a powerful "real-time" programmable fuel injection and ignition system computer designed to control most ignition-type engines. Whether 1-6, 8, 10, or 12 cylinders, 1-2 rotors, naturally aspirated, turbocharged or supercharged, the HALTECH E6S can control it.

The E6S is available in 2 configurations: E6S and E6S-8. The standard configuration is the 4 injector driver E6S, capable of controlling 4 low-impedance or 8 high-impedance injectors. The E6S-8 has 8 injector drivers capable of controlling 8 low-impedance or 16 high-impedance injectors. If necessary an additional driver box can be added for more injector outputs.

The HALTECH F9 is a powerful "real-time" programmable fuel injection system computer designed for those seeking optimum performance. No other system in the same class is as adaptable, easy to install, or program. The F9 System has up to 22 adjustable fuel maps each with 32 individual bars. The F9 will run up to 16000 rpm with better resolution and greater accuracy than ever before.

The F9 is available in 2 configurations: F9 and F9-8. The standard configuration is the 4 injector driver F9, capable of controlling 4 low-impedance or 8 high-impedance injectors. The F9-8 has 8 injector drivers capable of controlling 8 low-impedance or 16 high-impedance injectors. If necessary an additional driver box can be added for more injector outputs.

Injectors can be controlled directly, fired all together, in batches, or can be staged when running high boost turbo or superchargers. The F9 is upgradeable to F9A specifications which will allow: closed loop EGO (Exhaust Gas Oxygen) sensing, idle speed control, torque converter control, thermofan, turbo waste gate, and many more controls. The patented HALTECH system of programming virtually eliminates the input of numbers. You simply manipulate graphics in the form of bar graphs and by pressing arrows you increase or decrease the amount of fuel delivered at that particular load point. The process is repeated for all load points in each RPM range.

LC ENGINEERING

Pro Fuel Injection kits are now available for the Toyota 22R/22RE engine in three different configurations. Based on the SDS EM-2 system, the LC Pro Injection Kit is a fully programmable, stand alone, engine management system designed to replace the factory Toyota injection computer or convert your carbureted engine to fuel injection. While not for the everyday driver, the Pro Injection systems offer the performance enthusiast total control of fuel and ignition curves. This system does not require expensive software or a laptop computer for programming. Using speed density airflow sensing, the LC Pro Injection allows you to eliminate the bulky and restrictive OEM airflow meter. Full sensor diagnostics and programming.

LC Pro Injection has no limitations! It provides excellent results with naturally-aspirated engines, super chargers, turbo chargers, and all types of fuels. You can expect awesome driveability with the LC Pro Fuel Injection Kit.

Part #	Description
24-EM2D	Pro Fuel Injection, fuel only
24-EM2E	Pro Fuel Injection, fuel & ignition control
24-EM2F	Pro Fuel Injection, distributorless ignition

AIR FLOW METERS

DINAN

For those of you looking for even faster acceleration, this air flow meter package delivers additional power, particularly at higher engine speeds. The intake system benefits from a larger internal diameter air flow meter which allows more air into your engine at a faster rate. The package includes matched Performance Engine Software that optimizes fuel mixture and ignition timing for maximum power gains.

3 Series E46
3 Series E36
3 Series E30
328i (E46) 1999
323i (E46) 1999
M3 (E36) 1996-1999
M3 (E36) 1995
328i (E36) 1996-1999
325i, iC (E36) 1992-1995
323i (E36) 1998-1999
318i (E36) 1996-1998
318i (E36) 1992-1995
318ti (E36) 1996-1999
318ti (E36) 1995
M3 (E30) 1987-1991
325i, ix, Convertible (E30) 1987-1991
325, 325e (E30) 1984-1988
318i (E30) 1990-1993
318i (E30) 1983-1985
323i (E30) 1983-1991

WEAPON*R USA

Part#	Application
WRAFMTY	1984-1991 BMW 3 SERIES
WRAFMZD	1990-1991 Mazda Miata 1.6L
WRAFMZD	1988-1989 Mazda 626
WRAFMZD	1986-1989 Mazda 323
WRAFMZD	1984-1988 Mazda RX-7, all FI models
WRAFMNS	1989-1994 Mitsubishi Eclipse / Talon / Laser
WRF89EC	1995+ Mitsubishi Eclipse / Talon, turbo
WRAFMEC	1993+ Mitsubishi 3000GT / Stealth
WRAFMEC	1993-1998 Mitsubishi Mirage 1.8L
WRAFMNS	1991-1997 Nissan Sentra / NX / 200SX
WRAFMTY	1985-1989 Toyota Corolla 4AGE
WRAFMTY	1990-1993 Toyota MR2 turbo

OBX MASS FLOW ADAPTER

Product#	Description
M001	Mazda (Bosch Systems) Adapter
M003	Mitsubishi Adapter
M002	Nissan (4cyl) Adapter
M004	Nissan (6cyl) Adapter
M001	Toyota (Bosch Systems) Adapters

SPLIT SECOND

Split Second is your source for free flowing Mass Air Flow sensors (MAF). These flow sensors are made of a durable light-weight aluminum construction. By removing the restrictive stock Air Flow Meter (AFM), Karman Vortex, or Plunger-type air flow sensor and replacing it with a larger free flowing MAF sensor you are able to increase your horsepower. Mass Air Flow sensors (MAF) are sized to your engine's potential.

MAF sensor flanged
MAF 3.5"   450 hp
MAF 3"   300 hp
MAF 2.5"   240 hp
MAF Connector
MAF-con   Connector

MAF sensor non-flanged
MAF 3.5"   450 hp
MAF 3"   300 hp
MAF 2.5   240 hp
MAF Connector
MAF-con   Connector

FUEL INJECTORS

ACCEL

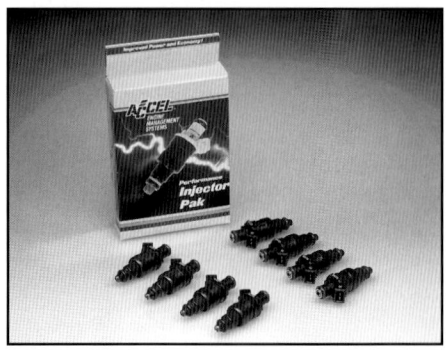

These are ACCEL's highest flowing, high-impedance injectors. Still compatible with the OE computer injector drivers. They also provide a full 30 degrees of cone spray angle which results in excellent atomization of the fuel, improved fuel economy and throttle response. The performance injectors are also the new anti-plugging type which will forever eliminate problems that were once associated with carbon buildup. Individually packaged.

Part #	Flow Rate	Type
74610	22 lb./hr.	High Imp.
74609	30 lb./hr.	High Imp.
74613	36 lb./hr.	High Imp.
74612	55 lb./hr.	Low Imp.
74607	83 lb./hr.	Low Imp.

Note: The 55 lb./hr. and 83 lb./hr. injector should only be used with the SEFI system.

MARREN MOTOR SPORTS, INC.

Fuel injectors are the essential element when running a performance EFI system. The motor cannot reach its full potential if the injectors that the engine management system control are not delivering the proper amount of fuel. Electronic fuel injectors are available in varying flow rates for all applications of high performance to racing specifications in auto and marine.

Static flow rates (lb./hr.) are estimated at 43.5 psi (3 bar) fuel pressure. All injectors are flow tested and put into matched sets with the flow rate tolerance of 0 to 2%. Injectors can also be purchased without being tested (factory tolerance).

Part #	Description	Ohms
0524	24 lb./hr.	High
0530	30 lb./hr.	High
0536	36 lb./hr.	High
0526	26 lb./hr.	Low
0534	34 lb./hr.	Low
0538	36 lb./hr.	Low Hose End
0542	42 lb./hr.	Low
0541	42 lb./hr.	High
0550	50 lb./hr.	High
0551	50 lb./hr.	Low
0552	52 lb./hr.	Low
0555	55 lb./hr.	Low
0572	72 lb./hr.	Low
0582	82 lb./hr.	Low
0596	96 lb./hr.	Low
05160	160 lb./hr.	Low

**These products are for racing use only and are not legal for use on emission-controlled vehicles.

If you do not see an injector that may meet your requirements, contact Marren Motor Sports; it is impossible to list all the injectors offered. Marren also offers stock fuel injectors.

GREDDY

Injectors/Injector Holders

Part #	Description
13500036	360cc Injector
13500055	550cc Injector
13500072	720cc Injector
13900001	Dummy Injector
13540001	Mazda RX-7 Turbo 1987-1992 1 (ONE) Injector Holder
13540002	Mazda RX-7 T/T 1993-1997 1 (ONE) Injector Holder
13530001	Mitsubishi Galant VR-4 1 (ONE) Injector Holder
13551011	Nissan 300ZX T/T 1990-1996 2 (TWO) Injector Holder
13510006	Toyota MR-2 Turbo 1990-1996 2 (TWO) Injector Holder
13510021	Toyota Supra Turbo 1987-1992 2 (TWO) Injector Holder
36055800	Toyota Supra T/T 1992-1997 2 (TWO) Injector Holder
13900451	Steel Injector Boss
13900452	Aluminum Injector Holder

TMW INDUCTION

Part #	Fuel Pressure psi				Driver Type	Resistance Ohms
	43.5	60	65	73.5		
Rochester 2900-2016	19	22	23	25	Sat	16
Bosch 2900-3302	19	22	23	25	Sat	16
Lucas 2500-1014	20	23	24	25	Sat	16
Lucas 2500-1028	20	23	24	25	P & H	2.2
Lucas 2500-1033	20	23	24	26	P & H	2.2
Lucas 2500-1012	20	24	25	26	Sat	16
Lucas 2500-1004	21	24	25	27	Sat	16
Lucas 2500-1001	21	25	26	27	P & H	2.4
Rochester 2900-2010	21	25	26	27	Sat	12
Lucas 2500-1000	21	25	26	28	Sat	16
Lucas 2500-1013	21	25	26	28	P & H	2.4
Rochester 2900-2017	22	26	27	29	Sat	16
Lucas 2500-1022	24	28	29	31	Sat	16
Bosch 2900-1302	25	29	30	32	Sat	16
Lucas 2500-1025	25	29	30	32	P & H	2.2
Rochester 2900-2011	26	31	32	34	P & H	2.0
Lucas 2500-1008	26	31	32	34	Sat	16
Bosch 2900-2302	31	36	38	40	Sat	16
Lucas 2500-1021	31	37	38	40	Sat	16
Lucas 2500-1016	32	38	40	42	P & H	2.2
Rochester 2900-2012	34	40	42	44	P & H	2.0
Bosch 2900-0803	36	38	44	47	P & H	20
Bosch 2900-4302	37	43	45	47	Sat	16
Lucas 2500-1018	37	43	45	48	P & H	2.2
Lucas 2500-1031	37	44	46	49	Sat	16
Rochester 2900-2018	38	45	46	49	Sat	12
Lucas 2500-1009	41	48	50	53	Sat	16
Lucas 2500-1030	42	49	51	54	Sat	16
Rochester 2900-2013	50	59	61	65	Sat	12
Lucas 2500-1032	51	60	63	67	P & H	2.2
Rochester 2900-2014	72	85	88	94	P & H	2
Rochester 2900-2015	96	113	117	125	P & H	2

TMW INDUCTION INJECTOR SUPPORT COMPONENTS

2900-2100 O-ring injector top and bottom, 8 per pkt.
2900-2400 Plug, harness to injector
2900-2121 Plug, injector pocket
2900-2120 Pocket, weld or epoxy to manifold
2900-5607 Clip injector retaining

HAHN RACECRAFT

With about 15% more fuel flow capacity than 550s, HRC's 625 cc injector offers a nice, safe edge. And you'll be pleased with the idle quality, and with the fact that they match stock injector impedance within 1/100 ohm! For BIG power, the 780 cc injector is also available (for serious competition only). Compatible with many brands of fuel system electronics.

HRC TEFI625 — 625 cc/min. fuel injectors, set of four: fits Talon, Eclipse, and many other Asian applications

HRC TEFI800 — 800 cc/min. fuel injectors, set of four: fits Talon, Eclipse, and many other Asian applications

JIM WOLF TECHNOLOGY

555 cc/min. Injectors:
fit 1990-1994 300ZX TT
Needed for upgrades from 420 hp to 620 hp. ECU programs are available for this injector in combination with most upgrades.

420 cc/min. Injectors:
fit 1984-1989 300ZX & 1981-1983 280ZXT

This injector set can deliver enough fuel for 450 hp. 1986+ requires the earlier 1984-1985 fuel rail. 1988+ requires dropping resistors.

370 cc/min. Injector:
fits SR20 & KA24D 4 cyl. engine. Used up to 270 hp for turbocharging and nitrous oxide systems.

RC ENGINEERING

RC Engineering can provide injectors in any format, any type of mounting or fuel rail configuration. These include hose end, large O-ring American / European fuel rail, small O-ring Japanese fuel rail, and custom additional controller units. All Flow numbers are taken at static settings.

**Peak and Hold Injectors
Low Resistance - 2.5 / 3 Ohms
(Measured at 43 P.S.I.G.)**

155 cc/min.
185 cc/min.
195 cc/min.
210 cc/min.
220 cc/min.
250 cc/min.
270 cc/min.
320 cc/min.
370 cc/min.
400 cc/min.
450 cc/min.
500 cc/min.
550 cc/min.
650 - 800 cc/min.
800 - 1200 cc/min.
1400 - 1600 cc/min.

**Saturated Injectors
High Resistance Approx. 12 - 16 Ohms (Measured AT 43 P.S.I.G.)**

160 cc/min.
185 cc/min.
200 cc/min.
210 cc/min.
225 cc/min.
240 cc/min.
270 cc/min.
310 cc/min.
370 cc/min.
440 cc/min.
500 cc/min.
600 - 800 cc/min.

Most all Gally or Side feed injectors can be modified up to rates of 100%. This is a partial listing of available injector sizes. Please call RC Engineering for information on particular applications or any unique requirements you may have.

VENOM

VENOM Stage I Injector is an off-the-shelf high-performance injector which is an exact fit, OEM design injector. Flow rate is increased up to 10% in order to maximize horsepower increase, while minimizing against too rich fuel mixture. Idle is maintained, while increasing overall performance throughout the RPM range. VENOM Stage II Injector is an OEM exact fit injector with matched specific flow rates balanced to required horsepower gains.

LC ENGINEERING

High volume Bosch Fuel Injectors for use with the Pro Injection. These new injectors are custom machined to fit in the stock Toyota fuel rail. Various flow rates available.

Part #	Description
24-200	Bosch 300cc Injector
24-201	Bosch 360cc Injector
24-204	Bosch 490cc Injector
24-206	Bosch 620cc Injector

SPLIT SECOND

Split Second stocks high precision, pintle style, multi-port fuel injectors of the latest design. These injectors feature accurate flow rates, low variation from one unit to the next, excellent fuel atomization, and wide dynamic range. They are available in both low- and high-resistance varieties and all have O-rings on both ends for safe, leak-free installation into your fuel rail and manifold. High resistance (>12 ohms) injectors are used where only one injector is driven by each driver, as in most true sequential fuel injection applications. Contact Split Second for assistance in sizing injectors for your application.

AIR-TO-FUEL RATIO METERS

ACCEL

Air/Fuel Ratio Meter with Oxygen Sensor

This unit is an excellent tuning aid for immediate response to air/fuel mixture changes. The 9 LEDs provide a wide range of operational information in order to tune any engine management system for any size engine using unleaded fuel. Mounts conveniently on the dash or in the passenger compartment. Includes air/fuel monitor, harness, oxygen sensor, and mounting nut.

Part #	Description
74550	Air/Fuel Ratio Meter with Oxygen Sensor
74551	Air/Fuel Ratio Meter w/o Oxygen Sensor (for unleaded fuel only)

EFI SYSTEMS

The EFI Systems, Inc. Injector Air/Fuel Monitor has a readout for both air/fuel ratio, and percentage of injector usage. The other display is for percentage of injector usage. This information is used to determine if your injectors are sized correctly. A reading of more than 80% is an indication that you need larger injectors.

LC ENGINEERING

Perform accurate fuel curve adjustments, on fuel-injected or carbureted engines with the Cyberdyne Mixture Meter and heated O2 Sensor.

Part #	Description
24-110	Cyberdyne Mixture Meter Gauge
24-114	Heated O2 Sensor

SPLIT SECOND

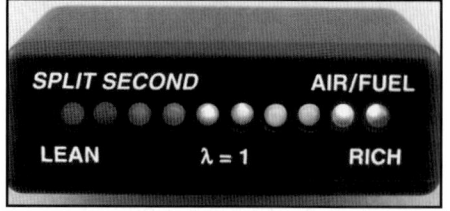

The ARM1 (Air/Fuel Ratio Meter) is a precision, miniature instrument that provides an easy-to-read, real time indication of the air/fuel ratio of an internal combustion engine. It features a brilliant, 5-color display that is automatically dimmed for night viewing. It is an ideal monitoring tool for calibrating engine air/fuel ratio or making adjustments while driving.

The EGO1 (Exhaust Gas Oxygen) sensor is a four-wire sensor that provides a very accurate output voltage which is directly correlated with air/fuel ratio. It is an ideal sensor for use with the ARM1 (Air/Fuel Ratio Meter). The EGO1 features an internal heater which assures accurate readings soon after engine start. EGO1 also features a signal ground which provides accurate readings through the driving cycle.

FUEL INJECTION PUMPS & FUEL FILTERS

HOLLEY

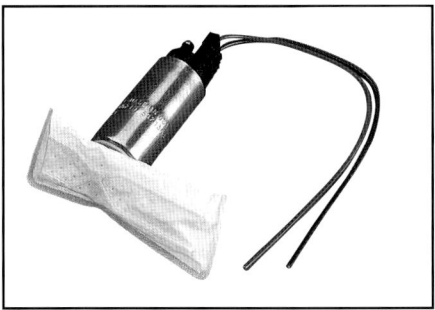

The Holley line of high-output in-tank electric fuel pumps delivers fuel at up to twice the flow rate of stock pumps for dramatically improved performance. These performers utilize a proven gerotor design. The outside pump dimensions, however, are compact enough to fit existing hanger assemblies, without modifications.

The addition of a high-output fuel pump is a necessity when other engine modifications such as camshaft, headers, larger injectors, higher flow throttle bodies, etc. are contemplated. These are complete fuel pump kits and include all drop parts, accessories, and installation instructions. Also included is an inlet filter that meets or exceeds original equipment specifications and provides improved filtration and durability.

Part # 12-906
In-Tank Electric 255 LPH Fuel Pump
Acura Integra 1994-1995 1.8L
Honda Civic 1992-1997 1.5L 4 cyl.
Honda Civic 1992-1997 1.5L
 4 cyl. VTEC
Honda Civic 1992-1997 1.6L
 4 cyl. VTEC

Part # 12-907
In-Tank Electric 255 LPH Fuel Pump
Eagle Talon 1995-1997
Mitsubishi Eclipse 1995-1997
 2.0L 4 cyl., turbo

Also carries same for Mazda and Toyota applications.

HAHN RACECRAFT

Fuel injection fuel pump upgrades

HRC TEFUPMP — Fuel Pump Upgrade, 1989-1994 T/E/L

HRC TEFUPMP95 — Fuel Pump Upgrade, 1995+ T/E

K&N

K&N's all new billet-aluminum washable fuel filter offers the highest filtration quality of any fuel filter on the market. The 81-0500 series filters contain a 304 stainless-steel filter disc which will stop particles as small as 10 microns (.000392") in size. The 1.375" diameter pleated disc provides 6.02 square inches of effective surface area to prolong service intervals. The finned 2" diameter billet-aluminum body is 4.25" long with AN fittings. Interchangeable threaded end caps sealed with rubber O-rings will withstand up to 6000 pounds per square inch of pressure. Bypass option will prevent total fuel starvation in race applications.

SPECIFICATIONS

Length: 4.25" (with AN fittings)
Diameter: 2"
Filter Medium:
304 stainless-steel pleated disc
Filter Diameter: 1.375"
Effective Filtering Area:
6.20 Square Inches
Filter Efficiency: 10 Micron
Operating Pressure:
up to 6000 PSIG
Flow Rate: 15.3 GPM*
15.3 GPM Flow Rate @ 20 PSIG,
7.3 PSID P w/#8 AN Fittings*

* Independent laboratory certified test results.

Part #	Description
81-0530	Filter w/-6 AN ends
81-0540	Filter w/-8 AN ends
81-0550	Filter w/-10 AN ends
81-0500	w/-1/4" barbed style
81-0510	w/-5/16" barbed style
81-0520	w/-3/8" barbed style

MARREN MOTORSPORTS

High Pressure Electric Fuel Pumps

43 GPH FUEL PUMP, IN-LINE
Specifications:
43 gph @ 40 psi, 12 volts/5.4 amps.
Has 3/8-inch hose nipple inlet,
5/16-inch hose nipple outlet, 500 hp.
60 GPH FUEL PUMP
Specifications:
60 gph @ 40 psi, 12 volts/12 amps;
10 amps, 3 bar; 1 amp, 5 bar; 650 hp.

Other pumps available include:
90 gph @ 45 psi.
150 gph @ 45 psi.

Other pumps available for unique applications.

High Pressure Fuel Filter: In-Line

There is no such thing as keeping an EFI fuel delivery system too clean! A well filtered fuel supply prevents clogging the injectors' internal fuel filter. This filter is a low-restriction, high-pressure filter with 140 square inches of filtering material area to ensure total entrapment of particles as small as 5 microns. It mounts in-line in any position with 5/16-in. hose inlet and outlet fittings.

VENOM

The electronic fuel pump is central to the fuel management system. It must deliver precisely pressurized fuel in exacting quantities at each and every level of performance. Venom has applications for the following vehicles:

Acura	Jeep
Audi	Mazda
BMW	Mitsubishi
Chevrolet	Nissan
Chevrolet/GMC	Pontiac
Trucks	Saturn
Dodge	Subaru
Ford	Toyota
Ford Trucks	Volkswagen
Honda	

LC ENGINEERING

High volume EFI fuel pumps will handle all the fuel your Pro Injection System demands. Recommended for most Pro Injection installations, a must for turbo and blown application.

Part #	Description
24-100	300 hp fuel pump
24-101	500 hp fuel pump

Paxton Fuel control units

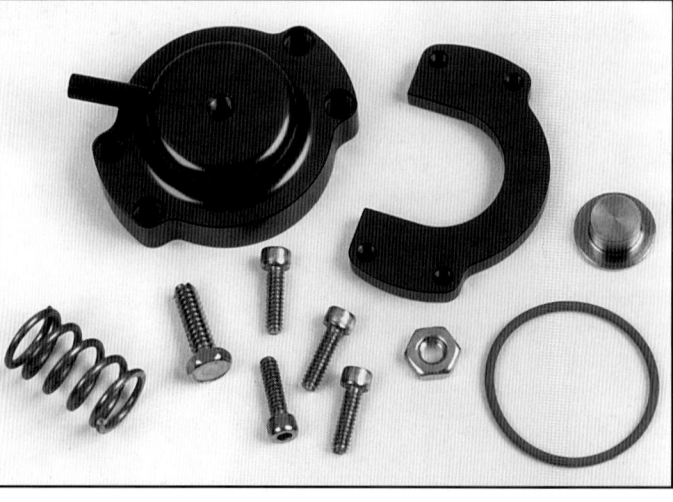

B&M CommandFlo billet-aluminum fuel flow modifier.

NOS

NOS carries a full line of fuel pumps to fit every performance level. From a small displacement fuel pump (#15760) that flows 18 gph at 4.0 psi to monster pumps capable of supporting 1200 horsepower.

SPLIT SECOND

Fuel pumps are crucial to the survival of your engine. This component maintains sufficient fuel delivery to your fuel rail and injectors. The flow rate of the pump is rated in gallons per hour. The pump must be sized to the fuel requirements of your engine. It is okay to have a pump that is too big, but not one that is too small. The excess fuel returns back to the tank from the fuel pressure regulator. Flow rating 1100 gpm.

VOLTAGE CONTROL UNITS

B&M

The PowerPlus Voltage Control Unit provides 18 volts for fuel pumps. Handles 15 amps continuous, 20 amps peak. The PowerPlus is for any vehicle utilizing electronic fuel injection. Designed and engineered for ultra-high performance racing applications, this unit provides up to 50% more energy for electric fuel pumps. The PowerPlus' internal voltage regulator keeps a constant 18-volt output and will provide full output even when input voltage drops below 12 volts! Fully epoxy encapsulated to survive the toughest racing environments and the anodized aluminum case requires only 3" x 5" to mount. Ideal for drag racing with alternator belt removal as this unit provides for no degradation in fuel pump performance.

Part # 46050   PowerPlus Voltage Control Unit

FUEL INJECTION PRESSURE REGULATORS

PAXTON

Fuel control units are a cost-effective way to provide an engine with additional fuel under boost. The only problem is not every engine or application has the same fuel curve requirements. Paxton's new fuel control units have different rates of gain to suit a variety of application.

B&M

The CommandFlo is a billet-aluminum fuel flow modifier. This unit is designed specifically for Hondas, Acuras, and Mitsubishi Eclipses. The CommandFlo allows modification of the fuel flow rate to properly tune the air/fuel ratio. Ideal for use with free flow intakes and exhaust systems. The CommandFlo offers these special features: bolt-on adjustable modifier for stock fuel regulators, 6061-T6 billet-aluminum case, CNC machined, allows pressure adjustments from 25-60 psi.

Part #	Application
46056	CommandFlo for 1988-1999 Honda Civic/CRX 1991-1999 Acura NSX 1990-1999 Acura Integra 1999 Honda S2000
46051	CommandFlo 1995-1999 Mitsubishi Eclipse

The B&M Fuel Pressure Gauge Set allows the user to accurately measure fuel pressure. Proper fuel pressure is critical at wide-open throttle to prevent lean conditions. Recommended to be used with the B&M CommandFlo fuel flow modifier.

Part #	Application
46054	Fuel Pressure Gauge Set 1988-1999 Honda Civic/CRX 1990-1999 Acura Integra
46055	Fuel Pressure Gauge Set 1989-1999 Mitsubishi Eclipse

APEX INTEGRATION FUEL SYSTEM COMPONENTS

Part #	Application
404-A022	Adjustable Fuel Press Reg. -6
404-A021	Adjustable Fuel Press Reg. Hose

HOLLEY

Holley fuel injection regulators have an adjustment range up to 65 PSI and they're capable of providing all the fuel pressure a high-performance, fuel-injected vehicle requires.

Two universal regulators are offered. The first is Part # 512-504.

Holley fuel injection regulator

Designed to be used on fuel injected, non-turbo-charged vehicles, it is machined from billet aluminum and has a range of adjustability from 15-65 PSI. It comes equipped with two -8 AN inlet fitting and one -6 AN outlet fitting and it can be used on any import or domestic fuel-injected vehicle. The other universal regulator is Part # 512-505. This one is designed for fuel-injected and turbo-charged engines. Because of its boost compensating design, it can provide more fuel under turbo-charger boost conditions. Its range of adjustability is from 20-65 psi.

Six regulators for dedicated applications round out the current product line. They each feature a range of adjustability from 35-65 psi and can accommodate engine modifications from the mild to the wild side. They're made to bolt in the stock regulator's location so installation problems are greatly simplified. Utilizing a special wave spring to maintain constant fuel pressure, these Holley-designed regulators will truly enhance the performance of other horsepower-creating components that you may have added to the fuel system, air flow system, and electronic system of your vehicle.

Pressure Regulators for Fuel-Injected Engines

Part#	Application
512-506	1997-92 Honda Civic 1.6L VTEC engine
512-504	Regulators for fuel-injected engines. Universal for all non-turbo-charged engines.

TMW INDUCTION ADJUSTABLE FUEL PRESSURE REGULATORS

Inline type	Inlet	Return	Pressure
2800-4401	-6 AN	-6 AN	35-45
2800-4404	-6 AN	-6 AN	55-65
Manifold	Inlet	Return	Pressure
2800-4411	-6 AN	-6 AN	35-45
2800-4414	-6 AN	-6 AN	55-65
Rail end mount	Inlet	Return	Pressure
2800-6401	-6 AN	-6 AN	35-45
2800-6404	-6 AN	-6 AN	55-65
Manifold	Inlet	Return	Pressure
2800-6411	-6 AN	-6 AN	35-45
2800-6414	-6 AN	-6 AN	55-65
Rail center mount	Inlet	Return	Pressure
2800-6402	-6 AN	-6 AN	35-45
2800-6406	-6 AN	-6 AN	55-65
Manifold	Inlet	Return	Pressure
2800-6412	-6 AN	-6 AN	35-45
2800-6416	-6 AN	-6 AN	55-65

Supplied with rail. Specify type when ordering, threaded both ends or thread one end and counterbore.

TMW INDUCTION THROTTLE LINKAGE COMPONENTS

Part#	Description
2900-3066	Throttle Cable with firewall fitting and threaded (M8x1) adjuster. Length 42" inner, 36" outer with trunnion.
3004-1701	Lever, DCNF
2900-1703	Throttle Stop fits 2900, 2930, 3000 series
3004-3038	Lever Interconnect fits 3004 series, pair with 3004-3039
2900-1701	Throttle Lever, enables counter-clockwise rotation of 3000 series. Use with spring 47610.110.
3004-3039	Lever Interconnect, pair with 3004-3038
2900-1700	Throttle Lever fits 2900, 2930, 3000 series
2900-3050	Throttle Cable Bracket fits 2900 series, locates cable for 2900-3038 lever. Swivel has M8x1thread for cable adjuster.
2910-3050	Throttle Cable Bracket fits 2910 series
2910-3038	Throttle Lever Standard on 2910 series, interconnects with 2900-3039
2900-3038	Throttle Lever Standard on 2900 series, interconnects with 2900-3039
2900-3039	Lever Interconnect, pair with 2910-3038
2900-3041	Throttle Position Sensor, cw
2900-3040	Throttle Position Sensor, ccw

Weld-on Boss with plug for oxygen sensor

Part#	Description
2799-0005	Plug
2799-0006	Bushing
2799-0007	Sealing washer
2799-0001	Oxygen Sensor, heated, 3 wire. Mount approx. 30" from the head. Ideal exh temp 680 - 1450 F.
2900-3042	Plug for TPS
2900-2310	Coolant Sensor
2900-2320	Intake Air Sensor

WEAPON*R

Dedicated to bringing you the best of the best, these fuel pressure risers are made from the highest quality materials and come in assorted colors. These fuel pressure risers will increase pressure in your fuel system to create more HP from your car.

Part#	Application
FPC1	HONDA /ACURA
FPC2	MITSUBISHI 2.0L-UP / MAZDA / TOYOTA
FPC3	MITSUBISHI 2.0L-LOWER / NISSAN
FPC4	VW / BMW / BENZ / UNIVERSAL

Available In Red/Blue/Yellow/Purple: Add $10 for color.

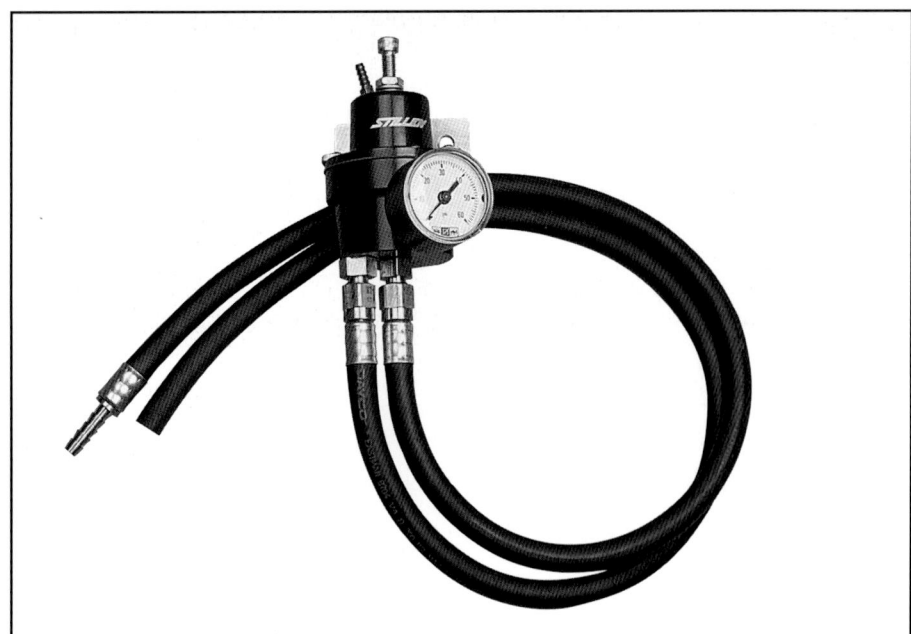

Stillen's Billet Aluminum Fuel Pressure Riser

STILLEN

Stillen's R&D department has been analyzing ways to richen the fuel mixture for a power gain on vehicles equipped with intake, headers, and exhaust. Such equipment leans out a motor and the typical cure is to update the fuel delivery schedule hidden within the engine's computer. The Fuel Pressure Riser (FPR) offered by the company has proven to be the answer. Tested and tuned on a Honda Civic equipped with intake, headers, and exhaust, Stillen's FPR showed a maximum gain of 6 horsepower on the company's DynoJet. The billet aluminum component is shipped with gauge, clamps, hoses, fittings, and instructions. The FPR installs in 30 minutes.

TMW INDUCTION

TMW offers several adjustable fuel pressure regulators machined from 6061-T6 aluminum, all designed for firewall or fuel rail mountings. All feature threaded fuel line fittings. All regulators will flow between 300 and 700 lbs. of gasoline per hour depending on the fuel pump configuration. Note: 300 lb./hr. is sufficient for a 600 hp engine (on gasoline).

MARREN MOTOR SPORTS

Adjustable Fuel Pressure Regulator

This adjustable fuel pressure regulator lets you fine tune the fuel pressure to the installation from 36-45 psi. Its versatility allows it to be adapted to any installation position.

Adjustable Pressure Reference Regulator

Adjustable from 29-87 psi. For turbo and supercharged engines. Marren has a wide variety of regulators, contact them with your specs and they will find one to suit your needs.

SPLIT SECOND

Fuel injection systems rely on a known fuel pressure differential across the injectors. To maintain that pressure, a manifold vacuum-referenced fuel pressure regulator is required. Fixed fuel pressure regulator maintains a fuel pressure of 45 psi referenced to intake manifold pressure. Adjustable fuel pressure regulator maintains a user adjustable difference between fuel pressure and intake manifold pressure.

B&M

The Fuel Pressure Gauge Set allows the user to accurately measure fuel pressure. Proper fuel pressure is critical at wide-open throttle to prevent lean conditions. Recommended to be used with the B&M CommandFlo fuel flow modifier.

Part #	Description
46054	Fuel Pressure Gauge Set 1988-1999 Honda Civic/CRX 1990-1999 Acura Integra
46055	Fuel Pressure Gauge Set 1989-1999 Mitsubishi Eclipse

FUEL INJECTION SYSTEM INSTALLATION ACCESSORIES

SPLIT SECOND

Split Second offers fuel injector bosses for adding multi-port fuel injectors to manifolds or throttle bodies. These billet-aluminum inserts come either threaded (3/4" - 16) or 3/4" O.D. non-threaded. The insert bore is machined to accept O-ring or port-type injectors. The bosses may be threaded or welded into your manifold. Fuel can be supplied with a fuel rail or with a billet-aluminum injector cap (using a standard AN-4 fitting) and hold down assembly.

CARBURETORS

LC ENGINEERING

From mild to wild, Pro and Street Performer kits have you covered. The Street Performer Single Carburetors offer great torque and power. For higher performance we offer a full selection of Weber sidedraft dual carburetor kits.

38mm Carburetor Kit

The new 38mm Street Performer Carburetor Kit is the best single carb kit for slightly modified 20R and 22R engines. For both 20R and 22R engines simply install this kit on the stock manifold by utilizing the supplied adapter kit. For 22R engines with a 20R head add a hi-flow open plenum aluminum performance manifold for superior high-RPM performance. Combine this 38mm Carburetor Kit with the Street Performer Cylinder Head, Street Performer Camshaft and Header Kit to improve performance throughout the entire RPM range with super quick acceleration.

Kit includes: 38mm Weber carburetor, complete linkage kit, electric choke, billet air filter adapter, massive 11" K&N air filter, gasket, hoses, clamps, and illustrated instructions.

Part #	Description
16-74638	38mm Deluxe Carb Kit w/ 20R Intake Manifold
16-3822	38mm Deluxe Carb Kit 20R/22R
16-3820	38mm Carb & Manifold Adapter Only

32/36 Carburetor Kit

The 32/36 Street Performer Carburetor Kit features a custom jetted 32/36 Weber carburetor designed to put the power back in your engine. Kit includes: 32/36 Weber carburetor, billet air filter adapter, massive 11-inch K&N air filter, complete linkage, gaskets, hoses, clamps, and fully illustrated easy-to-install instructions. You can expect increased low-end and mid-range throttle response with improved overall power from this powerful carburetor kit.

Part #	Description
16-746	32/36 Deluxe Carb Kit w/ 20 Intake Manifold
16-323622	32/36 Deluxe Carb Kit 20R/22R
16-323620	32/36 Carb & Manifold Adapter Only

Dual Sidedraft Pro Carburetor Kit

Big carburetors mean big Toyota Power! Check out LC Engineering's custom 40mm, 45mm, & 48mm Pro Carburetors! Available only from LC Engineering. These custom reworked carburetors are transformed into the ultimate carburetion package designed specifically for engines using the LC Pro Cylinder Heads, such as the Stage-2, Stage-3, and Stage-5 set ups. These kits include our long runner "Pro Manifold" for maximum air flow. Massive horsepower increases and better all-around performance are only a small part of the benefits this carburetor kit has to offer. The Pro Carburetor Kits have all of LC Engineering's many tricks included. Kits Include: two 40/45/48 carburetors; custom jetting; proper venturi sizing; idle circuit calibration; pump nozzle calibration; float level adjustment; Pro Manifold; complete throttle linkage; throttle cable upgrade; modified air horns; two large K&N air filters; PCV valve assembly; carburetor insulator mounts; intake gasket; mounting hardware.

Circle Track Carburetors

Circle-track racers running under track rules that require using a Holley 500 cfm or 350 cfm carburetor — this is for you. These carburetors are custom-built and calibrated to work with the Toyota 4 cylinder air flow characteristics. Each carburetor is assembled from new components — not rebuilt — and blueprinted. Fuel circuits are calibrated to match the air flow rate. The booster venturis are balanced and flow-matched. The acceleration circuit is modified to prevent fuel siphon. Choke and linkage are removed for improved air flow.

Part #	Description
16-4412	Holley 500 cfm Carburetor
16-7448	Holley 350 cfm Carburetor

2 Barrel Asian Carburetor

LC Engineering now offers the Asian Toyota OEM Carburetor for circle-track classes running under

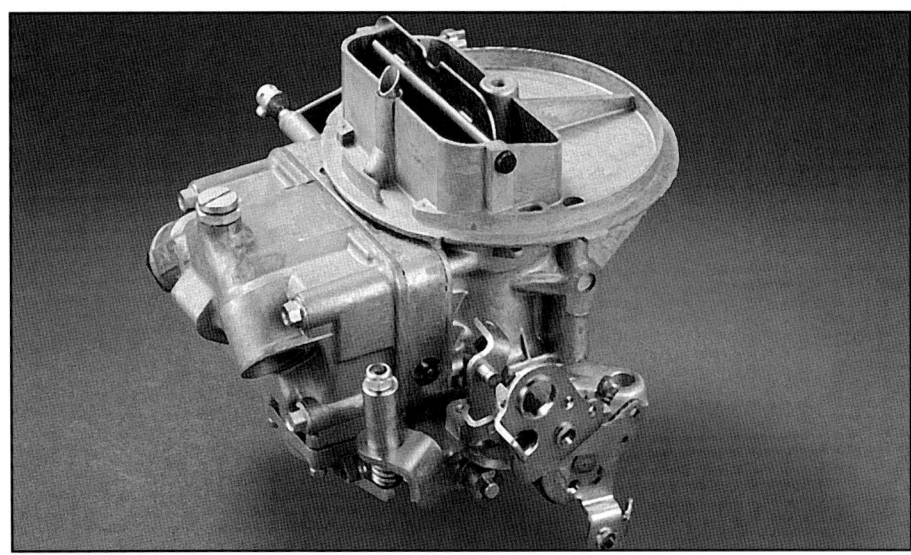

Holley 500 cfm Carburetor by LC Engineering.

2 Barrel Asian Carburetor for Circle Track Classes by LC Engineering.

this track regulation. LCE starts with select cores, then improves them by increasing the air and fuel flow delivered from the carburetor. Uses Holley jets. Features include: flowed and indexed booster venturi; choke & linkage removed; brass float and hi-flow needle and seats machined to accept Holley jets; vacuum ports plugged; positive mechanical secondary linkage.

Circle Track Manifold

LC Engineering makes these manifold to work with either the 350 or 500 cfm Holley carburetor. If your class requires you to run a "factory Toyota manifold," look no further. This trick manifold starts as a factory I intake and is then transformed by master machinists into a race manifold that will deliver peak horsepower at high RPM. Hi-flow open plenum design has proven to help top end power in both mini stock and modified engines. Available for both 20R and 22R cylinder heads.

Part #	Application
16-NC20	20R Manifold
16-NC22R	22R Manifold

Pro Fuel Pump

A Pro Fuel Pump is the only choice when using either a single- or dual-carburetor. Offering the quietest operation of any electric pump available, this custom calibrated fuel pump is set to provide an optimum 4 psi and does not require a pressure regulator. Supplied with fuel fittings, hose clamps, and installation instructions.

Part # 16-4070LP Pro Fuel Pump

REDLINE WEBER

DCOE Series Carburetors

Still the standard by which all other carburetors are measured, the DCOE is the ultimate side draft carburetor. It is unsurpassed for full-race use, yet interchangeable calibrated parts allow it to be tailored to suit even the mildest engine and application situation. Redline/DCOE kits include all necessary hardware, but are not supplied with air filters. Optional Redline air filters are listed in the Service Parts Section.

FUEL LINES, RAILS, AND FITTINGS

AEROQUIP

The new aluminum one-piece fitting, designed to be the next generation of high performance fittings, eliminates two potential leak points that can occur with fittings assembled using the standard braze process. The new fittings have an improved appearance and brighter overall finish. They are currently available in the most popular sizes and configurations and will soon be implemented in more than 80 percent of the performance fitting offerings from Aeroquip. In addition, Aeroquip offers a line of nickel-plated adapters and fittings. These give the look of polished stainless but with the weight-saving benefit of aluminum.

HOLLEY

Holley Performance Products has high-flow fuel injector rails (part # 534-87) for 1992-1997 Honda Civics. They provide 50 percent more fuel flow than OE fuel rails, reducing fuel pressure drop to the injectors. Holley's new high-flow fuel rails accept Holley, Bosch, and Siemens high-flow fuel injectors. They bolt on in the stock location and are designed for remote-mounted high output fuel regulators. The fuel rail inlet fitting is a low restriction AN-8. To prevent corrosion and provide a custom appearance, all Holley Honda high-flow injector fuel rails are anodized and available in five colors. Now Honda owners can match their paint and graphics themes with engine components.

Part #	Description
534-87	clear anodized satin aluminum finish
534-87-1	red finish
534-87-2	blue finish
534-87-3	green finish
534-87-4	purple finish

Holley Performance Products has high-flow fuel injector rails (part # 534-94) for 1992-1996 Acura Integras. They provide 50 percent more fuel flow than OE fuel rails, reducing fuel pressure drop to the injectors. Holley's new high-flow fuel rails accept Holley, Bosch, and Siemens high-flow fuel injectors. They bolt on in the stock location and are designed for remote-mounted high output fuel regulators. The fuel rail inlet fitting is a low restriction AN-8. To prevent corrosion and provide a custom appearance, all Holley Acura high-flow injector fuel rails are anodized and available in five colors. Now Acura owners can match their paint and graphics themes with engine components.

Part #	Description
534-94	clear anodized satin aluminum finish
534-94-1	red finish
534-94-2	blue finish
534-87-3	green finish
534-94-4	purple finish

Holley Performance Products has high-flow Keihin injector fuel rails (part # 534-86) for 1992-1997 Honda Civics. They provide 50 percent more fuel flow than OE fuel rails, reducing fuel pressure drop to the injectors. Holley's high-flow Keihin fuel rails accept OE or modified Keihin fuel injectors. They bolt on in the stock location and can be used with the OE fuel regulator or a close-coupled high output fuel regulator. The fuel rail inlet fitting is a low restriction AN-8. To prevent corrosion and provide a custom appearance, all Holley high-flow injector fuel rails are anodized and available in five colors. Now Honda owners can match their paint and graphics themes with engine components.

Part #	Description
534-86	clear anodized satin aluminum finish
534-86-1	red finish
534-86-2	blue finish
534-86-3	green finish
534-86-4	purple finish

Holley Performance Products has high-flow Keihin injector fuel rails (part # 534-93) for 1992-1996 Acura Integras. They provide 50 percent more fuel flow than OE fuel rails, reducing fuel pressure drop to the injectors. Holley's high-flow Keihin fuel rails accept OE or modified Keihin fuel injectors. They bolt on in the stock location and are designed for a remote-mounted high output fuel regulator. The fuel rail inlet fitting is a low-restriction AN-8. To prevent corrosion and provide a custom appearance, all Holley high-flow injector fuel rails are anodized and available in five colors. Now Acura owners can match their paint and graphics themes with engine components.

Part #	Description
534-93	clear anodized satin aluminum finish
534-93-1	red finish
534-93-2	blue finish
534-93-3	green finish
534-93-4	purple finish

STR

STR fast flow fuel rails are an easy way to upgrade a fuel system.

STR fuel rails provide better flow and larger volume of fuel to the injectors. All STR fuel rails are CNC machined from billet aluminum. STR fuel rails are well complimented with the STR AIRMAXX manifold for performance and looks.

Part #	Application
FR0101	1990-1998 Acura Integra GSR/Type R, B18 motor
FR0101	1993-1997 Honda del Sol VTEC, B16 motor
FR0102	1990-1998 Honda Prelude SI VTEC, 2.2 motor

SPLIT SECOND

Unique applications often require custom fuel rails. Unmachined aluminum extruded fuel rail stock is available in 6 ft. lengths. The fuel supply tube runs the length of the rail and has an inside diameter suitable for threading to AN-8 fitting.

XTREME RACING PRODUCTS

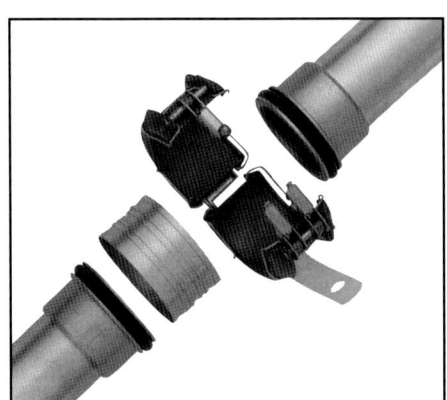

Pro racers who demand the latest technology in high flow and lightweight fluid flow control systems, will respect Xtreme Racing Product's (XRP) HS-79 Ultra-Lite flexible smooth-bore Teflon brand hose and aluminum quick disconnect clamshell couplings. Lightweight and flexible, HS-79 hose features a construction of teflon and silicone, with stainless steel reinforcement and a full Nomex brand outer braid. HS-79 is very flexible and routes easily and maintains full flow characteristics. It can be assembled with either 37° JIC fittings or aerospace-style aluminum quick disconnect clamshell couplings. Available in straight, 30°, 45°, 60°, 90°, 120°, 150°, and 180° fittings, and comes in -4, -6, -8, -10, -12, -14, -16, -18, -20 sizes.

TMW INDUCTION FUEL RAILS

FUEL RAIL KITS FOR 2000 SERIES THROTTLE BODIES

2000-6701	Dash 10 rail kit for 2000-0111 and 0122
2000-6702	Dash 10 rail kit for 2000-0123

FUEL RAILS FOR 2805 SERIES (FORMERLY 3005 SERIES)

3005-5710	Fuel rail with one injector, threaded both ends -6 AN
3005-572	Fuel rail with two injectors, threaded both ends -6 AN
3005-5711	Fuel rail with one injector, threaded -6 AN one end with O-ring counterbore other end
3005-5721	Fuel rail with two injectors, threaded -6 AN one end with O-ring counterbore other end
3005-5713	Fuel rail with one injector, with O-ring counterbore both ends
3005-5723	Fuel rail with two injectors, with O-ring counterbore both ends
3005-5630	Connecting tube, with O-rings, for center-to-center spacing 110-128mm (4.33-5.00")

FUEL RAIL COMPONENTS

3060-5607	Single rail mount for 3000 series (included with rail kit)
3060-5608	Dual rail mount (included with rail kit for four injectors)
2960-5605	Standard rail mount for throttle bodies prior to Sept. 1998
2960-5620	O-ring tube for 83-105mm centers, L. 50mm
2960-5630	O-ring tube for 100-124mm centers, L. 75mm.
2960-0112	O-ring
2960-5706	O-ring tube retainer
2960-6112	Screw M6 x 12
2960-5710	Screw M5 x 10

DCOE / IDF (2900, 2910, 2930 series) Fuel Rails

2960-5700	Fuel rail threaded both ends
2960-5701	Threaded one end, counterbore other end
2960-5703	Counter bore both ends

IDA (3000 series) Fuel Rails

3000-5700	Fuel rail threaded both ends
3000-5701	Threaded one end, counterbore other end

BLANK FUEL RAILS

TWM fuel rail is now available in two sizes, -6 and -10. The cross section shape enables the use of the injector retaining clips, used in TMW throttle body fuel rail kits. The design features additional material below the fuel gallery to facilitate the drilling of mounting holes.

2900-5602	Blank fuel rail, -6, 24-inch length (61cm)
2900-5603	Blank fuel rail, -6, 36-inch length (91.5 cm)
2900-5606	Blank fuel rail, -6, 72-inch length (183 cm)
3006-6602	Blank fuel rail, -10, 24-inch length
3006-6603	Blank fuel rail, -10, 36-inch length
3006-6606	Blank fuel rail, -10, 72-inch length

FUEL CELLS

MOMO CORSE

Fuel safety tanks with Safom open cell sponge. F.i.A. FT3 and FT5 homologations.

External anti-ageing treatment, reduced risk of explosion, minimal fuel surge, extreme lightness, fuel pickup under any condition. A full range of mounting accessories are also available. MOMO Corse fuel safety tanks can be ordered in standard sizes or can be made to measure. Contact MOMO Corse technical department for more details.

FUEL SAFE SYSTEMS

Fuel Safe Systems has an extensive line of fuel cells for almost any application. Approved by most racing sanctioning organizations.

Sport Compact Bolt-On Performance Guide Volume 1 — Ignition

PROGRAMMABLE IGNITION CONTROL

APEX I-USA

The Super ITC (Ignition Timing Control) allows the user to modify the crank angle signal and adjust the ignition timing of the vehicle. Ignition Timing can be modified more than 15%. By using the Super ITC in conjunction with the Super AFC fuel controller, a new level of performance and flexibility can be attained which was never before possible with entry-level sub computers.

The ITC allows the user to modify ignition timing according to RPM specific levels, much like the Super AFC modifies fuel. The five knobs on the face of the unit indicate a particular RPM level at which timing may be modified. Each timer harness has been designed for easy installation of the Apex Integration TIMER. All harnesses are made to clip in to the factory harness eliminating any excess wire cutting and connections.

Part # 401-A005   Super ITC

ELECTROMOTIVE

HPV Direct Ignition Systems

Electromotive's HPV ignitions outperform all other production and aftermarket systems. The HPV ignition fires the spark plugs directly from the coils. Multiple ignition coils and advanced, automatically adjusting dwell circuits assure fully-charged coils every time. The powerful spark of this patented system delivers 120 millijoules of energy to the plugs from idle to 10,000 rpm. Individual coils allow fast and accurate spark initiation, long burn times, and the highest spark energy available. Benefits of increased spark energy and timing accuracy include improved driveability, increased performance, and decreased fuel consumption and emissions. Electronics, power module, ignition coils, advance coils, and soft rev limiter are all contained in one engine compartment mountable unit. The lack of moving parts assures long-term reliability while virtually eliminating maintenance. Patent number RE. 43,183.

Part # HPV-3B   The Ultimate Stand-Alone Ignition

PC-computer based, menu-driven tuning sets the HPV-3B apart from every other ignition. Interactive calibration allows the user to tailor the spark advance throughout the engine's operating range. The HPV-3B lets you dial-in eight RPM break points, eight manifold pressure points, and 64 spark advance values. You set the perfect spark curve for your engine. Turbo and supercharged engines enjoy built-in boost retard and knock control. HPV-3B calibration software includes real time engine monitoring and timing adjustment, data logging, and graphics.

HALTECH

The Haltech IG5 is a powerful "real-time" programmable ignition system computer designed to control most ignition-type engines. Whether 1-6, 8, 10, or 12 cylinders, 1-2 rotors, naturally aspirated, turbocharged or supercharged, distributor or direct fired, the Haltech IG5 can control it. The IG5 is also compatible with most aftermarket ignition amplifier systems such as MSD, Jacobs, Crane, and M&W Ignitions edge-triggered CDI units.

The IG5 is much more than a programmable ignition management computer — it provides logging of engine data and allows access in real time to maximize performance and troubleshoot problems in a vehicle while running. It can also be used to control many programmable auxiliary functions such as NOS enable, etc. Typical applications include conversion from breaker points to electronic ignition, control of ignition timing on performance engines, race and rally applications of all description, and design and development purposes.

The patented Haltech system of programming virtually eliminates the input of numbers. You simply manipulate graphics in the form of bar graphs, and by pressing arrows you increase or decrease the amount of timing delivered at that particular load point. The process is repeated for all load points in each RPM range allowing the ignition timing to be "mapped" to obtain optimum performance across the range. The IG5 incorporates five output drivers of which four can be used as ignition channels, the fifth is a dedicated tach output. If these four outputs are not used for ignition they become available as programmable outputs. Spare outputs can be used for turbo wastegate control, dual intake valve control, torque converter lock-up, electric thermatic fan control, intercooler fan control, shift light, or anti-stall solenoid control.

The IG5 kit includes: Electronic Control Unit (ECU), flying lead wiring loom, 1x power relay, communication cable, programming software, and instruction manual.

SYSTEM FEATURES:

Number of Cylinders:
1-6, 8, 10, 12 and 1-2 Rotors.

Max Operating RPM:
16000 rpm.

RPM Range increments:
500/1000 rpm.

Max. Range: 10500/16000 rpm.

Number of Ignition Maps: 22/17.

Number of Bars per Map: 32.

Ignition Correction Maps:
Air temperature, coolant temperature, ignition crank.

Trigger Signal Type:
Inductive magnetic (with external adaptor) hall effect sensor; optical sensor.

Trigger Pattern:
Twin trigger, single pulse per cycle, Bosch Motronic (60t-2), multi-tooth.

Ignition Configuration:
Twin Distributor, twin rotor (Dist. or DF), single distributor, direct fire (1-4, 6, 8 cylinder), programmable charge time, or constant duty cycle output.

ECU Inputs:
MAP sensor, coolant temperature, air temperature, throttle position, primary trigger, secondary trigger, spec purpose digital, gen. purpose analog.

ECU Outputs:
Ignition output, tach output, up to 3 extra outputs.

Optional Extras:
Fully terminated wiring loom in lieu of flying lead loom, ignition/boost trim module,
air temperature sensor, coolant temperature sensor, igniter modules, manifold pressure sensor (1-, 2-, or 3-Bar).

Engine Data:
US or Metric Units for map storage and retrieval data logging.

MSD

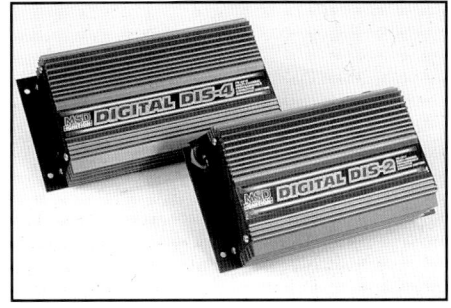

Ignition timing is always a compromise between cylinders. The dynamics of the flow of air and fuel into each cylinder is never exactly the same no matter how much machining magic has been done. This has always caused top engine builders to compromise their ignition timing. With the Programmable Digital-7's advanced Individual Cylinder Management (ICM) system and other exact timing programs, you will never need to compromise again.

Part # 7530 Digital 7 Ignition Control

ICM Timing Control

Adjust the ignition timing in each cylinder! Program up to 5° of timing retard into each individual cylinder in 0.1° increments. Plot a timing curve in 0.1° per 100 rpm throughout the entire RPM range of your engine! Program a timing curve exclusively for the launch! If the starting line conditions are less than adequate, you can set a completely different curve for the launch. Retard the timing up to 15° for 0 - 2.5 seconds after you launch the car. There are three steps of retard that can be activated with nitrous solenoids or switches. Program a timing retard up to 5° with every gear change! Ease engine cranking with an adjustable retard during start up.

No other ignition system comes close to matching the output power and the Individual Cylinder Management timing system of the Programmable Ignition. To effectively handle all of the ignition's tasks, a 15 Megahertz microcontroller reviews, manages, and analyzes every trigger signal up to 15,000,000 instructions each second! Capacitive discharge circuits combined with an IGBT coil driver deliver incredible energy to the coil creating a spark that will ignite even the highest cylinder pressures. Below 3,300 there is of course MSD's powerful series of multiple sparks. This spark series burns in the cylinder for over 20° of crankshaft rotation resulting in improved combustion for a smooth idle, great throttle response, and increased power.

Monitoring the engine's RPM allows you to set shift light points, activation points, and rev limits. The Programmable Digital-7 has MSD's proven Soft Touch rev-limiting controls built in and lets you program several RPM features. Program three rev limits in 100 increments for burnout, launch, and overrev protection. Program a different RPM setting for each gear change for up to six gears! Activate a circuit at an adjustable RPM such as a nitrous solenoid, then set another RPM level to deactivate the same circuit.

Don't let all of these accessories and adjustments worry you. MSD engineers developed two very useful and easy ways for you to program the ignition. You can use the hand-held programmer (Part # 7550) or MSD's Pro-Data+ software package on your PC.

The Programmable Digital-7 Ignition Control can be triggered with a points/ECU trigger, magnetic pickup in a distributor, or a non-magnetic pickup of a crank trigger. There is even a mag pickup compensation adjustment for absolute trigger accuracy! The single unit is fully potted for vibration protection and is easy to mount. It can be used on 4-, 6-, or 8-cylinder engines and is supplied with the Pro-Data+ software, PC harness, vibration mounts, wiring, and thorough instructions. The MSD HVC Pro Power Coil (Part # 8251) is the recommended coil.

Pro Data+ Software

This software program is designed exclusively for the MSD Programmable Digital-7 Ignition System. This easy-to-use program lets you plot your ignition curves, RPM limits, shift points, retards, and more! This only scratches the surface of what the Pro-Data+ software offers. The Pro-Data+ software can be used with any PC running Windows 95, 98, or NT. It is available on a 3.5 floppy or can be downloaded from the MSD web site.

Programmer/Monitor

If you do not have a laptop or PC, all of the Programmable 7 Ignition Control's optional programs can be set with this hand-held programmer/monitor. This programmer communicates to the programmable ignition via the 9-pin cable. The LCD will display the programming options which you can select to adjust or view the program that is already in the ignition. Adjustments are easily made with six positive-contact push buttons. The unit is easy to handle, even with race gloves on, and weighs in at under half a pound.

Part # 7550   Hand-held Programmer/Monitor

Manual RPM Launch Control

This handy controller lets you change the launch RPM setting of the Programmable 7 Ignition Control manually when you're strapped in the car. The controller plugs into the MSD Programmable Ignition Control through the 9-pin harness. There are two control knobs, one for 1,000 rpm and the other for 100 rpm. The launch setting can also be adjusted from 3,000 to 12,500 rpm in 100 rpm increments.

Part # 7551   Manual RPM Launch Control

Synchronization Pickup Kit

In order to take advantage of the Programmable Digital-7's Individual Cylinder Management system, a synchronization pickup must be incorporated so the ignition knows exactly which cylinder is firing. With this information the MSD can begin your unique timing sequence through each cylinder! MSD offers two ways to accomplish this: With the Cam Sync Pickup or the Spark Plug Wire Sync Kit.

Cam Sync Pickup

The Pickup Kit is supplied with a non-magnetic pickup, connectors, the magnet, and retainer. You will need to fabricate a bracket assembly and install the magnet.

Part # 2346   Universal Cam Sync Pickup Kit

Spark Plug Wire Sync Kit

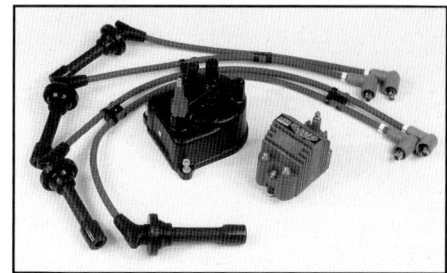

This pickup simply installs to the number one spark plug wire, then it senses the trigger signal and sends this information to the ignition through a fiber optic cable.

Part # 7555   Spark Plug Wire Sync Kit

OUTPUT SPECIFICATIONS

Spark Energy:
190 millijoules per spark
Primary Voltage: 535 volts
Output Voltage: 40,000 volts
Operating Voltage:
12-18 volts, neg. ground
Current Draw:
1.1 amp per 1,000 rpm
RPM Range:
12,500 rpm with 14.4 volt supply
Weight & Size:
4.7 lbs., 9.5" L x 4.5" W x 2.2" H

Tested with the Pro Power HVC Coil, Part # 8251

Digital 7 Plus Ignition Control

For drag racers, the MSD 7AL-2 has long been the standard ignition due to its reliability and power. By combining the 7AL-2's high performance with the proven digital technology from the Digital-6 Plus Ignition, MSD is once again raising the performance ignition standards by introducing the Digital-7 Plus Ignition Control.

State-of-the-art technology allows the 7 Plus to produce more power while using the same amount of current. The CD circuits combined with an IGBT coil driver deliver 520 - 535 volts to the primary side of the coil with up to 190 millijoules of energy at any RPM. Below 3,300 there is of course MSD's powerful series of multiple sparks, rather than a single spark. This spark series burns in the cylinder for over 20° of crankshaft rotation resulting in improved combustion and increased power.

Inside the familiar gold housing is a 15 Megahertz microcontroller, the fastest of any digital ignitions. This means that the controller analyzes up to 15,000,000 critical instructions per second to produce the most accurate timing control and rev limits possible! There are two smooth rev limits, one for top end overrev protection and another for a launch RPM. For nitrous applications or for racers looking for a little more MPH, there is a high-speed retard circuit that is adjustable by rotary dials up to 9.9°, plus there is a diagnostic LED. The Digital-7 Plus can be used on 4-, 6-, or 8-cylinder engines and should be used with an MSD HVC coil (Part # 8251 or 8252).

Part # 7520   Digital 7 Plus Ignition Control

DIS-HO Ignition Controls

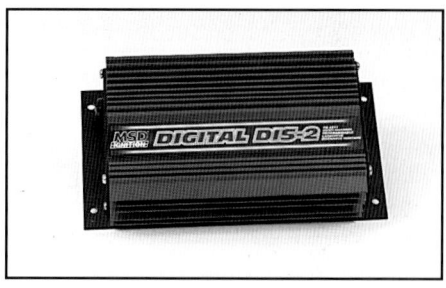

The popularity of small displacement, high RPM, turbocharged racing engines has created a need for an even higher output ignition for DIS systems. Wherever there's a demand for powerful sparks, MSD is there and the answer is the MSD DIS-HO Ignition Controls. Like the popular MSD DIS Ignitions, the DIS-HO models are designed for vehicles with distributorless ignition systems with two-, three-, or four-coil packs. The HO models produce 170 millijoules of energy and deliver 470 volts going to the coil packs, plus the CD circuits deliver a series of multiple sparks below 3,000 rpm! This combination is more than capable of completely burning the fuel mixture of engines with through-the-roof cylinder pressures.

Along with all of its spark power, the MSD DIS-HO Ignitions have some great built-in programmable features. There is an ultra smooth two-step rev control which gives you the ability to set two RPM limits so one can be set during a holeshot while the other comes in for top end protection. There is also a timing retard feature that allows you to pull timing out of your engine at a specific rate and RPM point to prevent engine damage from detonation.

Part # Description

62111 DIS-2 HO, 2-coil packs
62151 DIS-4 HO, 2-, 3-, or 4-coil packs

Operating Voltage:
12-18 volts, neg. ground

Current Draw:
DIS-2 3.5A @ 10,000 rpm
DIS-4 6.6A @ 10,000 rpm

RPM Range:
14,500 rpm with 14.4 volt supply

Spark Duration:
20° crankshaft rotation

Spark Energy:
105 - 115 millijoules per spark

Weight and Size:

DIS-2: 4 lbs., 8.5" L x 4.5" W x 2.2" H

DIS-4: 4.5 lbs., 9.5" L x 4.5" W x 2.2" H

Voltage Output Max:

Primary:
460 - 480 volts delivered to coil

Secondary:
40,000+ volts (MSD HVC Coil)

This product is legal to sell, distribute, or install in California according to Executive Order E.O. D-40-31; legal in all 50 states. CARB Approved, D-40-31.

RPM-ACTIVATED SWITCHES

The MSD RPM-Activated Switches allow you to activate an electrical device at an adjustable RPM. Turn on a shift light or nitrous solenoid at exactly the RPM you want!

Part # Description

8950 RPM-Activated Switch, provides or removes a ground to activate a circuit.

8956 RPM-Activated Window Switch, allows you to activate a circuit by supplying a ground path, then deactivate the same circuit at a different RPM!

LC ENGINEERING

Pro Distributor

The LC Pro Distributor is an absolute must for all performance applications. Especially circle track and off-road racing. Hours of dyno testing have proven the Pro Distributor will provide an increase in horsepower due to its proper ignition timing advance curve. Gains of 10 – 12 horsepower have been experienced as well as smoother acceleration through ignition timing improvements.

This distributor may be used with a factory igniter and coil, the LC Crane Ignition Kits, or most other high-output ignition systems. Two versions are available: the standard Pro Distributor and the LC Pro Distributor with vacuum advance for street applications.

Part # Description

17-100 LC Pro Distributor
17-100V LC Pro Distributor w/ vacuum advance

SPLIT SECOND

The TMC1 (Timing Map Controller) is compatible with modern engines with individual ignition coils and will not interfere with the protection and self-diagnostic features of the ignition system. The TMC1 provides the ability to precisely control ignition timing retard vs. both intake manifold pressure and RPM. It is especially useful for engines that have been converted to forced induction through the addition of either a turbocharger or supercharger. The TMC1 makes it possible to boost the manifold pressure without inducing harmful detonation (engine knock).

IGNITION AMPS

ACCEL

The 300+ ignition system was designed to be the most compact, lightest, most powerful, and most reliable ignition system available. Fully epoxy encapsulated for water and vibration resistance, the 300+ was designed to perform in extremely demanding environments. The 300+ has the lowest operating current draw, and supplies the highest energy into the coil when compared to other ignition systems in its class. The 300+ also features an integral rev limiter which can easily be changed with rotary dial — no need to use removable chips! Reliability is unsurpassed with the microprocessor-controlled, fully epoxy-encapsulated design. See High Performance Cap & Coil section of this chapter for details on external coil conversion kit.

B&M

The New Volt Coil Power Unit works with multi-coil applications as well as single-coil applications with one unit. Achieve significant results — even with a stock coil — as long as there is increased demand at the plug. For racing & street applications. Fits most import, domestic vehicles & race cars including GM (incl. HEI), most Fords (incl. multi-coil), Chrysler, Honda, Acura, Mitsubishi, Toyota, Nissan, Porsche, etc. OBDII friendly — OBDII equipped vehicles may not be compatible with many aftermarket ignitions.

Microprocessor controlled state-of-the-art internal power regulation. Output remains at 20 volts & up to 20 amps (or 400 watts) even when input voltage drops below 12 volts. Ideal for racing applications where no alternator is used. Handles 15 amps continuous, 20 amps peak.

Most stock high-energy systems deliver .05 amp at the plug. Some aftermarket ignitions provide 0.5 (ten times OEM). The B&M New Volt can deliver over 2 full amps at the plug! Lightweight unit aluminum housing that uses only 2.25" x 5" of space. Only three wires to connect. Fully epoxy encapsulated for protection against moisture & vibration. Components isolated to prevent affecting other vehicle electronics.

CARB E.O. number applied for OBDII vehicles.

Part # 46049 New Volt Coil Power Unit

While B&M may be new to the ignition products market, they are known for innovation. Here are a few basics you should know about ignitions in order to appreciate the B&M New Volt.

Any aftermarket ignition system regardless of output, will not provide a horsepower or torque gain over a stock ignition unless other modifications are done to the engine that require a more powerful ignition to fire the plugs effectively. The only way to make more horsepower is to induce more air and a proper corresponding amount of fuel for that increase of air into the engine (or a nitrous system). The exception might only be in the case of some carbureted engines where the fuel could be burned more efficiently by a better ignition. Simply put, you can only realize performance gains as a result of other engine modifications.

Results that are realized from an ignition system come from spark energy. Spark energy is wattage not voltage. Most aftermarket ignitions are a capacitive discharge type CD. The New Volt is an inductive design just like 99% of the OEM ignitions in the world. A CD design produces a quick delivery of energy, generally lasts for about 200 microseconds. The B&M New Volt delivers a long-lasting spark at higher energy for 2500 - 3000 microseconds which is more efficient with regard to a full burn in the combustion chamber.

An inductive ignition produces more energy overall over a longer period of time. CD systems compensate for poor coil saturation at high engine RPMs when the time to recharge is diminished. The New Volt more than compensates for the coil deficiency and maximizes the value of the inductive ignition.

Most ignitions are not "smart boxes," meaning they have no ability to feed more energy if the plug needs it or can use it. The B&M New Volt is a "smart box." It reads the system 100,000 times per second determining what the need is at the plug. For example if turbo boost is blowing out the spark, the B&M New Volt increases the energy delivery far more than it would if the vehicle had not needed the extra energy to ignite the mixture.

For maximum spark-gap energy output match with a Crane FireBall HI-6DSR, HI-6DS, HI-6TRC, (Fully Digital Capacitive Discharge CD ignitions), or HI-6S inductive ignition and high-output Crane FireBall LX-91 E-Core Coil.

When matched with the correct Crane FireBall ignition this kit provides the increased ignition efficiency needed for modified, supercharged, turbocharged, and nitrous-oxide applications! Perfect for everyday street performance or all-out competition! Can also be used with stock Honda and Acura ignitions.

Each Kit Contains: High density, phenolic-resin cap and rotor; locking coil wire; terminal connector and solderless terminals. Ignitions and coils sold separately. Applications available for: 1988-97 Honda Accord; Honda Civic; Honda Civic CRX; Honda del Sol; Honda Prelude; Acura.

HOLLEY PERFORMANCE

The HP Annihilator is the perfect ignition system for any vehicle that can use a high performance capacitive discharge, multiple spark ignition system with one rev limiter. It has plenty of power, 135 millijoules at 525 volts, therefore it is ideal for circle-track cars, street vehicles, motorhomes, towing vehicles, and 4x4s.

The HP Annihilator was engineered so it can be used in a variety of applications. By choosing the appropriate LaserShot coil, you have four ignition systems in one. When coupled with the LaserShot 500 coil, it is ready to take on the super speedways and high-banked oval tracks of the stock car racing world. Hook it up to the LaserShot Street coil and you have an excellent ignition system for street cars, RVs, and towing vehicles.

For serious street machines including Pro Street and Street Rods, run the HP Annihilator with the LaserShot Pro coil. Finally, for all out drag racing, connect the LaserShot Pro Strip coil and you have an excellent budget drag racing ignition system.

Because the HP Annihilator uses a microprocessor and our unique sequential rev limiting method, the spark plugs fire exactly when they're supposed to and the rev limiter is extremely smooth and accurate. The extruded aluminum housing is finished in black satin and has a thick stainless-steel base plate that is pre-drilled for easy mounting.

FEATURES

Microprocessor Controlled:
The microprocessor is extremely accurate at controlling the rev limiter because it is not affected by temperature and humidity.

Capacitive Discharge:
The capacitor quickly and efficiently outputs 135 millijoules of energy at 525 volts.

Multiple Sparks:
Each spark plug is automatically fired multiple times from idle to 3,000 rpm for 22-1/2° of crankshaft rotation.

Engine Friendly™ Rev Limiter:
The microprocessor controlled sequential rev limiter is very smooth and easy on your engine. It is adjustable from 1,000 to 9,900 rpm in 100 rpm increments and is designed for engines under 700 hp. Designed to be accurate to ± 10 rpm.

Coil Compatibility:
The HP Annihilator is compatible with any Holley LaserShot coil for outstanding versatility. It is also compatible with any aftermarket capacitive discharge coil.

Engine Compatibility:
Can be used on any 4-, 6-, or 8-cylinder, 4-cycle engine.

Distributor and Crank Trigger Compatibility:
Connects easily to any original equipment or aftermarket distributor including points, HEI, or magnetic pick-up. Can also be used with any brand of magnetic crank trigger.

Tachometer Compatibility:
Connects easily to any electric tachometer that uses a 12-volt square wave signal.

Battery Compatibility:
Compatible with any 12-, 16-, 18-, or 24-volt negative ground system. Will operate on as little as 10 volts. System shuts off at 7 volts.

Wiring Harness:
The wiring harness meets all the new rules for circle-track racing that require a color coded six-wire main harness. EO# D-115-5. Legal in 50 states.

Potted For Durability and Long Life: All systems are potted for long life and rugged durability.

Part #	Description
800-100	HP Annihilator for Honda/Acura 1990-98 1.5L and 1.8L VTEC, 2.2, 2.3
800-112	Ignition box with coil. Includes new distributor cap. Plug in harness. Fits factory ignition harness.

HKS

Twin Power Ignition Amplifier

The Twin Power Ignition Amplifier is engineered to produce a hotter and more efficient spark needed for high performance applications. The Twin Power continuously monitors the coil to allow the ignition system to reach maximum capacity without overcharging. The Twin Power also provides optimum spark duration and voltage output. The Twin Power combines a Capacitor Discharge Ignition (CDI) and a Transistor Ignition into one package. While the CDI is effective at producing high voltage, it can only do so for a short period of time. The Transistor Ignition controls current to the coil via an impedance-matching circuit, to produce a longer spark duration. This powerful combination creates greater horsepower at higher RPM levels and increased throttle response at lower RPM levels.

JACOBS ELECTRONICS

Pro-Street Ultra Team with Accessory Pak

The absolute ultimate ignition for a street-driven sport compact. Completely compatible with OEM computer, guaranteed more horsepower than with any other system at any price. Lots of pluses: throttle switch doubles spark energy only when at full throttle; driver-visible diagnostic LEDs; tells driver the state of engine and electrical system, both now, and looks forward in time to predict future trouble; sophisticated built-in anti-theft which can't be disabled by thief because it's part of the ignition; super-accurate rev limiter; quick-start circuitry; standard acceleration spark changes to maximum acceleration spark as soon as engine RPM increases.

Accessory Pak

Micro Throttle Sensing switch: mounts under gas pedal to generate the maximum engine power spark when under full throttle operation.

1st Micro Toggle switch: allows driver to adjust built-in RPM limiter at any time.

2nd Micro Toggle switch: controls built-in anti-theft system.

Driver Viewed LEDs: keeps you informed of engine's condition and performance at a glance.

Omni Torquer

The most economical ultra-high energy electronic ignition with the same features and benefits as Omni Magnum, except with a coil designed for lower RPM, but with tremendous boosts in torque, especially for 4- (8,800 rpm) or 6-cylinder (6,600 rpm) vehicles, under all driving conditions. CARB E.O. #D-19-30

Since their introduction over 15 years ago, sport compact cars have always had very tight engine compartments. To allow for ignition upgrades, Jacobs Electronics, with its Omni Torquer ignition, has achieved very high-spark energy into an easy-to-install unit with both ignition circuitry and coil in the same compact housing. CARB E.O. #D-19-30

MSD

Sport Compact enthusiasts will be excited to see MSD's newest ignition design! The MSD Sport Compact Ignition (SCI) is the ultimate ignition for the high-revving smaller displacement engines that are found in late-model sport vehicles. At higher RPM, stock-inductive ignitions cannot produce full power sparks resulting in a loss of power or even a top end miss.

The new MSD SCI Series Ignitions feature capacitive discharge circuits that are capable of full power sparks at any RPM! Whether you're idling through traffic or ripping through the gears at 10,000+ rpm, each spark of an SCI Ignition is at full power! High powered sparks mean complete combustion which puts more power to the ground.

Below 3,000 rpm, the SCI Ignitions produce a series of sparks that last for 20° of crankshaft rotation. This series of sparks will smooth the idle, produce quick starts, and deliver lightning-quick throttle response.

There are two models of the MSD SCI Ignition Controls offered: the SCI and the SCI-L. With these proven ignitions, your sport compact car will get the spark power it needs to outperform the competition on both the street and the track.

MSD SCI Ignition Control

The MSD SCI is the base SCI Ignition Control. The SCI will work on most engines equipped with a distributor and is supplied with detailed instructions and wiring.

Part # 6300 MSD SCI Ignition Control

MSD SCI-L Ignition Control

The MSD SCI-L Sport Compact Ignition shares the same powerful ignition design as the SCI, but also features MSD's popular built-in Soft Touch Rev Control feature. The Soft Touch Rev Control will precisely limit the RPM at an adjustable amount for overrev protection and is supplied with a 3,000, 6,000, 7,000 and 8,000 rpm module. This built-in feature also allows you to use an MSD Two-Step Module Selector so you can have a holeshot rev limit!

Part # 6320 MSD SCI-L Ignition Control

SPECIFICATIONS

Spark Energy:
105 - 115 millijoules per spark

Primary Voltage:
460 - 480 volts delivered to coil

Spark Series Duration:
20° crankshaft rotation

Operating Voltage:
12 - 18 volts, neg. ground

Current Draw:
1 amp per 1,000 rpm approx.

RPM Range:
14,000 rpm with 14.4 volt supply

Weight & Size for SCI:
2.75lbs., 8" L x 3.5" W x 2.25" H

Weight & Size for SCI-L:
3lbs., 8" L x 4" W x 2.25" H

Two- or Three-Step Module Selector

This compact unit plugs directly into the MSD SCI-L to give you two or three different RPM limits. This is a great feature to activate during the burnout or on the starting line to give you consistent, firm launches.

Part #	Description
8739	Two-Step Module Selector
8737	Three-Step Module Selector

HIGH PERFORMANCE CAP & COIL KITS

When you install an aftermarket ignition system, you'll almost always have to install an external coil. Most manufacturers have kits that make this conversion quick, easy, and inexpensive.

ACCEL

External coil conversion kit complete with new distributor cap, matched ACCEL Super Coil (#140019) and universal coil lead (#49310).

Applications include:
1992-1998 Acura Integra 1.8L DOHC 16V
1996-1998 Acura 2.2CL/2.3CL
1990-1998 Honda Accord 2.2L/2.3L SOHC 16V including VTEC
1992-1998 Honda Civic / del Sol 1.5L/ 1.6L SOHC 16V including VTEC
1992-1997 Honda del Sol 1.6L DOHC 16V VTEC
1992-1996 Honda Prelude 2.2L SOHC 16V / 2.3L DOHC 16V VTEC

Does not fit:
1992-1998 Acura Integra GS-R or Type R 1.7L/1.8L DOHC 16V VTEC

Everything you need to replace the stock Honda or Acura internal coil with a Crane FireBall LX-91, Low-Profile, Lightweight, E-Core Race & Street Coil, and a Crane FireBall "HI Series" multi-spark, digital CD ignition for increased HP, torque, RPM, and response! (HI-Series ignition and LX Series coil sold separately.)

Each kit includes: High performance, low-resistance, high-density phenolic resin distributor cap with correct matching rotor. Complete wiring harness and hardware for easy installation.

Heavy Duty CD Only E-Core Super Coil

Professional, continuous use racing coil specifically designed to work with CD ignition systems only. High energy, heavy gauge windings designed especially for optimum performance with an Accel, Mallory, Crane, Holley, or MSD capacitive discharge ignition system. E-core design minimizes inductance losses and maximizes energy output. Special high-temperature epoxy resists shock and vibration and provides excellent thermal conductivity. The extruded aluminum heatsink provides maximum cooling to ensure long life. SAE male tower offers greater coil wire retention and protection from arcing. Comes complete with insulated primary wire connector and universal Accel 8.8mm 300+ Race Wire coil lead and mounting hardware kit. This coil is effective to over 10,000 rpm.

SPECIFICATIONS

Tested with Accel 300+ Ignition

Primary Resistance: 0.2 Ohms

Turns Ratio: 95 : 1

Secondary Resistance: 3.6 k Ohms

Maximum Voltage: 48,000 volts

Peak Current: 300 mA

Spark Duration: 360 µS

Part # 140019 Heavy Duty CD only E-core Super

Superstock High Vibration Coil

Excellent choice for high performance, heavy duty, and off-road use. Canister-style can coil is completely encapsulated in high-temperature epoxy to protect the windings and internal connections from the harsh vibration and impacts that could destroy a typical oil-filled canister-style can coil. Engineered with special low resistance, high turns ratio windings to produce higher energy output with breakerless electronic ignition systems and replacement distributors. For points applications a 0.85 Ohms ballast resistor (not included) must be used in conjunction with the vehicle's original ballast resistor, if so equipped. Heavy duty black Alkyd over-molded tower provides "flashover" protection to primary terminals. Can be mounted in any orientation.

SPECIFICATIONS

Primary Resistance: 0.6 Ohms

Turns Ratio: 123 : 1

Secondary Resistance: 9.5 k Ohms

Maximum Voltage: 45,000 volts

SuperStock High Vibration coil: 8140HV

MOROSO

PlasmaPulse Ignition Coils

Moroso has taken 30-plus years of ignition experience and engineered an extremely powerful racing coil for both Capacitive Discharge (CD) and Inductive Discharge (breaker points, HEI, etc.) ignitions. Moroso PlasmaPulse Coils feature a unique winding and core design that generates ultra-high spark current for maximum horsepower and combustion efficiency! In addition to delivering exceptional ignition power, PlasmaPulse Coils are loaded with durability features that include double-layer insulation, corrosion-resistant connectors, and a durable alkyd case. The blue anodized extruded aluminum case not only gives the coil a distinctive appearance, but cooling fins dissipate damaging heat quickly. In fact, the entire coil can withstand continuous operation without overheating. A high-temperature epoxy filling allows you to mount the coil in any direction.

For Racing Only! Ultra-High Spark Current! Maximum Horsepower & Combustion Efficiency!

Part #	Description
72380	PlasmaPulse Ignition Coil, Inductive Discharge.
72381	PlasmaPulse Ignition Coil, Capacitive Discharge.

ACCEL

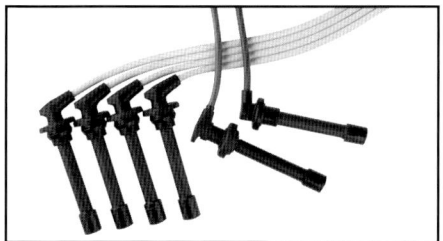

300plus ThunderSport Universal Coil Leads are designed to be used when converting Honda/Acura to an external coil ignition system. Each kit features a 42" ACCEL 300plus ThunderSport lead in your choice of three wire jacket colors: Blue, Red, and Yellow. The kit also includes distributor/coil boots and terminals for both male tower and female socket style coil applications.

Part #	Description
7990B	300plus ThunderSport Blue Universal Coil Lead kit
7990R	300plus ThunderSport Red Universal Coil Lead kit
7990Y	300plus ThunderSport Yellow Universal Coil Lead kit

MSD

Modified Distributor Caps for HONDA/ACURA Vehicles

Professional race engine builders have known for a long time that the only way to produce maximum horsepower from a Honda or Acura engine is to get rid of the weak coil mounted inside the cap. MSD's new Honda and Acura Modified Distributor Caps are specially constructed to allow the use of an external coil such as an MSD Blaster Series Coil. Each cap is specially fitted with an MSD Power Tower to accept a high-voltage coil wire.

Part #	Application
8291	1993-1997 Accord 2.2L w/Hitachi Dist. 1995-1997 Honda Civic 1.5L/1.6L w/VTEC & Hitachi Dist.
8290	1988-1991 Acura Integra 1.6L/1.8L 1988-1991 Honda Civic CRX 1.5L/1.6L8292
8292	1992-1997 Acura Integra 1.8L 1993-1997 Honda Civic 1.5L/1.6L 92-97/ Civic del Sol 1.6L
8293	1994-1997 Acura Integra 1.7L w/VTEC

IGNITION CABLES

Don't let your spark plug wires be the weak link in your high-performance ignition system. To get peak performance from your engine, you need spark plug wires that can handle the brutal power modern CD and inductive ignition systems produce. Fortunately there is an abundance of manufacturers with products capable of meeting your vehicle's needs.

AROSPEED

Arospeed spark plug wires feature an oversized 9.2mm wire for maximum amperage to the spark plugs. These wires also feature a high-temp resistant silicone outer sheath for added protection against the elements. All wires are constructed with double silicone and an extended EMI/KFI suppression coating to eliminate interference. Colors: Red, Blue, Yellow. (See table next page.)

LIGHTSPEED

Ignition Cables. All of the following applications are 9.5 mm in size and are yellow in color.

Part #	Application
HO3264	1990-1993 Acura Integra
HO3267	1994-1997 Acura Integra GSR
HO3263	1994-1997 Acura Integra RS, LS
HO3267	1990-1995 Honda Accord
HO3266	1992-1995 Honda Civic, non-VTEC
HO3264	1992-1997 Honda Civic VTEC
HO3265	1988-1991 Honda CRX/Civic

JACOBS

Jacobs supports sport compacts specifically, as well as imports in general, with a full line of its ultra-high conductivity metal core noise suppression Energy Core Spark Plug Cables, factory-cut and terminated to exact specifications to plug right in.

BLUE MAX™ SPIRAL CORE IMPORT/SPORT COMPACT WIRE SETS

Blue Max™ delivers ultra-high spark energy for maximum horsepower without interfering with audio systems and other electronics such as ignition boxes, navigation systems, instruments, etc. Wires are cut at the correct length and terminated at each end with locking steel terminals protected by high temperature boots bonded to the wire to seal out moisture, fuel, and oil.

Part #	Application
72708	1995-1998 Mitsubishi Eclipse/Eagle Talon, turbo, Blue
72709	1995-1998 Mitsubishi Eclipse/Eagle Talon, turbo, Red
72710	1995-1998 Mitsubishi Eclipse/Eagle Talon, turbo, Yellow

NEUSPEED

Double-layered, nylon-reinforced virgin silicone spark plug wires are custom cut to exact length for a perfect fit and show-car appearance. Lower electrical resistance, heat-resistant to over 600F, and factory-style end terminals.

LC ENGINEERING

LC's Pro Plug Wire set features the finest red 8.5mm wires available. These wire sets are custom-tailored to

AROSPEED SPARK PLUG WIRES

Part # Red	Blue	Yellow	Application
ACURA			
ARO400202	ARO400205	ARO400207	1996-1997 CL 2.2 16V VTEC 2.2L
ARO400202	ARO400205	ARO400207	1996-1997 CL 2.3 16V VTEC 2.3L
ARO400302	ARO400305	ARO400307	1990-1993 Integra 16V 130hp 1.8L
ARO400402	ARO400405	ARO400407	1992-1993 Integra GSR 16V VTEC 160hp 1.7L
ARO400402	ARO400405	ARO400407	1994-1998 Integra GSR 16V VTEC 170hp 1.8L
ARO400302	ARO400305	ARO400307	1997-1998 Integra LS, RS, 16V 142hp 1.8L
ARO400402	ARO400405	ARO400307	1994-1998 Integra Type R 16V VTEC 190hp 1.8L
BMW			
ARO401502	ARO401505	ARO401507	1993-1997 318i 1.8L
FORD			
ARO401202	ARO401205	ARO401207	1991-1994 Escort 1.9L
EAGLE			
ARO400502	ARO400505	ARO400507	1990-1997 Talon, turbo 2.0L
ARO400502	ARO400505	ARO400507	1990-1994 Talon, non-turbo 2.0L
ARO400502	ARO400505	ARO400507	1995-1998 Talon, non-turbo 2.0L
HONDA			
ARO400302	ARO400305	ARO400307	1990-1993 Accord DX, LX 16V 125hp 2.2L
ARO400202	ARO400205	ARO400207	1998 Accord DX, LX, EX 2.3L
ARO400202	ARO400205	ARO400207	1994-1997 Accord EX 16V VTEC 2.2L
ARO400302	ARO400305	ARO400307	1992-1993 Accord EX, SE 16V 130hp 2.2L
ARO400102	ARO400105	ARO400107	1988-1991 Civic 1.5L
ARO400102	ARO400105	ARO400107	1988-1991 Civic 1.6L
ARO400102	ARO400105	ARO400107	1992-1995 Civic CX, DX, LX 1.5L
ARO400202	ARO400205	ARO400207	1996-1998 Civic CX, DX, LX, HX 1.6L
ARO400202	ARO400205	ARO400207	1992-1995 Civic EX, VX, 16V VTEC 1.5, 1.6
ARO400102	ARO400105	ARO400107	1988-1992 CRX 1.5L
ARO400102	ARO400105	ARO400107	1988-1991 CRX HF 1.5L
ARO400202	ARO400205	ARO400207	1992 CRX HF, SI 16V VTEC 1.5, 1.6
ARO400102	ARO400105	ARO400107	1988-1991 CRX SI 1.6L
ARO400102	ARO400105	ARO400107	1993-1995 del Sol 1.5L
ARO400202	ARO400205	ARO400207	1993-1995 del Sol 16V VTEC 1.6L
ARO400402	ARO400405	ARO400407	1994 del Sol 16V VTEC 1.6L
ARO400202	ARO400205	ARO400207	1996-1997 del Sol 16V VTEC 1.6L
ARO400402	ARO400405	ARO400407	1996-1997 del Sol 16V VTEC 1.6L
ARO400302	ARO400305	ARO400307	1994-1995 Prelude S 16V 135hp 2.2L
ARO400302	ARO400305	ARO400307	1992-1996 Prelude SI, SE, SR 16V 160hp 2.3L
HYUNDAI			
ARO400502	ARO400505	ARO400507	1992-1995 Elantra 1.6L
ARO400502	ARO400505	ARO400507	1993-1997 Elantra 1.8L
ARO400502	ARO400505	ARO400507	1992-1997 Sonata 2.0L
INFINITI			
ARO100602	ARO100605	ARO100607	1991-1996 G20 2.0L
LEXUS			
ARO401802	ARO401805	ARO401807	1992-1996 SC300 3.0L
MAZDA			
ARO401902	ARO401905	ARO401907	1993-1996 626 2.0L
MERCURY			
ARO401302	ARO401305	ARO401307	1991-1993 Cougar 5.0L
MITSUBISHI			
ARO400502	ARO400505	ARO400507	1989-1997 Eclipse, turbo 2.0L
ARO400802	ARO400805	ARO400807	1995-1998 Eclipse, non-turbo 2.0L
ARO400502	ARO400505	ARO400507	1988-1994 Galant 2.0L/2.4L
ARO400502	ARO400505	ARO400507	1989-1992 Mirage 1.6L
ARO402002	ARO402005	ARO402007	1992-1995 Mirage 1.5L
NISSAN			
ARO400602	ARO400605	ARO400607	1995-1997 200SX 2.0L
ARO400702	ARO400705	ARO400707	1993+ Altima 1.6, 2.0, 2.4
ARO400102	ARO400105	ARO400107	1991-1995 Maxima 3.0L
ARO400602	ARO400605	ARO400607	1991-1994 Sentra 2.0L
PLYMOUTH			
ARO400502	ARO400505	ARO400507	1990-1994 Laser 2.0L
ARO400802	ARO400805	ARO400807	1995-1998 Neon 2.0L
ARO400802	ARO400805	ARO400807	1996-1998 Voyager 2.4L
PONTIAC			
ARO401102	ARO401105	ARO401107	1998-1999 Firebird 5.6L
SATURN			
ARO400902	ARO400905	ARO400907	1991-1998 Saturn 1.9L
TOYOTA			
ARO402202	ARO402205	ARO402207	1992-1995 Corolla AE100.4AFE
ARO402302	ARO402305	ARO402307	1982-1994 Tercel 1.5L
VOLKSWAGEN			
ARO402402	ARO402405	ARO402407	1998-1999 Beetle 2.0L
ARO402502	ARO402505	ARO402507	1990-1997 Golf/Jetta 2.0L

fit the Toyota 22R and 22RE engines. Includes red poly nylon wire isolators.

Part #	Description
17-103	1978-1992 Pro 8.5mm Plug Wire Set
17-104	1993-1995 Pro 8.5mm Plug Wire Set

MSD

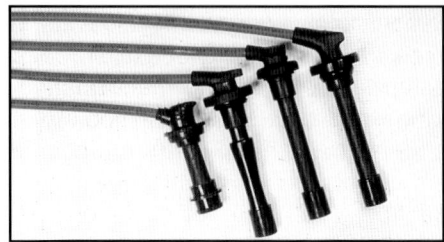

8.5mm Super Conductor Spark Plug Wire Sets

MSD is constantly adding more late-model custom plug wire sets for a variety of vehicles. Factory wires can have up to 3,000 ohms per foot of resistance while the MSD 8.5mm Super Conductor has less than 50 ohms per foot for increased spark delivery! When you also add the improved grip of the Dual Crimp Terminals, heavy-duty boots, and heat-resistant sleeve compound, you have the best performance spark plug wire available! This is just a sample of MSD's latest custom 8.5mm wire sets for 2000. New sets are constantly added so check back if you do not see your specific application.

MAGNECOR

KV85 Competition (8.5mm) and R-100 Racing (10mm) Ignition Cables

These cables feature Magnecor's exclusive 2.5mm high-capacity metallic inductance EMI-suppressed conductor consisting of stainless-steel wire precisely wound at 200 turns per inch over a ferromagnetic core. The insulating jacket is made entirely of Magnecor's exclusive TC-1500-HS high-strength aerospace grade silicone rubber, and its single layer construction will prolong the jacket's insulating ability by conducting extreme heat away from hot-spots that occur near over-the-limit heat sources.

The KV85 8.5mm jacket has a service heat resistance of 600 degrees F (320 degrees C) and up to 1,000 degrees F (540 degrees C) for short burst 3 minutes. The R-100 10mm jacket has a service heat resistance of 700 degrees F (380 degrees C) and up to 1,200 degrees F (650 degrees C) for short burst 3 minutes. Even if limits are exceeded, the silicone rubber will retain its insulating ability until wires are removed from the engine.

Magnecor Race Wires are primarily designed and constructed to be used in applications where it is essential to prevent the possibility of ignition wires compromising engine performance. Modern race engines, modified street engines, and stock street engines which rely on electronic devices to control the function of either or both the ignition and fuel systems are prone to interference from all other spiral conductor ignition wires sold through performance parts outlets, none of which can provide proper suppression for EMI, particularly if a high-output ignition system is used.

7mm and 8mm High Performance

Magnecor's 7mm and 8mm High Performance ignition cables consist of a 2mm diameter 120 turns per inch chrome alloy wire wound over a ferromagnetic core. These wires can be used with all stock and most racing ignition systems.

The conventional style insulating jacket consists of EPDM insulation, fiberglass reinforcing braiding, and a high-temperature, high-tear strength silicone rubber outer jacket. The RFI suppression and heat resistance ability of these cables is similar to the very best of our competitors' ignition wires and superior to all the rest!

The jacket color is black for 7mm and blue for 8mm cable. The jackets have a heat resistance of 400 degrees F (205 degrees C) for 7mm cable and 450 degrees F (232 degrees C) for 8mm cable.

These ignition wires are intended for use as factory replacement wires on carburetor and mechanical fuel injected street, race, commercial, and industrial stationary engines, and can be supplied as stock length replacement sets, individual leads in a variety of styles and lengths, universal sets, and to any length or style needed by the customer. Either cable can be ordered loose in any length.

Although these ignition wires are used successfully on many early EFI engines, their use is not recommended on late-model vehicles, as the conductors are not intended to provide the full EMI suppression of our KV85 and R-100 Race Wires.

A GUIDE TO IDENTIFYING RADIO-INTERFERENCE NOISES CAUSED BY IGNITION WIRES

Often, we are asked to describe how broadcast band noise can be identified as coming from ignition wires. Although it's difficult to describe in words, we'll try.

On the AM band, noise coming from spark plug wires is usually heard as a sharp "clacking" noise (from speakers) at idle that increases with engine speed to a "ZZZZ" sound at higher RPM. A faulty coil wire will always create a "ZZZZ" noise. A faulty or inadequately grounded antenna lead, or a heavily corroded antenna body can also cause the same sounds, even with good wires.

On the FM band, if you hear a ticking noise that increases with engine speed, it's more than likely that somewhere in the ignition system a spark is jumping to ground, or a spark is jumping a large gap inside a carbon conductor wire with the conductor burning back from the metal terminal.

Loose or badly fitted spark plug and coil wires, wires burnt through from header or turbocharger plumbing heat, ignition coil or coil packs with cracks in towers or bodies, cracks in distributor caps, and failed or excessively worn or gapped spark plugs (causing sparks to come out of spark plug boots and connectors) all can create open sparks that can be heard on the FM band.

WARNING about metal shielded and so-called "Built-in Capacitor" ignition wires: Although using a grounded metal shielding over the entire length of each ignition wire will certainly provide RFI suppression, and this style of wire is still used on low-revving piston-driven aircraft engines, it is common knowledge (from experience) amongst automotive electrical engineers that it's unwise to use ignition wires fitted with grounded metal shielding over ignition cable jackets on a high-revving automobile engine — as the problems caused by any style of ignition wires which need to be grounded have proven to be so great, that using them should be avoided at all costs!

This type of ignition wire forces the cable jacket to become an unsuitable dielectric for a crude capacitor (effect) between the conductor and the grounded braiding. While the wires function normally when first fitted, the cable jacket under the metal shielding soon breaks down as a dielectric, and progressively more and more spark energy is induced from the conductor (through the cable jacket) into the grounded shielding, causing the ignition coil to unnecessarily output more energy to fire both the spark plug gaps and the additional energy being lost in the grounded metal shielding. This situation leads to engine power loss, and eventually to ignition system overload failures as the insulating ability of the cable jacket (under the metal shielding) breaks down.

Ignition wires promoted as having "built-in capacitors" are nothing more than solid wire or spiral conductor wires over which grounded metal shielding is fitted to only part of the wires' insulating jacket. These wires have all the disadvantages of wires with grounded metal shielding over the entire length of each ignition wire — without being able to properly suppress either RFI or EMI!

MAGNECOR CN SERIES

KV85 Competition (8.5mm) and R-100 Racing (10mm) CN25 Ignition Cables

Specifically designed and constructed conductor provides maximum RFI suppression needed for problem mobile Ham radio, telephone and TV transmission, marine communication, high-powered sound systems equipment, etc.

CN Series 8.5mm KV85 Competition and 10mm R-100 Racing Ignition Cables

Magnecor Race Wires, if properly fitted, will provide excellent RFI suppression indefinitely for virtually all vehicles in which the original carbon conductor ignition wires provide adequate suppression. In severe cases, such as those experienced by mobile ham radio operators, where carbon conductor ignition wires (original and/or aftermarket) provide RFI suppression only for a short time before replacement is again needed, we recommend the use of CN Series Race Wires, the only ignition wires capable of indefinitely suppressing severe RFI without reducing spark current!

The majority of original equipment and aftermarket carbon conductor (suppression) wires will provide adequate RFI suppression until the wire conductors' limited suppression life is exceeded. Unfortunately, for mobile ham radio operators in particular, the effective RFI suppression life of most carbon conductor ignition wires is less than that required by anyone listening only to signals received on commercial AM and FM broadcast bands.

No spiral conductor "pro" etc. ignition wires sold in mass-merchandisers and speed shops will provide adequate (if any) RFI suppression for ham radios, TV, and sensitive sound equipment. Most provide token RFI suppression by coating the spiral conductor with a conductive latex or silicone compound, which, like a carbon conductor, is only effective for a limited time.

Magnecor's CN Series Race Wires feature Magnecor's exclusive 2.5mm metallic inductance suppressed CN25 conductor, consisting of a special alloy wire precisely wound at 200 turns per inch over a ferromagnetic core. The insulating jacket is identical to those used for our KV85 Competition and R-100 Ignition Race Wires. Magnecor CN Series wires can be identified by the designation "CN25" printed on the cable insulating jacket. IMPORTANT: Please specify you want "CN Series" wires at time of ordering.

Magnecor CN Series Wires can also be used on street vehicles that suffer extreme EMI problems from badly designed and easily-spiked engine management systems, and are normally supplied as the only alternative in Magnecor wire sets supplied for engines known to suffer these problems.

MAGNECOR PARTS

Any part of a Magnecor ignition wire can be purchased separately. Loose ignition cable (any type), boots, terminals, professional quality crimp tools, numbering sleeves and wire separator looms are available for installers preferring to assemble ignition wires in their own workshop and at the race track. No minimum quantity is required. Magnecor USA factory and the Australian and UK importer/distributors can supply custom tailored complete wires at short notice.

Crimping Tool

Heavy duty crimping tool designed specifically to crimp terminals to spark plug cable. The tool's steel crimping jaws (not mild steel or aluminum) are stepped from 6mm to 15mm thick to accommodate the full crimp section of the various heavy duty terminals sold by Magnecor. Can be used to crimp terminals onto ignition cables from 7mm to 10mm in diameter. The frame of the tool is made from quality materials with longevity in mind. Actual size of tool is 290 mm overall length.

This is not an inexpensive tool, but it's a worthwhile investment if you are always crimping terminals to ignition cables. This professional crimping tool is superior in every respect to the narrow-jawed mild-steel crimping pliers and the 2-piece aluminum closing tools (which are usually rendered useless after two crimp operations) currently available in the US aftermarket.

SPARK PLUGS

GREDDY RACING SPARK PLUGS

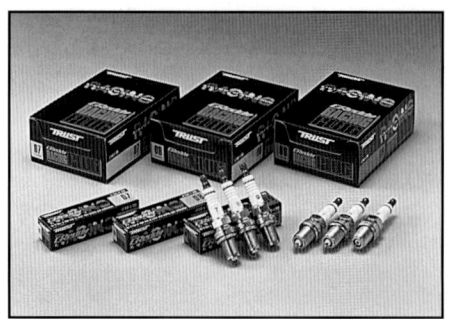

Part #	Description
13000007	JIS 07
13000027	ISO 07
13000008	JIS 08
13000028	ISO 08
13000029	ISO 09
13000030	ISO 10
13000049	RE 09
	For Rotary Engines
13000050	RE 10
	For Rotary Engines
13000051	RE 11
	For Rotary Engines

HKS

The HKS Super Fire Spark Plug is equipped with an iridium core, fine wire, center electrode, and a V-groove tapered side electrode. The HKS Super Fire spark plug is a high-performance plug, still allowing easy start ups and preventing misfires during warm up and day-to-day driving. The insulator is a perfect blend of materials, volumes, and measurements designed to prevent detonation. HKS Super Fire Plugs are the perfect compliment to the Twin Power Ignition Amplifier.

ZEX

Complete your power package with ZEX Performance Components to give you the winning edge. Don't settle for second-rate parts in your first-rate car. Get the performance you deserve from ZEX.

Originally designed to be used with the ZEX nitrous system, these plugs are specifically designed to maximize combustion cylinder efficiency in applications where nitrous — or a turbo — may be used. Short ground straps provide for a faster cooling process which promotes a more efficient burn and cooler cylinder temperatures. That means a safer environment for nitrous to operate and results in more torque and horsepower.

NGK FAST TECH TIPS FOR STREET/STRIP VEHICLES

1. INSTALLING SPARK PLUGS

Torque is one of the most critical aspects of spark plug installation. Torque directly affects the spark plugs' ability to transfer heat out of the combustion chamber. A spark plug that is under-torqued will not be fully seated on the cylinder head, hence heat transfer will be slowed. This will tend to elevate combustion chamber temperatures to unsafe levels, and pre-ignition and detonation will usually follow. Serious engine damage is not far behind.

An over-torqued spark plug can suffer from severe stress to the metal shell which in turn can distort the spark plug's inner gas seals or even cause a hairline fracture to the spark plug's insulator. In either case, heat transfer can again be slowed and the above mentioned conditions can occur.

The spark plug holes must always be cleaned prior to installation, otherwise you may be torquing against dirt or debris and the spark plug may actually end up under-torqued, even though your torque wrench says otherwise. Of course, you should only install spark plugs in a cool engine, because metal expands when hot and installation may prove difficult. Proper torque specs for both aluminum and cast-iron cylinder heads are listed below.

2. GAPPING

Since the gap size has a direct affect on the spark plugs' tip temperature and on the voltage necessary to ionize (light) the air/fuel mixture, careful attention is required. While it is a popular misconception that plugs are pre-gapped from the factory, the fact remains that the gap must be adjusted for the vehicle that the spark plug is intended for.

Those with modified engines must remember that a modified engine with higher compression or forced induction will typically require a smaller gap setting (to ensure ignitability in these denser air/fuel mixtures). As a rule, the more power you are making, the smaller the gap you will need.

A spark plug's voltage requirement is directly proportionate to the gap size. The larger the gap, the more voltage is needed to bridge the gap. Most experienced tuners know that opening gaps up to present a larger spark to the air/fuel mixture maximizes burn efficiency. It is for this reason that most racers add high-power ignition systems; the added power allows them to open the gap yet still provide a strong spark.

With this mind, many think the larger the gap the better. In fact, some aftermarket ignition systems boast that their systems can tolerate gaps that are extreme. Be wary of such claims. In most cases, the largest gap you can run may still be smaller than you think.

3. INDEXING

This is for racers only !! Indexing refers to a process whereby auxiliary washers of varying thickness are placed under the spark plug's shoulder so that when the spark plug is tightened, the gap will be pointed in the desired direction.

However, without running an engine on a dyno, it is impossible to gauge which type of indexing works best in your engine. While most engines like the spark plug's gap open to the intake valve, there are still other combinations that make more power with the gap pointed toward the exhaust valve.

In any case, engines with indexed spark plugs will typically make only a few more horsepower, typically less than 1% of total engine output. For a 500 hp engine, you'd be lucky to get 5 hp. While there are exceptions, the bottom line is that without a dyno, gauging success will be difficult.

4. HEAT RANGE SELECTION

Let's make this really simple: when you need your engine to run a little cooler, run a colder plug. When you need your engine to run a little hotter, run a hotter spark plug. However, NGK strongly cautions people that going to a hotter spark plug can sometimes mask a serious symptom of another problem that can lead to engine damage. Be very careful with heat ranges. Seek professional guidance if you are unsure.

With modified engines (those engines that have increased their compression), more heat is a by-product of the added power that normally comes with increased compression. In short, select one heat range colder for every 75-100 hp you add, or when you significantly raise compression. Also remember to retard the timing a little and to increase fuel enrichment and octane. These tips are critical when adding forced induction (turbos, superchargers, or Nitrous kits), and failure to address ALL of these areas will virtually guarantee engine damage.

An engine that has poor oil control can sometimes mask the symptom temporarily by running a slightly hotter spark plug. While this is a "Band-Aid" approach, it is one of the only examples of when and why one would select a hotter spark plug.

5. USING "RACING" SPARK PLUGS

Be cautious!! In reality, most "racing" spark plugs are just colder heat ranges of the street versions of the street spark plug. They don't provide any more voltage to the spark plug tip!! Their internal construction is no different (in NGK's case, as all of our spark plugs must conform to the same level of quality controls) than most standard spark plugs.

There are some exceptions, though. Extremely high compression cars or those running exotic fuels will have different spark plug requirements and hence NGK makes spark plugs that are well-suited for these requirements. They are classified as "specialized spark plugs for racing applications." Some are built with precious metal alloy tips for greater durability and for their ability to fire in denser or leaner air/fuel mixtures.

However, installing the same spark plugs Kenny Bernstein uses in his 300+ mph Top Fuel car (running Nitromethane at a 2:1 air/fuel ratio and over 20:1 dynamic compression) in your basically stock Honda Civic (running 15:1 air/fuel ratios with roughly 9.5:1 compression) will do nothing for you!! In fact, since Kenny's plugs are fully four heat ranges colder, they'd foul out in your Honda in just a few minutes.

NGK as a company tries to stay clear of saying that a racing spark plug (or ANY spark plug) will give you large gains in horsepower. While certain spark plugs are better suited to certain applications, NGK representatives try to tell people that are looking to "screw in" some cheap horsepower that, in most cases, spark plugs are not the answer.

To be blunt, when experienced tuners build race motors, they select their spark plugs for different reasons: to remove heat more efficiently, provide sufficient spark to completely light all the air/fuel mixture, to survive the added stresses placed upon a high performance engine's spark plugs, and to achieve optimum piston-to-plug clearance.

Some of these "specialized racing plugs" are made with precious metal alloy center/ground electrodes or fine wire tips or retracted-nose insulators. Again, these features do not necessarily mean that the spark plug will allow the engine to make more power, but these features are what allow the spark plug to survive in these tortuous conditions. Most racers know screwing in a new set of spark plugs will not magically "unlock" hidden horsepower.

6. USING HIGH POWER IGNITION SYSTEMS

Many of the more popular aftermarket ignition systems are of the capacitive discharge type. They store voltage, or accumulate it, until a point at which a trigger signal allows release of this more powerful spark. Companies like Mallory, MSD, Crane, and Accel, to name a few, offer such systems.

They affect spark plugs in that they allow the gaps to be opened up to take advantage of the increased capacity. The theory is that the larger and the more intense the spark you are able to present to the air/fuel mixture, the more likely you will be to burn more fuel, and hence the more power you will make. We encourage the use of such systems, but only on modified or older non-computer controlled vehicles.

In reality, computer-controlled vehicles do such a good job of lighting off the air/fuel mixture (as evidenced by the ultra-low emissions), added ignition capacity would do little to burn more fuel since the stock configuration is doing such a good job. Older non-computer controlled vehicles or those that have been modified with higher compression or boosted (nitrous, turbo, supercharged) engines can certainly take advantage of a more powerful ignition system.

Sport Compact Bolt-On Performance Guide Volume 1
Boosted Performance

TYPES OF NITROUS OXIDE SYSTEMS

Nitrous oxide injection systems come in several configurations. The primary difference between them is how the nitrous is delivered to the engine and mixed with the fuel.

The most common is a carburetor plate. This application involves a thin plate, which mounts below the carburetor and has thin brass tubes that are paired together. One tube is positioned over the other. The upper tube is usually nitrous and the lower tube is usually fuel. The high velocity of the nitrous as it comes out of the upper tube helps to atomize the fuel.

Carbureted port injection systems use a series of mixer nozzles. This type of nozzle combines the nitrous and the fuel as they are injected into the engine. Port systems use individual nozzles per cylinder allowing you to tune each cylinder differently if necessary.

A carbureted hybrid system uses a plate and port mixing schemes usually staged, i.e., the plate system is active off the start, then as the chassis settles, it is switch off and the second stage, in this case the port system is activated.

Fuel-injected plate systems are virtually the same as the plate systems used with carburetors. The difference being the plate mounts between a throttle body; or in some designs the plate is spliced into the intake runners in some fashion.

Fuel-injected nozzle system types use a mixer nozzle to deliver nitrous oxide and fuel to the engine. An example of this system type is the NOSTurbo Nitrous system for various turbocharged applications.

Fuel-injected port systems are essentially the same as the carbureted port systems discussed above.

A fuel-injected dry manifold system uses a spray nozzle to deliver nitrous oxide only to the intake. The additional fuel is supplied by increasing fuel pressure when the nitrous system is activated. It is called a dry manifold system because there isn't any fuel present in the intake manifold. A dry manifold is safer than a wet manifold because nitrous by itself is not explosive. It's when you mix nitrous with fuel in the manifold that you get spectacular manifold and hood, removals. In the last few years several manufacturers have developed this system type into easy-to-install, fast and fun systems.

NITROUS OXIDE SYSTEMS INC. (NOS)

Lightweight 1.6-Pound N$_2$O Bottle

Looking to save weight while you squeeze? Nitrous Oxide Systems Inc. (NOS) has introduced a brand-new lightweight carbon fiber-wrapped nitrous bottle. It holds 1.6 pounds of liquid nitrous — and offers close to 2 pounds of weight savings over the bottle it replaces. If you're on a weight-saving campaign, this is one of the least expensive ways you can shave off a couple of pounds.

To achieve the weight savings, NOS has introduced aerospace technology to the world of nitrous. The 1.6-pound bottle is made from very lightweight thin-wall aluminum, which is wrapped in lightweight carbon fiber to add strength. It also comes with NOS's new-style valve, to assure high flow. The lightweight bottle is perfect for motorcycle racers, and it's NHRA, IHRA, and AMA-PROSTAR legal.

NOS 2000 Catalog

For the latest information on Nitrous Oxide Systems, Inc. products, check out its 2000 catalog with 68 pages jam-packed with everything that has made NOS the industry leader for over 20 years: the highest-quality, best-engineered, and most thoroughly-tested nitrous oxide systems, components, and accessories available.

From the mildest 90 hp plate systems all the way up to the full-boogie Pro Shot Twin Fogger system (capable of adding 1,000 hp), NOS has all the ingredients necessary to wake the sleeping demon in your vehicle. Lightweight carbon-fiber bottles, progressive nitrous controllers, remote-control bottle valves, bottle warmers, pressure gauges, all varieties and sizes of nozzles, plumbing, solenoids, fuel pumps and fuel pressure regulators, fittings, and of course, specifically-designed kits for your application. Anything you'll need to do nitrous right, you'll find it here.

More than just a list of part numbers and pretty pictures, NOS' 2000 catalog also features ten pages of solid tech, frequently asked questions, and system recommendations, combined with easy-to-understand application charts, product summaries, and first-rate color illustrations and photos. The NOS 2000 catalog is a must-have reference tool for the serious racer and boulevard destroyer.

VTEC Kit #02040

The easiest way to add massive amounts of power to any engine is by adding nitrous, and Nitrous Oxide Systems Inc. (NOS) has just introduced a nitrous system designed specifically for the popular Honda VTEC engine. This new system can be adjusted to provide from 75 to 200 additional horsepower with the touch of a button.

NOS's VTEC system features the company's highly effective Big Shot injector plate, which attaches to the OEM Honda plenum. The Big Shot benefits from a unique "fogging" plate design that vastly improves nitrous flow, fuel atomization, and mixture distribution. How much of a difference can nitrous make? Kurt Gordon's street-driven Honda Civic runs 11.55 at 122 mph in the quarter-mile, thanks to an NOS #2040 nitrous system.

NOS's new VTEC kit includes a 10-pound nitrous bottle, the Big Shot injector plate, fuel and nitrous solenoids, high-quality fittings and braided stainless lines, wiring, jets to adjust the amount of nitrous flowing through the system, and hardware -- everything needed for a professional-quality installation.

| 02040 (A, B) | 1997-1999 Acura Integra GSR 1.8 VTEC |
| 02045 (A, B) | 1997-1999 Honda Prelude 2.2 VTEC |

NOS Dry Manifold Import Kit

Owners of imported vehicles can benefit from nitrous power, as NOS has developed safe, reliable, and highly effective kits that produce from 40 to 60 hp for a large number of applications. Most of these employ "dry" injection techniques, where the OEM fuel injection provides the required additional fuel only when the nitrous system is armed and activated at W.O.T. These systems provide excellent fuel/nitrous distribution to each cylinder, as opposed to the "wet" kits from other manufacturers. However NOS does recommend "wet" type kits for most turbocharged and supercharged applications due to the increased air velocity and extra heat from the forced induction.

Pro Race Fogger

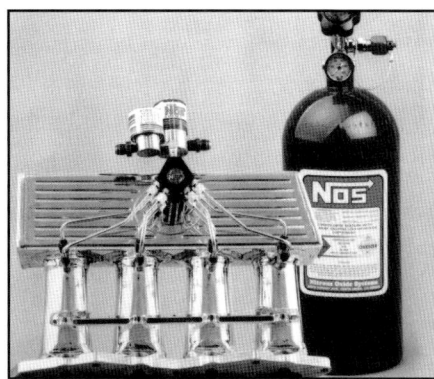

Nitrous Oxide Systems Inc. (NOS), offers a killer system for competition-spec import 4-cylinder and Rotary. The adjustable, state-of-the-art Pro Race Fogger system provides from 80 to 225 additional horsepower on properly built race engines. The Pro Race Fogger features the industry's best flowing valves, stainless hard lines and the Pro Race bottom discharge solenoid.

Nitrous Express

Nitrous Express reportedly has taken nitrous injection to the "next generation" level. The company claims to have solved all the current problems that are associated with the use of nitrous oxide. No more uneven distribution from injector plates, difficult fuel atomization, unstable bottle pressure, to mention a few.

Every Nitrous Express system is flow-bench designed, dyno tested, and track proven. Nitrous Express offers safe, reliable, "next generation" nitrous systems from 50 horsepower sportsman systems to 1,000 plus horsepower professional drag race systems. Nitrous Express is backed by a motivated team with a combined 50 years of design, manufacturing, sales, and use of nitrous systems.

Part #	Application
20413	Acura (50-75hp)
20414	Honda (50-75hp)
20415	Mazda RX (50-75hp)
20416	Mazda Miata (50-75hp)
20417	Toyota MR2 (50-75hp)
20514	Toyota, all including turbo (50-75hp)
20614	Nissan (50-75hp)
20615	Nissan, all ZX & SX series except turbo (50-75hp)
20616	Nissan 300 ZX, twin turbo (35-50-75hp)
20714	Mitsubishi Eclipse (50-75hp)
20715	Mitsubishi 3000 GT, all including VR4 (50-75hp)
20716	Mitsubishi Eclipse, turbo (35-50-75hp)
20814	BMW 4 & 6 cyl. (50-75hp)
20815	BMW 8 cyl. (50-75-100-150hp)
20816	BMW 12 cyl. (50-75-100-150hp)
20817	BMW M3 2.3L (35-50-75hp)
20816	Infinity (50-75-100hp)
20913	Lexus V-8 (50-75-100-150hp)
20914	Lexus (50-75hp)
20010	Porsche, non-turbo (50-75hp)
20011	Porsche, turbo (50-75hp)
20917	VW Corrado/Golf/Jetta (50-75hp)
20918	VW Beetle, watercooled
20915	All Other EFI Sport Compact Cars
15499	Pro Wiring Kit (includes all hardware for dual solenoid system)

UP215	Upsize (from 10 lb. to 15 lb. bottle)
00011	Bottle Downsize (from 15 to 10 lb. bottle)
00010	10 lb. Bottle Discount (for use with pre-existing bottle)
00015	15 lb. Bottle Discount (for use with pre-existing bottle)

SYSTEM CONTENTS

10 lb. bottle with Pure-Flo valve
Lifetime guaranteed large solenoids
Hinged steel bottle brackets
14 foot stainless-steel braided supply line
Heavy duty 40 amp anti-flyback relay
All necessary hardware

NITROUS WORKS

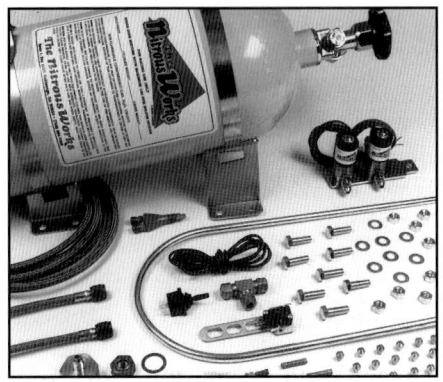

After dominating America's two top nitrous racing divisions last season, NitrousWorks applied the latest nozzle technology to a new range of performance kits for smaller displacement imports and domestics. These new nitrous systems minimize air flow turbulence in the port, provide superior atomization, and can be installed anywhere in the intake tract before the plenum. The kit comes complete with fuel tuning jets and doesn't harm driveability or emissions. It's the best power-to-dollar ratio kit on the market. Each kit contains Power Wing nozzle, calibrated jets, solenoids, stainless line and fittings, filter, hardware, instructions, 14 ft./ -4 AN stainless bottle feed line, and a 10-lb. capacity bottle.

ZEX

Possibly, the world's most engine friendly nitrous kit ever! The ZEX Nitrous Oxide Kit is so simple to install, your Mom could do it. When armed, the ZEX Nitrous Kit kicks in electronically off the T.P.S. and tells the fuel pressure regulator how much extra fuel to deliver. Results are the most constant nitrous-to-fuel ratio of any kit available. So while the other guy is trying to find the Nitrous switch, you have already won! The ZEX Nitrous Oxide Kit is the ultimate in Plug & Play performance.

JIM WOLF TECHNOLOGY

Making horsepower has always been a basic game of getting extra oxygen to the cylinders, adding the proper amount of fuel, and tuning the engine to safely handle it. Along this pursuit, W.W.II fighter planes were the first to use N_2O to gain instant horsepower. Inducing pure oxygen in a liquid form would have been very unstable, but nitrous oxide has two stabilizing nitrogen molecules to one oxygen. Sprayed in a liquid form, N_2O's oxygen is available to burn with the fuel in the cylinders. The "Holy Grail" of using this stuff is accurate control of the fuel ratio and ignition timing.

The JWT N_2O systems consist of a conventional solenoid-operated nitrous oxide spray nozzle. However, the supplemental fuel is not added by a separate fuel spray nozzle, as with most conventional N_2O systems. Older conventional "wet" systems sprayed supplemental fuel through the intake manifold along with the nitrous oxide, requiring the addition of an extra solenoid, line, and fuel source. Most fuel-injected engines have intake runners that are designed to run "dry" and will not distribute fuel droplets evenly, causing some cylinders to run dangerously lean during nitrous usage.

The JWT system eliminates the need for add-on fuel injectors or spray nozzles, since additional fuel is added through the existing injectors, as intended by the engine designer. A custom program module is installed inside the ECU that switches between two engine control programs. Program #1 is a normal performance program, used to produce maximum power when nitrous oxide is not used. Program #2 is activated only when the nitrous arming switch is on, and the throttle has been fully depressed. On turbo cars, the system is designed as a supplemental system to fill in the low-end power missing from high-output turbocharged cars. The system automatically shuts itself off when the turbochargers have sufficiently spun up to carry the power demand.

JWT has integrated, computer-controlled, Nitrous Oxide applications for the Infiniti G20, Infiniti Q45, Sentra, Sentra SE-R, 200SX SE-R, NX2000, 240SX, Maxima, Pathfinder, and Nissan trucks. While costing more, only Pro-grade nitrous solenoids are used for maximum reliability.

JACOBS

Nitrous oxide has always been a popular method of gaining horsepower on high-revving sport compact cars. However, reality has proven nitrous can be hard on small engines. That is, until now. Jacobs' Nitrous Mastermind Team offers tremendous protection, as well as power boosts, when using nitrous. Yes, you can have both power and engine safety! Omni Magnum Team CARB E.O. #D-19-30 Nitrous Mastermind CARB E.O. #D-19-10 .

VENOM™

The VCN-2000 Programmable Nitrous Board

The VENOM™ PC Nitrous System has several key advantages. The system is completely programmable by the end user. The user simply plugs the Nitrous Controller into the serial port of a PC. Using VENOM™ software, the user can configure the nitrous to operate in three various modes of operation.

Drag Mode: In this mode, the nitrous operates in the same mode as current nitrous systems operate. Full nitrous is delivered to the engine when the control mode has sensed wide open throttle.

Linear Mode: In this mode, the user programs the throttle angle for the starting point for the introduction of nitrous. The control module then adds a proportionate amount of nitrous in relation to throttle angle. The higher the throttle angle, the greater the nitrous flow. This is expected to be the most popular mode of operation.

Timed Mode: In this mode, the user programs at what throttle angle the nitrous should be introduced and how much nitrous should be added (in terms of %). The user also enters a time delay (pause after the throttle angle is reached) and an injection time (how long to inject the nitrous for). This is ideal for turbo-charged engines. The nitrous can be energized while the turbo reaches optimized boost levels and, after a certain amount of time, it is deactivated.

Electronic Low Bottle Detection

The control module monitors the vehicle's existing oxygen sensor to determine if proper nitrous was introduced. The module electronically detects when the bottle is low and automatically disables the system. A low bottle LED is illuminated on the control pad to inform the driver.

Optimal Air Fuel Ratio At Any Bottle Pressure

When nitrous is introduced, additional fuel is required to ensure the proper air/fuel mixtures obtained. Without this additional fuel, the mixtures can become too lean, causing pre-detonation, which leads to severe engine damage. The VENOM system uses existing injectors to enrich the fuel mixture when nitrous is introduced. This system adds an injection pulse after the computer has finished its pulse. The pulse added is a product of how much nitrous is entering the engine. The user only needs to program the amount of nitrous, the control module will automatically calculate the additional amount of fuel required. The module ensures the proper air/fuel ratio by monitoring the vehicle's existing oxygen sensor. If bottle pressure becomes too low, the system is disabled and no additional fuel is needed.

SUPERCHARGERS

JACKSON RACING

Honda Civic Si DOHC B16A2 Jackson Racing Supercharger System

Fuel management is utilized through proprietary Jackson Racing fuel regulator. Installation is as simple as bolting it on. That's what a Jackson Racing supercharger delivers. Not some high strung, fancy, drag-strip-queen sort of power. We're talking street smart, hole shot, 0 to 60, and 0 to 40 dominating kind of torque and horsepower, all down low and running right to the fuel cutoff. All day, every day, every time you mash the pedal to the metal. Reliable, lock-the-hood power with an Eaton supercharger and a dedicated cast aluminum intake manifold, just the way Honda would have done it.

Jackson Racing-equipped Civics make more torque at 2,000 rpm than a stock motor makes at peak; torque that makes for unmatched Honda performance in a launch and drag strip race. Impossible to bog down, impossible to be surprised on the street. No waiting for the turbo to spool, no lag. Mash the pedal and go in any gear. Jackson Racing's roll on power is unequaled by any other system ever. Instantaneous boost, low heat rise, trouble-free operation; that's the principle of usable power, the principle of Jackson Racing.

Forget headers or cams, even trick cylinder heads or pistons, they'll never be as strong as simply bolting on a Jackson Racing supercharger. Get 40% more horsepower in one afternoon. No pushing buttons, no tweaking with controllers, this one has it all on the fly.

The Jackson Racing supercharger system is CARB legal (EO# D-344-5) for the 1988-1999 model years. However, in order to maintain its CARB certification, you MUST run Premium grade fuel.

HONDA CIVIC/CRX/DEL SOL Applications

Civic/CRX systems 1.6 SOHC VTEC and non VTEC, 1.5 SOHC where applicable. Multiport injection only. No throttle body injection fitments.

1999 Civic SI
1997-1998 CR-V
1999 CR-V, no HF or HX fitments
1992-1995 del Sol, SI, S
1994-1997 del Sol DOHC
1988-1991 EX, SI
1992-1995 EX, SI, LX, DX, CX
1996-1998 EX
1996-1998 LX, DX, CX

ACURA INTEGRA Applications

Subsequent to the successful release of the Integra GS-R supercharger system, JR has added the following applications:

1994-1999 Integra GS-R
1994-1999 Integra GS/LS/RS
1997-1998 Integra Type-R

ADVANCED MOTORSPORT SOLUTIONS

VR6 Supercharger System for the Volkswagen Golf/Jetta/ Passat and Eurovan VR6

This system brings the base 172 hp 6-cylinder platform to 272 hp. The system is conservative and has longevity in mind. Complete kit runs low boost and standard compression and has an easy installation. Complete vehicle conversions are also available as per the customer's request.

ABT Sportsline for the Volkswagen/Audi 1.8 Valve Turbo

This engine is currently in the new Passat and also the A4. ABT Sportsline currently offers 6 stages ranging from 193 hp to the Ultimate 310 hp 2.0L conversion. Complete vehicle conversions are also available as per the customer's request.

TURBO KITS

ACTIVE AUTOWERKE

If you drive an RHD model (right-hand drive), such as 320i or 325i in countries such as Great Britain, South Africa, Australia, etc. now there's a turbo kit to equal the HP gain of a US spec Turbo M3. As a BMW tuner, AA specializes in performance products to improve both handling and power for your BMW E36, from front & rear strut braces to 500 hp turbo kits.

Specially prepared turbocharger with external wastegate. Custom cast-iron, crack-resistant exhaust manifold. Large hi-flow air filter system. Black powder-coated steel plumbing with rolled end. Custom aluminum front-mounted intercooler. Complete hardware, including hoses and clamps. Revised steering shaft included. Detailed instruction manual. Custom software program / Performance Turbo chip. 6 Hi-Flow injectors, 7 Psi boost.

E36 320i / 325i Right hand drive Turbo Kit
300 hp @ 6580 rpm;
295 lbs./ft. @ 3900 rpm
1/4 mile: 13.5 @ 105;
0-60: 5.5 sec.
Top Speed: 145+ mph
RPM Limitation: 6800-7200 rpm

APEX INTEGRATION

Apex Integration has combined forces with IHI Turbos to create one of the most dynamic turbo kits available today. The heart and soul of the turbo kit is the legendary IHI RX6 series turbo. This turbo is the exact same version that led Honda to the F-1 Championships. All RX6 turbos are ball bearing and reduce shaft motion to a minimum allowing quick spool up and good top end.

The AX turbos are also a product of a joint venture with IHI turbos. Designed with an internal wastegate, the AX turbo boasts an industry first "abradable seal." This seal surrounds the compressor blade for minimum clearance. As the turbo begins to wear, it slowly grinds away at the seal enabling the turbo to keep maximum efficiency throughout its life.

All kits come complete with a cast-iron exhaust manifold which has a higher resistance to heat than stainless steel. Wastegates, piping, hose clamps, air filter (not available in some kits), gaskets, lines, nuts, and bolts all come with the kit to allow easy installation.

HOTSHOT

The HotShot Turbo system for Sentra SE-R, 200SX SE-R, Sentra SE (1999), and NX2000 owners provides 80 extra horsepower at the drive wheels, yet retains all the stock smog equipment and air conditioning system. In HotShot's two test cars, boost comes on at 3500 rpm, and stays strong all the way to redline.

The HotShot turbo system includes: Turbonetics T3 Turbo (rated for over 300 hp); custom intercooler with bolt-on mounting brackets; mandrel bent and bead rolled intercooler tubing; silicon couplers / stainless-steel hose clamps; Nissan 370 cc injectors; boost and oil pressure gauges with A-pillar mount; HotShot 304 stainless, ceramic-coated turbo tubular manifold; 2-1/2" downpipe runs to stock converter; Turbonetics adjustable Deltagate wastegate; Turbonetics blow-off valve; and K&N filter. Safely Boost 7psi with stock MAF. Uses Jim Wolf Modified ECU.

HAHN RACECRAFT

HRC has redesigned the 16G and 20G upgrades for Diamond Star with innovative features and excellent quality. For starters, the Super G does NOT boost creep, unlike the conventional 16G. Boost pressure can be set as low as 10 psi, all the way to maximum RPM. And this is achieved without requiring any expensive porting, clipping, or flapper valve mods. Boost level is so consistent with RPM changes you'll think your boost gauge needle is stuck!

The conventional 16G used for years on these cars has become increasingly prone to boost creep. Boost creep is a condition which involves boost pressure "creeping" or rising with RPM to unsafe, excessive (potentially dangerous!) levels. This condition is a direct result of the higher engine airflow being developed by today's aftermarket accessories (i.e.: 3" exhausts, high-flow intercoolers, 3" downpipes, etc.). Combined with a conventional 16G, these high-flow components will lead to boost creep issues which did not exist with the older, lesser airflow components (i.e.: 2-1/2" exhausts and downpipes, stock intercoolers, etc.).

The problem lies with the too small turbine section of the conventional 16G. It produces excessive exhaust pressure due to its limited airflow. This excessive backpressure also limits horsepower. Even when porting, clipping, and modified flappers are employed, the conventional 16G will still creep. The larger turbine attacks these issues at their root cause and the results are impressive. The Super 16G develops full boost by 2700 rpm, yet will not creep at all, all the way to 7000 rpm!

You've probably heard of HRC's Eliminator downpipes, which prevent the need for porting of the restrictive O2 housing by replacing it with mandrel-bent tube. The new Super series turbo takes a similar approach. Included with each HRC Super turbo is a 2-1/2" tubular O2 housing which is compatible with standard 2-1/2" or larger downpipes! If you have already purchased a downpipe upgrade (other than HRC's standard Eliminator), it will bolt directly to the Super's tubular O2 housing! And HRC now offers a version of its well-known Eliminator downpipe called the Eliminator Jr. which is compatible with both the new Super turbo as well as stock O2 housings used with other turbos!

And for you high-horsepower types, the Super series features a turbine housing configuration which is available in larger TD05 and TD06 A/R ratios and turbine wheel options for BIG airflow! This interchangeability is achieved without any custom machining of the housing -- just install the wheel or housing of your choice! All Super series housings are machined exclusively by Mitsubishi, retaining the fabulous quality and accuracy only their state-of-the-art factory can produce.

Unlike other turbo upgrades which utilize custom-machined versions of the 7 cm housing, the HRC Super series uses these standard Mitsubishi parts. You will never have to worry about parts availability or quality in the future, as your Super series turbo is not limited in repair options by custom machining of its internal components.

KNIGHT ENGINEERING

Iceman Turbo Kit

Iceman turbo kits feature a tuned equal-length turbo manifold which is reportedly 60% more efficient than the typical log-style manifolds. The kit is fully bolt-on -- no welding or other engine mods required. They offer Intercooler, blow-off valve, and external wastegate as available accessories.

The internal wastegate is set at 3.5 psi, though boost potential is 18 psi. This boost level however is done at your own risk. The kit is 49 State smog legal and looks to be extremely durable. The Knight Engineering test vehicle has been driven with the Iceman Turbocharger for a hard 90,000 miles and the turbocharger kit is still strong.

The tech details show this to be a very complete kit. It comes with: two-piece mandrel bent chrome-plated steel pressure tube exhaust downpipe; braided stainless-steel nylon core oil feed line installed between engine block and oil pressure sensor (near oil filter). The kit's oil drain line, from engine block to turbocharger unit, includes all oil fittings, oil adapters to turbocharger, and an adapter plate to oil pan.

Fuel is managed with a pressure sensitive fuel regulator using high pressure fuel lines. A map sensor inline check valve and remote map sensor adapter are also used.

The TE04H Turbocharger's exhaust flows through a mandrel-bent 2.25" dia. steel tube, chrome-plated discharge pipe. High-temperature silicone hose couplings and clamps secure the exhaust circuit. And a polished aluminum heat shield isolates air conditioner and power steering pumps. Of course the system comes with an Iceman Intake System and complete installation manual, as well as a 6-month limited warranty.

Available for these vehicles:

1990-1993 Acura Integra RS LS GS-R
1994-1998 Acura Integra RS LS GS-R
1988-1991 Honda Civic SI CRX
1992-1995 Honda Civic All
1996-1998 Honda Civic EX
1994-1997 Honda Accord DX LX EX

LC ENGINEERING

LC Engineering introduces a Turbo Kit designed for Toyota 20R/22R/22RE powered Celicas. For street use or competitive drag racing, LC Engineering can configure a custom Turbo Kit for your specific needs.

The LC Engineering Pro Turbo Kit is designed to utilize the Pro Fuel Injection System (Part # 24-EM2E or 24-EM2F). Along with bigger injectors, the Pro Fuel Injection can be programmed to provide the correct fuel and ignition curve for a performance turbo engine.

The base kit (Part # 26-100) features a Garret T3/T4 super series turbo, a tig-welded stainless-steel ceramic-coated turbo header with down tube, Delta adjustable waste gate, variable boost controller for in-cab adjustments, and the necessary gaskets, fittings, lines, and hardware for installation. Kit includes the following items:

Qty.	LC Part #	Description
1	26-150	Turbo Header
1	26-5034	Turbo Charger T3/T4 Super
1	26-5035	Turbo Inlet Gasket
1	26-506	Delta Waste Gate - 9-13 psi
1	26-507	Variable Boost Controller
1	26-510	Oil Drain Flange 1/2" FPT
1	26-512	Oil Drain Gasket
3	26-520	Hose Clamps 2"
3	26-522	Hose Clamp 2.75"
1	26-523	Hose Couplers 2" id x 2" ID BLUE
1	26-524	Hose 2-1/2" ID 45 Elbow
1	26-528	2-3/4" to 2" Hose Adapter
1	26-606	Turbo Oil In 1/8 NPT -4AN Straight
2	26-608	Turbo In/Block Out 90 Swivel
1	26-610	Oil Drain Weld Fitting -8 Male
2	26-611	Oil Drain Hose Ends 45 Swivel
1	26-612	Block to Oil Out Fitting -4/ 26BST
1	26-613	Turbo Oil Drain 45 1/2" NPT
3	26-614	Oil In Hose 3'
2	26-615	Turbo Oil Drain Hose 1/2 x 2'
2	26-616	Turbo Oil Drain Hose Guard 2'
2	26-622	2 Fitting -6AN Swivel
1	26-700	K&N Air Cleaner Inlet 2.5"
1	26-740	U Bend 2"
1	26-744	Straight Tube 2" x 24"
1	26-746	Air Inlet Extension Tube
1	14-769	Exhaust Manifold Gasket
1		Turbo Hardware Kit

LC Turbo Header

The LC Turbo Header is designed for the Toyota Celicas powered by the 20R/22R/22RE engines and is flanged for Garrett turbo chargers. The tig-welded Turbo Header features mandrel-bent 14-gauge stainless-steel tube runners, laser flanges, and is ceramic coated. The ceramic coating will withstand temperatures to 1,500 degrees. It increases header life and improves turbo performance. Includes turbo head pipe with wastegate connection.

Part # 26-150   LC Turbo Header

Garrett T3/T4 Turbo

The Garrett T3/T4 Hybrid offers the low inertia and fast boost response of the light-weight T3 turbine wheel and the high-airflow characteristics of the T4 compressor family making the T3/T4 hybrid the turbo of choice for higher performance import applications.

Part # 26-5034   Garrett T3/T4 Turbo

Delta Waste Gate 9 - 13 psi

Designed for durability, with a 1.250" stainless-steel valve, nomex/silicone diaphragm and with a unique "stand-off" actuator section, the Deltagate can control boost on engines that develop 250 - 300 hp.

Part # 26-506   Delta Waste Gate 9 - 13 psi

Variable Boost Controller

Change your boost level from the cockpit of your car with the Variable Boost Controller. The controller can adjust boost pressure on any Deltagate.

Part # 26-507   Variable Boost Controller

Bypass Valve

Great insurance for upgraded turbos and streetable high-performance engines. Manufactured by Bosch, this OEM quality light-weight compressor bypass valve features 1" hose connections and the highest flow capacity of any unit offered in this size.

Part # 26-508   Bypass Valve

Dump Valve

This billet-machined surge protector is available in anodized red or natural aluminum finish. It combines the great look, an awesome sound, and ease of installation at an affordable price.

Part # 26-509   Dump Valve

Street Turbo Camshaft

Designed for low boost or Toyota RET engines. The Street Turbo Camshaft will work with all of the stock valvetrain components while extracting that extra power from your low boost turbo application. Works with the stock RET EFI system and components without modification. Get the extra power and torque your turbo engine was designed for.

Part # 18-101T   Street Turbo Camshaft

Custom Ground Turbo Camshafts

LC Engineering custom grinds and designs camshaft profiles for many special applications.

Turbo charging any engine increases the strain on all of the engine components. At each level of additional boost, new issues for engine configuration develop and need to be addressed. Keep in mind, it is the combination of matched components that will deliver a reliable high-horsepower engine. What works for a low-boost application may not take the strain of high levels of boost.

Camshaft

LC Engineering offers specially designed camshafts to achieve full benefit of your turbo engine. They offer custom-grind camshafts for all levels of boost and RPM ranges. For most low-boost street applications, the Street Turbo Cam (Part # 18-101T) is an excellent choice.

Valves, Valve Springs and Cylinder Head

For the most performance, valve size, valve springs, and cylinder head porting need to match the desired level of boost and camshaft profile used. LC Engineering's Street Performer cylinder head (Part # 13-100) will be adequate for most low-boost street applications. For drag strip and high RPM use, even at low-boost levels, we recommend using the Stage 2 Head (Part # 13-2201) with Pro Dual Valve Springs and Titanium Retainers. The Pro Cam Kit (Part # 13-200) should be used for most applications if you are rebuilding your cylinder head.

Compression Ratio

To achieve a reliable turbo-charged engine, you will need to lower your mechanical compression ratio to 8:1. This can be done on a stock EFI engine by changing the pistons during a rebuild. LC Engineering offers both cast and forged piston kits that will achieve this compression ratio. Cylinder head and block modifications can change the compression ratio. Always cc your components during assembly to verify the mechanical compression ratio.

Bottom End

The stock bottom engine has adequate strength for low boost and low RPM applications. For higher levels of boost and performance LC Engineering's Pro bottom end components (Pro Crank, Pro Rods, Forged Pistons) should be used. A Pro Bottom End (Short-Block Kit Part # 19-085PK) will provide adequate strength to 250 hp.

Fuel & Ignition Management

LC Engineering offers the SDS fuel management system that will control the fuel curve and ignition timing. Generally you will need larger injectors and additional sensors for higher boost applications.

Intercoolers

Intercoolers allow the use of high boost levels and increased performance. There are many different intercooler designs and locations to position them. LC Engineering suggests a 3.5" x 8" x 13" core unit. These units are available with different tank configurations.

Turbo Engine Recommendations

The following recommendations are a guideline for the type of modifications needed to build a strong and reliable engine for the desired level of boost and performance.

0-10 psi Boost Accessory Recommendations

LC Part #	Description
13-100	Street Performer Cylinder Head
13-106	Cylinder Head Studs
19-85111	Pro Oil Pump
18-101T	Street Turbo Cam
13-110	Street Performer Valve Springs

Special Order Low Compression Street Pistons

19-3194	Turbo Gapless Ring Set
19-111	Pro Rod Bolts
24-EM2E	Pro Fuel Injection
13-2201	Stage 2 Cylinder Head
13-106	Cylinder Head Studs
19-85111	Pro Oil Pump

Special Order Custom Turbo Camshaft

13-200	Pro Cam Kit w/ Dual Valve Springs
19-9485SC	8:1 Forged Piston Kit
19-3194	Turbo Gapless Ring Set
19-111	Pro Rod Bolts

Labor O-Ring Block & Cylinder Head

P2293	Copper Head Gasket
19-108T	LC Pro Rods
19-205	Timing Chain Conversion Kit
30-101	3-Core Radiator
24-EM2F	Pro Fuel Injection

RPS

RPS is now offering a Single Turbo Conversion kit for Toyota twin-turbo Supras. The kit features everything you need to convert a twin-turbo car to a single turbo set-up. This is the same kit used by Vinny Ten in his 9-second Supra.

The standard kit includes: header (equal length stainless-steel header), Turbonetics T04S04 Turbo, Turbonetics Racing Wastegate, oil lines (in and out) / water lines (in and out), air intake system, 3" diameter downpipe, HKS bypass valve, and all necessary hardware.

There is a 2-3 week processing time required on all orders placed. The nice thing about this kit is that the turbo option can be variable. You can use any of the Turbonetic's family of turbos with this kit, not just the T04S04. This will give you the flexibility to fit the right turbo for your style of driving.

REV HARD

Rev Hard has been on the leading edge of high-quality and high-performance turbocharger kits for Civics, CRXs, Integras, VTECs, and Hybrids since 1992. Narrowing down the scope of their research and development to these selected cars, allows R-H to design the best high-performance turbo kit for your dollar. For whatever degree you wish to push your Honda or Acura, R-H has a turbo kit for you.

Stage I

Standard bolt on/non-intercooled kit includes an R-H cast-iron manifold, T3/T4 hybrid turbo, aluminized piping, 2.5" down pipe, purosil hoses and clamps, high-volume fuel pump, boost-dependent fuel regulator, and steel braided -3 oil line and fittings.

Stage II

Street race ready kit includes Stage I bolt-on kit with the addition of a front-mounted R-H intercooler, piping, and Greddy Blow-Off Valve. Available for 1992+ Civic and 1994+ Integra.

Stage III

Fully race ready kit includes an R-H tuned turbo manifold; premium R-H T3/T4 hybrid 500 hp turbo; front-mounted R-H intercooler; external wastegate; all necessary pipes, hoses, and clamps; blow-off valve; high-pressure fuel pump; and large injectors. Stand-alone DFI or TEC II.

11-second Motor Packages

All 11-second motor packages are engine dyno tested before shipping and are VERY capable of accomplishing 10-second timeslips if traction is accomplished. Optional upgrades available for stainless-steel turbo manifold, chrome piping, racing bypasses, and racing wastegates.

DRAG PERFORMANCE PRODUCTS

Generation III Turbo systems feature a 4-into-1 cast manifold with external wastegate for optimum durability without sacrificing performance and consistent boost control. The Gen-111 Hybrid TO4/T3 turbo will flow more horsepower than your engine can probably hold, so you won't have to upgrade. Plus the system includes two-piece intercooler piping that makes installing one of the largest, most efficient intercoolers (that fits stock without major mods) as well as an HKS sequential blow-off valve, electric fuel pump, and fuel pressure regulator.

GREDDY

The Greddy TD04 is the centerpiece of its Honda Civic and Mazda Miata turbo systems. The TD04 is twice the fun as upgrades on Nissan and Mitsubishi's dazzling twin-turbo machines. At Greddy, they know the key to a killer-combination is balance. Peak horsepower never takes precedence over torque and engine response, what you really use in day-to-day driving.

You need to check the integrity of the engine and drivetrain. All the extra pressure won't do any good if it leaks past the valves, seals, or rings. Is your cooling system in good condition? Turbochargers tend to increase oil temperature. They live long on clean, synthetic oil.

Finally, don't rush into a turbocharger add-on or upgrade if you're going to be doing extensive modifications. A planned approach to building a performance machine minimizes downtime, labor (time and charges), and maximizes gratification.

Greddy offers more than 40 turbo configurations. If you want the most performance-per-dollar, investigate a Greddy turbo solution for your car. Chances are, they've got just the turbo to complement your driving style and budget.

TURBO ASSEMBLIES

AERODYNE CORPORATION

The AEROCHARGER is the world's only variable-geometry, self-contained, ball-bearing turbocharger. Components, kits, and turn-key installations are available for a variety of applications.

APEX INTEGRATION, INC.

IHI RX-6 BB   Turbocharger Assembly

MAJESTIC TURBOCHARGERS, INC.

Remanufacture of all popular and not-so-popular models: Schwitzer, Cummins, Holset, Mack, Mitsubishi, Warner, Garrett (AiResearch), Rajay, KKK, and IHI.

Turbo balancing is available and is done within .005 grams. Balancing is available and is included in competition prepping. Spindle/Wheel lightening is available and yields up to 600 rpm drop in spool up time and up to two lbs. of extra boost at maximum turbo charge output. A complete line of superchargers and accessories for vortex systems, prochargers systems, and Prodyne is also available.

HAHN RACECRAFT

All new HRC / Mitsubishi turbos are sold with a 12-month manufacturers warranty. See table next page.

HKS

HKS offers Turbo and Sport Turbo upgrades as well as Full-Cartridge Ball Bearing GT Turbochargers. Turbo and Sport Turbo upgrades are designed to improve the efficiency of air flow, thus improving power and reducing thermal stress on engines. These upgrades also increase exhaust manifold flow and turbine shaft velocity which increases boost range capability, and allows for greater power potential.

GT Turbos

HKS and Garrett Turbochargers in Japan have collaborated to produce one of the most impressive commercial turbochargers available. Offered exclusively through HKS, GT Turbos are the first affordable true ball-bearing turbos. Standard turbochargers use bronze bushing-type bearings on the center shaft. The GT Turbos are engineered with a full ball-bearing cartridge system. Weight and friction are reduced on the center shaft allowing for quicker spool-up times and better response, thus reducing turbo lag. GT Turbo durability is equal to or greater than conventional designs.

HAHN RACECRAFT TURBOS

HRC 16G10CM2 — Runt TD05H-16G-10CM2 Turbo Assembly: Excellent for up to 350 hp. T-3 Turbine inlet. Fittings / flanges available.

HRC 16GUPGR — TD05H 16G Compressor Upgrade: Direct bolt-on upgrade for stock 1989-1994 T/E TDO5.

HRC 20GCONV — Convert 16G to 20G: Rebuild unit, replace bearings, machine for 20G, clip turbine wheel, remove internal wastegate, machine/port t/hsng, balance, and assemble.

HRC 20GUPGR — TD05-TD06H-20G Compressor Upgrade: 650 cfm @ 15 psi. Machining required (available through HRC) to mount on TDO5 center housing.

HRC 25G17CM2 — Mad Dog TD07-25G-17CM2 Turbo Assembly: 850 cfm @ 15 psi, no internal wastegate.

HRC 3000L — 3000GT/Dodge Stealth Upgrade (Left): TD04L-13G-6CM2, 360 cfm @ 15 psi (720 cfm as a pair).

HRC 3000R — 3000GT/Dodge Stealth Upgrade (Right): TDO4L-13G-6CM2, 360 cfm @ 15 psi (720 cfm as a pair).

HRC 30V18CM2 — Rabid Dog TF08L-30V-18CM2 Turbo Assembly: 1200 cfm @ 15 psi, no internal wastegate.

HRC 95TETD06 — 1995+ Talon/Eclipse 20G Turbo Upgrade: 400+hp Direct bolt-on Mitsubishi turbo; all installation components included (requires fuel system and wastegate upgrades).

RC 95TETURBO — TD05H-16G Turbo Upgrade for 1995+ Talon / Eclipse: 350 hp Direct bolt-on Mitsubishi, all installation components included (fuel pump upgrade recommended).

HRC STARCON1 — 1985-1986/87 Conquest/Starion Upgrade Turbo: Direct bolt-on TD05H-14G-8CM2, 300+ hp, 505 cfm @ 15 psi, for upgrade or service replacement.

HRC STARCON2 — 7/1987-1989 Conquest/Starion Upgrade Turbo: Direct bolt-on TD05H-14G-8CM2, 300+ hp, 505 cfm @ 15 psi, for upgrade or service replacement.

HRC SUPUPG — 1987-1992 Supra 20 G Turbo Upgrade: Economical direct bolt-on Mitsubishi performance conversion, TDO6H-20G-14CM2, 400+ hp, 650 cfm @ 15 psi.

HRC SYSTOCK — Typhoon / Syclone Service Turbo Assembly: Stock service replacement. Custom installations: T-3 inlet, 300-375 hp @ 8 psi boost (3.5-6 liters).

HRC SYUPGR — Typhoon / Syclone Turbo Upgrade: Bolt-on performance, TDO6H-20G-14CM2, 400-450 hp, 650 cfm @ 15 psi. Custom: T-3 inlet, fittings/flanges available from HRC.

HRC TEMANKIT — 1989-1994 T/E Manual Trans Turbo Install Kit: All gaskets and seals needed to install 16G upgrade, includes special 7CM2 seal ring and manifold to cyl. head gasket.

HRC TEMAUTOKIT — 1989-1994 T/E Auto TDO5 Turbo Conversion Install Kit: Includes TEMANKIT (see above) as well as all needed components to convert from stock TD04 to TDO5.

HRC TETD05 — Turbo Upgrade for 1989-1994 Talon Eclipse: The ever-popular bolt-on TDO5H-16G-7CM2, 350 hp, great response as well as top-end power.

HRC TETD0620 G — Turbo Upgrade for 1989-1994 Talon Eclipse: Direct bolt-on TDO6H-20G-7CM2C, 400+ hp, clipped turbine wheel (fuel and wastegate upgrades required).

HRC TETDOIL — 1989-1994 T/E/L Oil Line Upgrade: Converts early T/E to late-model style improved oil feed. Stainless line and fittings. Great insurance when replacing turbo.

Note: Turbocharger sizing is a very complicated process of measuring temperatures and air flow in a variety of locations to arrive at a turbo size that is suitable for a particular application. It is also a game of compromises. A larger turbo gives up bottom-end response for top-end power. A smaller turbocharger is the opposite. A properly sized turbo will offer the best compromise possible between response and power.

JIM WOLF TECHNOLOGY

It's no secret that real horsepower simply comes from making higher air flow and using it efficiently in the engine. Once the boost is raised beyond the design of the stock turbo, the compressed air's temperature rises rapidly and the exhaust manifold pressure skyrockets, causing super-heated exhaust gases to reverse direction back into the cylinder. (Without special camshafts, it can actually enter the intake runners!) Not only will this severely limit horsepower, but may damage the engine and the turbocharger.

Sport 500 Turbocharger

Bolts on without modification using all stock components. Gives 25% more air flow over stock (at same turbine inlet pressure). Offers superior spool-up compared to other turbos of this size. Preset for 12 psi base boost. Must use a boost control device for higher boost. The Sport 500 turbo upgrade offers superior spool-up characteristics with a 500 hp potential. This upgrade makes an excellent choice for good all-around performance where no internal engine mods are made.

Sport 600 Turbocharger

Significant air flow increase from 4200 rpm. Relatively good spool-up with dual POP-Charger system installed. Bolts on without modification using all stock components. The Sport 600 is designed for engines capable of up to 600 hp. They produce a significant air flow increase at moderate to high boost levels due to their low back-pressure design.

Sport 650 Turbocharger

Excellent match for JWT #400 cams and spring package. Requires exhaust pre-cats to be modified for the five-bolt mounting flange. This turbo is excellent for fully-built engines that use the JWT #400 race cams to extract full potential. Spool-up is slower to 4500 rpm, but things get real serious from there on up! Lag is eliminated completely when using the POP computer-controlled N2O system. Dual-ported wastegates are used to ensure excellent boost control at higher levels. Requires minor modification for clearance and a five-bolt exhaust flange is needed. 650 hp potential.

TURBONETICS PERFORMANCE

T3-Series Turbochargers

Available in any combination of compressor trim (including the exclusive Turbonetics Super 60) and turbine section in standard, Stage II, or Stage III turbine wheel trim. The T3-series gives you the choice of wet or dry bearing housing and dynamic or carbon seal. Blueprinted assembly is standard. With airflow ratings from 150 hp to 325 hp the Performance T3-Series is ideal for small displacement engines. Basic unit does not include wastegate -- please see "installation accessories" listed below. For specific applications, contact a Turbonetics specialist.

Part #	Description
10565	Performance T3 Turbocharger, except Super 60
10566	Super 60 Turbocharger
10567	Performance T3 Charger
10568	Super 60 Charger
10672	Polished Compressor Housing Option

NOTE: When ordering part numbers above, you must specify wet or dry bearing housing, dynamic or carbon seal, compressor and turbine trim.

Turbonetics ceramic ball-bearing turbochargers are winning races and setting new records all over the world. Rapid "spool up," excellent transient response and unequalled durability combine to make the ceramic ball-bearing turbo the ultimate turbocharger for successful race-cars and boats on tracks everywhere.

TURBONETICS PERFORMANCE

TURBINE HOUSINGS

Aspect Ratio	Part # Standard Trim	Stage II Trim	Stage III Trim
.36	20369-72	20369-02	20369-03
.48	20357-72	20357-02	20357-03
.63	20358-72	20358-02	20358-03
.82	20359-72	20359-02	20359-03

NOTE: All Turbonetics Performance T3 Series turbine housing of the same trim are physically interchangeable. (Identical pattern to late Ford 2.3L Garrett).

Compressor Trim	Comp. Housing Part #	Comp. Wheel	Part #
40	20372		20267
45	20373		20263
50	20374		20268
60	20375		20272
Super 60	20376		20324

3" inlet available on T3-Series

TURBINE WHEEL/SHAFT

Standard Trim	Stage II Trim	Stage III Trim
20279	30361	30310

Compressor Wheels

Part # Std. Shaft	Trim T3	Inducer Diameter	Major Diameter
20266	35	1.396	2.367
20267	40	1.484	2.367
20263	45	1.595	2.367
20268	50	1.674	2.367
20264	55	1.76	2.367
20272	60	1.83	2.367
SUPER 20424	60	1.9	2.367

COMPRESSOR HOUSINGS

Part #	Inlet Diameter	Part #	Inlet Diameter
20499	2.350"	20499-3	3.000"
20372	2.350"	20372-3	3.000"
20373	2.350"	20373-3	3.000"
20374	2.350"	20374-3	3.000"
20500	2.350"	20500-3	3.000"
20375	2.350"	20375-3	3.000"
20376	2.350"	20376-3	3.000"

TO4B STD. SHAFT

Model	Part #	Inducer Dia.	Major Dia.	Part #	Inlet Dia.
S	20330	1.904	2.75	20202	2.750"
SUPER-S	20394	1.904	3	20202	2.750"
T5/6	20345	2.032	2.75	20346	2.750"
V	20325	2.18	2.75	20203	2.750"
SUPER-V	20364	2.18	3	20203	2.750"
H	20235	2.298	2.75	20192	2.750"
SUPER-H	20288	2.298	3	20192	2.750"
60-1 HI-FI	20230	2.324	3	20210	2.750"
60-1	20177	2.324	3	20190	4.000"
62-1	20255	2.441	3	20249	4.000"

TO4B BIG SHAFT

Model	Part #	Inducer Dia.	Major Dia.	Part #	Inlet Dia.
SUPER-V	20364T	2.180	3.000	20203	2.750"
SUPER-H	20344T	2.298	3.000	20192	2.750"
60-1	20177T	2.324	3.000	20190	4.000"
60-1 HI-FI	20230T	2.324	3.000	20210	2.750"
62-1	20255T	2.441	3.000	20249	4.000"

TO4E

Model	Part #	Inducer Dia.	Major Dia.	Part #	Inlet Dia.
40	30373	1.870	2.950	30425	3.000"
46	30374	2.003	2.950	30426	2.750"
46	30374	2.003	2.950	30427	3.000"
50	30375	2.122	3.000	30428	4.000"
54	30376	2.170	2.950	30429	2.750"
57	30377	2.230	2.950	30430	2.750"
57	30377	2.230	2.950	30431	3.000"
60	30378	2.290	2.950	30432	3.000"

T-SERIES BIG SHAFT

Model	Part #	Inducer Dia.	Major Dia.	Part #	Inlet Dia.
TS04	30335	2.300	3.304	20450	4.000"
T-61	30423	2.382	3.544	20498	4.000"
T-64	30325	2.490	3.670	20451	4.000"
T-66	30327	2.580	3.584	20452	4.000"
T-70	30329	2.720	3.850	20453	4.000"
T-72	30336	2.840	4.030	20454	4.000"
T-76	30372	3.020	4.030	20466	4.000"

Now available in the T3 series and the popular T3/T4 hybrid series in addition to the standard TO4B/TO4E, 60 Series and "T- series."

TURBONETICS PERFORMANCE

T3/T4 BEARING HOUSINGS

	Part #	Shaft	Water Connection	Size
WET	20371	Big Shaft		3/8" FPT
	20234	Standard		3/8" FPT
	20234-2	Standard		16mm
	20234-1	Standard		18mm
DRY	20360	Standard		
	20327	Big Shaft		

Aspect Ratio	Trim Configuration	Turbonetics Part #	Garrett Part #
.36	Standard	20369-72	430410-0011
	Stage II	20369-02	N/A
	Stage III	20369-03	N/A
.48	Standard	20357-72	431262-0012
	Stage II	20357-02	N/A
	Stage III	20357-03	N/A
.63	Standard	20358-72	430225-0013
	Stage II	20358-02	N/A
	Stage III	20358-03	N/A
.82	Standard	20376-72	N/A
	Stage II	20376-02	N/A
	Stage III	20376-03	N/A

T4 SERIES ON CENTER TURBINE HOUSING SUMMARY

Aspect Ratio	Trim	Turbonetics Part #	Garrett Part #
.58	N	20258-1	407414-0004
	O	20258-2	407414-0024
	P	20258-3	407414-0034
	Q	20258-4	N/A
.69	N	20269-1	407414-0003
	O	20269-2	407414-0023
	P	20269-3	407414-0033
	Q	20269-4	N/A
.81	O	20281-2	407414-0022
	P	20281-3	407414-0032
	Q	20281-4	N/A
.96	O	20296-2	407414-0021
	P	20296-3	407414-0031
	Q	20296-4	N/A
1.30	P	20237-3	442534-0001
	Q	20237-4	N/A

TANG/UNDIVIDED

Aspect Ratio	Trim	Turbonetics Part #	Garrett Part #
.50	N	30252-1	407264-0008
	O	30252-2	407264-0028
.58	O	30253-2	407264-0027
	P	30253-3	407264-0037
.68	O	30254-2	407264-0026
.68	P	30254-3	N/A
.81	O	30255-2	407264-0021
	P	30257-3	407264-0031
	Q	30257-4	N/A
.96	O	30258-2	407264-0022
	P	30258-3	407264-0032
	Q	30258-4	N/A
1.71	P	30263-3	407264-0039
1.71	Q	30263-4	N/A

TANG/DIVIDED

Aspect Ratio	Trim	Turbonetics Part #	Garrett Part #
.58	O	30253-2D	410401-0023
	P	30253-3D	407263-0036
.70	O	30254-2D	410401-0024
	P	30254-3D	410401-0034
	Q	30254-4D	N/A
.84	O	30255-2D	407316-0043
	P	30257-3D	410401-0035
	Q	30257-4D	N/A
1.00	O	30256-2D	407316-0022
	P	30256-3D	407263-0033
	Q	30256-4D	N/A
1.15	O	30259-2D	407316-0021
	P	30259-3D	432183-0002
	Q	30259-4D	N/A
1.32	P	30261-3D	407263-0035
	Q	30261-4D	N/A
1.52	P	30262-3D	407263-0039
1.52	P	30262-4D	N/A

TANG/DIVIDED ("Euro" Style Small Inlet)

Aspect Ratio	Trim	Turbonetics Part #	Garrett Part #
.84	O	30456-2D	407402-0051
	P	30456-3D	407402-0033
	Q	30456-4D	N/A
1.00	O	30457-2D	407402-0050
	P	30457-3D	407402-0032
	Q	30457-4D	N/A

The NASA-inspired angular contact, ceramic ball-bearing design (patent pending) practically eliminates thrust bearing and operational surge failures. The ceramic ball-bearing system can safely handle 50 times more thrust loading than conventional turbochargers, making it ideal for severe transients and extreme pressure ratio applications.

All Turbonetics ceramic ball-bearing turbochargers are manufactured to the strictest aerospace standards by the most experienced technicians in the trade. Quality control is maintained throughout the precision assembly process to assure adherence to the closest tolerances in the industry. All ceramic ball-bearing turbochargers are VSR balanced at rated speeds to less than .05 G -- the toughest specification in the performance turbocharger industry.

Turbonetics ball-bearing turbochargers are matched and manufactured for your specific application. Contact a Turbonetics Turbo Specialist for a computer-generated analysis and a recommendation on the hardest pulling, quickest spooling, most durable turbocharger available to the performance aftermarket.

T3/T4 Hybrid Turbochargers

Turbonetics presents a complete line-up T3/T4 Hybrid turbochargers consisting of a T3 turbine section, (standard, Stage II, or Stage III trim) and a T4 compressor section (T04B trim or T04E trim). The T3 / T4 Hybrid offers the low inertia and fast boost response of the lightweight T3 turbine wheel and the high airflow characteristics of the T4 compressor family, making the T3/T4 Hybrid the turbo of choice for high-performance "import" applications.

For the ultimate street/strip performance import enthusiast. The Turbonetics ceramic ball-bearing T3/T4 Hybrid series offers the fastest spool-up available. Coupled with extreme durability, the ceramic ball-bearing concept provides unparalleled performance never before experienced by the import turbocharging aftermarket.

All T3/T4 hybrid's are custom matched for specific applications. Airflow ratings from 250 hp to 450 hp are available. Contact a Turbonetics Turbo Specialist for application assistance and availability.

Part #	Description
10673	T3/T4 Hybrid Turbo Assembly, std. TO4B
10674	As above, less turbine housing
10675	As above, CHRA only
10676	T3/T4 Hybrid Turbo Assembly, TO4E/TO4B "Super"
10677	As above, less turbine housing
10678	As above, CHRA only
10660	Ceramic Ball-Bearing Option, T3/T4 std. shaft

Exclusive "T-Series" Competition Turbochargers!

For serious competitors only! Turbonetics offers custom-matched and custom-built turbochargers designed to get you across the finish line first! Designated the "T-SERIES," this turbo family incorporates the latest "state of the art" turbocharger aerodynamics and the toughest durability available to the maximum performance engine builder.

With a wide range of flow capacities (TSO4, T61, T64, T66, T70, T72, and T76) capable of supporting 600 to 1200 hp with a "single" turbo, the T-SERIES is the only true custom turbo family designed exclusively for racing applications!

All T-SERIES turbos are custom built to your specific application and include the Turbonetics "Tuff-Turbo" option. Dynamic seal is standard. Your choice of O or P trim turbine; .58, .69, .81, or .96 A/R on-center turbine housing; dry or water-jacketed bearing housing (specify when ordering). 1.30 A/R on-center and a full range of tangential style turbine housing are optional. "Q" trim and the exclusive Turbonetics ceramic ball-bearing option are available. Contact a Turbonetics Turbo Specialist for a computer generated analysis of your application and get the turbo that will put you in the winners circle!!

Tuff-Turbo Option (Standard on 68-1 And T-Series Turbochargers)

Durability can be enhanced greatly by ordering the Tuff-Turbo option for your new turbocharger. The Tuff-Turbo option is available for all T4 series, 60-1, and 62-1 turbochargers. This Turbonetics exclusive option utilizes O, P, or Q trim turbine wheel shafts, and the "stagger gap" piston ring. Specially developed for competition applications, the Tuff-Turbo option includes the big shaft with a larger bearing structure, larger thrust bearing, and a left-handed nut. The big shaft virtually eliminates the destructive shaft motion normally associated with high boost. The Tuff-Turbo option is available with dynamic seal only.

Part # 10570 Tuff-Turbo option (add to price of standard turbo or CHRA)

"Q" Trim Option

Recognizing the need for a higher flow capacity turbine to match the capabilities of the 68-1 and the T-Series compressor wheels, Turbonetics has developed the "Q" trim. Incorporating all of the features of the Tuff-Turbo option, the "Q" trim represents the largest diameter turbine wheel that can be mated to a properly machined TO4B turbine housing. The result is a 12 - 15% increase in choke-flow limitation which significantly reduces turbine backpressure.

TURBONETICS PERFORMANCE "T-SERIES" COMPETITION TURBOCHARGERS

Part #	Description
10681	TSO4 Turbocharger Assembly
10682	As above, less turbine housing
10683	As above, CHRA only
10684	T61/T64/T66/T70/T72 Turbocharger Assembly
10685	As above, less turbine housing
10686	As above, CHRA only
10689	T76 Turbocharger Assembly
10690	As above, less turbine housing
10691	As above, CHRA only
10680	Polished comp. hsg. option, T-Series
10573	T-Series "Q" trim option, CHRA only
10577	T-Series "Q" trim option, turbo assembly
10661	T-Series Ceramic Ball-Bearing option

Turbine Wheels

Model	Part #	Trim	Exducer Diameter	Major Diameter
T3	20279	Standard	1.898"	2.319"
	30361	Stage II	2.122"	2.559"
	30310	stage III	2.229"	2.559"
T4 std. shaft	20301	N	2.071"	2.922"
	20302	O	2.296"	2.922"
	20303	P	2.544"	2.922"
T4 big shaft	20460	O	2.296"	2.922"
	20333	P	2.544"	2.922"
	20366	Q	2.693"	3.111"

Part #	Description
10573	"Q" trim option (add to price of Tuff-Turbo CHRA)
10577	"Q" trim option (add to price of Tuff Turbo Turbocharger)
20366	"Q" trim big shaft Turbine Wheel Assembly
20349	"Q" trim heat shroud (must be used with above)

Turbin-end piston ring oil leakage has plagued the turbocharger industry since "day one." Conventional piston rings utilize a standard ring-gap configuration for ease of manufacture and installation. Such rings, by design, leave an open path through the exposed gap for any oil reaching it to pass into the turbine section. The result is smoke, raw oil leakage, oil consumption, messy oil on tracks, etc. These problems are further aggravated by turbo installs with marginal oil drain provisions, high turbo lube oil flow, low oil viscosity, high oil temps, and low-mounted turbochargers.

The new unique Turbonetics Stagger Gap piston rings minimizes these concerns by offering a closed gap path to any oil attempting to escape from the bearing housing. This simple but effective design is accomplished by a stepped-end cut instead of the conventional through-cut utilized by stock ring manufacturers. Normal pressure differential between the bearing housing and the turbine section force the opposing faces of the Stagger Gap ring together, thus eliminating the open path normally encountered.

Stagger Gap rings are standard in all Turbonetics performance turbochargers and are fully interchangeable with standard factory rings for all T2, T25, T28, T3, and T4 production turbos.

Part #	Description
20440	Stagger Gap Turbine End Piston Ring For T3, T4, and Tuff-Turbo
20479	Stagger Gap Turbine End Piston Ring For T2, T25, and T28

WATER INJECTION

ERL LIMITED

Aquamist is ERL's latest generation of water-injection equipment. The main function of these systems is to suppress detonation caused by high temperature and pressure developed within the combustion chamber when the effective compression ratio has been taken beyond the auto-ignition point by either a turbo or a supercharger. Water, with its high latent heat content, is extremely effective for controlling not only the onset of detonation but also the production of oxides of nitrogen in the modern leanburn engines. ERL's latest products are designed with great care to ensure each system meets the highest standards of both electronic and mechanical reliability.

The concept of injecting water into the internal combustion engine has been around for over 50 years. But the desire to extract more power from the standard production engine has increased at a neck-breaking speed. ERL has just revived this old principle, applying the latest techniques in both electronic and mechanical engineering to take water injection into the next millennium.

Water exists mainly in a liquid state because that is its most stable inter-molecular structure. When we apply heat energy to it, its molecules begin to expand. A great deal of heat is absorbed during this process owing to water's specific heat capacity of approximately 4.2 kJ/(kg.K). At 100°C the water begins to evaporate, at which point a large amount of heat energy is consumed in sustaining the process. The latent heat of evaporation is 2256 kJ/kg, approximately six times more than gasoline!

Because of its huge specific- and latent-heat capacity, water is the perfect liquid for regulating excess heat under certain engine-operating conditions, for example induction charge air cooling; but its biggest contribution is inside the combustion chamber where, under excessive loading, pre-ignition and detonation can otherwise occur. Such abnormal combustion is particularly common in forced-induction engines, where exhaust temperature can exceed 1100°C!

SYSTEM 1 and SYSTEM 1s consist of an ERL high-pressure electro-magnetic water pump, adjustable pressure switch, plus all the necessary hardware to form the basis of a starter kit.

SYSTEM 2s is a fully-mappable water-injection, pre-pressurized system, equipped with diagnostic circuitry, able to detect blocked water-jet and abnormal operation problems.

SYSTEM 2c is designed for use with a third party engine management system. The kit provides all the necessary hardware to interface with the PWM output signal.

MF2 injector driver is a small controller that will go beyond what any EPROM chip can ever dream of. It can control four high-impedance injectors to flow enough fuel for up to an extra 200 hp!

TURBO MANIFOLDS

X-TEC MOTORSPORTS

X-TEC Motorsports Honda/Acura tubular turbo manifolds are designed to be used with either T3, or T3-T4 hybrid turbos in cars with or without air conditioning. The manifolds are manufactured with mandrel-bent tubular exhaust runners, and 1/2" thick machined flanges. They can be used with either internal or external wastegates and come standard with mount for the Turbonetics "Deltagate" wastegate. If you plan to use a different wastegate (Turbonetics "Racegate," HKS wastegates, etc.), mounting for these and others can be made to order. Each manifold comes complete with both gaskets for installation. Available with ceramic coating, or bare for your choice of coating.

REV HARD

Rev Hard cast manifolds are made from high-quality, ductile-high nickel iron. These cast and tubular manifolds are simply the best turbo manifolds in the market. These manifolds are not the typical log-type manifolds. Rev Hard can also custom make tubular manifolds made of carbon-cast steel and stainless steel that are fully warranted against cracking. Used in some of the fastest Hondas around, these manifolds give maximum flow for higher boost and horsepower levels.

Available in cast iron, cast tubular steel, stainless steel, equal length tuned stainless, or mild steel.

RPS

Turbo Manifolds Custom made to specific applications. Supra, Civic, VTEC and more.

GREDDY PERFORMANCE

Greddy Performance offers full stainless turbo manifolds for popular Japanese turbocharged vehicles.

TURBOCHARGER INSTALLATION ACCESSORIES

TURBONETICS

V-Band Turbine Discharge
Turbonetics can provide modified slip-joint TO4B tangential turbine housings with V-band discharge configurations. V-band sets are available in 2-1/2" or 3" diameter for any standard slip-joint housing. Components are available individually or as an assembly, including welding of discharge flange to the turbine housing.

Part #	Description
10597-25	2-1/2" V-band Turbine Discharge Set, installed
10597-30	3" V-band Turbine Discharge Set, installed
30230	Housing Weld Flange, 2-1/2"
20244	Housing Weld Flange, 3"

Part #	Description
30231	Tube Weld Flange, 2-1/2"
30241	Tube Weld Flange, 3"
30232	Clamp Assembly, 2-1/2"
30242	Clamp Assembly, 3"

TO4B Turbine Inlet Flange

20167	1/2" thick weldable steel alloy, 2-1/4" center hole

TO4B Turbine Discharge Weld Flange

20168	5" OD X 2-1/2" ID
20174	5" OD X 3" ID 5/16" thick weldable steel alloy (for all on-center units)

Housing Gaskets

Part #	Description
30263	T3 Turbine Inlet Gasket, stainless steel
30143	T4 Turbine Inlet Gasket, stainless steel
30142	T4 Turbine Discharge Gasket
30142S	T4 Turbine Discharge Gasket, stainless steel
30238	T3/T4 Oil Inlet Gasket
30141	T3/T4 Oil Drain Gasket
20142A	Deltagate "Fire-Ring" Flange Gasket
20396A	Racegate "Fire-Ring" Flange Gasket
20217	Pressure Plenum (Part #20200) Flange Gasket

Installation Fittings

Part #	Description
30133	3/8" MPT x 5/8" Hose Fitting, straight
30134	3/8" MPT x 5/8" Hose Fitting, 90°
30224	"H" Fitting 5/8" Hose
30244	1/2" MPT x 5/8" Hose Fitting, straight
30245	1/2" MPT x 5/8" Hose Fitting, 90°
30306	Brass Fitting 1/8" MPT x 5/32" Hose, straight
30307	Brass Fitting 1/8" MPT x 5/32" Hose, 90°
30308	Brass Fitting 5/32" Hose x 5/32" Hose x 5/32" Hose, "T"

T3/T4 Oil Drain Flange

Part #	Description
20259	1/2" FPT, straight
20382	3/8" FPT, straight

T3/T4 Turbocharger Clamps/Clamp Set

Dress up your turbo with Gold-Lustre Finish compressor and turbine clamps/clamp set complete with self-locking plated compressor fasteners and grade 5 turbine bolts. Locking compressor fasteners and unique turbine clamps eliminate the need for awkward lockplates.

Part #	Description
20193	TO4B Compressor Clamp
20198	TO3 Compressor Clamp
20194	TO3/TO4B Turbine Clamp, standard
20195	TO3/TO4B Turbine Clamp, crescent
20207	TO4B Compressor Fastener, 5/16 USC
20208	TO3 Compressor Fastener, metric
20209	TO4B Turbine Fastener, 5/16 USC
20206	TO3 Turbine Fastener, metric
10413	Complete TO4B Clamp Set
10414	Complete TO3 Clamp Set

T-Bolt Clamps

Made of heavy-duty stainless steel these are many times stronger than conventional clamps! Inner band protects hose. Measures 3/4" wide. Includes self-locking nut.

Part #	Hose Inner	Size Dia.	Range (Dia.)
30275-175	1.75"	1.94"	- 2.25"
30275-200	2.00"	2.19"	- 2.44"
30275-225	2.25"	2.44"	- 2.75"
30275-238	2 3/8"	2.58"	- 2.83"
30275-250	2.50"	2.63"	- 2.94"
30275-275	2.75"	2.94"	- 3.25"
30275-300	3.00"	3.19"	- 3.50"
30275-325	3.25"	3.44"	- 3.80"
30275-400	4.00"	4.19"	- 4.55"

Silicone Connects
Silicone 90° Elbows

Part #	Size
30447	2"
30448	2-1/4"
30449	2-1/2"
30450	2-3/8"
30451	2-3/4"
30452	3"

Silicone 45° Elbows

Part #	Size
30441	2"
30442	2-1/4"
30443	2-3/8"
30444	2-1/2"
30445	2-3/4"
30446	3"

Silicone Transition Hoses

Part #	Size
30436	2" to 2-1/4"
30437	2" to 2-3/8"
30438	2" to 2-1/2"
30439	2-1/2" to 2-3/4"
30440	2-1/2" to 3"

Silicone Hump Hoses

Part #	Size
30379	2"
30433	2-1/4"
30434	2-3/8"
30380	2-1/2"
30312	2-3/4"
30435	3"

Silicone Hose Couplings

Top quality high-strength, high-temperature hose couplings. Multi-layered fluro-silicone with fiberglass reinforcements. Additional sizes and lengths are available.

Silicone Hose, standard, orange, 1/8" wall

Part # 2 ft. long	Part # 3 ft. long	Inner Diameter
3012862-200	30352-200	2"
3016162-225	30352-225	2-1/4"
3030462-238	30352-238	2-3/8"
3017262-250	30352-250	2-1/2"
3012962-275	30352-275	2-3/4"
3016262-300	30352-300	3"
3030262-400	30352-400	4"

Silicone Hose, heavy duty, blue, 1/4" wall

Part # 2 ft. long	Part # 3 ft. long	Inner Diameter
30282	30353-200	2"
30283	30353-225	2-1/4"
30305	30353-238	2-3/8"
30284	30353-250	2-1/2"
30285	30353-275	2-3/4"
30286	30353-300	3"
30453	30353-350	3-1/2"
30303	30353-400	4"

Performance T3 Installation Accessories

Part #	Description
20365	T3 Turbine inlet weld flange
30263	T3 Turbine inlet gasket
20367	T3 Turbine discharge weld flange
30298	T3 Swing valve assembly
20368	T3 Swing valve discharge flange
30314	T3 Adjustable swing valve actuator, single port
30326	T3 Adjustable swing valve actuator, dual port

DOWN PIPES

HAHN RACECRAFT

By eliminating the O2 housing and offering a true 3-inch path from the turbo outlet to the catalytic converter

HRC DOWNPIPES

Part #	Description
ATR TE114	1989-1994 TE AWD 3" stainless exhaust
ATR TE114A	1995+ TE AWD 3" stainless exhaust
ATR TE115	1989-1994 T/E FWD 3" stainless exhaust
ATR TE115A	1995+ T/E FWD 3" stainless exhaust
GRE 109406	1995+ TE FWD exhaust
GRE 109407	1995+ T/E AWD 60-130mm single-tip exhaust
GRE 109408	1989-1991 T/E/L FWD 60-130mm exhaust
GRE 109409	1989-1994 T/E/L AWD 60-130mm exhaust
GRE 109412	1995+ TE non-turbo 50-130mm exhaust
HKS LET-M02	1989-1994 Talon Eclipse Laser 60mm FWD exhaust
HKS LET-M03	1989-1994 Talon Eclipse Laser 60mm AWD exhaust
HRC TE8994SS	1989-1994 TE AWD 3" stainless exhaust
HRC TE95SS	1995+ TE AWD 3" stainless exhaust
HRC TEAPIPE	3" Piping with Flanges, misc. length
HRC TECA3MOD	Modify 3" Exh. for 3" Cat. Convertor
HRC TECAT	T/E Max Flow Catalytic Convertor, 3" In/Out
HRC TECATF	1995+ T/E FWD MaxFlow Catalytic Convertor, 3" In/Out
HRC TECATFLNG	3" Weld-On Flange (for adding 3" convertor to existing three-inch systems)
HRC TECATG	Max Flow Catalytic Convertor, Talon / Eclipse, 2.5" In/Out
HRC TEDWNPIPE	1989+ T/E 3" stainless Eliminator downpipe
HRC TEDWNPIPEF	1995+ T/E FWD 3" stainless Eliminator downpipe
HRC TEDWNPIPEFH	1995+ T/E FWD 3" stainless Eliminator downpipe, HKS Wastegate
HRC TEDWNPIPEFS	1989+ T/E FWD 3" stainless Eliminator downpipe, Deltagate equipped, stock turbo cars only
HRC TEDWNPIPEH	1989+ T/E AWD 3" stainless Eliminator downpipe, HKS Wastegate
HRC TEDWNPIPEJ	1989+ T/E AWD 3" stainless Eliminator Jr. downpipe
HRC TEDWNPIPEJF	1995+ T/E FWD 3" stainless Eliminator Jr. downpipe
HRC TEDWNPIPES	1989+ T/E AWD 3" stainless Eliminator downpipe, Deltagate equipped, for stock turbo cars only

inlet, Hahn Racecraft has designed one of the highest flowing downpipes. There is an added benefit also. Through careful redesigning of the wastegate port and forward section, Hahn Racecraft has developed a downpipe which positively controls boost creep and overboost problems associated with upgraded versions of the Talon and Eclipse! Saves money otherwise spent on porting a stock 02 housing which would never flow as much as this pipe — no matter what!

Not to be confused with other lesser engineered three-inch downpipe designs which actually worsen boost creep or do not replace the O2 housing! To prevent exhaust/turbo system strain due to drivetrain movement on rubber mounts, a robust flex-section is provided for ultimate durability. This pipe's modular design allows interchangeable options for catalytic converters or off-road configurations. Combine it with HRC's High Flow convertor and three-inch stainless exhaust for a bumper-to-bumper three-inch system!

Meticulously hand-crafted from mandrel-bent, 16 gauge 304 stainless steel, it offers the added benefit of eliminating the highly restrictive (and heavy!) cast iron O2 sensor housing (of course, a screw in socket for your O2 sensor is provided).

Eliminator Jr. Downpipe

HRC took its best-selling HKS wastegate equipped Eliminator downpipe and made it better! By low mounting the wastegate under the turbocharger, this latest version of the noted 3" Eliminator series offers excellent engine compartment clearance with all components. Allows complete retention of stock left side cooling fan for air conditioning use. Forget about boost creep forever. This is the cure, and like all Eliminators, it also replaces the restrictive 02 housing for mega flow while offering modular catalytic converter options as well as a huge flex joint. TIG welded, mandrel bent, 16 gauge 304 stainless, naturally. Due to engine mount differences, the Low-Mount fits 1995-1999 DSM only.

Super 16g and Super 20g Turbo Upgrades

HRC starts with a long tapered inlet (2-1/2" to 3") for zero turbulence and great mounting nut access. From there on back it's pure 3" Eliminator, with a big flex joint for excellent durability of turbo and exhaust system components. Modular catalytic converter options give you flexibility both now and in the future.

If you're looking for the flow of an open exhaust system, but still have to maintain emissions legality and reasonable sound levels, Hahn Racecraft has the solution. The company's high-flow three-inch in/out catalytic converter bolts directly to the Eliminator downpipe, and provides an increase in airflow of 30% over the stock catalytic converter. This is a cat specifically designed for high-performance applications, not a stock replacement type with three inch tubes welded in like some others.

Its outlet is a three-inch / three-bolt flange which bolts directly to the three-inch stainless-steel exhaust system (flange available separately if you already have a three-inch system). The three-bolt flanges enable you to easily install and remove the cat to allow the use of an off-road pipe in appropriate situations. When used in conjunction with the HRC Eliminator downpipe and exhaust, your Talon or Eclipse can have a true three-inch bumper-to-bumper exhaust system! Much quieter (and legal!) than running no cat and flows almost as much!

This converter is also 50 state legal and warranted! When using the HRC Eliminator downpipe with a stock-type catalytic converter, the HRC Powercone will provide the proper tapered non-turbulent transition to the catalytic converter's smaller inlet. Beware of other downpipes which do not offer this option for providing a proper transition to the smaller inlet of a stock converter. TIG welded from tapered 304 stainless tubing, this part also carries a lifetime warranty.

INTERCOOLERS

APEX INTEGRATION

The unique design of this intercooler has the fins at the base of the delta wedge tightly packed, while the fins at the top of the delta wedge are loosely packed. This allows the channeled air flow at the base of the delta wedge to cool more air while the loosely packed fins on top prevent any unnecessary wind turbulence.

Because of it's purpose-built front mount design, all the fins are extended to the same length at the rear of the intercooler. This allows the air to pass through without causing wind turbulence in the rear of the intercooler and cool the remaining radiator and engine. The RS Series incorporates the same technology but adds a new dimension of performance with its thicker core sizes.

Part #	Application
532-KM02	1995-1998 Eclipse Turbo I/C Kit (with silicone)
532-KM03	1995-1998 Eclipse Turbo (upper piping)
531-T002	1993-1998 Supra I/C Kit (lower piping only)
531-A020	GTR I/C Core 2
531-A030	Silvia R/S I/C Core 3
531-B010	Tank 1
531-B020	Tank 2
531-B040	Tank 3
531-B030	Tank 4
531-B070	Tank 6
531-B060	Tank 7
531-B050	Tank 8
531-B150	Tank 15 (new version for C2 Core)
531-C880	90° 60mm elbow
531-C910	90° 70mm elbow
531-C890	135° 60mm elbow
531-C891	120° 60mm elbow
531-C940	90° 80mm elbow
531-C870	45° 60mm elbow
599-A001	Cap Plug
9920-0280	Rubber Transition 65-70mm
9920-0450	Rubber Transition 70-90mm

STILLEN

If you thought all the possible power improvements had already been developed for the Mitsubishi Eclipse Turbo, think again! Stillen has upped the size of the intercooler, reduced the pressure drop, reshaped the internal contour, and converted it to an in-your-face front mount to be the absolute best. These developments, combined with a new state-of-the-art intercooler core, will extract more reliable-horsepower from a 1995-1998 Eclipse GST than any other intercooler previously offered.

The new size (20" L X 6" H X 4.5" W), translates into more cooling efficiency. As intake temperatures are reduced, more air and fuel molecules can be drawn in per intake stroke (referred to as a denser charge). This creates a more potent mixture for the power stroke (read more horsepower) even at the same relative boost level.

HAHN RACECRAFT

The largest, most efficient sidemount intercooler ever developed for the 1995-1999 Eclipse and Talon is now available from Hahn RaceCraft. HRC completely redesigned the intercooler upgrade, and the result is what you would expect: ultimate performance and exceptional quality.

HRC started with a super-efficient core specifically designed for this intercooler, so efficient that it produces only one-PSI pressure drop at 400 horsepower of airflow! The core was repositioned to take advantage of all the room available in the fenderwell. Trick fabricated sheetmetal end tanks were added for ultra-light weight. The outlet tube was straightened out for optimum flow while making it a full 2-1/4" to match aftermarket intercooler pipes. And the mounts were redesigned to take stress off the intercooler pipes. Front-mount intercoolers are also available!

Stock intercooler piping is designed for stock power levels and not much more! The increased airflow your engine achieves through exhaust and air intake upgrades quickly outflows the stock pipes. Replacing them will always net a gain in power.

HRC intercooler pipe upgrades are the highest quality available, engineered for power and torque, amply sized yet not oversized. All HRC pipes feature mandrel bent, TIG welded construction, and are powder-coated gloss black for long-lasting beauty. And you can upgrade them in stages or buy them as a set, always enjoying the best in HRC performance at the right level for your car. They also directly fit stock, HRC, and other intercooler upgrades, as well as offering options for any turbo combination.

Stage II Upper and Lower Pipe Upgrades

For the ultimate flow and appearance, add HRC's Stage II upper and lower pipe upgrades! The lower pipe replaces the stock hose (and on some cars, plastic silencer) from the turbo to the intercooler, and can be ordered two ways: to work with stock and stock-type compressor outlet turbos, or to work with HRC and other HRC-type 16G turbo upgrades!

The Stage II upper pipe completes the free flow air path from the Stage I pipe to the throttle body. With this pipe, a large reduction in turbulence and increase in airflow is realized by replacing the poorly-designed aluminum "elbow" (bolted to your car's throttle body) with a high-flowing mandrel bend.

Stage II pipes are usually used on cars with upgraded turbos and an attitude, but are also effective on stock turbo cars as well as for those who crave a more muscular underhood appearance.

HRC STAGE II UPPER & LOWER PIPES	
Part #	Description
HRC 89-94TEIC	1989-1994 Talon/Eclipse Laser Side Mount Intercooler
HRC 89-94TEICFM	1989-1994 Talon/Eclipse Front Mount Intercooler
HRC 95 TEIC	1995+ Talon/Eclipse Side Mount Intercooler
HRC 95 TEICFM	1995-1996 Talon/Eclipse Front Mount Intercooler
HRC 957TEICFM	1997+ Talon/Eclipse Front Mount Intercooler
HRC 95TEIP1	Stage 1 Intercooler Pipe Mounts Greddy Type S or Modified 1st Gen BOV
HRC 95TEIP2	1995-1999 Talon/Eclipse Stage 2 Intercooler Pipe Upper, replaces throttle body elbow
HRC 95TEIP3	1995-1999 Talon/Eclipse Stage 2 Intercooler Pipe Lower, for Stock, HRC Super 16G and 20G turbos
HRC 95TEIP4	Stage 2 Intercooler Pipe Lower, for HRC conventional 16G and like setups (Super Turbos use HRC 95TEIP3)
HRC 95TEIP5	I/C 1995-1999 Talon/Eclipse Piping, full set of three, Stock T-25 and HRC Super Series Turbos
HRC 95TEIP6	I/C Piping, full set of three, for HRC and similar conventional 16G turbos which utilize HRC type J-pipe

GREDDY

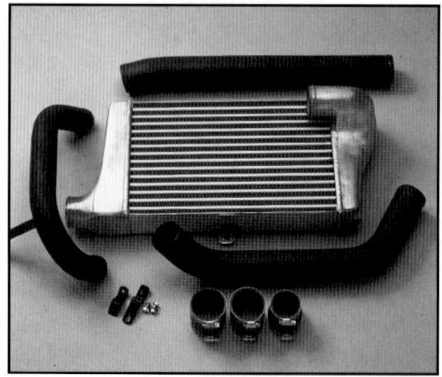

Greddy 1995-1997 Mitsubishi Eclipse front-mount intercooler kit EO#D-397-2 is an upgraded intercooler that supplies the proper efficiency for most street-driven vehicles. This intercooler allows less of a pressure drop than the factory unit, thus allowing better performance to be realized from the turbocharger. Since it is front mounted, maximum fresh air volume is taken advantage of so maximum calories per hour can be dissipated. The 1995-96 models require some trimming due to the difference in front openings.

Greddy also has kits for 1992-2000 Honda Civic EX/Si SOHC, 1999-2000 Honda Civic Si DOHC, 1994-2000 Acura Integra GSR, Toyota Supra and MR2, Nissan 300ZX twin turbo, 1987-1999 Mazda RX-7 turbo.

HKS

The HKS intercooler systems are designed to rapidly and consistently draw heat away from the intake charge by passing it through what is best described as a radiator for air. This produces power gains throughout the powerband, and reduces thermal stress in turbocharged engines.

Intercooler Pipe Upgrades

Where entire intercooler upgrades are not available, HKS offers intercooler pipe upgrades designed to reduce pressure loss through OEM intercooler systems. HKS offers individually-welded intercooler assemblies as well as miscellaneous cores and end tanks all designed to complete any custom intercooler system. HKS tube and fin intercooler cores offer maximum heat dissipation with minimum pressure loss.

JIM WOLF TECHNOLOGY

300ZX Twin Turbo Intercoolers

Diamond Blackstone core material makes this one of the most efficient intercoolers available. These intercoolers are a direct bolt-in replacement.

MZ320-IC000   300ZX Twin Turbo Intercoolers

BLITZ

REMIX Intercoolers

One of the best ways to increase the horsepower on a turbocharged engine is the addition or upgrade of your vehicle's intercooler. The Blitz REMIX utilizes its innovative offset fin core to provide maximum cooling ability and to minimize pressure drop. Blitz offers a complete line of factory replacement intercoolers for selective vehicles. They also offer custom-sized intercoolers for custom applications.

REV HARD

The Rev Hard intercoolers come with custom cast-end tanks. These cores are familiar to the world's fastest Hondas. These come in three sizes and are also available in a polished finish.

Size 24.5" x 3.5" x 8": This core is Rev Hard's most popular and is seen in most fast Hondas. We've seen these cores reduce intake charge and stay efficient at 30 psi of boost and above 500 horsepower levels.

Size 18.5" x 3.5" x 8": This core is popular with Rev Hard's 1.6 Civic/CRX kits. Efficiency is maintained at 20 psi of boost and good up to 350 horsepower.

Size 29" x 3.5" x 7": This is an extra-wide intercooler with the same efficiency as Rev Hard's 500 hp intercooler. This intercooler gives an extra "intimidating" look.

Rev Hard intercoolers are also available in these sizes: 28 x 10 x 2.75, 25 x 10 x 2.75, 25 x 5 x 2.75.

WASTEGATES

The wastegate is commonly a spring-loaded valve fitted just before the turbine. The valve opens and bleeds off excess exhaust pressure when the compressor reaches a pre-determined boost. The wastegate performs three jobs: 1. Controls boost to keep the engine intact; 2. Controls the speed of the turbo to keep it from self-destructing; and 3. Helps tailor the turbocharger's performance to the requirements of the engine.

GREDDY

Power without control isn't performance. It's dangerous. The wastegate is a critical component of Greddy's total power system. Greddy's precision, premium-crafted wastegates help ensure maximum power, flexibility, responsiveness, and safety.

Greddy's CNC-machined wastegates never "waste" exhaust-gas energy. The Type S wastegates are designed for street/performance applications. They're ideal for smaller engines (1.6 to 2.0 liters) and smaller turbocharger applications. The Type R is for larger-capacity turbos and engines in the 300+ hp range. The Type C is ideal for "highly motivated" vehicles of between 400 and 1000 hp.

HAHN RACECRAFT

Wastegate Actuator Upgrade for Stock 1995-1999 T-25 Turbo

In HRC's endless experimentation on the DSM, it discovered that a widely held belief was in fact only partially true: that the stock T-25 turbo "ran out of steam" in the midrange and upper RPM ranges due to being too small. In reality, more was going on. HRC uncovered an easy-to-fix problem: at higher RPM, exhaust pressure would force the wastegate valve open due to inadequate spring pressure in the stock wastegate actuator! The wastegate would open and limit boost anyway, even if you removed the entire boost pressure signal from the actuator (which, of course, is all a boost controller can do!) This actuator package is easy to install and will give a major wallop in seat-of-the-pants torque. Combine it with a boost controller for even better results!

HKS

HKS External Poppet Type Wastegates are available in standard and racing configurations. Both feature stainless valves, die-cast mounting bases, valve seats, fully sealed shafts, high temperature resistant diaphragms, and large outlet pockets. Standard wastegates available with 40mm valve and racing wastegates available with 50mm valves.

The GT Wastegate features a large 60mm diameter valve for use with vehicles producing extreme horsepower levels. The GT wastegate spring is engineered to provide ample resistance to the excessive exhaust pressure developed by these high-horsepower applications. These features help to decrease turbo lag and prevent spikes in boost pressure. Despite its complex structure, the GT Wastegate is very compact and its adjustable V-band structure provides tremendous flexibility for custom installations.

BLITZ

To achieve maximum boost response, a properly selected wastegate size is important. Blitz offers several different sizes for you to choose from. Blitz wastegate utilizes a die-cast housing with external heat sink fins to withstand high temperature operating conditions. All waste-gates can be used in both street and race applications. Different valve spring rates are available.

TURBONETICS

Deltagate Mark II

Designed for durability, with a 1.250" stainless-steel valve, nomex/silicone diaphragm, and a unique "stand-off" actuator section, the Deltagate can control boost on engines that develop 350 - 400 hp. With the addition of a Variable Boost Control Regulator (Part #10402) the Deltagate is fully adjustable over a wide boost range.

Racegate

This high-flow wastegate will control engines that develop 900+ hp, with a 1.625" (42mm) stainless-steel valve and the proven Deltagate actuator. "Boost creep" is practically eliminated. Fully adjustable with the Variable Boost Control regulator listed below.

GREDDY'S CNC-MACHINED WASTEGATES

Part #	Description	Press Range
11501500	External Wastegate Type S	
11501528	External Wastegate Type R	0.8-1.2 kg/ cm2
11501531	External Wastegate Type R	1.1-1.5 kg/ cm2
11501534	External Wastegate Type R	1.4+ kg/ cm2
11501548	External Wastegate Type C	
11501551	External Wastegate Type C	
11501554	External Wastegate Type C	
11501560	External Wastegate Type C	High Flow
11501600	Actuator P565 11 psi	
11501610	Actuator P765 14 psi	
11900260	Spring Type-R/ C	0.8-1.2 kg/ cm2
11900261	Spring Type-R/ C	1.1-1.5 kg/ cm2
11900262	Spring Type-R/ C	1.4+ kg/ cm2

TURBONETICS RACEGATES

Adjustable Range	Deltagate Single Flange Discharge	Deltagate Dual Flange Discharge	Racegate Part #	Spring Only Part #
3 - 5 psi	10101-3FF125	10101-3FFF125	10307-3	10113 (Green)
5 - 7 psi	10101-5FF125	10101-5FFF125	10307-5	10115 (Blue)
7 - 9 psi	10101-7FF125	10101-7FFF125	10307-7	10117 (Silver)
9 - 13 psi	10101-9FF125	10101-9FFF125	10307-9	10119 (Black)

Part #	Description
20142A	Deltagate "Fire-ring" gasket
20396A	Racegate "Fire-ring" gasket
20260	Deltagate Weld Flange, drilled
20261	Deltagate Weld Flange, tapped
20397	Racegate Weld Flange, drilled

BLOW-OFF, BYPASS, AND POP-OFF VALVES

HKS

HKS Adjustable Pop-Off Valves provide secondary overboost protection in the event of wastegate malfunction or failure. These valves simply pop open at a preset amount of boost pressure allowing excess boost to blow off to the atmosphere.

APEX INTEGRATION

The Apex Integration Twin Chamber Blow-Off Valve incorporates a revolutionary design in boost pressure release systems. Blow-Off valves allow built up boost pressures to escape into the atmosphere when the engine is no longer under load. This prevents the pressure from backing up into the turbine compressor housing, causing it to rapidly stop, and causing potentially destructive damage to the turbo. The blow-off valve is also adjustable to allow desired amounts of boost response between shifts.

Unlike conventional single-chambered blow-off valves, the Twin Chamber Blow-Off Valve uses two separate chambers with an assisting pressure hose. This design allows for a short and highly sensitive spring in the first chamber that controls a piston and a valve in the secondary chamber. The result is quicker valve response under low AND high boost pressures. The blow-off valve also gives the user the ability to adjust the blow-off sound. By turning a disk near the base of the unit, the exhaust gas release volume can be adjusted to normal, loud, and extra loud.

Part #	Application
550-A001	Universal Blow-Off Valve
551-Z001	1993-1996 Mazda RX-7
551-Z002	1986-1991 Mazda RX-7
551-M005	1991-1995 Mitsubishi 3000GT (5 Speed)
551-KM01	1995-1998 Mitsubishi Eclipse
551-N007	1990-1996 Nissan 300ZX
551-T014	1991-1996 Toyota MR-2
551-T001	1993-1998 Toyota Supra

GREDDY

Blow-Off Valves and Installation Accessories

Part #	Description
11501710	Relief Valve
11501650	Blow-Off Valve Type "S"
11501661	Blow-Off Valve Type "R"
11501660	Blow-Off Valve Type "R"
11541010	1987-1992 Mazda RX-7 Turbo B.O.V. Kit
11541011	1993-1996 Mazda RX-7 T/T B.O.V. Kit
11531010	1995-1997 Mitsubishi Eclipse B.O.V. Kit
11511000	1990-1996 Toyota MR-2 turbo B.O.V. Kit
11511011	1987-1992 Toyota Supra turbo B.O.V. Kit
11511050	1993-1997 Toyota Supra T/T B.O.V. Kit
11900510	Stiff Spring
11900450	Steel Mounting Flange
11900451	Aluminum Mounting Flange (Type "S" or "R")
11900490	Outlet Adapter 40mm for Type"R"
11900491	Outlet Adapter 45mm for Type"R"
11900470	Outlet Adapter 19-21mm for Type "R"
11900471	Outlet Adapter 28-35mm for Type "R"
11900481	Outlet Adapter 16mm for Type "S"
11900482	Outlet Adapter 19mm for Type "S"
11900483	Outlet Adapter 29mm for Type "S"
99900061	Type-S Replacement Diaphragm
99900062	Type-R Replacement Diaphragm
11900520	Relief Valve Adapter

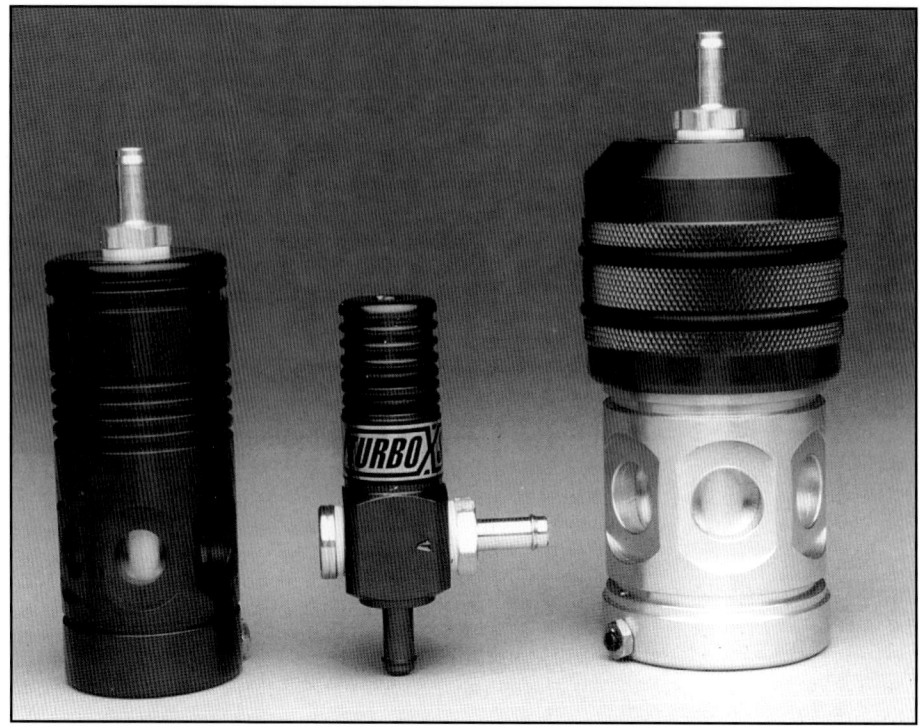

TurboXS Blow-Off Valves

TURBOXS

TurboXS Blow-Off Valve Type H

Designed for high performance, the TurboXS Blow-Off Valve Type H relieves compressor pressure surge caused by changing gears or backing off the throttle quickly. This valve is an extremely important part of any turbo system allowing quick boost response and greatly increasing the life of a turbocharger. The BOV Type H provides greater venting flow than the Type S and is designed for turbocharged engines running 10 psi or higher boost. There is no limit to the maximum boost pressure this unit can hold.

The TurboXS Blow-Off Valve Type H Kit includes: TurboXS Blow-Off Valve Type H, mild steel zinc-plated weld-on adapter, aluminum weld-on adapter, spring adjusting packers / washers, hex key, installation guide, and display box.

The TurboXS Blow Off Valve Type H is installed directly into the connecting pipe running between the turbo and the throttle body housing. The valve vents to atmosphere at sound pressure levels in excess of 110 db making it one of the loudest on the market. It is fully adjustable by adding packer / washers with the unique set-and-forget system. No two ways about it, this unit looks, sounds, and performs like no other blow-off valve available.

TurboXS Blow-Off Valve Type S

The TurboXS Blow Off Valve Type S is designed to release compressor pressure surge caused by changing gears or backing off the throttle quickly. This valve is an extremely important part of any turbo system allowing quick boost response and greatly increasing the life of a turbocharger. The BOV Type S is designed for small- to medium-sized turbo charged engines running from 5-15 psi boost, however, when properly installed and adjusted, there is no limit to the maximum boost pressure this unit can hold.

The TurboXS Blow-Off Valve Type S Kit includes: TurboXS Blow-Off Valve Type S, mild steel zinc-plated weld-on adapter, aluminum weld-on adapter, spring adjusting packer washers, installation guide, hex key, and display box.

The TurboXS Blow-Off Valve Type S is installed directly into the connecting pipe running between the turbo and the throttle body housing. The valve vents to atmosphere at sound pressure levels in excess of 106 db when measured 3 feet from the valve. The unit is fully adjustable by adding adjustment packer / washers included with the kit. The high-grade aircraft aluminum body is anodized bright purple to provide outstanding looks and superior corrosion resistance.

Super Sequential Blow-Off Valve

The Super Sequential Blow-Off Valve is a pull-type relief valve, unlike other blow-off valves which are push type. This valve is actuated by pressure alterations only, ensuring quick valve response and complete closure during idle. Standard blow-off valves must utilize large valves in order to accommodate high boost (high horsepower) applications. However, these large valves react slowly and require high activation pressure to open. Smaller, fast reacting valves, do not permit the air flow required for high horsepower. The Super Sequential Blow-Off Valve incorporates both for maximum performance. It is engineered utilizing a small primary valve for ultra-quick activation along with a secondary valve for additional relief capacity. The Super Sequential Blow-Off Valve is made of billet aluminum and emits a unique aggressive sound.

BLITZ

Super Sound Blow-Off Valve

The Blitz Super Sound Blow-Off Valve is the king of all blow-off valves. It not only relieves the excess pressure inside the intake track when letting off on a hard run, it will amplify and tone the air being released into a sound of superior power and authority. With the Blitz Blow-Off Valve, you can have function, looks, and head-turning sound.

ZEN BILLET RACING

Zen Billet Racing Blow-Off Valve is made with the best manufacturing technique available today. Zen Racing uses only the best possible material to assure the quality of its product. Zen Racing BOV is designed on MasterCam software and is carved from a solid piece of aircraft-grade aluminum by a precision CNC machine.

ZEN Racing BOV is designed to be used for a turbo vehicle that is generating high boost level. Many other BOV have been tested that claim to hold at high boost, think again. With its high-precision piston port design the ZEN Racing BOV seals shut the valve when its needed and still provides excellent vacuum response for safeguard operation. Piston port design. Compact size. Awesome sound. 100% made in the U.S.A.

Part #	Applications
ZMBV-1	ZEN Billet Racing Blow-Off Valve (Universal Kit)
ZMBV-2	1990-1995 Toyota MR-2 Turbo Adapter Kit
ZMBV-3	1995+ Mitsubishi Eclipse GST/X Adapter Kit

Universal kit includes a steel mounting flange with extension, silicone vacuum hose, and hardware. Adapter kit comes with a dump-back adapter for those who want the performance, not the sound.

APEX INTEGRATION

Part # 721-A001 Racing By-Pass Valve

TURBONETICS

A totally unique design! The "Godzilla" bypass valve assembly offers the ultimate in surge protection and cosmetic appeal. Highest flow capacity available! Aircraft-quality construction featuring a 1-1/2" diameter all stainless-steel valve assembly and a totally sealed actuator assembly. All polished aluminum with a unique V-band mount that allows a full 360 degree orientation. Includes 2" diameter discharge for system connection and weldable steel alloy mounting flange.

Part # 10656 Competition Bypass Valve

For the enthusiast who likes to "hear" what is happening! Fully polished discharge horn assembly sounds as good as it looks. Bolts directly to "Godzilla" in place of 2" discharge.

Part # 10692 "Godzilla" Discharge Horn

BOSCH

Street / Strip Bypass Valve

Great insurance for upgraded turbos and streetable high-performance engines. Manufactured by Bosch this OEM quality light-weight compressor bypass valve features 1" hose connections and the highest flow capacity of any unit offered in this size.

Part # 30359 Street/Strip Bypass Valve

TURBO TIMERS

APEX INTEGRATION

The Apex Integration Timer is designed to keep the engine idling after the ignition key is removed. This prevents hot oil from clogging up the oil lines of the turbo. Turbos need time to let oil pass through its lines to cool down. Failure to do so results in burning oil eventually leaving burnt deposits along the inside of the oil lines. This will eventually cause the oil to clog and damage the turbo. The Apex Integration Timer is recommended for any turbo vehicle. Factory turbos are just as susceptible to damage from oil "coking."

The Apex Integration Timer comes with variable time settings. Each setting can be adjusted for the specific driving type. Time Settings start at 30 sec. and rise to 9 min. 59 sec. All display is through an easy-to-read LED display with a visible countdown timer. Easy commuting does not require as much after idling as hard racing. A theft prevention feature of the timer shuts off the engine when the hand brake is released while the key is not in the ignition.

The Apex Integration Timer can be used on any normally-aspirated vehicle. Several uses for the timer would be to warm up the vehicle on a cold day or cool down the interior of the vehicle on a hot summer day without having to stay inside the vehicle.

Part #	Description
405-A004	Apex Timer Black
405-A005	Apex Timer Gold

GREDDY

If you have a turbocharger — whether it's factory, added, or upgraded — the Greddy Turbo Timer should be included in your budget under the category "peace of mind." The Turbo Timer allows you to leave your vehicle while the timer leaves your engine running anywhere from 10 seconds to 9.99 minutes. The gradual cool-down prevents bearing damage that can occur when a turbocharged engine is shutdown abruptly after normal driving. ("Spirited" driving and its more extreme temperatures would be even worse.)

The turbo's bearings rely on a generous supply of clean engine oil. All oil pressure is lost when the engine isn't running. With temperatures of about 250F/106C -- and at the turbine shaft, 300-350C (540-630F) — a hard, destructive varnish or "coke" can form on the bearings or seals. With the one-quarter DIN-sized Greddy Turbo Timer tucked in an unobtrusive location, you can leave and lock your car with confidence. No "baby-sitting" your prized machine or being late to work or a movie.

Turbo Timers

Part #	Color
15500011	Black
15500002	White
15500003	Blue
15500004	Silver-Red
15500005	Silver-Blue
15500006	Red
15500007	Sky Blue

HKS

The HKS Turbo Timer is a must for any turbocharged vehicle. The HKS Turbo Timer is designed to extend turbocharger life by allowing the engine to idle for a pre-set amount of time after the ignition key has been turned off and removed from the key cylinder. This permits the engine oil to circulate through the turbocharger

GREDDY TURBO TIMER HARNESSES

Part #	Application	Spec
15940002	1987-1991 Mazda RX-7, turbo	TT-14-32
15940003	1993-1996 Mazda RX-7, twin turbo	TT-14-33
15930002	1989-1994 Mitsubishi Eclipse	TT-14-42
15930003	1989-1994 Mitsubishi Eclipse	TT-14-43
15930003M	1995-1997 Mitsubishi Eclipse	TT-14-43M
15920001	1981-1983 Nissan 280SX, turbo	TT-14-21
15920002	1984-1989 Nissan 300ZX, turbo	TT-14-22
15920002M	1990-1996 Nissan 300ZX, twin turbo	TT-14-22M
15910001	1987-1992 Toyota Celica, all-trac	TT-14-11
15910001	1985-1989 Toyota MR-2 S/C	TT-14-11
15910003	1990-1992 Toyota MR-2, turbo	TT-14-13
15910001	1987-1992 Toyota Supra, turbo	TT-14-11
15910004	1993-1996 Toyota Supra, twin turbo	TT-14-14

Blitz Turbo Timer

bearing housing, drawing heat out of the bearings and impeller shaft in order to bring the temperature down to a safe level before the engine is shut down.

Some features include 15 preset times up to 9.99 minutes, audible alarm with a "beep" that can be activated or deactivated to "hear" the countdown, an hour display that can be reset which maintains a continuous total of engine running time in hours (because routine maintenance should be based on engine running time not necessarily vehicle mileage). Available in Red, White, Green, Blue, and Black.

Turbo Timer Harnesses

The HKS Turbo Timer Harness allows for quick and easy Turbo Timer installation. Most popular applications available.

BLITZ

The Blitz Turbo Timer allows your engine to idle down after you have removed the key from the ignition. This will allow fluids to flow through the engine and turbo to gradually cool down to safe levels after long drives or aggressive driving. Idle time can be set from 10 sec. up to 10 minutes 50 sec. The built in safety circuit will automatically shut off the engine when the parking brake is released.

The Blitz Dual Turbo Timer has all the key features as Blitz's standard turbo timer, plus it also adds the very useful digital boost readout in its display. Now you can protect the turbo when shutting down your engine and protect your turbo from boost spikes.

LEVOC

Levoc manufactures the most affordable timer in the market today, made with Levoc's tradition of high quality. If the regular turbo-controlling devices are functionally too limited, Levoc also offers LV72, which not only keeps your turbo healthy, but also automatically warms your engine every morning.

BOOST CONTROLLERS

APEX INTEGRATION

The AVC-D is the low-cost, high-performance Drag Racing boost controller from Apex Integration. The AVC-D is an "open loop" boost controller with no pressure sensor. This allows the user to specify any boost level that the engine can handle. The AVC-D calculates boost from three RPM-specific boost duty settings at 3000, 5000, and 7000 rpm. The AVC-D also features a speed-sensitive boost adjustment for better traction off the line by utilizing the vehicle speed signal. By adding an optional nonlocking button, the AVC-D also features a scramble boost feature that allows the user to either lower or raise the boost level for a specified amount of time. Both the speed sensitive boost adjustment and scramble boost feature may be turned off when not in use.

Part # 420-A003 AVC-D Boost Controller

Digital AVC-R

The new Digital AVC-R exceeds all other boost controllers on the market today with new parameters never available until now. Some of its impressive functions include: RPM-based boost and solenoid duty cycle control, scramble boost, gear-based functions, self learning, 2D map trace mode, analog display, real time and peak hold data, quick response, and stable boost control. The AVC-R allows the user to control virtually every aspect of boost control whether it is RPM based or gear based.

Since many factory turbochargers lose peak boost due to inefficient factory wastegates, the RPM-based duty cycle adjustment can help squeeze out the maximum stable boost possible. (Some physical limitations will apply.) Larger turbocharger applications can benefit from maximizing low-end boost response without sacrificing high-end stability. Graphic playback modes assist the user in identifying problem points in the boost curve. Scramble boost can be used either to increase boost or decrease boost levels for a certain period of time.

Part # 420-A004 AVC Type-R Boost Controller, Digital

GREDDY

Greddy has taken all the features of fuzzy logic and packaged them in an elegant, compact unit: the PRofec. It's outfitted with a high-speed processor, a warning alarm, LED display, and an overtake boost system as developed on turbocharged Formula 1 cars. Overtake boost will let you run a specified higher boost pressure for better economy. When you need to accelerate for passing, the PRofec allows maximum boost for a period you control, then returns to the lower boost level automatically. This provides the best engine and turbo life without sacrificing on-demand performance.

The PRofec is an electronic boost controller that employs fuzzy logic. Its powerful CPU allows your engine to be at the razor edge of performance more often, safely. In its learn mode, Greddy's hardware and software process data from the vehicle and, using this more intelligent, interactive "mapping," the PRofec's stepping motor not only controls, but anticipates boost spikes. Unlike most computers that only operate in "black and white" (1s and 0s), fuzzy logic can "think" in shades of gray and "learn" direct answers to problems. Where normal computers stair-step in "yes" and "no," fuzzy logic can go straight to the answer.

In recent years, fuzzy logic has gained popularity on everything from the famous bullet trains in Japan to washing machines and thermostats. The latter is a great example when we look at fuzzy logic's application in the PRofec. Standard on/off thermostats will turn on the heating or air conditioning when the air reaches the set temperature. Fuzzy logic thermostats turn on the A/C or heat as the temperature approaches the specified value.

When it comes to boost control, standard electronic controls will open the wastegate at a specified boost pressure. In some cases, the desired boost can be reached too fast for the controller to act, and harmful overboost can occur. Fuzzy logic, on the other hand, actually learns how fast your engine approaches maximum safe boost and starts to open the wastegate at the appropriate time so you never get into an overboost condition. Fine-tuning your vehicle to the highest safe boost setting eliminates the need for a wide safety margin to compensate for potential overboost.

Part #	Description
15500203	PRofec Fuzzy Logic Boost Controller
15500202	PRofec B-Spec (Electronic Boost Controller)
15500351	Remote Switch For PRofec And PRofec B-Spec.
15500361	Remote Switching Optional Harness 5-Volt.
15500362	Remote Switching Optional Harness 12-Volt
11501700	T.V.V.C. (Mechanical Boost Controller)
15900512	PRofec Wire Harness 4.5 meters
15900526-4	PRofec Replacement filter 4mm
15900526-6	PRofec Replacement filter 6mm

Boost Cut Controllers

Part #	Application
15540001	1990-1991 Mazda RX-7, turbo
15540006	1993-1996 Mazda RX-7, twin turbo
15510006	1990-1996 Toyota MR-2, turbo

Speed Limiter Controllers

Part #	Application
15520201	1990-1996 Nissan 300ZX, twin turbo 5M/T N-1
15520202	1990-1996 Nissan 300ZX, twin turbo 4A/T N-2
15510201	1987-1992 Toyota Supra, turbo T-1
15510202	1990-1996 Toyota MR-2, turbo T-1

Blitz Dual Solenoid Boost Controller (Dual S.B.C.)

Street Spec Boost Controller (Street S.B.C.)

HKS

EVC (Electronic Valve Controller) and EVC EZ

In order to achieve the maximum potential from a turbocharged engine, it is necessary to control the boost levels. The EVC units provide immediate push-button selection of preset levels of boost pressure, plus a return to factory boost level, by switching the EVC units off. All boost selections and adjustments are accessible from within the cockpit of the vehicle, which gives the driver the ability to change boost pressure on the fly. Aided by fuzzy logic, the EVC also possesses the ability to memorize the vehicle's boost pressure curve and optimize it. This learning feature allows a maximum reduction in turbo lag without overboosting. Adjustable up to 2.5 kg/cm or 35.55 psi.

Features include digital real time vacuum and boost meter, direct boost input, low and high preset modes, liquid crystal display, external scramble boost trigger interface, visual and audible overboost warning. Scramble boost feature allows added boost pressure for a preset amount of time. Can be used with internal- or external-type wastegates.

Variable Boost Controller

The HKS Variable Boost Controller (VBC) is a boost control system utilizing a pneumatic relief or regulator valve depending on the application. These VBCs are designed to work with either single- or dual-port actuator wastegates. While many manufacturers offer only a one size fits all, HKS vehicle specific VBCs include all components necessary for the installation of an effective boost control system.

JIM WOLF TECHNOLOGY

A very basic adjustable control that includes a block-off plug to remove the boost limiter valve on the intake manifold, a pressure regulator, and fittings.

Part #	Description
MMADJ-10000	1981-1989 Nissan ZX Manual Boost Controller

BLITZ

Dual Solenoid Boost Controller (Dual S.B.C.)

The Blitz Dual SBC is a revolutionary electronic boost controller that features a dual solenoid design which provides better response and increased boost pressure. Boost pressures are determined by preset ratios or percentages. This eliminates the need to cycle the car through several test runs to determine correct boost pressure. Boost curve varies with ambient air temperature.

This Dual SBC also features a boost meter offering a display of manifold pressure and vacuum. This allows the driver to monitor pressure drop or boost spikes. A warning function is set to "beep" when actual boost pressure exceeds the desired warning limit. The peak hold function is used to record the highest boost reading. It is set for all channels and can be checked any time. A limiter function works with the warning function and reduces the boost pressure to desired setting when warning function beeps. A scrambler function can be set to raise the boost pressure with time limit when just a little more boost is needed. Boost pressure is raised for the set time starting from the moment it reads boost.

Four Channel Dual SBC offers four programmable channels to set your boost. Four channels can be set for your own low/high manual and one more for your extra need. The boost pressure is set by ratio. Off - Off function allows you to set your vehicle back to stock boost pressure when maximum boost pressure is not desired. This unit features a compact 1/4 DIN size head unit that is mounted in the interior cockpit of the vehicle. It is compatible to external wastegate or integral wastegates with switch actuator. It can hold boost pressure up to 2.5 kg/cm2 (37 psi).

Street Spec Boost Controller (Street S.B.C.)

The Blitz Street SBC is a simpler electronic boost controller system that allows you to alter the boost pressure from within the cockpit of the vehicle. The unit features two preset knobs that allow you to preset your "Lo" and "Hi" settings. The mode selector switch allows the driver to alternate between the "Lo" and "Hi" setting. The off button allows the driver to shut off the system and allow the vehicle to operate under stock boost pressure. The unit is compatible with external or integral waste-

TurboXS Standard Boost Controller

gates. It can hold up to 1.2 kg/cm2 (18 psi). This unit is the best value for the money. It allows you to have all the advantages of an electronic boost controller at an affordable price.

TURBONETICS

Variable Boost Control Regulator

Change your boost level from the cockpit of your car with the Turbonetics VBC kit. The VBC kit can adjust boost pressure on any Deltagate, Racegate, or factory dual-port actuator. Adjustable from stock to the indicated pressure above stock. All kits come complete with fittings and blue silicone vacuum hose.

Part #	Description
10402-10	0 - 10 psi
10402-25	0 - 25 psi
10402-50	0 - 50 psi

TURBOXS

TurboXS Standard Boost Controller

Possibly the most effective way to generate more power from your turbocharged vehicle is to simply increase the boost pressure. This can be achieved quickly and very cost effectively with the TurboXS Standard Boost Controller.

The TurboXS Standard Boost Controller is installed inline with the pressure hose running from the positive pressure side of the turbo to the wastegate actuator system. It can be used on vehicles with internal and external wastegate systems and on vehicles fitted with factory electronic boost control systems.

The Turbo XS Standard Boost Controller is quick and easy to install. Cut the wastegate pressure hose and insert the supply pressure hose onto the silver colored nipple of the boost controller. Insert the wastegate supply hose onto the blue colored nipple. Secure the hoses with hose clamps. Alternatively, use the hose extension which negates the need to cut the pre-existing pressure hose. The boost controller can be mounted with mounting bracket.

The boost pressure is adjusted via the adjusting screw located internally on the top of the TurboXS Boost Controller. The vehicle's boost pressure can be increased by winding the adjusting screw in the counter-clockwise direction. Once the boost pressure has been increased, winding the adjusting screw in the clockwise direction will decrease the boost pressure. Typically, one (1) full turn of the adjusting screw in the counter-clockwise direction will result in a turbo boost increase of one psi.

Note: No internal engine components can be warranted at greater than original equipment specifications. This product is for racing use only. Not applicable nor intended for use on emission-controlled vehicles.

ADDITIONAL INJECTOR CONTROL

HKS

The HKS Additional Injector Controller (AIC) III is designed to supplement upper-end fuel requirements for most forced-induction vehicles. The AIC controls up to eight additional injectors, offering the most comprehensive adjustments available.

GREDDY

When a turbocharger and intercooler deliver more air to the engine, more fuel is needed to extract the potential power, especially in street/strip/race applications. The Rebic IV is an auxiliary fuel-injector controller that works independent of the factory electronic control unit. Greddy's "black box" can be used in any forced-induction setup to supply more fuel under high boost. The Rebic IV maintains safe air/fuel ratios, while supplying up to eight additional injectors. Its modular designs lets you use the Rebic IV with other Greddy control devices. Enthusiasts rave about the Rebic IV graphical, dynamic user-interface and how it adds a "cool" factor to even the best interiors.

Part #	Description
15500110	Rebic IV
15900012	Additional Injector Driver Harness
15900013	Additional Injector Driver Harness
15900016	Injector Driver Harness 2.5 Meters

Boost Pressure Switch

Three-pole unit switches on 0-30 psi adjustable pressure setting. Easily installed anywhere on engine or under dash. Can be used for any pressure-actuated circuit for any purpose. 1/8" MPT connection. Use with Boost Gauge (Part #30458).

Part # 30459 AutoMeter Boost Pressure Switch

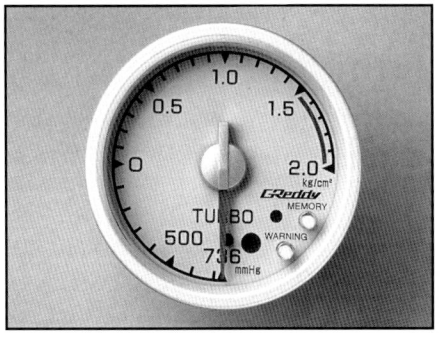

AutoMeter 2" Boost Gauge Kit offers 30" HG, 0 - 20 psi 270 degree sweep, chrome bezel, panel mount. Complete with illumination and installation kit.

Part #	Description
30150	AutoMeter 2" Boost Gauge Kit

Engine Reliability Components

REMANUFACTURED ENGINES

LC ENGINEERING

Toyota 20R/22R/22RE

All Long-Block engines are fully assembled by LCE's technicians. Engines are complete with valve cover, oil pan, pickup tube, timing cover, water pump, and oil pump installed. Each assembled engine is inspected, tested, and dyno run to ensure the highest level of quality control.

BOTTOM END, STROKER KITS

LC ENGINEERING

The stock bottom engine has adequate strength for low boost and low RPM applications. For higher levels of boost and performance LCE's Pro bottom end components (Pro Crank, Pro Rods, Forged Pistons) should be used. A Pro Bottom End (Short-Block Kit part # 19-085PK) will provide adequate strength to 250 hp. For higher horsepower levels or turbo/nitrous applications please call LCE technicians for specific recommendations.

CROWER STROKER KITS

Crower is the world's largest manufacturer of high-performance crankshafts and now offers a stroker kit for the Honda/Acura B16 and B18 blocks. Instantly turn your 1.6L into a 2.0L...or your 1.8L into a 2.1L+. Kits include a

Part #	Application
ACURA	
D16A1	1986-1987 Integra 522, DOHC, 16 valve, 3-bolt mount for TDC sensor on rear of exhaust camshaft, 22mm crank snout, with water pump, brown, 1590. Also see 522A.
D16A1	1988-1989 Integra 522A, DOHC, 16 valve, 2-bolt mount for TDC sensor on rear of exhaust camshaft, 22mm crank snout, with water pump, black, 1600. Also see 522.
D16A1	1988-1989 Integra 522B, DOHC, 16 valve, 2-bolt mount for TDC sensor on rear of exhaust camshaft, 24mm crank snout, with water pump, 1600.
C25A	1986-1988 Legend/Sterling 523, CA25 engine, with water pump, 2493.
C27A	1986-1990 Legend/Sterling 524, 2.7L, without oil level sensor hole in block, with water pump, 2675. Also see 524a.
C27A	1988-1990 Legend/Sterling 524A, 2.7L, with oil level sensor hole in block, with water pump, 2675. Also see 524.
B18A1	1990-1993 Integra 527, 1835cc, DOHC, 16 valve, with water pump, 1835.
C32A	1991-1992 Sedan/Coupe 528, SOHC, 24 valve, with oil cooler, w/p has 2 outlets for cooler, cam angle sensor has a female connector, 3206.
C32A	1993-1995 Sedan (not for GS or Coupe) 528A, SOHC, 24 valve, no oil cooler, water pump has 1 outlet, cam angle sensor male connector, 3206. Also see 528.
C32A	1993-1995 Sedan GS/Coupe, 528B, V-6, SOHC, 24 valve, with oil cooler, water pump has 2 outlets for cooler, cam angle sensor has a male connector, 3206.
C32A6	1995+, TL-3.2L, 528C, V-6, SOHC, 24 valve, 3206.
G25A1	1991-1995 Vigor, 529, 5 cyl., SOHC, 20 valve, with water pump, 2500.
G25A4	1995+ 2.5TL, 529A, 5 cyl., SOHC, 20 valve, cam and crank angle sensors without oil cooler mount block, no water pipe out of block, 2451.
B18B1	1994-1995 Integra, 535, 1834cc, DOHC, non-VTEC, 16 valve, 1834.
B18C1	1994-1995 Integra, 535A, 1834cc, DOHC, VTEC, 16 valve, 1834.
B18C5	1997+ Integra, 535B, Type R, 1834cc, DOHC, VTEC, 16 valve, crank angle sensor, 1834.
B18B1	1996-1999 Integra, 535C, 1834cc, DOHC, non-VTEC, 16 valve, crank angle sensor, 1834.
B18C1	1996-1999 Integra, 535D, 1834cc, DOHC, VTEC, 16 valve, crank angle sensor, 1834.
C35A1	1996+ 539, 3.5RL, V-6, SOHC, 24 valve, 3473.
C30A1	1990-1996 NSX, 540, DOHC, 24 valve, 2977.
C32B1	1997+ NSX, 3.2L, 544, 3200cc, DOHC, VTEC.

BUILDING RELIABILITY

Hahn Racecraft

Mitsubishi 4G6

The stock engine components in the Mitsubishi 4G6 Turbo engine are exceptionally strong. This durability, even when the power is turned up, is a large reason why the Mitsu is so popular among those desiring increased power. Instances exist of completely stock engines running at 450 hp with the right components! While it is possible, it's not always a given that stock engine internal components will endure this type of strain at 400+ hp without mishap. Even though the stock Mitsu parts are most excellent for stock components, they do have their limits. Three primary areas, which can be improved for high HP durability, are:

1. Stronger, less brittle forged pistons instead of stock cast pistons. Stock cast pistons are unforgiving to detonation, a condition which can cause them to crack easily.
2. A stronger connecting rod, precision machined from billet, manufactured to very stringent tolerances. A con rod failure is to be avoided, as it is always spectacularly destructive to the engine.
3. Eliminating variables of stock production tolerances. This is the hardest area to control, or even predict the possible outcome. Although those stock pieces are great, they are still only produced to tolerances of acceptable standards for a 200 hp engine. This means that you may get weaker parts than the next car, or you may get lucky and get stronger ones. But you just won't know which! This is why we see occasional, but not widespread, problems in stock engines producing 350 hp or more.

These factors point out the benefits of replacing the stock components with heavier duty pieces better designed for the task at hand. If you are building a 350 hp or more engine, give these pistons and rods serious consideration. They give excellent durability as well as peace of mind. The cost of replacing one broken engine will far outweigh the cost of these components. And even if you are rebuilding an engine in the 300-400 hp range, oversized pistons and reconditioned connecting rods will be required, so get an edge in durability at the same time.

420A Chrysler

Hahn Racecraft has been evaluating the 420A engine in turbocharged form since early 1998, and has already produced almost 400 hp with Stage III systems on this excellent powerplant. The stock engine will handle up to 275 hp without incident. HRC's stock engine prototypes have withstood tens of thousands of road miles and high performance use and looked fabulous internally when disassembled for inspection.

But you need not be limited to only 275 hp. When rebuilding the engine or preparing it for over 300 hp use, the use of these forged pistons and billet connecting rods is a must. The stock powdered metal rods in these engines are excellent but will not safely withstand repeated use over 300 hp. The stock pistons are high-quality Mahle units, but can be improved upon with forged pistons if high HP is your goal. The durability these components add is all you need to do to this exceptional engine to prepare it for 400 hp use.

Len Ayala's World's Quickest Neon engine is completely stock other than these pistons and rods; and he's already run 11.80s with his Stage III Turbo system equipped Neon! Yes, the remainder of the engine is completely stock, even the throttle body. No porting or cams. Hahn Racecraft didn't even take the manifolds off the cylinder head when these pistons and rods were installed, and Ayala still drives it regularly on the street. This makes the DOHC 420A economical for high HP use. Any competent mechanic and engine rebuilder / machinist can install these heavy-duty components with excellent results, without limiting the car's potential for daily street use.

JE Forged Pistons

Stock cast pistons can often withstand high power levels without failure. However, they also can be easily and instantly broken by unintended but destructive detonation episodes, even momentary ones. Detonation can occur from a number of factors or combinations of these factors. Usually these factors add up to an incorrect tuning condition, and if sufficient detonation occurs, the resultant violent, extremely high-pressure uneven loading can crack the piston.

These HRC/JE forged pistons are custom designed for the 420A engine, and are highly recommended for use with HRC's Stage III systems. They are many times more resistant to the damage detonation can produce than stock cast pistons, which are really quite brittle in comparison. They also employ features better suited to the higher HP engine, as well as a more robust ring set and wrist pin. Sold in sets of four with rings, wrist pins, and pin locks included.

Part #	Description
HRC EC-4000	JE Forged Pistons with pins and locks, 2.0L 420A engine, 8.8:1 compression ratio, 3.465" bore. For use in Talon, Eclipse, Neon, Avenger, and Sebring. Use with EC-4050 rings.
HRC EC-4050	Ring set. For use with JE Forged Pistons for 420A Chrysler.
HRC EC-4100	JE Forged Pistons with pins and locks, early Mitsu 4G6 (.827" wrist pin), 8.6:1 compression ratio, 3.366" bore (.020" over). Uses EC-4175 ring set.
HRC EC-4150	JE Forged Piston set with pins and locks, late Mitsu 4G6 (.866" wrist pin), 8.6:1 compression ratio, 3.366" bore (.020" over). Uses EC-4175 ring set.
HRC EC-4200	Crower Billet Connecting Rods, 420A Engine, bushed for floating wrist pin. For use in Talon, Eclipse, Neon, Avenger, and Sebring.
HRC EC-4300	Crower Billet Connecting Rods, Mitsubishi 4G6 Engine, bushed for .827" floating pin. For use in Talon, Eclipse, Laser, Galant, and Lancer.
HRC EC-4350	Crower Billet Connecting Rods, Mitsubishi 4G63 Engine, bushed for .866" floating pin. For use in Talon, Eclipse, Laser, Galant, and Lancer.

Crower 4340 steel billet or factory crankshaft; Crower 4340 steel billet rods; custom JE pistons; premium pins, rings, locks, and bearings; and Crower system balancing for easy, drop-in installation.

Crower Billet Stroker Rods

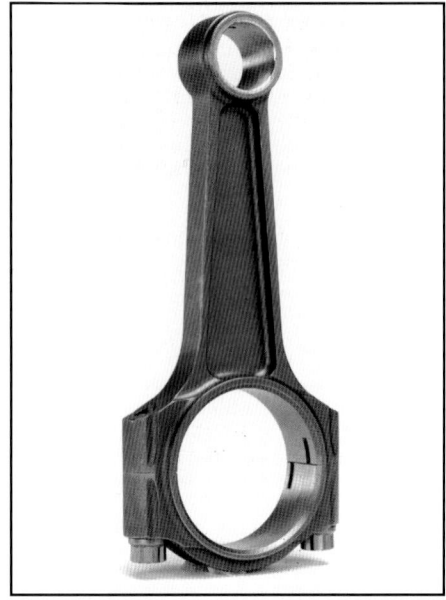

Custom length w/Maxi-Light stroker design. JE custom pistons. Modified pin boss for longer rod, specify compression. Premium tool steel pins, rings, locks, spacers, and rod bearings. Crower internal balancing for drop-in installation.

For block sleeving, contact Benson Performance Machine at 714-241-1284 for info and pricing. In Texas, call Performance Auto Supply at 214-324-0602.

Custom billet crankshafts are available for any make (Nissan, Toyota, Mitsubishi, Porsche, etc.). However lead times are 2-3 months for delivery; 50% deposit required.

HIGH PERFORMANCE ENGINE PACKAGES

LC ENGINEERING

STREET PERFORMER

If it's time to replace your engine due to excessive mileage or just plain old age, the LC Engineering Street Performer stock replacement engine surpasses anything you'll get at your Toyota dealership in both performance and value. LCE used experience and knowledge to produce an engine that will deliver more performance than the stock motor, with all the durability and driveability that you expect from the OEM stock product.

Features: 130 hp
Uses Stock Radiator and Mounts
AC / Power Steering Okay

EFI PRO

LC Engineering's EFI Street Performer engine is designed to get the maximum performance from the stock Toyota fuel injection. The EFI Street Performer engine uses the factory fuel injection system, mounts, and radiator. It maintains the stock A/C and power steering too! Like every LC Engineering product, it's designed for performance and reliability.

Features: 135-145 hp
Great Low-RPM Torque
All Stock Accessories Okay
AC / Power Steering Okay

PRO Series Engines

LC Engineering's pro series engines offer the peak performance tailored to meet your exact demands. Each engine is custom built to the customer's specifications. These engines can be configured in both low and high compression for both street and race only applications.

Stage-2 PRO

Adding performance doesn't mean giving up reliability and driveability. The Stage-2 Pro engine offers excellent torque capabilities along with many of the performance features found on LCE's more powerful engines. A Stage-2 engine is the perfect match for your 4x4 or hot street 2WD mini truck.

Features: 140 hp
Strong, Low-RPM Throttle Response
Perfect for Both 4WD and 2WD
AC / Power Steering Okay

Stage-3 PRO

LC Engineering's Stage-3 Pro Engine can be custom tailored to meet many applications including street, off-road, and circle track. Available in both "pump gas" and "race gas" configurations. The mid-range torque and acceleration of the Stage-3 engine makes it a great performer on smaller 1/8 and 3/8 mile circle tracks. In street applications, the Stage-3 Pro Engine gives stoplight-to-stoplight accelerations that will keep you and your passengers planted in your seats.

Features:
175-190 hp @ 5800-6800 rpm
Superb Mid-Range Torque
Brute Mid-Range Throttle Response

Stage-5 PRO

LC Engineering's Stage-5 Pro Engine offers the most powerful out-of-the-box performance your money can buy! This no compromise engine is winning NASCAR Modifieds, off-road trucks, rally, hill climb, and circle track races across the country and around the world. Other customers use the awesome power of the Stage-5 Pro Engine for sand rails, 4x4 Trucks, and custom street cars.

Features:
200-245 hp @ 6000-7200 rpm
2.3 to 2.6 Liter Displacement
Incredible RPM Range
Unmatched Acceleration

Build-It-Yourself

LC Engineering offers a complete selection of Master Rebuild Kits and components for your 20R/22R/22RE Toyota 4 Cylinder. Pistons, cranks, rods, cylinder heads, bearings, and gaskets for the home mechanic.

Master Rebuild Kits

LCE's Master Rebuild Kits include only the highest-quality components to keep the Toyota dependability you have relied on. These are the same quality components used in the Street Performer Engines. Kits include silvolite pistons; total seal racing rings; clevite bearings; LC Pro oil pump; timing chain kit; new water pump; brass freeze plugs; and a Fel-Pro gasket kit.

Part #	Description
19-8184MK	Master Kit
19-8595	Master Kit
19-205MK	Timing Chain Conversion Kit Upgrade
19-104	Oil Pump Drive Spline, 84 Only
10-103	Forged Piston Upgrade

ELP

Sport high-performance engine packages are available for most imports brands.

GUDE

Racing Packages

Kits include ported and polished, high-compression cylinder head; racing valve grind; ported intake manifold; high-velocity throttle body; racing header; optional ECU (if applicable), and cams.

Part #	Application
Honda/Acura	
AIRP01	1986-1989 1.6 DOHC
AIRP02	1990-1995 1.8 DOHC
AIRP03	1990-1996 1.7/1.8 DOHC

Bullfrog Race Packages

Each race package consists of a ported and polished, high compression cylinder head; a racing valve grind; a ported intake manifold; a high velocity throttle body; racing headers for the exhaust system; a matched ECU; and the camshaft of your choice. Up to 35 hp gains with one of these packages.

REV HARD

R-H 11-second Motor packages

All 11-second motor packages are engine dyno tested before shipping and are very capable of accomplishing 10-second timeslips if traction is accomplished.

ENGINE SWAP KITS

PLACE RACING

Before you can build your motor, add a turbo, or squeeze nitrous, you have to start with a good base. This is why the 10-second Hondas use 1.8L or larger Honda/Acura motors in place of stock motors to maximize performance. Place Racing offers motor upgrades for just about any Honda. Whether you just want some more pep from your car or you're going for all-out race, Place Racing has the solution for you.

Place Racing offers various engine upgrades for your Honda Accord giving it sports-car acceleration. The most popular installation is a 2.0L DOHC motor.

Place Racing offers numerous engine upgrades for your Honda Civic. Place Racing has HF to 1.6 SOHC upgrades to 2.2L and even Honda V-6 engine upgrades. The popular 1.8L DOHC upgrade is cost-effective and can instantly give your Civic 14-second performance without any other upgrades.

Greatly enhance your Civic's low-, mid-, and high-end performance with a Prelude 2.2 VTEC motor. The stock version of this motor offers 195 hp. With Place Racing's cold air intake and an exhaust system, you can push those numbers well over 200 hp.

Acura Integras are a popular candidate for motor swaps as well. Most older non-VTEC Integras will easily accommodate a 1.8L GS-R VTEC or 2.2L Prelude VTEC engines.

SPEED IMAGE

Engine swaps are available for applications shown in chart.

Conversion also available from Auto to 5 speed for most Hondas and Acuras.

Engines Only

1988-1991 Civic/CRX with trani
1992-1995 EX/Si with trani
B16A automatic
B16A with cable trani
B16A with hydraulic

SPEED IMAGE ENGINE SWAPS	
Engine Swap From	To Engine
1988-1991 Civic/CRX DX	1990-1991 Integra
1988-1991 Civic/CRX DX	1992-1993 Integra
1988-1991 Civic/CRX DX	1994-1995 Integra
1988-1991 Civic/CRX DX	1994-1995 GSR
1988-1991 Civic/CRX DX	SiR VTEC
1988-1991 Civic/CRX Si	1990-1991 Integra
1988-1991 Civic/CRX Si	1992-1993 Integra
1988-1991 Civic/CRX Si	1994-1995 Integra
1988-1991 Civic/CRX Si	1994-1995 GSR
1988-1991 Civic/CRX Si	SiR VTEC
1992-1995 DX/CX/VX/EX	1994-1995 Integra
1992-1995 DX/CX/VX/EX	1994-1995 GSR
1996-1998 DX/CX/VX/EX	1994-1995 GSR TYPE R Motor only
From most Honda/Acura	Prelude

LS/GSR - B18C1
ZC16 with trani
JAP Type R

Swap Accessories

AXLES:
H22 motor into 1992-1995 Civic
MOTOR MOUNTS:
Prothane motor mount bushings
MOTOR MOUNT KITS:
SI 1988-1991 Civic/CRX to
B Series motors
MOTOR MOUNT KITS:
PRI 1988-1991 Civic/CRX to
B Series motors

HASPORT PERFORMANCE

These mounts make DOHC VTEC B16A swaps into EF a simple, bolt-in process. Every kit is engineered to race specifications. Engine movement is minimized by controlling the durometer of the polyurethane bushings and as such, only 3 mounts are required for the engine swap. This kit is available in steel or lightweight aluminum.

Engine & Transmission Exchange

Specialist in supplying recycled Japanese Automobile engines and transmissions. Engine and Transmission Exchange has an extensive range of engines and transmissions for most Japanese cars.

RODS

AEM

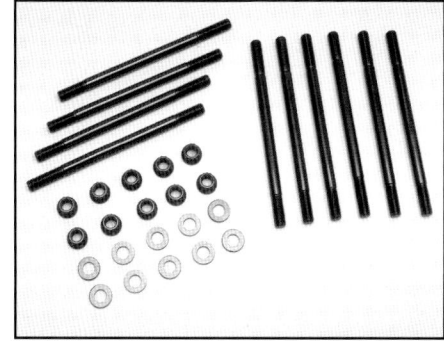

AEM's Hyper Rods are made from forged steel and are capable of handling extreme conditions with reliability. Hyper Rods from AEM are the lightest, strongest rods available and are designed for engines capable of exceeding 9,000 rpm. All are forged 4340 Chrome Moly, machined to precise specifications.

CROWER CONNECTING RODS

Part #	Application	C-to-C Length	B.E. Bore	B.E. Width	Pin Dia.	Pin Width
ACURA						
B93726B	Integra 1.6	5.394"	1.890"	0.892"	0.747" (19mm)	0.710"
B93727B	Integra 1.7	5.208"	1.890"	0.935"	0.826" (21mm)	0.785"
B93728B	Integra 1.8 non-VTEC (B18A/B18B)	5.394"	1.890"	0.935"	0.826" (21mm)	0.785"
B93729B	Integra 1.8 VTEC (B18C)	5.433"	1.890"	0.858"	0.826" (21mm)	0.725"
HONDA						
B93741B	Civic 1.5	5.279"	1.772"	0.897"	0.748" (19mm)	0.710"
B93742B	1342cc	5.436"	1.693"	0.897"	0.748" (19mm)	0.710"
B93743B	1237cc	5.065"	1.693"	0.856"	0.669" (17mm)	----
B93744B	1.6 VTEC (B16A)	5.290"	1.890"	0.935"	0.827" (21mm)	0.710"
B93745B	1.6 (D16Z6, D16A)	5.394"	1.890"	0.892"	0.748" (19mm)	0.716"
B93747B	Accord/Prelude Si	5.580"	2.008"	0.935"	0.866" (22mm)	0.940"
B93748B	Prelude 2.2 VTEC	5.636"	2.008"	0.935"	0.866" (22mm)	0.940"

CROWER

4340 Steel Billet Connecting Rods

Crower is the industry leader in high-performance connecting rods. Choose from the largest selection of import makes available including Honda/Acura, Mitsubishi, Toyota, Porsche, Nissan, Saturn, Neon, and Volkswagen. CNC machined from premium quality 4340 chromoly steel, Crower billet rods are the only choice when running nitrous oxide, high boost, or high RPM in your "all motor" application. See chart next page.

Honda/Acura rods are listed below and usually in stock (B16, B18). Mitsubishi, Nissan, Toyota, and other makes also available. Contact Crower Tech for more information, including availability. Billet titanium rods run $440 per rod. Allow 8 weeks for delivery.

CUNNINGHAM

From steel to titanium rods, Cunningham has the experience to design any connecting rod for your specific application.

The desire for more horsepower by installing turbochargers has put a demand on the engine's bottom end. To help engine builders keep-it-together, Cunningham has redesigned the connecting rod. In addition to quality control and The Cunningham Difference, the H-I Beam design is stronger and more durable than traditional rods. The thickness of the web at the beam is increased. This reduces early signs of fatigue, providing a long-life rod that can withstand the rigors of high-rev engines.

Cunningham steel rods are made from pure 4340 chromoly, not from a mix of other materials. Cunningham Titanium connecting rods are superior to any other rods in the industry. For the serious racer who demands more horsepower and wants a lightweight rod, this is your best choice.

Should you require more oiling at the pin ends, Cunningham's Rifle Drill procedure will keep the pistons running cooler. This will also increase your horsepower. Another Cunningham exclusive is a 45-degree modification. This procedure re-positions the end cap for added clearance when installing larger base caps or larger cap bolts.

Cunningham can produce any rod, in any size, in any quantity you need, from imports to domestics, tractor engines to antique engines.

GREDDY

Forged Connecting Rods

Part #	Application
13510756	Toyota Supra T/T 2JZ-GTE
13520766	Nissan 300 ZX T/T VG-30DETT

MALVERN RACING

Carrillo connecting rods available for all 4- and 6-cylinder import engines. Also available for exotic and vintage applications. Custom titanium connecting rods available as well.

CRANKSHAFTS

CROWER

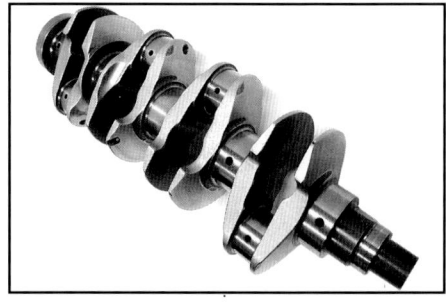

Crower billet stroker crank or reworked factory crank 95mm for B18 or 89mm for B16.

Custom billet crankshafts are available for any make (Nissan, Toyota, Mitsubishi, Porsche, etc.) however lead times are 2-3 months for delivery; 50% deposit required.

PISTONS

AEM

Race teams and street performance enthusiasts rely on AEM's product and industry knowledge to develop serious horsepower with superior reliability. Each application is designed and manufactured to exacting specifications and quality standards delivering top-level performance under the most extreme conditions.

Power Pistons are manufactured to precise specifications to insure optimum performance. These are serious components for serious competitors. Made to exacting tolerances, AEM pistons are designed for extreme use. For drag racing, road racing, or maximum street performance, these are the products.

AEM Power Pistons are offered in three different compression ratios for naturally-aspirated engines and engines assisted by superchargers, turbochargers, and/or nitrous oxide. These piston sets have been especially engineered by AEM, incorporating the same tolerances used in engines for Cosworth and Honda's Formula One race cars. These 4032 alloy pistons are designed for turbocharged and nitrous-assisted performance engines.

All AEM piston sets are made from 4032 High Silicon. Each are fully skirted for superior strength and durability. All AEM R-Series pistons come with instructions for setting ring gaps, bore finishing, and final block preparation.

Tech Tip: When installing a supercharger, turbocharger, and/or nitrous oxide, the use of pistons, rods, and studs with superior fatigue properties becomes vital. Factory components are not designed to accommodate the added cylinder pressure resulting from superchargers and turbochargers or nitrous oxide systems.

GREDDY

Forged Pistons

Part #	Application
13511612	Toyota Supra T/T 2JZ-GTE 87mm BORE
13511611	Toyota Supra T/T 2JZ-GTE 86.5mm BORE
13521631	Nissan 300 ZX T/T VG-30DETT 89mm BORE
411116	Nissan 300 ZX T/T VG-30DETT 90mm BORE

AEM PISTON SETS

Application	Low C/R	O.E. C/R	High C/R
ACURA			
B17A1	23-116	23-118	23-125
B18A1	23-116	23-118	23-125
B18B1	23-116	23-118	23-125
B18C1	23-116	23-118	23-125
B18C5	23-116	23-118	23-125
D16A1	23-103	23-104	23-105
HONDA			
B16A2	23-116	23-118	23-125
D16A6	23-103	23-104	23-105
D16Y5	23-106	23-107	23-108
D16Y7	23-106	23-107	23-108
D16Y8	23-106	23-107	23-108
D16Z6	23-103	23-104	23-105
F22A1	23-131	23-132	23-133
F22A4	23-131	23-132	23-133
F22A6	23-131	23-132	23-133
F22B1	23-131	23-132	23-133
F22B2	23-131	23-132	23-133
H22A1	23-110	23-114	23-115
H23A1	23-110	23-114	23-115
MITSUBISHI			
4G63 2.0L 1994-1998 8:1		23-130	
TOYOTA			
2JZGTE Turbo		23-160	

D16Z pistons are also used on Honda D16A engines, reduce compression factor by 0.5:1

Low Compression Pistons are 8.5:1.
O.E. Compression Pistons are O.E. specification.
High Compression Pistons are 12.5:1.
All Pistons are sold as sets with rings and wrist pins.

JE

Stock cast pistons can often withstand high power levels without failure. However, they also can be easily and instantly broken by unintended but destructive detonation episodes, even momentary ones. Detonation can occur from a number of factors or combinations of these factors. Usually these factors add up to an incorrect tuning condition, and if sufficient detonation occurs, the resultant violent, extremely high-pressure uneven loading can crack the piston.

JE Forged pistons are considerably more resistant to the damage detonation can produce than stock cast pistons, which are really quite brittle in comparison. They also employ features better suited to the higher HP engine, as well as a more robust ring set and wrist pin. Sold in sets of four with rings, wrist pins, and pin locks included.

MALVERN RACING

Cosworth forged racing pistons available for Nissan, BLMC, Triumph, Jaguar 3.8 and 4.2, Porsche 911 and 356, and 23% small-block Chevrolet engines flat top and dome.

JE & Wiseco forged pistons available for all Nissan/Datsun, Fiat X 1/9 1300 + 1500 cc, British Leyland 1275 A series, MGA, MGB in bore sizes 71mm to 83.5mm, Standard Triumph Spitfire, TR's 3 + 4 + 6, GT-6, VW 1600 + 1800 + 2000 Rabbit/Scirocco, and BMW.

AEM FASTENERS

Application	Rod Part #	Cyl. Head Stud Part #
ACURA		
B17A1	23-308	23-506
B18A1	23-306	23-504
B18B1	23-306	23-504
B18C1	23-308	23-506
B18C5	23-308	23-506
D16A1	---------	---------
HONDA		
B16A2	23-309	---------
D16A6	23-300	23-500
D16Y5	23-301	---------
D16Y7	23-301	---------
D16Y8	23-301	---------
D16Z6	23-300	23-500
F22A1	23-302	---------
F22A4	23-302	---------
F22A6	23-302	---------
F22B1	23-302	---------
F22B2	23-302	---------
H22A1	23-303	---------
H23A1	23-302	23-502
MITSUBISHI		
4G63 2.0L 94-98 8:1	23-320	---------
NISSAN		
L16	---------	23-541
L18	---------	23-541
L20	---------	23-541
L24	---------	23-516
L26	---------	23-516
L28	---------	23-516
TOYOTA		
2JZGTE Turbo	23-330	---------
3SGTE 2.0 L Turbo	---------	23-524
4AG	23-322	23-523
4AGZE	23-323	23-523
7MGTE	23-321	23-522
22R	---------	23-521

FASTENERS

AEM

Tru-Torque Head Studs from AEM are made to handle the extreme cylinder pressures encountered during high RPM performance driving. These fasteners are made from 8740 Chrome Moly Steel to withstand the massive pressures of racing. Ideal for use with metal head gaskets. Provides extra clamping loads. A must for nitrous-equipped engines.

LC ENGINEERING

The factory exhaust manifold studs have a shoulder in the center that can interfere with proper header tightening. For better holding strength, LCE's 45mm long heat-treated header mounting studs are stronger than stock. Kit includes 8 studs, washers, and nuts.

Part # 14-100   Cylinder Head Stud Mount Kit 20R, 22R

AUTOMOTIVE RACING PRODUCTS

Driveline Fasteners From ARP

When most people think of Automotive Racing Products (ARP), they think of engine fasteners. But ARP also offers a complete line of driveline fasteners, including flywheel/flexplate bolts, torque converter bolts, pressure plate bolts, bellhousing studs, automatic transmission pan bolts, ring gear bolts, rear end cover bolts, brake hat bolts, wheel studs, and drive plate bolts.

Like all ARP fasteners, the company's driveline bolts and studs are strong and tough. Most have a nominal tensile strength rating of 170,000 or 190,000 psi, which is substantially stronger than Grade 8 fasteners. And unlike hardware store bolts, each ARP driveline fastener is designed for the specific application — and to endure the rigors of a racing environment.

Race teams have been using ARP driveline fasteners for years to solve a number of common problems. For instance, you don't have to worry about shearing a torque converter bolt when you install one of ARP's 190,000 psi bolt kits for GM and Chrysler applications. And you won't be cross-threading ARP's bellhousing studs, which are designed with a radiused head to position the bellhousing and come with nuts and flat washers. Likewise, the company's ring gear bolts and wheel studs are designed to handle the tremendous shock loads generated in drag racing applications.

ARP Perma-Locs™ are forged in-house from premium grade 8740 chrome moly steel, and they feature a tensile strength of 190,000 psi (substantially stronger than Grade 8 fasteners). Most ARP driveline fasteners are made from a premium-grade 8740 chrome moly steel that is rated far superior to "aircraft" quality. Unlike other manufacturers, ARP places each bolt or stud vertically in special racks for heat treating to ensure complete heat penetration. What's more, ARP rolls the threads on all bolts and studs after heat treating, which gives them roughly 1,000% better fatigue strength than fasteners that are threaded prior to being heat treated (a very common industry practice).

High-Performance Fastener Catalog

Automotive Racing Products (ARP) has released its new 60-page, full-color, high-performance fastener catalog for 2000, filled with top-quality fasteners for racers, engine builders and street performance enthusiasts — domestic and import. You can depend upon each of these fasteners to be the absolute best product possible for its application.

Crammed full of technical information, including step-by-step illustrations covering the proper way to install rod bolts, head studs, main studs, and head and main bolts, ARP's catalog is much more than the sum of its parts. Charts also cover recommended torque specs and rod bolt stretch guidelines.

The latest catalog includes every fastener you need to assemble your engine — from premium-performance connecting rod bolts to head and main studs and bolts. Other top-quality fasteners include Perma-Loc rocker arm adjusters that provide the proper valvetrain geometry and don't loosen like ordinary poly locks; valve cover, oil pan, intake manifold, and carb bolts and studs that ensure proper sealing; oil pump bolts and studs that make sure your pump doesn't fall into your pan; distributor stud kits that resist vibration; and even highly-specialized break-away blower studs for professional racing.

ARP also offers such vital components as harmonic damper bolts, fuel pump pushrods, oil pump driveshafts, cam bolts, flywheel and flexplate bolts, torque converter bolts, bellhousing studs, motor mount bolts, ring gear bolts, rear end cover bolts, wheel studs, and much more.

Stud Kits

ARP recommends the use of main studs over bolts whenever possible for several key reasons. First is the

ARP HEAD STUDS

Part #	Application
ACURA	
208-4302	B18A1, 11mm
208-4303	B18CI VTEC
HONDA	
208-4301	D16, 10mm
MITSUBISHI	
207-4201	2.0, 4-cyl., 16 valve, 12mm, 4G63 up to 1994
207-4701	12-point
207-4203	2.0L, 4-cyl., 16 valve, 11mm, 4G63 1994+
207-4702	12-point
207-4202	2.6L 4-cyl.
NISSAN	
202-4201	L20 series, 4-cyl.
202-4202	A-12 engines
202-4203	A-14 engines
202-4206	L24, L26, L28 series, 6-cyl.
TOYOTA	
203-4201	22R
203-4202	7M GTE-Supra
203-4701	12-point
203-4203	4AG, 16 valve
203-4702	12-point
203-4204	3SGTE
203-4205	2JZA80 Supra
VOLKSWAGEN	
204-4201	1600cc air-cooled
204-4202	Super Vee
204-4203	Golf/Jetta, 1.8L & 2L, 8 valve
204-4701	12-point
204-4204	Golf/Jetta, 1.8L & 2L, 16 valve
204-4702	12-point

ARP MAIN CAP STUD KITS

Part #	Application
CHRYSLER	
141-5401	2.2L, 4-cyl., 11mm
MITSUBISHI	
207-5401	2.0L, 4-cyl., 16-valve, 4G63
207-5402	2.6L, 4-cyl.
NISSAN	
202-5401	L20 series, 4-cyl.
202-5406	L24, L26, L28 series, 6-cyl.
TOYOTA	
203-5404	3SGTE
203-5402	Supra 7M GTE
203-5403	4AG, 16 valve
VOLKSWAGEN	
204-5402	Rabbit, Golf and Jetta, 1.6L-2L

ARP ROD BOLTS

Application	Head Style	Hi-Perf 8740 (complete)	Hi-Perf 8740 (2-PC)	HP Wave 8740 (complete)	HP Wave 8740 (2-PC)	Pro Wave ARP2000 (complete)	Pro Wave ARP2000 (2-PC)
HONDA							
1.2L to 1.6L, 8mm	A	208-6001					
1.8L, 9mm	C					208-6401	
MITSUBISHI							
4G63, pre 1994, 9mm	C	107-6001	107-6021				
4G63, 1994+, 8mm	C	107-6002	107-6022				
2.6L	C	107-6003	107-6023				
3.0L V-6, 3.5 V-6 6674	C	107-6004	107-6024				
NISSAN							
L16 Series	C	102-6001					
L20 Series, 4-cyl.	C	202-6001					
L24 (early), 8mm	C	202-6002					
L24 (late), L26, L28 6-cyl., 9mm, V G30E & VG30ET	C	202-6003					
VG30 V-6 D (Four Cam), DET, DETT	C	202-6004					
TOYOTA							
4AGE, 9mm	A	203-6001					
22R	A	203-6002					
2TC, 3TC, 2TG	A	203-6003					
Supra, 7MGTE	A	203-6004					

ability to obtain more accurate torque readings because studs don't "twist" into the block. All clamping forces are on one axis. By the same token, there is less force exerted on the block threads, which contributes to improved block life (very critical on aluminum blocks). Finally, there are factors of easier engine assembly and proper alignment of caps every time.

There are many important reasons to use ARP main stud kits, including the elimination of main cap walk and fretting, as well as protecting the threads in your engine block. The studs are manufactured in ARP's factory using the best materials, processes, designs, and engineering. Every ARP main stud kit exceeds the most stringent aerospace specifications.

All kits come complete with hardened parallel-ground washers and aerospace quality nuts. Some applications have provisions for mounting windage trays and have specially designed standoff studs with serrated lock nuts to position the windage tray and lock it securely in place. The studs are manufactured from 8740 chrome moly steel, heat treated in-house to 190,000 psi tensile strength, and precision J-form threads rolled after heat treat to create a fastener that has threads 1000% stronger than others.

STAGE 8 AUTOMOTIVE PRODUCTS

The following application kits have been developed by Stage 8 to solve some of the more common fastening problems faced in the automotive industry.

Exhaust Header bolt kits continue to be Stage 8's most popular item, because loose headers without Stage 8 Locking Safety Bolts continue to be a problem! Each kit comes with an exclusive double hex and socket head configuration for installation with any of three tools: socket, open end wrench, or Allen hex wrench.

Oil pan and valve covers must maintain clamping force to stop leaks, but cannot be too tight or they will crush the gasket and distort the pan or cover. If they loosen, messy leaks and serious engine problems may result. Stage 8 Oil Pan & Valve Cover Kits will eliminate this problem.

A spinning flywheel contains incredible inertia and stored energy that helps your vehicle leave the starting line and perform. This energy is enough to actually cut the vehicle in half and even kill you if the bolts fail and become shrapnel! A Stage 8 Locking Flywheel Bolt Kit will remove this risk.

Nothing can leave you stuck, or more angry, than a starter that doesn't work. But, a loose starter motor also damages the flywheel starter ring, and

TITANIUM PERFORMANCE BOLTS

Part #	Description
HF0510	Hex flange M5X10
HF0515	Flanged Hex Head M5X15
HF0520	Flanged Hex head M5X20
HF0525	Flanged Hex head M5X25
HF0530	Flanged Hex head M5X30
HF0535	Flanged Hex head M5X35
HF0540	Flanged Hex head M5X40
HF0610	Flanged Hex M6X10
HF0615	Flanged Hex M6X15
HF0620	Flanged Hex M6X20
HF0625	Flanged hex M6X25
HF0630	Flanged Hex M6X30
HF0635	Flanged Hex Head M6X35
HF0640	Flanged Hex Head M6X40
HF0645	Flanged Hex Head M6X45
HF0650	Flanged Hex Head M6X50
HF0655	Flanged Hex Head M6X55
HF0660	Flanged Hex Head M6X60
HF0810	Flanged Hex Head M8X10
HF0815	Flanged Hex Head M8X15
HF0820	Flanged Hex Head M8X20
HF0825	Flanged Hex Head M8X25
HF0830	Flanged Hex Head M8X30
HF0835	Flanged Hex Head M8X35
HF0840	Flanged Hex Head M8X40
HF0845	Flanged Hex Head M8X45
HF0850	Flanged Hex Head M8X50
HF0855	Flanged Hex Head M8X55
HF0860	Flanged Hex Head M8X60
HF1020125	Flanged Hex Head M10X20X1.25
HF1025125	Flanged Hex Head M10X25X1.25
HF1030125	Flanged Hex Head M10X30X1.25
HF1035125	Flanged Hex Head M10X35X1.25
HF1040125	Flanged Hex Head M10X40X1.25
HF1045125	Flanged Hex Head M10X45X1.25
HF1050125	Flanged Hex Head M10X50X1.25
N06	Nut M6
N08	Nut M8
T0415	Tapered Socket Head Cap Screw M4X15
T0610	Taper Socket head cap screws M6X10
T0615	Taper Socket Head Cap Screw M6X15
T0620	Taper Socket Head Cap Screw M6X20
T0625	Taper Socket Head Cap Screw M6X25
T0630	Taper Socket Head Cap Screw M6X30
T0635	Taper Socket Head Cap Screw M6X35
T0640	Taper Socket Head Cap Screw M6X40
T0645	Taper Socket Head Cap Screw M6X45
T0650	Taper Socket Head Cap Screw M6X50
T0655	Taper Socket Head Cap Screw M6X55
T0660	Taper Socket Head Cap Screw M6X60
T0810	Taper Socket Head Cap Screw M8X10
T0815	Taper Socket Head Cap Screw M8X15
T0820	Taper Socket Head Cap Screw M8X20
T0825	Taper Socket Head Cap Screw M8X25
T0830	Taper Socket Head Cap Screw M8X30
T0835	Taper Socket Head Cap Screw M8X35
T0840	Taper Socket Head Cap Screw M8X40
T0845	Taper Socket Head Cap Screw M8X45
T0850	Taper Socket Head Cap Screw M8X50
T0855	Taper Socket Head Cap Screw M8X55
T0860	Taper Socket Head Cap Screw M8X60

GREDDY METAL HEAD GASKETS

Part #	Engine	Bore	Thickness
13511123	4A-G	82.5mm	2.0mm
13511171	7M-G	83mm	1.0mm
13511172	7M-G	83mm	1.5mm
13511173	7M-G	83mm	2.0mm
13511174	7M-G	83mm	3.0mm
13511181	7M-G	85mm	1.0mm
13511182	7M-G	85mm	1.5mm
13511183	7M-G	85mm	2.0mm
421171	3S-G	87mm	1.0mm
421172	3S-G	87mm	1.5mm
421173	3S-G	87mm	2.0mm
421174	3S-G	87mm	3.0mm
421175	3S-G	89mm	1.0mm
421176	3S-G	89mm	1.5mm
421177	3S-G	89mm	2.0mm
421178	3S-G	89mm	3.0mm
13551101	D16A	76mm	2.0mm

nothing could be more scary than a starter coming out from under a vehicle and bouncing down the highway at 65 mph! Get a Stage 8 Locking Starter Kit for your vehicle.

If an intake manifold leak is a problem, imagine what a loose carburetor can do to your engine! A Stage 8 Locking Carburetor Mounting Nut Kit is insurance against leaks, without carburetor flange distortion.

CV joint bolts require a high amount of shear or side load strength. Most CV joints use 8mm or 5/16 fasteners. Anyone who has raced Baja knows how easily these sizes shear off. Stage 8 recommends 3/8 bolts. The extra security is worth the effort to drill and retap the bolt holes.

The timing of your engine is critical to performance. A loose distributor can stop you dead and destroy your engine! Use the Stage 8 kit made especially for distributor fastening.

GASKETS

APEX INTEGRATION ENGINE PARTS

Part # 4814-N102   SR-20 Metal Head Gasket

TRD

Metal Head Gaskets available for these applications:

1988-1993 Celica Turbo
1988-1991 Corolla GTS
1985-1987 Corolla GTS
1987-1988 Corolla FX
1985-1989 MR2, Normally Aspirated
1988-1989 MR2, Supercharged
1990-1995 MR2 Turbo

HKS

HKS Metal head gaskets are constructed from multiple layers of steel to ensure proper head-to-block sealing, even under the most severe conditions. The special metal used in the construction of the head gaskets is resistant to both heat and corrosion. All gaskets are coated with a special fluorine rubber coating to provide the ultimate sealing.

EARL'S

Earl's Pressure Master Gaskets include header flange, header collector, and head gasket sets for most popular high performance vehicles.

SEALS

STR PROSEALS

STR patented ProSeals help solve the dirty problem Honda Acura DOHC motors experience with the stock cam seal. The OEM plastic seal can corrode, harden, and breakdown. This in turn leads to major oil leakage from the seal and a very dirty motor. The STR ProSeal solves this problem with style. STR ProSeals are constructed from high-quality CNC machine billet aluminum. They are then matched with a dual rubber 0-ring that keeps oil in the engine and out of the engine bay.

When ordering STR products available in colors please add a letter to the end of the part number to designate your desired color. i.e.: R = red /

B = blue / P = purple / Y = yellow. With no letter it will be shipped with a polished finish.

Part #	Application
CS0100	1990-1998 Acura Integra GSR/Type R B18 DOHC
CS0100	1993-1997 Honda del Sol VTEC B16 DOHC
CS0100	1990-1998 Honda Prelude Si VTEC 2.2 DOHC

LUBRICATION SYSTEM COMPONENTS

DYSON

Dyson Oil, Inc. has been researching lighter-weight synthetic engine oils since the late 1980s. Dyson refused to sacrifice protection while reducing the horsepower robbed by engines having to "push" heavy-weight oils. Starting with LTS 3w30 Racing Oil, Dyson's research team of racers and chemists have progressed to what they call 0 Weight Oils. As hands-on knowledge increased, successful testing was completed on 0w-16 wt., 0w-8 wt. and 0w-4 wt. engine oils. The culmination of ongoing research is the development of Synergyn® "Quad-0" or LTS 0000 Racing Engine Oil. Dyson's 0 Weight Engine Oils produce more horsepower to the ground than any other engine oil on the market today. Following recommended change intervals will provide complete protection to expensive racing engine parts.

Royal Purple

Royal Purple® is proud to introduce Racing 51, the latest addition to its line of premium-quality synthetic motor oils with Synerlec™. Racing 51 comes in the heavier 20W50 weight preferred in a number of competition applications. Thanks to the addition of this new viscosity, Royal Purple® now offers an optimum lubrication solution for virtually every internal combustion engine on the planet!

Extensive dynamometer testing conducted by leading professional engine builders confirms that Royal Purple® Motor Oil provides increases in horsepower over other lubricants. In fact, power increases of at least 5% have been obtained with no changes other than switching to Royal Purple's racing oils with Synerlec™, the slippery, super-tough synthetic film that greatly reduces power-robbing friction.

Royal Purple® Motor Oil also has a very high-load carrying ability, which reduces ring, cylinder, and bearing wear. And Royal Purple® is so tough that it can withstand the effects of heat far beyond other motor oils.

RED LINE

Red Line Engine Oils

Derived from Red Line's Race Oils, Red Line Synthetic Engine Oils were formulated specifically for street use in all kinds of passenger cars and light, medium, and heavy trucks. Red Line Engine Oils outperform all petroleum-based oils and all other synthetics on the market today.

Red Line Engine Oils are designed to provide highest performance, best durability, ultimate protection, and outstanding cleanliness along with lowest friction to your automotive, motorcycle, marine, or stationary engine running on gasoline, diesel, alcohol, or natural gas fuel.

Red Line lubricants are unique because they contain polyester base stocks, the only lubricant base stock type that withstands the incredible heat present in the hot sections of jet engines. This high-temperature stability makes Red Line Engine Oils a necessity for proper lubrication of high-performance engines, turbocharged engines, heavily loaded truck engines, or any engine that runs high engine oil temperature.

Red Line is not just for high-performance and racing. Ordinary cars and trucks that see "daily driver" duty benefit greatly when their engines are lubricated with Red Line engine oils. More performance, better fuel economy, and increased durability come with use of these oils in daily drivers.

Because of the robust polyester base stock and high-performance anticorrosive additive package in Red Line oils, they are ideal for use in street-driven vehicles at extended drain intervals. Red Line recommends oil changes for engines that are in good condition and do not see frequent starts without warm-ups or short-trips at between 10,000 and 18,000 miles for gasoline engines, 10,000 and 12,000 miles for diesel engines, or every 12 months, whichever is shorter.

Red Line 5W30

Provides the quickest starts and fastest oil pressure rise. Will reduce turbo lag and provides more power and best economy in an engine in good condition. Replacement for OE factory-fill oils in passenger cars and most light trucks. Thicker oil film at operating temperature than a petroleum 10W40. Best choice for engines operated in extreme cold weather.

Red Line 10W30

Best all-weather viscosity grade for gasoline engines in cars and light trucks that are driven on the street on a daily basis. Reduces turbo lag and provides more power and economy while providing thicker bearing oil films at operating temperature than a petroleum 10W40. Best all-round, synthetic oil for stock or slightly modified engines in high-performance cars that are street-driven. Best choice to replace a 5W30 or 10W30, petroleum-based, or other-brand synthetic oil if maximum durability is preferred. Acceptable for engines that are occasionally operated in extreme cold weather.

Red Line 10W40

Best choice for engines that typically run high oil temperature. Best choice for engines in daily drivers operated in very hot weather on a regular basis. Best choice for medium- and heavy-duty gasoline engines in trucks. Best choice for high-performance engines that see street as well as frequent racetrack duty. Thicker oil film at operating temperature than a petro-based 20W50.

Red Line 15W50 & 20W50

The ultimate high-temperature protection in Red Line engine oils recommended for street use. Good for engines that regularly run very high oil temperatures. Best for engines that run large clearances such as air-cooled engines or large-displacement, all-out racing engines that see occasional street use. Provides 25% more viscosity in bearings than petroleum 20W50s. Not recommended for use in cold climates where temperatures are at or below 10°F or -12°C. Not recommended for street use in production engines that see sustained oil temperatures below 225°F. Those engines should use Red Line 10W30 or 10W40.

Red Line 15W40 Diesel Engine Oil

Highly resistant to thermal breakdown. Provides double the detergent and acid-neutralizing ability of conventional petroleum diesel engine oils for maximum engine cleanliness. Ideal for diesels that run high oil temperature, such as those operated in hot weather or those in light truck applications where heavy loads are carried or towed. Best choice in medium- and heavy-duty diesel truck engines when maximum durability is required. When used at extended drain intervals, it is an excellent value for long-haul, fleet use.

Red Line Race Oils

Red Line Race Oils have gained a reputation as the ultimate racing lubricant. Marketers of other lubricants unsuccessfully claim to be "as good as Red Line." Red Line's lubricants are used by many teams who have found that the improved performance and equipment durability is the key to winning.

Red Line race oils are made with the most thermally stable synthetic base stocks available and provide the best high-temperature lubrication and a higher film strength than any petroleum or synthetic product marketed. The ability of Red Line Oil to lubricate hot metal has enabled many cars to not only finish, but to win races after losing coolant, without serious damage to the engine.

Even though Red Line Race Oils are straight grades, their low-temperature properties make them exceptional multigrades. Red Line Race Oils allow 2-4% more power than an oil of similar viscosity, while providing much more protection. Each reduction in viscosity grade allows 1-2% more power. To reduce the chance of detonation, these race oils contain very few detergents and are not recommended for street use.

SAE 5 (0W)

For drag racing and circle track qualifying where the lowest internal friction is desired.

SAE 10 (0W10)

For drag racing and circle track qualifying where the lowest internal friction is desired.

SAE 20 (10W20)

For drag racing, circle track qualifying, and race engines designed for low-viscosity oils.

SAE 30 (10W30)

Suitable in well-balanced racing engines for sustained high-speed use where low internal friction is desired.

SAE 40 (15W40)

For use where temperatures may be high and when a wide range in RPMs and speeds will be encountered.

SAE 50 (15W50)

For use where extremely high temperatures may be encountered and when engine durability is the primary concern.

SAE 60 (20W60)

For alcohol fuel engines.

SAE 70 (25W70)

For top-fuel engines.

Synthetic Grease

Red Line Synthetic CV-2 Grease possesses a very high melting point, excellent water washout resistance, and superior antiwear which makes it excellent for high temperatures and extreme loads. CV-2 contains an organic moly and is for wheel bearings, high-angle and conventional CV-joints, chassis lubrication, and high-temperature, high-speed industrial equipment.

Power Steering Fluid

Red Line Power Steering Fluid provides much improved wear protection and resists thermal breakdown. Provides continued high pump output at high temperatures and resists evaporation and foaming at high temperatures. Suitable in most power steering units.

Assembly Lube

Red Line Assembly Lube provides three-times greater film-strength than conventional black Molybdenum Disulfide greases and will not clog oil filters. This product clings to all surfaces and is an excellent rust inhibitor, allowing the storage of parts for years.

Compressor Lubricants

Red Line provides a complete line of synthetic industrial and shop air compressor lubricants. These lubricants provide excellent resistance to carbon formation, last typically five times longer, and can provide approximately 5% improvement in compressor efficiency.

Suspension Fluids

Red Line Suspension Fluids change very little with temperature and provide lower operating temperatures. The foaming resistance is excellent and the slippery synthetic basestocks provide little seal drag. Available in five different grades. The LikeWater provides the least viscosity change of any commercial suspension fluid and will operate unchanged many times longer than other suspension fluids.

4-Cycle Alcohol Fuel Lube

This product provides excellent lubricity for alcohol to prevent upper cylinder wear and fuel system corrosion. Not detectable by normal fuel tests.

OIL PANS

MOROSO

Road Race Pan

Road Race Pan available for Honda 1.3L & 1.5L engines used in stock 1984-1987 CRX models without chassis modifications. Fully fabricated all-aluminum construction offers exceptional strength without the added weight and provides several design advantages over stock-core pan.

A cluster of four trap-door baffles completely surround the pickup to ensure ample oil supply and oil pressure regardless of hard acceleration, braking, or quick left/right cornering. Special oil control features are critical because the stock pan causes oil to move away from pickup during hard driving.

Double kicked-out sump increases capacity to 5.5 quarts, while maintaining stock depth for ample ground clearance. Removable sump tray allows for easy cleaning, cools and de-aerates return oil, and keeps excess oil off of the rotating assembly to prevent horsepower-robbing windage.

Includes 1/2" NPT bung at rear for fitting a temperature sender and 1/2" NPT bung at front for plumbing an oil return line for those running turbos (also includes two 1/2" NPT plugs if required).

Includes magnetic drain plug with extra copper washer. Also includes pan mounting kit with hex-drive steel studs to eliminate stripping the engine block and serrated-face flare nuts to withstand vibration. Accommodates stock pan gasket and dipstick with existing oil level marks. Use with stock oil pump and pickup.

| Part No. 20905 | Road Race Pan for Honda 1.3L & 1.5L |

Street/Strip Pan for Honda/Acura 1.6L

Street/Strip pan available for Honda/Acura 1.6L found in 1986-1989 Acura Integra, 1992-1995 Civic EX & SI, and 1988-1992 Civic/CRX Si.

Fully fabricated, all-aluminum construction improves oil control, increases power, and provides adequate header and stock exhaust clearance. Double kickouts increase pan capacity to 5.5 quarts with the rear kick out collecting oil during acceleration, serving as an ideal oil pickup location to prevent starvation. Rotating crank and rods direct oil into the enlarged kickout area helping to reduce power robbing windage and improves scavenging.

Dynamic trap-door baffling allows oil to flow "one-way" into the pickup area during acceleration keeping it there during braking. One piece, 1/4-inch thick 6061-T6 billet aluminum pan rail provides a rigid flange for leak-free sealing. Includes 1/2-inch NPT bung for plumbing turbo oil return line, magnetic drain plug with extra washer and plugs for unused bungs. Also includes pan mounting kit with hex-drive steel studs to eliminate stripping the engine block and serrated-face flare nuts to withstand vibration. Accommodates stock pan gasket and dipstick with existing oil level marks.

| Part # 24016 | 1986-89 Acura Integra |
| Part # 24017 | 1992-95 Civic EX & Si, 1988-92 all Civic/CRX Si |

Street/Strip Pan for Acura 1.8L

This pan fits 1994-1998 Acura Integra with 1.8L engines, VTEC and Non-VTEC.

Fully fabricated, all-aluminum construction improves oil control, increases power, and provides adequate header and stock exhaust clearance. Back-side kickout increases pan capacity to 5 quarts and collects oil during acceleration, serving as an ideal oil pickup location to prevent starvation.

Rotating crank and rods direct oil into the enlarged kickout area helping to reduce power robbing windage and improves scavenging. Dynamic trap-door baffling allows oil to flow "one-way" into the pickup area during acceleration keeping it there during braking. One piece, 1/4-inch thick 6061-T6 billet aluminum pan rail provides a rigid flange for leak-free sealing. Includes 1/2-inch NPT bung for plumbing turbo oil return line, magnetic drain plug with extra washer and plugs for unused bungs. Also includes pan mounting kit with hex-drive steel studs to eliminate stripping the engine block and serrated-face flare nuts to withstand vibration.

| Part # 20901 | Acura 1.8L |

6-quart Street/Strip Pan for Toyota 3TC, 2TC

This pan fits 1986-1989 Acura Integra, 1992-1995 Civic EX & SI, and 1988-1992 Civic/CRX Si.

Fully fabricated, all-aluminum pan was thoroughly track and dyno tested to ensure optimum oil control, increased power, and optimum performance. Main-cap-mounted louvered windage tray with built-in crank scraper and block zinc finish, strips oil from rotating assembly, drains oil into the sump area, and keeps sump oil isolated to reduce power robbing windage. A perforated sump tray helps prevent oil from splashing back onto the rotating assembly to further reduce windage; also de-aerates oil returning from turbo.

Dynamic trap-door baffling allows oil to flow "one-way" into the pickup area during acceleration keeping it there during braking. Kickouts increase pan capacity to 6 quarts without restricting ground clearance. Rotating crank and rods direct oil into the enlarged kickout area helping to reduce power robbing windage and improves scavenging. One piece, 1/4-inch thick 6061-T6 billet aluminum pan rail provides a rigid flange for leak-free sealing. Includes 1/2-inch NPT bung for plumbing turbo oil return line, two magnetic drain plugs with extra washers and plugs for unused bungs. Also includes pan mounting kit with hex-drive steel studs to eliminate stripping the engine block and serrated-face flare nuts to withstand vibration.

| Part # 20930 | 6-quart Street/Strip Pan for Toyota 3TC, 2TC |

Deep sump Aluminum, 6.25-quart Street/Strip Pan

Fits Mazda 13B rotary engines used in Mazda RX-3, RX-4, and several rotary conversions including 1981-1984 Toyota Starlet, 1964-1983 Toyota Corolla, 1971-1973 Datsun 1200, and others with little or no crossmember mods; and tube chassis cars.

Fully fabricated, all-aluminum pan follows the same design as the 6-quart street/strip pan mentioned above. This pan's kickouts increase pan capacity to 6.25 quarts with minimal ground clearance impact (adds .25-inch sump depth). Rugged 3/8-inch thick 6061-T6 billet aluminum pan rail with internal cross brace provides a rigid flange for leak-free sealing as well as reinforcing the entire engine assembly to reduce flex under hard driving. Includes 1/2-inch NPT bung for plumbing turbo oil return line, two magnetic drain plugs with extra washers and plugs for unused bungs. Also includes pan mounting kit with hex-drive steel studs to eliminate stripping the engine block and serrated-face flare nuts to withstand vibration.

| Part # 20942 | Deep sump Aluminum, 6.25-quart Street/Strip Pan |

LUBRICATION SYSTEM ACCESSORIES

GREDDY

Oil Block Adapters

Part #	Application
12002703	Honda Type
12002700	Toyota & Nissan Type
12002712	Mitsubishi & Mazda Type

B&M

Import Engine Oil Coolers

Fits all engines utilizing a 20 mm x 1.5 mm thread oil filter such as Honda and Acura (1988+). Adapter is 1 3/4" thick. Be sure adequate clearance is available for removal of oil filter.

| Part # 70261 | Import Engine Oil Coolers |

Temperature Gauge

Most transmission and converter failures can be traced directly to excessive heat. The extremely accurate and dependable B&M Temperature Gauge comes with a light kit, color coded dial face, showing a temperature range from 100 to 350 degrees. Includes anti-glare ABS enclosure, all wires and terminals, a special sending unit, and T-fitting for easy installation.

| Part # 80212 | Transmission temp gauge kit |
| Part # 80214 | Replacement sending unit |

Thermostatic Control Valve

This remote oil thermostat will help maintain proper oil temperatures required in today's high-performance vehicles outfitted with auxiliary oil coolers.

| Part # 70259 | Thermostatic control valve |

Cooler Mounting Kit

This easy mounting kit included with most B&M coolers is available separately for remounts of additional cooler support. Includes 4 nylon mounting rods, 4 nylon slip-on locking nuts, and 4 sponge rubber pads.

| Part # 80278 | Easy mounting kit |
| Part # 70269 | Cooler fitting kit |

GREDDY

Oil Cooler Kits

See chart below.

TD PERFORMANCE

TD Performance invented the oil filter relocation kit. These kits allow you to relocate your oil filter to make filter changes quicker and easier. Perfect for applications where the filter is difficult to reach. The dual filter unit doubles filtering capabilities for a cleaner engine.

EARL'S

Earl's offers a complete selection of sizes of Temp-A-Cure™ Oil Coolers & New Cleanable Oil Filters.

FLUID LINES, HOSES, AND FITTINGS

EARL'S

Earl's complete line of high-performance hoses include Fabric and Steel Braid-Reinforced Hoses, Hose Ends, and Hose Coverings. Earl's offers Speed Flex™ Hoses, Speed-Seal™ Hose Ends, Pre-assembled Speed Flex™ hoses, Speed-Flex II™ hoses, and Speed-Seal II™. Earl's complete line of hose ends includes the patented Swivel Seal™, AutoFit™, and QuickFit™ brands. They are all available in a variety of sizes and configurations to handle any fluid flow need. In addition, the firm's line of Aluminum & Steel Adapter Fittings and QuickFit™ Fuel Line Hose Kits are available anodized blue, red, or clear.

VACUUM LINES AND FITTINGS

HOSE TECHNIQUES

Super Series Starter Kit

HoseTechniques is proud to present a silicone vacuum hose starter kit, designed especially for car enthusiasts who plan to upgrade an engine bay with silicone hose in vivid color.

Each starter kit contains:

1. One color hose in the following lengths and sizes: 10 ft. of 3.5mm, 15 ft. of 4.0mm, 6 ft. of 6.0mm, 4 ft. of 8.0mm

2. Vacuum Hose Cutter

3. Thirty (30) nylon tie wraps in matching color

4. One HoseTechniques die-cut decal

5. Do-it-yourself installation instructions

Extreme Starter Kit

GREDDY OIL COOLER KITS

Part #	Application	Description
ACURA		
12051520	1994-1998 Integra GSR	10 Row
HONDA		
12051510	1994-1997 Accord EX	10 Row
12051500	1992-95 Civic EX/Si	10 Row
MAZDA		
12041000	1989-1993 Miata 1.6L	10 Row
12041500	1989-1993 Miata 1.6L	10 Row
12041510	1994-1996 Miata 1.8L	10 Row
MITSUBISHI		
12031520	1995-1998 Eclipse Turbo	10 Row
12031523	1995-1998 Eclipse Turbo	16 Row
NISSAN		
12024580	1990-1996 Nissan 300ZX T/T	10 Row
TOYOTA		
12011036	1993-1996 Supra T/T Remote Filter	16 Row
12011590	1993-1996 Supra T/T	10 Row
12011596	1993-1996 Supra T/T	16 Row

For an all-out showcar, we recommend you order HoseTechniques' Extreme Starter Kit which contains:

1. 10 ft. of 3.5mm, 20 ft. of 4.0mm, 10 ft. of 6.0mm, 10 ft. of 8.0mm, or 20 ft. of 10.0mm

2. Vacuum Hose Cutter

3. Sixty (60) tie wraps

4. 2+2 Decals

5. Installation instructions

AUTOLOOK

Sports Parts Series Silicone Hose

Part #	Size	Color
MG-401	4mm	Red
MG-402	6mm	
MG-403	4mm	Yellow
MG-404	6mm	
MG-417	4mm	Blue
MG-418	6mm	

Length:
2 meters

Temperature range:
-26 to 260 degree C.

Maximum pressure:
8 kg/cm square

RACING SPORTS

Since 1994, Racing Sports has been marketing its Akimoto Performance Silicone Hose and has had an incredible response to it. When designing this product, Racing Sports took into account many different variables. It needed to be durable, pliable, heat resistant, tear resistant, and most importantly, resistant to distortion.

As in most rubber and silicone vacuum hose, the problem is that the wall thickness is too thin. The resulting problem is that under high vacuum operation the hose collapses on itself, ultimately creating a blockage. Performance decreases as the vacuum passage reduces in size until the time it is completely closed. That obstruction is present only at high vacuum conditions and is very difficult to diagnose. Racing Sports uses a wall thickness of 3/16" which eliminates the possibility of that happening. And the 3mm vacuum hose is a true 3mm instead of the 4mm that is readily available on the market.

You will not have to tie or clamp any of the connections and the orifice through the hose will not collapse on itself even in a 1" 180° bend. One added bonus is that this vacuum hose is offered in eight colors, making it possible to color code your engine compartment or dress it up and match your vacuum hose to the color of your car. The hose is available in a variety of lengths as well. It can be purchased in 10' lengths for individuals, 25' lengths for shops, and for installers there are 100' rolls for optimum savings. See chart below for part numbers. Please order by length and color (add fifth digit numeric color code). Available in Blue = 6, Lt. Blue = 9, Yellow = 5, Red = 4, Orange = 7, Black = 1, Lavender = 0, Green = 8.

Part #	Description
5001	3mm Vacuum Hose (10' Roll)
5011	3mm Vacuum Hose (25' Roll)
5021	3mm Vacuum Hose (100' Roll)
5002	6mm Vacuum Hose (10' Roll)
5012	6mm Vacuum Hose (25' Roll)
5022	6mm Vacuum Hose (100' Roll)
5003	8mm Vacuum Hose (10' Roll)
5013	8mm Vacuum Hose (25' Roll)
5023	8mm Vacuum Hose (100' Roll)
5004	10mm Vacuum Hose (10' Roll)
5014	10mm Vacuum Hose (25' Roll)
5024	10mm Vacuum Hose (100' Roll)
52015	6mm High Pressure Coolant Hose (Yellow Only)
52115	6mm High Pressure Coolant Hose (Yellow Only)
52215	6mm High Pressure Coolant Hose (Yellow Only)
5100	"Driveway Kit" Vacuum Hose Kit

OBX

Silicone Hose Kits

Part #	Description
SHK01	10' Silicone Hose 4mm Kit
SHK02	10' Silicone Hose 6mm Kit
SHK03	10' Silicone Hose 10mm Kit
SH187R	100' Silicone 0.187" I.D. Hose Red
SH187Y	100' Silicone 0.187" I.D. Hose Yellow
SH187B	100' Silicone 0.187" I.D. Hose Blue
SH280R	100' Silicone 0.275" I.D. Hose Red
SH280Y	100' Silicone 0.275" I.D. Hose Yellow
SH280B	100' Silicone 0.275" I.D. Hose Blue
SH375R	100' Silicone 0.375" I.D. Hose Red
SH375Y	Silicone 0.375" I.D. Hose Yellow
SH375B	Silicone 0.375" I.D. Hose Blue

COOLANT

EVANS

NPG Cooling is a new technology, a system initially developed for cooling race engines to reliably increase power. It does that and much more. It's a racing-tested engine cooling breakthrough!

The technology is centered around a revolutionary new coolant, non-aqueous propylene glycol (NPG). In addition to Evan's own race teams and testing programs, NPG technology has been proven in many different racing vehicles from 2000 hp drag cars, cross country vintage racers, and big-block modified cars. Some of today's high-performance street machines put just as many demands on your engine and its cooling system as some race cars. With required engine pollution and emission control systems, air conditioning, and other such drains, street engines can experience tremendous stresses. NPG is ideal for such applications.

Engines have the capacity of operating at much higher efficiencies which lead to higher power production. The limiting factor has always been the conditions imposed by water-based coolants, including low boiling point and excessive vapor generation. These conditions cause localized coolant boiling, vapor blanketing at hot spots, and the resultant destructive detonation and pre-ignition. In some applications, coolant alone will improve fuel economy and reduce emissions; in other applications, simple mechanical modifications may be required.

When vapor blankets the surface, water-based coolants lose their ability to absorb heat from the hot spots in the combustion chambers, leading to high metal temperature spikes well above critical levels. The result is loss of power from detonation or component structural failure from pre-ignition in the form of piston damage, head gasket failure, and/or warped or cracked heads.

Water-based coolant is operated near its boiling point. Cylinder liner cavitation erosion is caused by vibration-induced high frequency pressure changes at the metal-coolant interface. Coolant, near its boiling point, makes vapor bubbles that abruptly collapse against the metal surface, causing erosion of the metal. Evans' NPG Coolant contains no water and is not operated near its boiling point.

The boiling point of Evans' NPG Coolant is 370 degrees F in a non- or low-pressurized system. The coolant is normally controlled at conventional temperatures but functions perfectly well at higher temperatures, even considerably higher temperatures. Detonation/pre-ignition control and previously forbidden combustion chamber pressures and temperatures are no longer the danger they were to thermal engine efficiency and durability.

Evans' NPG Coolant is 100% inhibited Propylene Glycol. It can maintain substantially vapor free, liquid-to-metal contact at all coolant temperature and engine loads. By bathing the entire combustion chamber with coolant 100% of the time, metal temperatures are controlled to such an extent that critical levels of detonation and pre-ignition are never reached. Because of NPG's naturally high 370 degree F boiling point, the need for adding high pressure to the cooling system is eliminated. Without pressure (or low pressure, i.e. 2 to 5 psi) in the system, gasket seals, hose connections, and even the radiator core, operate safer and longer.

ROYAL PURPLE

Purple Ice radiator super coolant lowers engine temperatures to increase power and dependability. Just pour one 16-ounce bottle of Purple Ice into your cooling system, and your radiator will transfer heat more efficiently and reduce coolant and engine temperatures. Purple Ice works well in both gasoline and diesel applications.

Purple Ice can be used with a typical 50/50 mix of antifreeze and water, but it reduces coolant temperatures even further when used with less antifreeze. For street vehicles, Royal Purple recommends running at least 15% antifreeze, but Purple Ice has been used successfully with water alone in racing applications. That's because Purple Ice contains an exclusive ingredient, Molybdate, which forms a protective coating on the surface of aluminum parts to prevent corrosion and erosion. In fact, Purple Ice is the only coolant additive on the market today that passes ASTM (American Society of Testing Materials) D-2570 Simulated Service Corrosion Tests in a straight water mixture (without the benefit of any of the corrosion inhibitors found in antifreeze).

Purple Ice also prevents the formation of scale and deposits in the radiator caused by hard water and other contaminants, enabling optimum coolant flow. Plus, it lubricates water pump seals to prevent premature failures, and Purple Ice won't gel if coolant seeps into the crankcase, preventing damage to bearings.

Extensive testing has confirmed that Purple Ice reduces coolant temperatures better than any comparable product, and it provides extra levels of protection. For example, when dyno tested with different coolants, the average operating temperature of a 350-cid Chevy V-8 (equipped with a 160° F thermostat) is 228° with a standard 50/50 mix of water and antifreeze. With a 50/50 mix and Purple Ice, the average temperature drops to 222°. When run with straight water (with no corrosion protection), temperatures average 220°. Add Purple Ice to the water and this drops down significantly to just 200°.

RED LINE

Red Line WaterWetter® is a unique wetting agent for cooling systems which reduces coolant temperatures by as much as 30°F. This liquid product can be used to provide rust and corrosion protection in plain water for racing engines, which provides much better heat transfer properties than glycol-based antifreeze. Or it can be added to new or used antifreeze to improve the heat transfer of ethylene and propylene glycol systems. Designed for modern aluminum, cast iron, copper, brass, and bronze systems.

FANS AND ACCESSORIES

ACCEL

This harness adapter kit lets you specify the exact coolant temperature at which the electric coolant fan is switched on. This kit connects your vehicle's fan to your Accel harness and also uses OEM-style wiring and connectors for trouble-free installation and reliable operation. Using your PC or laptop computer and Accel's CALMAP software, simply enter the ECU Configuration section and type in the desired "Fan On" temperature. The ECU will store the number and automatically switch the fan on whenever this temperature is reached.

Part # 74171 Spark/Fuel Management with electric coolant fan

MR. GASKET

High-Performance Electric Cooling Fans

These fans provide more efficient cooling at low speeds where it is needed most. With high torque and low amperage draw motor, they free up more usable horsepower to the drive wheels and increase fuel economy. The motor rides on dual ball bearings, not on bushings like some other models. The reversible fan blades are engineered to provide maximum air flow. The extremely low-profile design of these fans makes installation easy even in very limited space. With three sizes to choose from, all being reversible, it makes it easy to find the correct fan for your specific application.

Adjustable Electric Fan Control Thermostat

Allows electric fan(s) to operate automatically at different temperature settings. Features adjustment ranges

MR. GASKET HIGH PERFORMANCE ELECTRIC COOLING FANS

Part #	Air Flow	Description	Blades	CFM	RPM	Draw
1984	Puller/Pusher	9" Diameter	10	700	2600	5.5
1985	Puller/Pusher	10" Diameter	10	950	2650	8.3
1986	Puller/Pusher	12" Diameter	10	1400	2300	10.2
1987	Puller/Pusher	14" Diameter	10	1800	2100	10.3
1988	Puller/Pusher	16" Diameter	10	2000	1900	11.31

broad enough to meet any requirements, precise control from 140 - 220°F, 100 percent solid state, anodized aluminum radiator probe that senses external surface temperature and plug-in custom wire harness.

Part # 1995   Adjustable Electric Fan Control Thermostat

Illuminated Manual "On/Off" Switch

Switch bypasses and overrides the thermostatic sensor and allows fan(s) to be turned on manually at any temperature. Switch is illuminated any time fan(s) are in operation.

Part # 1993   Manual "On/Off" Switch

Thermostatic Sensor Kit

Designed to allow fan(s) to operate automatically. Includes a 30 amp relay, wiring kit w/fuse, thermostatic temperature sensor, brass radiator probe. Fan turns on at 190°F and off at 170°F.

Part # 1992   Temperature Sensor Kit

FLEX-ALITE

Honda Civic Fan

This fan replaces the original electric fan in 1992-1999. It requires 505 of depth and pulls 30% more air. Operates using car's on-board thermo controls.

Part # 125	Black
Part # 125Y	Yellow Shroud
Air Flow (CFM):	1250
Blade Diameter:	12"
Fan Dimensions: 15" X 13 1/2" X 2 3/4" thick	
Amp Draw:	10
Fan RPM @ 13.5VDC:	2000
Number of Blades:	10
Fan Blade Angle:	160

Other applications

| Part # 310 | 1986-1996 Acura Integra L4, 1.8L |
| Part # 310 | 1986-1993 Acura Legend V-6 2.7, 2.5 |

Twin Line Electric Fans

The Wrangler fan and model 310 include an adjustable thermostat and a/c relay. An optional manual override switch may also be ordered for water crossings and/or mud racing.

Part # 31148   Illuminated Switch

FLEX-A-LITE FANS

Application	Type	Engine	Litre	Rotation	Aux. Elec. Fan	Primary Elec. Fan
NISSAN						
1987-1988 200 SX, 240SX, 260Z,	L6	VG30E	3	CW	130	150
1984-1988 280Z, 280ZX,	L4	CA20E, CA18ET	2.0, 1.8	CW	130	30
1989-1996 Maxima, 810	L4	KA42DE, KA42E	2.4	CW		
1974	I6	L24	2.4	CW	130	30
1975-1983	I6	L26	2.8	CW	130	30
1990-1996	V-6	VG30DE VG30D	3	CW	114	210
1983-1989 300ZX	I6	VG30T VG30	3	CW	30	30
1990-1993 300ZX	V-6	VG30E	3	CW	114	210
TOYOTA						
1976-1981 Celica	L4	20R	2.2	CW	110	110
1979-1985 Celica	L4	22R	2.4	CW	110	110
1984-1987 Corolla	L4	4AGEC	1.6	CW	110	110
1980-1982 Twin Cam GTS	L4	3TC	1.8	CW	110	110
1983-1985 Twin Cam GTS	L4	4AC	1.6	CW	110	110
1979 1800	L4	2TC	1.6	CW	110	110
1975-1980 Corona 1200	L4	20R	2.4	CW	110	110
1981-1982	L4	22R	2.2	CW	110	110
1978-1979 Cressida	I6	4M	2.6	CW	114	210
1980+ Cressida	I6	4ME	2.6	CW	114	210
1981-1982 Cressida	I6	5ME	2.8	CW	114	210
1983-1984 Cressida	I6	5M	2.8	CW	114	210
1985-1988 Cressida	I6	5MGE	2.8	CW	114	210
1989-1993 Cressida	I6	7MGE	3	CW	114	210
1987-1993 Supra	I6	7MTGE	3	CW	130	150
1979-1985 Supra w/turbo	I6	5MGE, 5ME	2.6,2.8	CW	130	30
1986-1996 Supra w/turbo	I6	7MGE	3	CW	130	30

HONDA CIVIC FAN

	Part # 310 Reversible	Part # 320 Reversible	Part #375 Puller
Mounting Surf. Req'd	22" x 11 1/4" x 4 1/8"	22" x 11 1/4" x 4 1/8"	22" x 11 1/4" x 4 1/8"
Fan Diameter	2 x 10"	2 x 10"	2 x 10"
Fan RPM @ 13.5VDC	2500	2500	2500
Number of Blades	10	10	10
Fan Blade Angle	20°-40°	20°-40°	20°-40°
Airflow-Cu. Ft./Min at 0° Static Pressure	2000	2000	2000
Amp Draw	18	18	18
Mounting System	Through Core	Through Core	Custom Brackets
Adj. Thermostat 180°-240°	Yes	No	Yes
Air Conditioning Relay	Yes	No	Yes
Honda Prelude, Accord 1991-1995 V-6, 3200cc	3.2	Electric	110
1985-1995 L4, 1955cc - 2100cc	2.1, 2.0	Electric	110
1973-1995 L4, 1169cc - 1787cc	1.5 - 1.3	Electric	110

| Part # 310 & 320 | Universal fit dual reversible fan |
| Part # 375 | Custom fits 1987 through 1997 Jeep Wranglers |

Twin Line electric fans offer greater control over engine temps during long idles, low speed climbs. Replaces stock steel fan.

PERMA-COOL

Perma-Cool Turbo-Flex Fan

The new Turbo-flex high-performance electric fan has a high-RPM pancake motor with dual ball-bearing arature supports, lightweight blades, and open steel housing. Sizes range from 10 to 18 inches in diameter and flow rates to 290 cfm.

Driveline

SHIFTERS

B&M

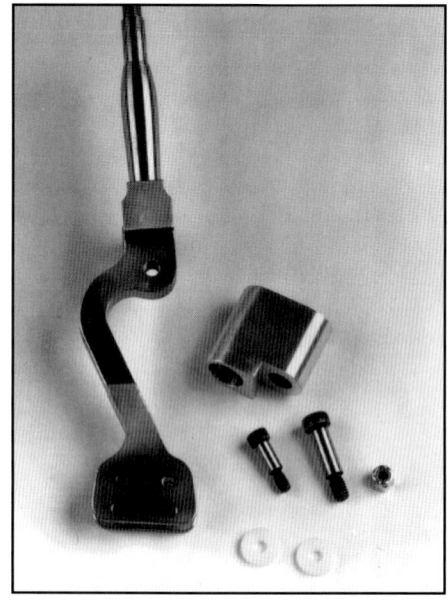

The Edge Shifter is a CAD-designed and engineered direct bolt-in replacement shifter for Honda and Acura. The only tools needed to install it are a 10mm and a 12mm wrench. Threaded for use with both factory and aftermarket knobs, the Edge features a counter-balanced bottom end for more precise shifts. Extremely tight tolerances and special, long-lasting, high-performance red silicone bushings make the Edge the smoothest, most accurate shifter available. The CNC-machined, super-tough billet alloy steel straight shaft provides the absolute best leverage and reduces shift throw by over 2 inches. The Edge is also highly polished and show-chromed to provide the best in beauty and wear. And B&M offers you a lifetime warranty; if you ever break this shifter, B&M will replace it.

Part #	Application
45075	1990-1999 Acura Integra
45076	1994-1998 Dodge/Plymouth Neon
45077	1995-1997 Eagle Talon
45075	1988-1999 Honda Civic & CRX
45075	1993-1997 Honda del Sol
45077	1995-1998 Mitsubishi Eclipse

Pro Edge Shifter

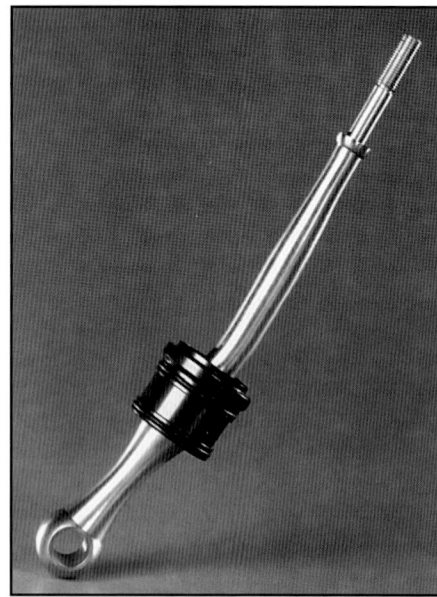

B&M has just introduced the Pro Edge racing shifter. The Pro Edge racing shifter was the natural evolution of the popular Edge line of shifters. Working with some of the top import racers, B&M's engineers took what they learned in the real-world racing environment and designed a professional level shifter system. By keeping the key features that has made the Edge such a success (such as counterbalanced bottom end) and incorporating a billet aluminum bearing mount (with a trick aerospace polymer spherical bearing), the Pro Edge has become the professional's choice. The CNC-machined stick has also been upgraded to 303 billet stainless steel!

Part #	Application
45074	1990-1999 Acura Integra
45079	1989-1999 Ford Escort/ZX2
45078	1993-1997 Ford Probe
45074	1988-1999 Honda Civic/CRX
45074	1993-1997 Honda del Sol
45078	1993-1997 Mazda MX-6GT
45079	1992-1997 Mazda MX-3

The Edge Shift Stabilizer System

The B&M Shift Stabilizer System will improve the shift feel and responsiveness on 1988-1997 Honda Civics/CRX and 1990-1997 Acura Integras. This easily-installed kit eliminates the soft rubber factory change extension bushings. The anodized rear shifter mount replaces the soft, spongy factory rubber mount and is precision engineered to remove all flexing common to rubber and plastic type bushings which lead to shifter movement and missed shifts. The B&M shift stabilizer system allows the neutral stick position to be adjusted so the driver can determine the ultimate position of the stick. This system will work with the B&M Edge Shifter as well as the factory shifter and other aftermarket shifters. Patent pending.

Part #	Application
45061	1990-1997 Acura Integra
45060	1988-1997 Honda Civic/CRX
45061	1990-1997 Honda del Sol

The Edge Short Shifting System

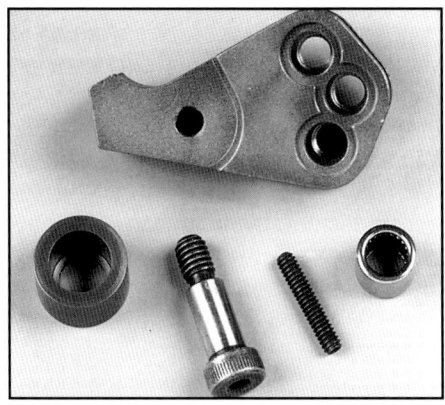

Easy, bolt-on kit can be installed in less than 30 minutes. It is CNC machined and bright anodized. Adjustable neutral position (45062, 45063). True roller bearing at pivot point for precise shifts. Backed by B&M's lifetime warranty.

Short Shifting System Shift Adapter

The B&M Edge Short Shifting System shift adapter is CNC machined from aerospace quality 6061-T6 aluminum and allows the user to reduce shift throw by over 25%! Another innovation not found in other shift adapters is the "neutral adjustment." This allows the user to custom fit the shifter for a more natural feel.

Part #	Application
45062	1994-1997 Honda Accord w/5 speed
45064	1998-1999 Honda Accord w/5 speed
45063	1992-1996 Honda Prelude w/5 speed

HURST

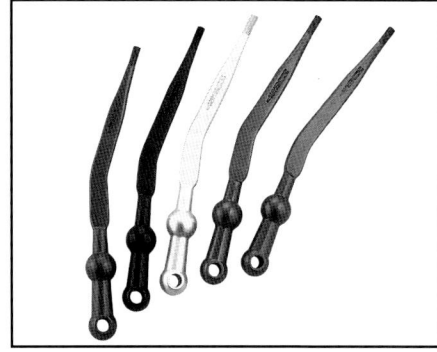

Providing a shorter shifter throw and quicker, more positive shifts, the Quick/Stick from Hurst is the shifter of choice for Honda Civic, CRX, and Acura Integra sport compact cars with manual transmissions. The curved stick design brings the shifter closer to the driver for a more comfortable position.

The Quick/Stick is CNC machined from billet aluminum to precise tolerances, and then cold-forged to shape for strength with the traditional Hurst look. Designed to accept the stock shifter knob, the Quick/Stick will also accept most custom aftermarket knobs in addition to the famous Hurst T-Handle. Available in trend-setting anodized colors including black, silver, blue, red, and purple. The Quick/Stick shifter installs easily using simple hand tools.

Part #	Application
1990-1997 Acura Integra	
391 4000	Black
391 4002	Silver
391 4004	Blue
391 4006	Red
391 4008	Purple
1988-1997 Honda Civic/CRX	
391 4000	Black
391 4002	Silver
391 4004	Blue
391 4006	Red
391 4008	Purple

B-1 Boot & Plate
Designed for use with round stick shifters. Complete with chrome ID plate and mounting hardware.

Part # 114 7336   4-3/8" x 5-1/2"

B-4 Boot & Plate
Hurst's most popular boot is adaptable to most shifter installations. Complete with chrome trim plate and mounting hardware.

Part # 114 4580   3-1/2" x 4-1/2"

ACCEL

Urethane Shifter Stabilizer Kit

This kit replaces the soft factory rubber shifter rod mount and bushing, providing a more positive feel of the shifter to help eliminate missed shifts under competition. A must when using the Hurst Quick/Stick Shifter or other aftermarket performance shifters. Easily installed.

Part #	Application
332 1000	1990-1997 Acura Integra
332 1000	1984-1987 Honda Civic/CRX
332 1002	1988-1997 Honda Civic/CRX

AROSPEED

Arospeed short-shifters are designed to give you shorter shift throws and quicker response. With less distance between throws, you can shift faster and more accurately on the track and on the street.

Part #	Application
ACURA	
ARO500502	1994+ Integra, Blue
ARO500505	1994+ Integra, Red
ARO500506	1994+ Integra, Polish
HONDA	
ARO500102	1988-1998 Civic, Blue
ARO500105	1988-1998 Civic, Red
ARO500106	1988-1998 Civic, Polish

DC SPORT

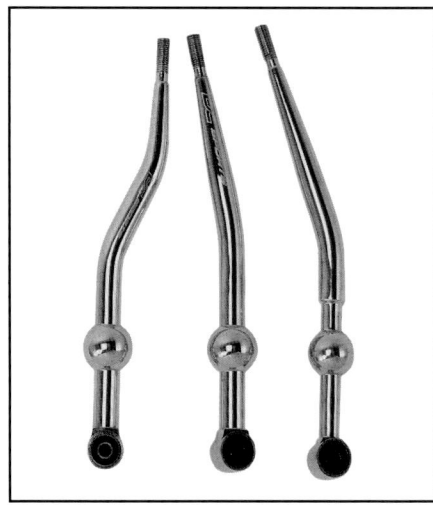

Reduce the time between shifts by installing a DC Sports Short Throw Shifter. The time you spend between shifts is time you're not on the throttle. The Short Throw Shifter can help you get through the gears quicker by reducing the shift throw by 45-50%

over the factory shift lever. CNC Machined. Sealed Bearing Bottom Bracket. Laser Engraved DC Sports Logo. Polished 6061 Aircraft Quality Aluminum.

Accord Prelude

Reduce the shift throw on your Honda Accord and Prelude by 30-35% by installing a DC Sports Short Shift Adapter. Simple installation. All hardware included right down to the allen wrench.

Billet Shift Knob

Anodized finish with a laser engraved DC Sports logo. Available in red, blue, and gun metal gray.

ENERGY SUSPENSION SHIFTER STABILIZER BUSHINGS

Energy Suspension's new performance polyurethane shifter stabilizer bushings for manual transmission cars provide precise, positive shifting under all conditions. Available for all popular Honda and Acura cars, as well as Mitsubishi Eclipse, Ford Escort/ZX2, and Nissan Sentra/200SX.

NEUSPEED

Neuspeed was the first to develop a true short shifter with a re-engineered pivot point (as opposed to a simple cut-down handle), and this unit proves Neuspeed technology is still in the lead. Applications: Honda/Acura/Audi/VW, including Beetle.

ABD RACING

The ABD Racing Short Shift Kit was ABD Racing's first production accessory. Now many years later, it is still one of the most popular items offered. By changing the geometry of the current shift linkage, the Short Shift Kit will reduce the shift throw by either 25, 45, or up to 65% less than the original pattern. Powder coated in bright silver for corrosion protection, the ABD Racing Short Shift Kit will bring you years of driving pleasure. Using O.E. linkage specifications, a counter weight is added to improve gear selection.

ABD Racing Short Shift Kit

Part #	Application
40;10	Rabbit / Scirocco / Jetta I (4 & 5 speed)
40;20	Golf / Jetta II (4 & 5 speed)
40;30	Golf / Jetta III 4 cyl. (comes with power shifter)

ABD Racing Power Shifters

Part #	Application
40;01	Rabbit / Scirocco / Jetta I
40;02	Golf /Jetta II & III 4cyl

Shift Linkage Components

Part #	Application

RABBIT / SCIROCCO / JETTA I 5-SPEED

171.711.574B	Shift linkage short rod
171.711.593E	Shift linkage long rod
171.711.163E	Shift rod selector
171.711.247	Gear shift lever w/ ball & spring
171.798.211	Complete shift bushing kit

GOLF / JETTA II 5-SPEED

191.711.595A	Shift linkage short rod
191.711.574	Shift linkage long rod
191.711.173B	Relay rod shaft
191.711.075A	Gear shift lever w/ ball & spring
191.798.211A	Complete shift bushing kit

Other shift kits

| 3.66.10.88 | Beetle / Golf / Jetta IV 5-speed (Neuspeed) |
| 3.66.10.55 | All VR6 & G60 Cars 5-speed (Neuspeed) |

LIGHTSPEED

Short Shifters

HO3035	1988-1998 Civic
HO3035	1990-1993 Integra
HO3094	1994-1998 Integra

STILLEN

A short shifter can make the whole driving experience more satisfying. The Stillen Short Throw Shifter bolts perfectly in place of the factory set up. All of the shifters have a precise feel with the confidence of knowing that your next gear pull will be right there.

TRD

Quick Shifter Kits

Applications:

1994-1997 Celica
1988-1991 Corolla GTS/SR5
1985-1987 Corolla GTS
1985-1989 MR2
1990-1995 MR2
1996 RAV4

MAZDATRIX

The price from suppliers just kept going up and up on short shifters, so Mazdatrix is now producing its own. The one-piece lever is made on an NC lathe from billet steel. Mazdatrix retains original shift knob threads for each year/model, and shifters are supplied with new upper AND lower bushings, plus a new inner shift lever boot. Each lever comes with needed hardware and installation instructions. The shorter throw of these Short Throw Shifters is accomplished by changing the pivot point of the lever. The distance the knob travels when shifting is shortened to 3-1/2" from the original 6".

Part #	Application
752-0126A	1981-1988
752-0114B	1989-1992
752-0113C	1993-1995

STR

STR Short Shifters are designed with the GSR shifter in mind. The special angle of the shifter gives that cool, easy shift feeling associated with GSR shifters. The STR shifter also allows four different adjustments for shift throw according to your driving habits and preference. All STR cool shifts are CNC machined and are the only anodized short shifter on the market.

When ordering STR products available in colors, please add a letter to the end of the part number to designate your desired color: R= red, B = blue, P = purple, Y = yellow. With no letter it will be shipped with a polished finish.

Part #	Application
SS0100	1988-1998 Acura Integra
SS0100	1988-1998 Honda Civic
SS0100	1988-1991 Honda CRX
SS0100	1993-1997 Honda del Sol

OBX

Performance Short Throw Shifters

Part #	Application
SS8898	1990-1993 Acura Integra
SS9498	1994-1998 Acura Integra
SS9497	1994-1997 Honda Accord*
SS8898	1988-1998 Honda Civic/CRX/del Sol
SS9497	1992-1997 Honda Prelude*
SS8994	1989-1994 Mitsubishi Eclipse*
SS9599	1995-1999 Mitsubishi Eclipse*
SS9700	1997-2000 Mitsubishi Mirage*
SS8999	1989-1999 Nissan 240SX*
SS9597	1995-1998 Nissan Sentra/200SX*
SS9397	1993-1997 Toyota Corolla*

Available in 3 Colors: Silver, Anodize Red, or Anodize Blue.
*Available in Silver ONLY.

GEARS

DINAN 3-SERIES

Acceleration is improved by lowering the gearing of the manual 323i and 328i to a shorter 3.15:1 final drive ratio.

3 Series E46
3 Series E36
3 Series E30
328i (E46) 1999
323i (E46) 1999
M3 (E36) 1996-1999
M3 (E36) 1995
328i (E36) 1996-1999
325i, iC (E36) 1992-1995
323i (E36) 1998-1999
318i (E36) 1996-1998
318i (E36) 1992-1995
318ti (E36) 1996-1999
318ti (E36) 1995
M3 (E30) 1987-1991
325i, ix, Convertible (E30) 1987-1991
325, 325e (E30) 1984-1988
318i (E30) 1990-1993
318i (E30) 1983-1985
323i (E30) 1983-1991

QUAIFE

Transmission Gear Kits

These kits have been designed to fit the standard gear cases of most popular competition cars. Available with dog-type engagement or synchromesh. Some kits replace four, with five gears or five with six gears. Gear kits for competition use are available for a wide range of vehicles, including:

Ford Escort
Honda Civic
Mazda RX7, turbo
Nissan Silvia

Nissan Skyline
Nissan Sunny/Pulsar Gti
Toyota Celica GT4
Toyota Corolla RWD AE86
Volkswagen Golf/02A and 02J type

Six Speed Front Wheel Drive Sequential Gearbox

Straight-cut gears with open-face dog engagement. Additional shaft support bearings for extra strength. More compact design allows easier installation. Differential accessed through separate cover for quick servicing.

ATB or Plate-Type Differentials

Compact drum-type sequential design for even faster gear shift. Range of detachable bellhousings from stock or manufactured as required. Driveshafts made to suit your installation. Large choice of gear and final drive ratios. Supplied with extension shafts and tube for equal driveshaft lengths. 100mm or 108mm output flanges fitted. Digital gear position display available. Remote gear lever with various length operating cables.

KAAZ

Close Ratio Gearsets

1994+ Integra and Civic DHOC VTEC
Stock — 1st: 3.231, 2nd: 2.105, 3rd: 1.458, 4th: 1.103, 5th: .848, Final: 4.400

MCH1850 — 1st: 2.667, 2nd: 2.118, 3rd: 1.682, 4th: 1.333, 5th: 1.069, Final: 4.400

FGH1841 — 1st: 2.667, 2nd: 2.118, 3rd: 1.682, 4th: 1.333, 5th: 1.069, Final: 4.063

FGH1835 — 1st: 2.667, 2nd: 2.118, 3rd: 1.682, 4th: 1.333, 5th: 1.069, Final: 3.500

FOR 1992 CIVIC SOHC

Stock — 1st: 3.250, 2nd: 1.909, 3rd: 1.250, 4th: .909, 5th: .750, Final: 4.250

MCH1650 — 1st: 2.533, 2nd: 1.864, 3rd: 1.385, 4th: 1.065, 5th: .824, Final: 4.250

FINAL GEARS FOR 1988 CIVIC SOHC

FGH1547 -- 4.688
FGH1545 -- 4.500

DIFFERENTIALS

DINAN

Limited Slip Differentials

If you could freeze time, imagine all the physical forces at play on your BMW when it is in the middle of negotiating a tight turn as opposed to when it is parked and sitting motionless. It all has to do with the physics of movement and the resulting forces and counter forces that affect weight distribution and a myriad of other things. One counter force that we employ is to improve the distribution of power between the two rear "drive" wheels when the car is cornering. A limited slip differential gives your 3 Series greater cornering ability and propels it out of a turn with authority.

TRD

Limited Slip Diffs available for these applications:

TOYOTA
1994-1997 Celica, clutch
1994-1997 Celica, helical
1984-1987 Corolla and Corolla GTS, clutch
1985-1989 MR2, clutch
1985-1989 MR2, helical
1990-1995 MR2, clutch
1990-1995 MR2, helical
1993-1997 Supra, clutch

QUAIFE

Automatic Torque Biasing Differentials

The unique design of the Quaife patented A.T.B. differential provides smooth constant traction for racing or slippery road conditions.

Suitable as a replacement for any rear or four-wheel-drive application, these differentials have the added benefit of no adverse effect on the steering of a front-wheel-drive vehicle. The A.T.B. differential is widely used from Formula 1 to emergency vehicles and public utilities where all weather mobility is essential.

Available to suit a very wide range of vehicles, including Ford, BMW, Mercedes, Land Rover/Range Rover, and light commercials. The differential progressively locks as torque increases; there are no plates or clutches to wear out as more conventional limited-slip designs. Is particularly effective in combating the effects of FWD torque steer.

With an ordinary open differential, standard on most cars, a lot of precious power is wasted during wheel spin under acceleration. This happens because the open differential shifts power to the wheel with less grip, along the path of least resistance.

The Quaife, however, does just the opposite. It senses which wheel has better grip, and biases the power to that wheel. It does this smoothly and constantly, and without ever completely removing power from the other wheel.

In drag-race style, straight-line acceleration runs, this results in a close to ideal 50/50 power split to both drive wheels, resulting in essentially twice the grip of an ordinary differential.

In cornering, while accelerating out of a turn, the Quaife biases greater power to the outside wheel, reducing inside wheel spin. This allows the driver to begin accelerating earlier, exiting the corner at a higher speed.

The Quaife also controls loss of traction when the drive wheels are on slippery surfaces such as ice and snow or mud, providing the appropriate biased traction needed to overcome these adverse conditions. The Quaife Differential provides constant and infinitely variable drive. Power is transferred automatically without the use of normal friction pads or plates seen in other limited-slip designs.

The Quaife's unique design offers maximum traction, improves handling and steering, and puts the power where it is needed most. A definite advantage whether on the track or on the street. The Quaife is extremely strong and durable and since the Quaife is gear operated, it has no plates or clutches that can wear out and need costly replacement.

The Quaife is great for street driving or racing. Racers don't have to put up with locking mechanisms or spools that tear the steering wheel out of their hands when cornering. Because it behaves like an open differential during ordinary driving, street drivers will have trouble telling it's there until pushing the car's limits.

The Quaife has been proven in everything from SCCA Rally to Formula 1. It provides autocrossers with such an advantage, it has become "required" equipment for a winning effort.

Quaife A.T.B. differentials are available throughout the world from various Quaife agents. Quaife's main agent in the US is Autotech in California.

Applications:

BMW 325/2002
BMW 5/7 Series
Chrysler (various applications)
Datsun R180/R200
Ford Taurus (USA)
Honda Civic/Accord/Integra
Ref: PL3/P80/P20/P21/PX5
Mitsubishi Eclipse 2WD
Nissan Primera
Toyota MR2, turbo
Toyota MR2, non-turbo
VW Beetle 1302/1303
VW Beetle swing axle
VW Golf/Scirocco/Jetta/Passat, with 020 transmission
VW Golf/Corrado/Jetta/Vento/New Beetle/Audi A3 & A4/Seat Ibiza/Skoda Octavia, with 02A or 02J transmission

KAAZ

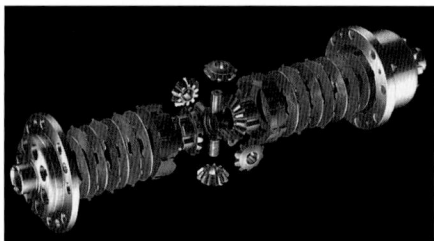

With a normal differential, the operation is very basic. The differential simply separates the power from the engine to the two wheels. The wheel which is simpler to turn gets more power so that the two wheels are running at different speeds, thus providing easier turn for the car. But, when the car is turning at higher speeds, the car will tilt to one side, and you hear the squelching sound. The car doesn't tilt as much as you see in the action movies, but tilting still occurs. When this happens, the normal differential puts more power on the wheel that is in the air, which is useless until the car is out of the turn. This is where a KAAZ limited slip differential can help to reduce the loss of power transferred to the wheel.

As you may already know, a race driver wins a race from gaining time when cornering. For this reason, many car manufacturers keep trying to make cars turn more efficiently at a faster speed without slipping out of the course.

As you can see, the side gears, pinion gears, and the pinion are all located inside the two pressure rings. Behind each pressure ring are several clutch plates "A" and "B." When the accelerator is stepped on, the differential case spins and pushes the pinion in between the pressure rings. The pressure rings are then pushed out against the clutch plates making the plates bind together and lock on both drive shafts making both wheels turn at the same speed. The cone spring is installed at the very end of each multi-clutch plate. The cone springs apply some initial torque to the plates so that the pinion doesn't need to be pushed too far to make the limited slip differential come into effect.

A special blend oil made by KAAZ named PowerTrain Gear Oil can be used to keep your limited slip differential running for long hours under the best condition. The oil helps the clutch plates to grip and slip when needed.

GEAR OIL & ADDITIVES

DYSON

Dyson Oil's Syngear II is designed to meet and exceed all known requirements for a lubricant in today's racing gear systems. It is formulated for both manual transmissions and differentials (rear ends). It has proven itself to be the gear lubricant of choice in all types of racing, from NASCAR Winston Cup to the smallest class in drag racing. It was tested in repeated runs at over 300 mph.

Syngear II is an 80w140, GL-6 rated gear lube blended from the highest quality base oils and extreme pressure additives. It incorporates an adhesive/cohesive component; adhering to metal surfaces for boundary layer protection and cohering to itself for greater film strength. It literally "climbs" the gears for maximum protection. Syngear II runs cooler in quick change differential racing gear systems. For maximum protection and minimum loss of horsepower, Syngear II is the very best. Proven in racing, Syngear II is excellent for all general automotive applications.

RED LINE

Red Line Gear Oils and Transmission Lubricants are designed to provide excellent low-temperature shiftability and improved gear protection at higher temperatures. Red Line Gear Oils will reduce differential temperatures 10-70°F. Efficiency improvements between 1-5% are typical. The synthetic base stocks used have tremendous thermal stability and provide the best film strength available. The unique combination of base stocks and additives allow Red Line gear and transmission oils to carry higher loads compared to petroleum lubricants. The stability of these products allow them to be used for extended periods.

MTL® Manual Transmission Lubricant

A 75W/80W GL-4 gear oil (SAE 5W30/10W30 engine oil viscosity) designed for use in manual transmissions and transaxles. Provides excellent protection of gears and synchronizers and its balanced slipperiness provides a perfect coefficient of friction, allowing easier shifting.

MT-90 Manual Transmission Lubricant

A 75W90 GL-4 gear oil designed for use in manual transmissions and transaxles. Provides excellent protection of gears and synchronizers and its balanced slipperiness provides a perfect coefficient of friction, allowing easier shifting.

75W90 Gear Oil

Recommended for most street-driven and racing differentials. Excellent performance in conventional and limited-slip units. Also for limited-slip manual transaxles which require a 90 weight oil. Contains limited-slip friction modifiers.

75W90NS Gear Oil

Recommended for manual transmissions and non-limited-slip transaxles that recommend 90 weight oils. Can be used in racing limited-slip units to increase lockup and reduce wheel spin. Street-driven rear-wheel drive cars should use regular Red Line 75W90 or 80W140.

75W140NS Gear Oil

Recommended for manual transmissions and non-limited-slip transaxles that recommend 140 weight oils. Can be used in racing limited-slip units to increase lockup and reduce wheel spin. Street-driven rear-wheel drive cars should use regular Red Line 75W90 or 80W140.

80W140 Gear Oil

Recommended for heavily-loaded and low-speed differentials, including limited-slip, and where reduction of limited-slip chatter or gear noise is required.

Shockproof™ Gear Oil

Recommended for heavily-loaded racing differentials and transmissions which see shock-loading. ShockProof contains a unique solid dispersion which cushions gear teeth to help prevent tooth breakage and allows the use of lower viscosities. Available as Superlight, Lightweight, and Heavy grades.

Differential Friction Modifier & Break-In Additive

This friction modifier is designed to reduce limited-slip noise and to aid the proper break-in of any differential. This can be added to any gear oil to reduce temperature during break-in and prevent gear softening. Replaces manufacturers' limited-slip additives. Can be used to perfectly tune a limited-slip unit. Red Line 75W90 and 80W140 Gear Oils already contain this additive.

Automatic Transmission Lubricants

Red Line Transmission Lubricants are designed to provide excellent low-temperature shiftability and improved gear protection at higher temperatures. Efficiency improvements between 1-5% are typical. The synthetic base stocks used have tremendous thermal stability and provide the best film strength available. The unique combination of base stocks and additives allow Red Line gear and transmission oils to carry higher loads compared to petroleum lubricants. The stability of these products allows them to be used for extended periods.

Synthetic ATF

Synthetic Dexron II, Mercon, and Mercedes-Benz approved fluid. Superior stability allows high-temperature operation without varnishing valves and clutches. Also provides improved shifting in cold weather.

D4 ATF

Synthetic Dexron III and Mercon fluid meeting the requirements of most transmission manufacturers, while satisfying GL-4 gear oil requirements. Superior stability allows high-temperature operation without varnishing valves and clutches. Also provides tremendously improved shifting in cold weather. The best low-temperature shiftability for manual transmissions and transaxles which require ATFs.

High-Temp ATF

A synthetic ATF which is a GL-4 gear oil for use where Dexron III or Mercon is recommended. A higher viscosity allows optimal operation at 70°F higher temperature, providing better torque converter efficiency. Perfect for heavily-loaded vehicles. Superior stability allows high-temperature operation without varnishing valves and clutches.

Racing ATF

A synthetic ATF for automatic and manual transmissions which need the positive shift of a TYPE-F ATF. This ATF contains no slipperiness additives, producing faster shifts and quicker lock-up. A higher viscosity at high temperatures provides greater efficiency and provides better wear protection than other ATFs.

CLUTCH AND PRESSURE PLATES

ADVANCED CLUTCH TECHNOLOGY

Advanced Clutch Technology (ACT) uses the latest in technology to manufacture custom performance clutch assemblies for racing and street applications. ACT has helped some of the world's top import drag racers to record-setting times. Applications for Acura, Dodge, Eagle, Geo, Honda, Infiniti, Mazda, Mitsubishi, Nissan, Subaru, Suzuki, and Toyota.

BORG WARNER

Brute Power Clutch and Flywheel

Part #	Application
DODGE	
90353	1996-1998 Dodge, Plymouth Neon 8 1/2-15/16-17T
EAGLE	
300924	1992-1996 Talon O.E. #MD188162 Flywheel
300925	1992-1996 Talon O.E. #MO194278 Flywheel
HONDA	
300927	1990-1996 Honda Accord 2.2L, 1992-93 Prelude 2.2L O.E. #22100-PT7-003 Flywheel
300928	1992-1996 Honda Civic 1.5L, 1.6L, 1993-1996 del Sol 1.5L, 1.6L O.E. #22100-P08-000 Flywheel
92333	1996-1997 Honda del Sol w/o VTEC eng. 7 7/8-27/32-20T
92329	1996-1997 Honda del Sol w/VTEC eng. 8 5/8-1 1/32-24T
MAZDA	
92078C	1986-1989 Mazda 323 1.6L exc., turbo 7 1/2-7/8-20T
92331	1989-1991 Mazda RX7 1.3L exc., turbo 8 7/8-1-22T
MITSUBISHI	
300924	1992-1996 Eclipse O.E. #MD188162 Flywheel
300925	1992-1996 Eclipse O.E. #MO194278 Flywheel
NISSAN	
92335	1996-1998 Pathfinder 3.3L 9 7/8-1-24T
92330	1996-1998 Truck 2.4L 9 1/2-1-24T
92334	1997-1998 2005X 2.0L 8 1/2-13/16-18T
PLYMOUTH	
300924	1992-1996 Plymouth Laser 2.0L, turbo 2WD O.E. #MD188162 Flywheel
300925	1992-1996 Plymouth Laser 2.0L, turbo 4WD O.E. #MO194278 Flywheel

CLUTCHNET USA

3 Button "Kwik Lok" Clutch Disc

This race clutch disc is designed for drag and road race use. It incorporates (3) sintered copper pucks bonded and riveted to a heat-treated high carbon steel plate. A rigid hub is also made of high carbon solid bar material for quick positive engagement, greater fatigue resistance, and improved heat dissipation. This disc is not intended for street use.

4 Button "Kwik Lok" Clutch Disc

This race clutch disc is designed for drag and road race use. It incorporates (4) sintered copper pucks bonded and riveted to a heat-treated high carbon steel plate. A rigid hub is also made of high carbon solid bar material for quick positive engagement, greater fatigue resistance, and improved heat dissipation. This disc is not intended for street use.

6 Button "Kwik Lok" Clutch Disc

This race clutch disc is designed for drag and road race use. It incorporates (6) sintered copper pucks bonded and riveted to a heat-treated high carbon steel plate. A rigid hub is also made of high carbon solid bar material for quick positive engagement, greater fatigue resistance, and improved heat dissipation. This disc is not intended for street use. Made for more slippage and ease in drive train.

3 Button "E-Z Lok"

Same as a 3 Button "Kwik Lok" but with a spring hub. The result is a positive lock up unit where steel has a degree of cushioning to prevent excessive driveline shock and breakage. A spring hub is made of high carbon solid bar material and turned on a CNC turret lathe for precise accuracy. Also heat treated. Needs less pressure; used for strip and street racing.

4 Button "E-Z Lok"

Same as a 4 Button "Kwik Lok" but with a spring hub. The result is a positive lock up unit where steel has a degree of cushioning to prevent excessive driveline shock and breakage. A spring hub is made of high carbon solid bar material and turned on a CNC turret lathe for precise accuracy. Also heat treated. Needs less pressure; used mostly for Off-Road Racing.

6 Button "E-Z Lok"

Same as a 6 Button "Kwik Lok" but with a spring hub. The result is a positive lock up unit where steel has a degree of cushioning to prevent excessive driveline shock and breakage. A spring hub is made of high carbon solid bar material and turned on a CNC turret lathe for precise accuracy. Also heat treated. Made for slippage and ease in drive train; used for Hi-Performance street.

"Air-Lok" Type, Organic Lining

A clutch disc assembly having a clutch plate assembly mounted between the clutch flywheel and pressure plate. The clutch plate assembly is made of a solid, heat-dissipating aluminum plate, a hub for axial movement relative to one another and to the hub, and clutch facings on the outer sides of the outer plates engageable with clutch facings on the flywheel and pressure plate.

"Kush-Lok" Type, Organic Lining

A progressive engagement clutch disc having a compressible clutch plate assembly mounted between the clutch flywheel and pressure plate. The clutch plate assembly has a pair of outer aluminum, heat-dissipating plates, a center wave spring plate coaxially mounted on a hub for axial movement relative to one another and to the hub, and clutch facings on the outer sides of the outer plates engageable with clutch facings on the flywheel and pressure plate. During clutch engagement, the clutch plate assembly and its spring are progressively compressed between the flywheel and pressure plate until the clutch plates are firmly gripped between the flywheel and pressure plate to permit torque transmission through the clutch without chattering, excessive stress on the clutch or transmission couplet to the clutch, and other problems associated with conventional clutches.

DINAN

3-series Lightweight Clutches

For those who want even faster acceleration and throttle response. These clutches give you faster engine revs and acceleration as a result of significant weight reduction. The Stage 1 Sport Clutch reduces weight by about 20%. The Stage 2 Performance Clutch reduces weight by about 30% and increases clamp load for improved lock-up, better harnessing the extra power of supercharged engines.

GUDE

Racing Clutches

Part #	Application
AICP01	1986-1989 1.6 DOHC
AICP02	1990-1995 1.8 DOHC
AICP03	1990-1996 1.7/1.8 DOHC

JACKSON RACING

Performance Clutch Assemblies

Rather than take a stock clutch, throw in a couple half-hearted mods, and call it a "performance" item, the Jackson Racing Clutch has been engineered from scratch as a complete package.

Designed for supercharged power levels, the pressure plate offers substantially increased clamping force without an undue rise in pedal pressure. The clutch disk features a carbon-kevlar lining for smooth engagement and extended life. Kit includes pressure plate, clutch disk, heavy-duty throwout bearing, pilot bearing, and clutch alignment tool. High performance engines burn up clutches. Highly recommended for street use in modified cars.

Part #	Description
900-130	1990-1993 Clutch Kit
900-125	1994+ Clutch Kit

CENTERFORCE

The dual-friction clutch assembly has up to 90% more holding power than stock clutches at higher RPM! The dual-friction clutch incorporates a non-asbestos synthetic composite material on one side, and a specially formulated RD200 thermal-resin compound on the other side. The dual-friction design, combined with a centrifugally assisted diaphragm, results in light pedal pressure, smooth engagement, and long clutch life.

ELP

Extreme-Duty Clutch Assembly

Stock OEM clutch components can experience a shortened life when they contend with increases in horsepower, and extended periods of hi-performance driving such as spirited street use, drivers schools, and drag racing. ELP offers the latest in clutch technology with the "Extreme-Duty" clutch assembly with its Carbon Kevlar disc. It was developed to thrive under harsh conditions. Club Racing? Supercharged or turbocharged engine? Using Nitrous Oxide? Drag racing? It's expensive, but this is the clutch package solution for you. The Carbon Kevlar material that is used in the "Extreme-Duty" clutch assembly is virtually bullet-proof, yet is very streetable allowing smooth engagement from standing starts.

TRD

Kevlar Performance Clutches

1994-1997 Celica, ST only
12/84 - 5/85 (Production Dates) MR2, normally aspirated
6/85 - 12/89 (Production Dates) MR2, normally aspirated
1988-1989 MR2, supercharged

Turbo Perf. Clutches
1986-1992 Supra, turbo
1993-1997 Supra, twin-turbo

LC ENGINEERING

LC Engineering offers a full selection of performance clutch kits and flywheels. Designed and built to custom specifications, the LC Pro Clutch Kits offer a full range of holding power from Street Performance to Racing applications. All LC Engineering clutch kits include: pressure plate, throw-out bearing, clutch disc, and installation tool.

Pro Clutch Kit

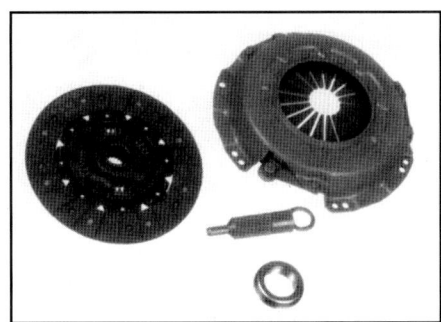

The LC Pro Clutch Kit features a heavy duty pressure plate combined with LC's custom disc. This disc, with small particles of brass impregnated into it, provides tremendous heat resistance and holding power. This clutch provides smooth operation and a slightly stiffer pedal with tremendous holding power for fast shifts and hard starts.

Part # 15-101P   Pro Clutch Kit

Dual Composite Clutch Kit

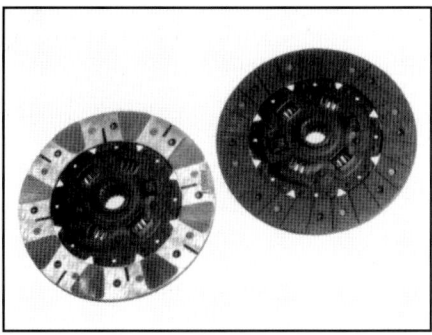

The Dual Composite Clutch Kit was developed for street racers requiring a more aggressive clutch without giving up everyday driveability. The key is the design of the clutch disc material — one side has metallic pucks for a positive hold and the other has the Pro Clutch Lining providing a smoother release to retain driveability.

Part # 15-106   Dual Composite Clutch Kit

Pro Metallic Clutch Kit

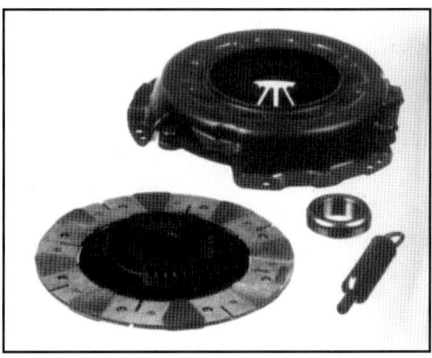

For race applications such as drag strip, circle track, and off-road, this is the clutch to run. A 1400 lb. pressure plate for maximum holding power, combined with a bullet proof metallic disc, and your clutch problems are over.

Part # 102M   Pro Metallic Clutch Kit

NEUSPEED

Raise your clamping force from the factory's 800-900 psi up to 1800 psi, with amazingly little difference in pedal pressure. Great for weekend racers, but thoroughly streetable for daily drivers.

RPS PERFORMANCE PRODUCTS

Thanks to the aftermarket and enthusiasts' continuing need for speed, 600+ horsepower Twin Turbo Zs, 320+ horsepower Eclipses/Talons/Lasers, and near 500 horsepower Hondas are becoming more and more common. But until recently, getting this much serious power to the wheels was no easy task. Enter RPS and the Turbo Clutch. This clutch is specifically designed for enthusiasts who want maximum holding power with smooth engagement.

Unlike other performance clutches which use stock pressure plates, the Turbo Clutch uses the patented "Power Plate" pressure plate that features a diaphragm which is 45 to 50 percent stiffer than stock. In addition, the clutch disk features a full 360 degrees of contact area with bonded riveted organic, brass impregnated facings. How does this translate into performance? The Turbo Clutch's maximum power handling capability is well over one and a half times stock. Surprisingly, the Turbo Clutch offers this performance without the tradeoffs usually associated with other performance clutches.

For example, many race style clutches only allow for high RPM, neck straining starts and so they are unsuitable for daily driving. Other performance set-ups often use buttons or pads of friction material which don't have the holding power or durability of a 360 degree full contact clutch plate facing. These problems are avoided in the Turbo Clutch, since the Turbo Clutch attains its additional clamping force by means of a considerably stiffer pressure plate instead of a special compound clutch disc.

Carbon Claw, Superlite High Performance Clutches

RPS Performance Products has released an exciting new clutch line for use with almost any year import car and even a few American cars. It features faster shifting due to its extremely light weight, unbelievable heat capabilities, and strength. It is the only type of its kind available on the aftermarket parts scene, and are surprisingly affordable. They are targeted for use in vehicles having up to 100 hp over stock. A super-light aerospace Carbonite disc material is the main feature, which will be coupled with a heavy-duty pressure plate.

At the same time RPS has released a new flagship line called the Turbo Clutch Carbon. These units feature the same great pressure plate technology already in use with the Turbo Clutch Classic kits, but also include the new Carbonite discs used in the Carbon Claw kits. These bad boys provide even more holding power, lighter weight, added durability, and incredible heat resistance capabilities. Available for Acura, Dodge, Eagle, Honda, Mazda, Mitsubishi, Nissan, Toyota, and Volkswagen.

UNORTHODOX RACING, INC.

Ultra Grip Clutch Sets

Stage 1
Matched heavy-duty pressure plate. Full-faced, 100% pure kevlar solid disc. Throw-out bearing.

Stage 2
Matched lightweight aluminum flywheel. Matched heavy-duty aluminum pressure plate (strapped for street/pinned for race). Single Disc. Up to 700 hp and 400 ft./lbs.

Stage 3
Matched lightweight aluminum flywheel. Matched heavy-duty aluminum pressure plate (strapped for street/pinned for race). Dual Disc. Up to 1000 hp and 700 ft./lbs.

Applications for:

Acura
Audi
BMW
Honda
Mazda
Mitsubishi
Nissan
Subaru
Saturn
Toyota
Volkswagen

CLUTCHMASTERS

Clutchmasters offers competition clutches for five levels of performance driving. Stage 1 has a heady duty cover, organic sprung hub, performance disc, that's good for entry-level performance mods. Stage 2, adds a full face kevlar disc, that'll take more and fade less. Stage 3 adds trapezoid kevlar into the friction surface. Good for a street/strip car and healthy nitrous shots. Stage 4 gets into a 4-puck ceramic button disc. Designed for larger turbos and big doses of nitrous. Stage 5 is a severe duty single- or dual-diaphragm and rigid sintered iron or 3- or 4-puck disc. This is a full-blown racing clutch, not recommended for the street and is sold as a race-only piece. Applications for most popular sport compacts including several engine transplant configurations.

REV HARD

After experimenting with numerous combinations of pressure plates and clutch discs, Rev Hard has discovered the optimum in clutch performance for your Honda/Acura. Extensive testing on turbo-nitrous race cars, has lead RH to produce a clutch set with maximum grabbing power with only a minimal increase in pedal stiffness. All RH clutch sets utilize a double diaphragm pressure plate and a metallic disc. These high-performance clutches have proven themselves on the street and track for years and now they are available for your import racer. Good for up to 400 hp.

Applications for:

Acura
1986-1989 Integra
1990-1991 Integra
1992-1993 Integra
1994+ Integra

JIM WOLF TECHNOLOGY

300ZX TT Clutch Set

With 1100KG clamping force, the need for a harsh, non-organic friction material is eliminated. This clutch makes a solid connection even with the nitrous spool-up kit to 570+ hp, while maintaining a smooth engagement.

Part #	Description
LZ320-TM000	300ZX TT Clutch Set
EZ320-NM000	300ZX Non-Turbo 700 KG Pressure Plate (Can be used with stock disk.)

300ZXTT Severe Duty Disc

Metallic pads on the pressure side maintain friction during hard launches, with a less aggressive material toward the flywheel for smoother engagement.

Part #	Description
LZ314-TM1MD	300ZXTT Severe Duty Disc

FLYWHEELS

ELP MOTORSPORTS

ELP's lightweight steel flywheel is primarily intended for hot street use, but it's also an economical road racing alternative to an aluminum flywheel. This lightweight steel flywheel retains enough mass for comfortable standing starts in street use, yet is sufficiently lighter to afford a noticeable improvement in low-speed acceleration and offer lightening quick throttle response.

ELP's aluminum flywheel is intended primarily for serious road racing and rallying, due to its substantial reduction in inertia and flywheel weight. ELP's flywheels are specially CNC machined and feature bolt-on ring gear for added longevity and a bolt-on tuftrided steel friction surface for long clutch life. All flywheels include necessary installation hardware. These units are custom built to order.

FIDANZA ENGINEERING

Fidanza is proud to offer the world's highest quality and best engineered aluminum flywheels. Fidanza's engineers are always working on new flywheels to expand an ever-growing product line.

AFH16

Attention 1.6L SOHC Civic owners: Your aluminum flywheel is in stock and ready to ship. At only 6.5 lbs., this flywheel will have your Honda flying.

AFH16DC

The 1.6L DOHC is already a potent engine. Fidanza has an aluminum flywheel that will make it a world class engine.

AFH18DC

This aluminum flywheel for the 1.8L DOHC engine will help rocket your Acura/Honda past the competition.

Saturn - Ready to ship

BMW M3

Misc. Porsche

Miata

Fidanza Engineering is more than happy to create one off, custom flywheels for almost any application. If you can provide Fidanza Engineering with your factory flywheel, then Fidanza can provide you with a high-quality performance unit.

ZEX INNOVATION

Zex Light & Ultra Light Flywheels

Constructed from 100% chromoly steel and designed to be 200% stronger than stock. These flywheels are ideally suited for any racing or hi-performance street application. Two different weights are offered based on your setup requirements.

Part #	Application
C82412	1990+ Acura Integra light weight flywheel
C82418	1990+ Acura ultra light weight flywheel
C82410	1990+ Honda Civic light weight flywheel
C82416	1990+ Honda Civic ultra lightweight flywheel
C82414	Infiniti G20 lightweight fly wheel
C82420	Infiniti G20 ultra light weight flywheel
C82414	Nissan Sentra SER, GXE, 200SX lightweight flywheel
C82420	Sentra SER, GXE, 200SX ultra lightweight flywheel

LC ENGINEERING

LC Engineering performance flywheels are available in both lightweight and heavyweight versions. The 9 lb. aluminum and 12 lb. steel race flywheels deliver excellent acceleration and performance while retaining a stock-style clutch assembly. The LC Engineering Heavyweight Hi-Torque flywheel will give your 4WD the extra inertia to pull those bigger tires and crawl over the toughest obstacle. CNC machined to close tolerances, each flywheel comes complete with a new ring gear and is balanced ready for installation.

If you circle track, drag race, or have a street slammer with small tires, add the 9 lb. Aluminum Flywheel and hang on. You'll feel acceleration like you never thought possible even with a stock engine. It idles smooth and revs super fast, just the thing for 2WD trucks and Celicas! This highly specialized custom flywheel features a replaceable steel "wear plate" the clutch disc rides on. Many circle track racers have won with this bullet-proof flywheel!

Part # 15-104   9 lb. Aluminum Flywheel

Racers who have to run a steel flywheel with a factory-type clutch kit, this is the flywheel for you. This 12 lb. Billet Steel Flywheel — not "cast iron" — accepts a stock clutch and pressure plate. Combine this flywheel with a LC Pro Metallic Clutch Kit and your are off to the races.

Part # 15-112   12 lb. Billet Steel Flywheel

The 30 lb. High Torque Flywheel increases the rotating inertia of the engine. It helps freeway performance.

Part # 15-103   30 lb. Hi-Torque Flywheel

For circle track open class racers, this 11.5 lb. clutch and flywheel assembly is the ultimate. It consists of an aluminum flywheel, pressure plate, and kevlar clutch disc to provide a reliable lightweight performance package. Fits 20R & 22R applications.

Part # 15-107   Gold Star Aluminum Clutch

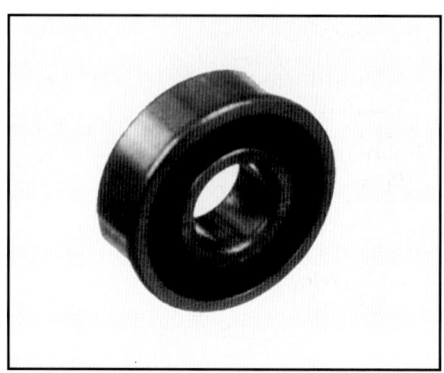

The pilot bearing is installed in the crankshaft end to support the transmission pilot shaft. It should be replaced whenever installing a new clutch, flywheel, or engine.

Part # 15-105   Pilot Bearing

UNORTHODOX RACING, INC.

ULTRA Light Aluminum Flywheels available for:

Acura	Mitsubishi
BMW	Nissan
Chrysler	Saturn
Dodge	Subaru
Eagle	Toyota
Ford	Volkswagen
Honda	
Lexus	
Mazda	

CLUTCHMASTERS

Clutchmasters new precision CNC machined, billet aluminum flywheels are specifically designed for performance or daily driver applications. All flywheels include new starter ring gear, replaceable heat shield, new pressure plate bolts, and pilot bearing if applicable.

Acura Integra	9 lbs.
Honda Civic	8 lbs.
Honda Accord/Prelude	10 lbs.
Mitsubishi VR-6	7 lbs.
Nissan SER 2.0	10 lbs.
Nissan 300ZX, twin turbo	13 lbs.
Toyota Supra, turbo	9 lbs.
Toyota MR2-T/All Trac	11 lbs.
Toyota Supra, twin turbo	14 lbs.

COMPTECH SPORT

Lightweight Aluminum
Flywheel
(GSR, RS, GS, LS)
6.75 pounds
Replaceable Friction Surface
For Years: 1994+

Lightweight Aluminum
Flywheel
(Type R)
6.75 pounds
Replaceable Friction Surface
For Years: 1997-1998

CONVERTERS

HKS

The ALC (Automatic Line Controller) has been developed for the computer-controlled automatic transmission, as equipped on the Nissan 300ZX. The ALC is designed to maintain line pressure within the transmission for consistent, high performance shifting. Should the pressure begin to drop within the transmission, the ALC will adjust to maintain an acceptable level.

DUNRITE CONVERTERS

Dunrite Converters offers modified converters. These high-stall converters help automatic trans-equipped machines perform on the street and strip.

SAFETY-SCATTERSHIELDS, TRANS BLANKETS ETC.

B&M SCATTERSHIELD

Finally a scattershield for the import racer! This heavy-duty plate steel shield provides the "hard core" import

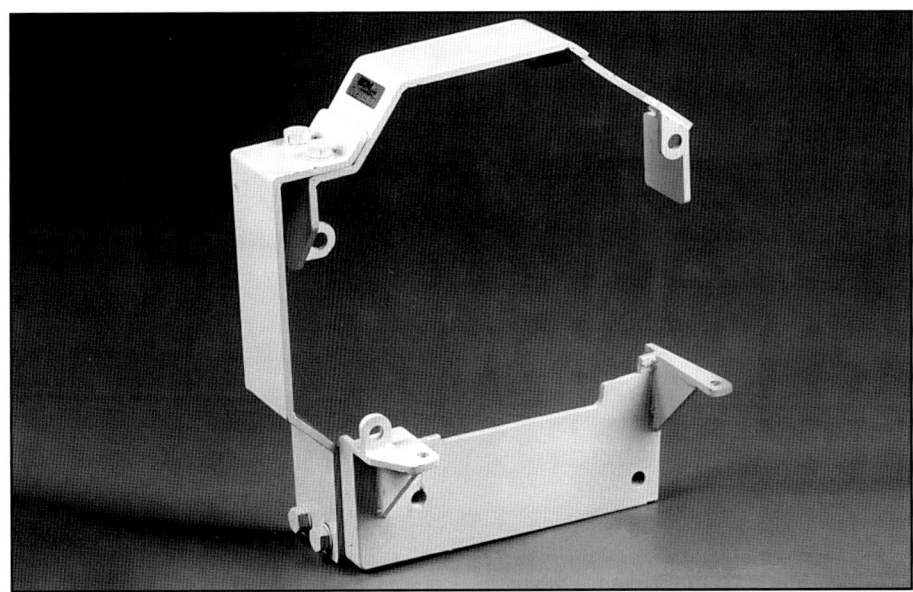

B&M Scattershield for Acura Integra

racer with the protection needed for today's ultra-high output engines. The unit is constructed of 1/4" plate steel and is designed to directly bolt on to the transmission using the supplied class 10.9 fasteners. The three-piece design allows ease of mounting while retaining full protection and strength. REQUIRED BY NHRA AND NIRA FOR ALL 11.99 SEC. OR QUICKER CARS.

Part #	Application
22148	1990-1993 Acura Integra
22149	1994-1998 Acura Integra

MOTOR MOUNTS

ENERGY SUSPENSION

Urethane Motor Mount Inserts

Many front wheel drive vehicles are breaking their stock torque-limiting motor mounts. Breakage is common not only at the strip but also on the street! If you're heavy-footed, check under the hood! Torn mounts allow the entire power train to jerk and flop around.

Made of HYPER-FLEX™ polyurethane construction, these inserts protect your existing O.E.M. rubber mounts form tearing, controls torque, and diminishes wheel hop. A must to use with modified motors! Can be removed for stock running if so desired. Even works with torn O.E.M. mounts. The motor mount insert sets are available for these front wheel drive vehicles with manual transmissions in red or black color:

**1990- 1999 Acura Integra
1998-1999 Ford Contour
1997-1999 Ford Escort & ZX2
1990-1997 Honda Accord
1988-1999 Honda Civic
1993-1997 Honda del Sol
1992-1996 Honda Prelude
1999 Mercury Cougar
1995-1999 Mitsubishi Eclipse
1991-1994 Nissan Sentra**

As shown, the motor mount inserts are typically easy to install, because the motor mounts are usually located at the underside of the vehicle. Once the vehicle is on a safety ramp, installations can be made in approximately 5 to 10 minutes each mount for Accords and Civics and no more than 1 hour with others.

TRD

Bushing and Motor Mounts

TOYOTA
1997-1999 Camry/Camry Solara
1985-1987 Corolla
1/92-10/93 (Production Date) MR2
11/93-1995 (Production Date) MR2
1985-1989 MR2
1990-12/91 (Production Date) MR2

BRAKE SYSTEMS

AEM

AEM High-Performance brake kits deliver precise control providing improved driver confidence. Turns become more manageable and straight-aways can be used to the fullest. Uniquely designed, AEM engineered these kits with exclusive MGS technology featuring larger diameter rotors. The kits allow for upgrades from original calipers to AEM two- and four-piston calipers. These new products carry the same level of quality and function as AEM engine performance products.

AEM Performance Brake Pads are designed to exact performance specifications by AEM and manufactured in Japan by an O.E. supplier to insure precise fit and performance. The program begins with Stage One, which includes oversized cross-drilled and gas-slotted rotors. This stage allows for the relocation of factory calipers. Stage Two features AEM two piston calipers for improved braking. Stage Three steps up with top-of-the-line four-piston calipers. Both Stage Two and Stage Three calipers come preloaded with AEM performance brake pads. All AEM High-Performance Brake Kits feature oversize cross drilled rotors with billet aluminum hats in a choice of three anodized colors: red, blue, or silver. Note: All kits require the use of wheels which are larger than stock diameter. All kits are 100% bolt-on requiring no drilling, cutting, or grinding to install.

AROSPEED

Arospeed big brake upgrades are now available for Honda Civic and Integra. These massive 13" rotors will shorten your stopping distance. These are high performance brake kits for street vehicles.

Arospeed's big brake upgrade features larger calipers with a 6-piston design and large 13" rotors that are both cross drilled and slotted to provide proper cooling and displacement of brake dust. The upgrade also includes stainless steel brake lines and metallic brake pads. Rotors can be mounted using a 4 lug pattern or a 5 lug pattern. All necessary parts are included.

The calipers come in two different anodized colors: blue and red. Each caliper is laser etched with the Arospeed logo and are great for fast cars or show cars. If you have 18" wheels with little brakes, upgrade to these big brakes and notice how much better they look.

BAER RACING

Offering weight savings in addition to dramatic performance enhancements over most OE performance car brake systems, SS systems are popular for cars that run on both the street and the strip. SS systems feature a 12" diameter x .810" ventilated rotor and 2 piston PBR DOT legal aluminum calipers. SS packages can be used with many aftermarket 15" and most 16" wheels.

Fitting most of the same wheels as SS systems, SPORT versions feature a heavy-duty 12" x 1.1" thick directionally ventilated rotor. SPORT systems also feature the newer pressure cast Baer logo version of the aluminum PBR caliper and are the legal specification for SCCA A-Sedan competition. SPORT systems are essentially identical in every respect except rotor diameter to TRACK systems.

Baer's TRACK system's 13" diameter rotor and logo version PBR caliper combine to produce solid, reasonably priced, and very serious performance.

GRAND TOURING (GT)

Employ a new design, larger, black, PBR pressure cast, Baer logo caliper with a substantially greater pad volume that also accepts rotors of up to 1.25" thick. GT systems are ideal for use on heavier vehicles such as the Impala SS.

GRAND TOURING+ (GTP)

Utilizing the large PBR as in GT Systems, GTP versions for cars feature a 14" diameter x 1.25" directional two-piece rotor with a 9" diameter billet aluminum hat. Serious performance and strong visuals make GTP systems a cost effective alternative to PRO+ systems for obtaining huge rotors on street rod applications.

PRO

Alcon 4 piston B-Type caliper-based systems are built with a cost effective one-piece 13" diameter and 1.1" thick directionally ventilated rotor. The Alcon calipers feature staggered pistons (1.5/1.625") to minimize potential pad taper, a radial mount configuration, and a proper bridge bolt for maximum rigidity, as well as having appropriate road going dust and weather seals. The exceptional caliper coupled to a rotor which is very cost effective have made this system very popular with enthusiasts who charge hard at the track or in canyons.

PRO+

Baer's top-of-the-line 4-piston system. Standard with 13.5" (or optional 14") diameter x 1.25" thick, Alcon 48 vane directionally ventilated rotors.

PRO+ systems deliver outrageous braking performance and repeatability simply not available from other 4-piston systems. PRO+ packages are only eclipsed by Baer's own EXTREME+ systems. PRO+ systems provide a significant upgrade for tuner cars.

EXTREME+

Featuring Trans Am 6-piston calipers homologated for street use. EXTREME+ systems are the most potent road going brake systems

AEM HIGH-PERFORMANCE BRAKE KITS

Stock Rotor Dia.	AEM Rotor Dia.	Big Brake Kit Part #	Big Brake 4 Pst. Cal. Kit Part #
ACURA			
1990-1999 Integra, exc. Type R			
F:10.31"	12.10"	29-500	29-800
R: 9.41"	11.10"	29-600	N/A
HONDA			
1990-1993 Accord			
F:10.24"	12.10"	29-511	29-820
R:	N/A	N/A	N/A
1994-1997 Accord, 4 cyl.			
F:10.24"	12.10"	29-511	29-820
R:	N/A	N/A	N/A
1998-1999 Accord, 4 cyl.			
F:10.22"	12.10"	29-512	29-822
R:	N/A	N/A	N/A
1998-99 Accord, V-6			
F:10.22"	13.25"	29-514	29-824
R:	N/A	N/A	N/A
1992-99 Civic EX, 1992-1995 SI w/ABS, 1999 SI			
F:10.31"	12.10"	29-500	29-800
R:9.41"	11.10"	29-600	N/A
1992-1996 Prelude			
F:11.09"	12.10"	29-516	N/A
R:	N/A	N/A	N/A
1997-1999 Prelude			
F:11.10"	13.25"	29-518	N/A
R:	N/A	N/A	N/A
MITSUBISHI			
1995-1999 Eclipse, 2WD (Drum in Disk for Rear Kit)			
F:10.08"	11.70"	29-560	29-861
R:10.31"	11.50"	29-630	N/A
1995-1999 Eclipse, AWD (Drum in Disk for Rear Kit)			
F:10.83"	12.50"	29-561	29-861
R:10.31"	11.50"	29-630	N/A

Notes: When ordering insert "B" for blue, "C" for clear, or "R" for red after part number to indicate color desired.
-1 Incorporates the existing O.E. caliper. All brackets and hardware included.
-2 Replaces existing caliper with high performance 4 piston unit.
-3 All Big Brake kits can be upgraded to a 4 piston caliper with the following:

AEM HIGH-PERFORMANCE CALIPER KITS

Stock Rotor Dia.	AEM Rotor Dia.	Big Brake 4 Pst. Cal. Kit*F:(4)
ACURA		
1990-1999 Integra, exc. Type R		
10.31"	12.10"	28-400
HONDA		
1990-1993 Accord		
10.24"	12.10"	28-410
1994-1997 Accord, 4 cyl.		
10.24"	12.10"	28-410
1998-1999 Accord, 4 cyl.		
10.22"	12.10"	28-411
1998-1999 Accord, V-6		
10.22"	13.25"	28-412
1992-1999 Civic EX, 1992-1995 SI w/ABS, 1999 SI		
10.31"	12.10"	28-400
MITSUBISHI		
1995-1999 Eclipse, AWD		
10.83"	12.50"	28-430

Notes:
-4 Includes all brackets, hardware, 4 piston calipers, and pads
All AEM High Performance Brake Kits feature CNC machined 6061 T-6 billet aluminum center hubs anodized in Blue, Clear, and Red.

All Honda and Acura brake kits can only be used with larger than stock wheels.
*Rotor kits, specify color of rotor hat by inserting a B for blue, C for clear, or R for red at the end of the part number to indicate color desired.

(1) All O.E. caliper upgrades include bracket and hardware to reposition the O.E. caliper to accommodate the larger two-piece rotor.
(2) All two-piston upgrades include a pair of two-piston calipers, brackets, pads, and hardware to replace the O.E. calipers.
(3) All four-piston upgrades include two four-piston calipers, brackets, pads, and hardware to replace O.E. calipers or two-piston calipers.

BAER CLAW SYSTEMS

Type	Part	Caliper, # Pists.	Rotor Dia.	Rotor Width	Rotor Type	Surface Spec
ACURA						
Integra all except "Type-R" - 1991 & up						
FRONT:						
TRACK	F1AI-10150-4HN	PBR, 2	13.00	1.10	36V-Dir	None
PRO	F1AI-10170-4HN	Alcon, 4/B	13.00	1.10	36V-Dir	None
PRO+	F1AI-10180-AMS	Alcon, 4/B	13.50	1.25	48V-Dir	Rev-Slot
REAR:						
ENHANCE	F0AI-10631-EAN	no caliper	9.40	0.40	Solid	None
Integra Type-R - 1996-1998						
FRONT:						
TRACK	F6AG-10150-5HN	PBR, 2	13.00	1.10	36V-Dir	None
PRO	F6AG-10170-5HN	Alcon, 4	13.00	1.10	36V-Dir	None
PRO+	F6AG-10180-AMS	Alcon, 4	13.50	1.25	48V-Dir	Rev-Slot
HONDA						
Civic Coupe 93-97 EX, del Sol 93-97 w/V-Tec, Hatchback 94-95 w/ABS, Sedan 90-97 EX, Sedan LX 94-97 w/OE rear discs & ABS						
FRONT :						
TRACK	F0HC-10150-4HN	PBR, 2	13.00	1.10	36V-Dir	None
PRO	F0HC-10170-4HN	Alcon, 4	13.00	1.10	36V-Dir	None
PRO+	F0HC-10180-AMS	Alcon, 4	13.50	1.25	48V-Dir	Rev-Slot
Civic Coupe 93-97 DX & HX, CRX 90-91, del Sol 93-97 except V-Tec, Hatchback 94-95 CX, DX, VX & 96-97, Sedan DX 90-97, Sedan LX 90-93 & 94-95 w/OE drum, Sedan LX 96-97 w/o-ABS, Wagon 90-91						
FRONT:						
TRACK	F0HC-10151-4HN	PBR, 2	13.00	1.10	36V-Dir	None
PRO	F0HC-10171-4HN	Alcon, 4	13.00	1.10	36V-Dir	None
PRO+	F0HC-101810-AMS	Alcon, 4	13.50	1.25	48V-Dir	Rev-Slot
Civic - All w/OE rear disc - 1992-1997						
REAR:						
ENHANCE	F2HC-10631-EAN	no caliper	9.40	0.40	Solid	None
Prelude W/O V-TEC- 1997 & up						
FRONT:						
TRACK	F7HP-10151-5HN	PBR, 2	13.00	1.10	36V-Dir	None
PRO	F7HP-10170-5HN	Alcon, 4	13.00	1.10	36V-Dir	None
PRO+	F7HP-10180-AMS	Alcon, 4	13.50	1.25	48V-Dir	Rev-Slot
Prelude W/V-TEC 1993-96						
FRONT:						
TRACK	F3HP-10151-5HN	PBR, 2	13.00	1.10	36V-Dir	None
PRO	F3HP-10170-5HN	Alcon, 4	13.00	1.10	36V-Dir	None
PRO+	F3HP-10180-AMS	Alcon, 4	13.50	1.25	48V-Dir	Rev-Slot
Prelude - 1992-1997						
REAR:						
ENHANCE	F2HP-10631-EAN	no caliper	10.25	0.40	Solid	None
MAZDA- Miata - MX5 - 1989-1998						
FRONT:						
SPORT	E9MM-10120-4GN	PBR, 2	12.50	1.10	36V-Dir	None
PRO	E9MM-10170-4HN	Alcon, 4	13.00	1.10	36V-Dir	None
PRO+	E9MM-10180-AMS	Alcon, 4	13.50	1.25	48V-Dir	Rev-Slot
REAR:						
ENHANCE	E9MM-10631-EAN	no caliper	10.25	0.40	Solid	None
MITSUBISHI (Diamond Star)						
Eclipse, Talon & Laser - 1995-1999						
FRONT:						
SPORT	F5ME-10120-5EN	PBR, 2	12.00	1.10	36V-Dir	None
TRACK	F5ME-10150-5HN	PBR, 2	13.00	1.10	36V-Dir	None
PRO	F5ME-10170-5HN	Alcon, 4	13.00	1.10	36V-Dir	None
PRO+	F54ME-10180-AMS	Alcon, 4	13.50	1.25	48V-Dir	Rev-Slot
Eclipse, Talon & Laser - 1989-1994						
FRONT:						
SPORT	E9ME-10120-5EN	PBR, 2	12.00	1.10	36V-Dir	None
TRACK	E9ME-10150-5HN	PBR, 2	13.00	1.10	36V-Dir	None
REAR - 94 AWD Eclipse, Talon - 2wd Turbo from 1/94-on, 4wd Turbo 11/94-on						
ENHANCE	F4ME-10631-EAN	no caliper	10.30	0.45	Solid	None
REAR - Eclipse, Talon - 4wd Turbo 1/94 - 10/94						
ENHANCE	F4ME-10631-EBN	no caliper	11.18	0.80	Vented	None
REAR - Eclipse, Talon - All from 5/88-12/93						
ENHANCE	E8ME-10631-EAN	no caliper	10.45	0.35	Solid	None

ever offered. Alcon dominates Trans-Am, with 6 consecutive championships and wins in all but one race in six years. So don't confuse the billet Alcon with massive 7793 series pads with 6 piston units offered by any other company. If you require the best, you have found it.

WORLD CHALLENGE (WC)

Built to exploit 1999 SCCA Pro-Racing World challenge rules, this system features Alcon 4 piston (maximum allowed by rules) K-Type calipers featuring stainless pistons and thermal barrier caps, ceramic disc path coating. These are mated to Alcon pre-bedded 2-piece discs of 13 x 1.25". Race systems are designed for use with tandem master cylinder and pedal assemblies with a balance bar and are shipped without pads or hoses.

ENHANCE

Order an ENHANCE rear with any front system and then optionally order slotted or cross drilled/slotted & zinc washed rotor upgrades for all four, so all will cosmetically match.

ENHANCE+ units include a performance rotor which solves an OEM rotor problem witnessed in hard street or track use.

BREMBO

All Brembo high-performance brake kits come complete with four-piston calipers and pads, cross drilled and/or slotted 12 to 14 inch discs, stainless-steel braided brake lines, and hats and brackets made specifically for your type of vehicle.

STILLEN

Stillen Brake Pros have announced the release of its newest Big Brake kit.

The Stillen engineered brake system has been designed to bolt on in place of the OE rotors and calipers. The ABS compatible system features new fixed-mount AP Racing six-piston calipers and two massive rotors measuring (330mm x 28mm Mitsu Eclipse) (343mm x 35.5mm 300ZX and Supra). The calipers and rotors meet DOT and TUV specifications. The kits are complete with everything needed for installation including performance brake pads, stainless steel brake lines, mounting hardware, and instructions.

STILLEN / AP RACING 6-PISTON CALIPER SYSTEM

AP Racing 6-piston caliper is made of lightweight cast aluminum and has a fixed mount for minimal caliper flex. Differential piston sizes (2x27/32/38mm) minimize pad taper and maximize even friction pressure. Anti-rattle springs reduce pad noise. Calipers have inner wiper and outer dust seals for everyday use. AP Racing 332/343/355 x 35.5mm Rotors. Directionally curve vented for maximum cooling; cross drilled and slotted for aggressive pad bite and proper out-gassing; two-piece modular disc brake pad with a pad area of 76.3cm squared x 2 per caliper; pad material designed for high performance road and track use. Consistent friction co-efficient at low and high temperatures.

STILLEN / PBR SINGLE PISTON REAR DISC CONVERSION

PBR Single Piston Caliper is made of lightweight cast aluminum and has a pin-guided floating mount. Piston sizes are 54mm. Anti-rattle springs reduce pad noise. Calipers have inner wiper and outer dust seals for everyday use. Stillen Sport Rotors (313x26mm) are vented for maximum cooling; cross drilled and slotted for aggressive pad bite and proper out-gassing. Brake pad area is 28cm squared x 2 per caliper. Pad material designed for high performance road and track use. Parking brake mechanism is the patented Banksia Parking Brake which has a drum-style single hoop shoe and automatic adjustment.

PBR 2-Piston Caliper is made of light weight cast aluminum and has a pad-guided floating mount. Piston sizes are 2x38m. Pad taper is minimized and even friction pressure maximized. Anti-rattle springs reduce pad noise. Calipers have inner wiper and outer dust seals for everyday use. Stillen Sport Rotors (328x28mm) are directionally curve vein vented for maximum cooling; cross drilled for aggressive pad bite and proper out-gassing. Brake Pad area is 53.2cm squared x 2 per caliper. Pad material is designed for high performance road use.

BREMBO

4-piston caliper lightweight cast aluminum with fixed mount for minimal caliper flex. Differential piston sizes are 2x36/40mm; minimizes pad taper and maximizes even friction pressure. Anti-rattle springs reduce pad noise. Inner wiper and outer dust seals are for everyday use. Brembo 328 x 28mm rotors are directionally curve vein vented for maximum cooling; cross drilled for aggressive pad bite and proper out-gassing. The two-piece modular disc kit (# 305550) uses a 330 x 28mm directionally curve vein vented cross drilled single piece rotor. Kit # 030308 uses a 313 x 28mm two-piece rotor. Kit # 305850 uses a 320 x 28mm two-piece rotor. Brake pad area is 54.2mm squared x 2 per caliper. Pad material is designed for high performance road and track use. Consistent friction co-efficient at low and high temperatures.

SMC
KWIK STOP BIG BRAKE KITS

Cars that have been modified to higher levels of performance can have the stock braking system fall short on stopping power. Braking forces needed to stop a typical car are generally as much as 4 times the horsepower of the engine. The Kwik Stop System will provide improved braking through larger size cross-drilled brake rotors, calipers, pads, and stainless braided brakelines.

RM RACING

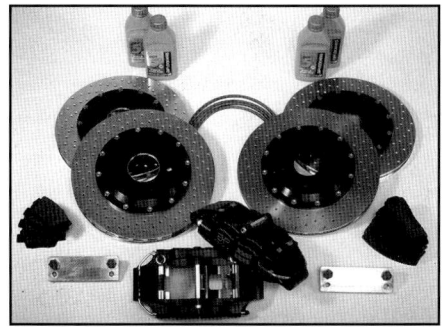

Over the past two years, RM Racing has had several requests to supply a big brake upgrade that would correct the problems of the kits currently available. The first problem to overcome was wheel fitment. The big brake kits required extra clearance where the caliper meets the rim section. This means the use of one-piece wheels which limited owners to very few wheel choices. Also large offsets and even spacers are used to set the front wheels outward. By using the AP 38.1 X 41.2 caliper, RM Racing's kit is able to clear most wheels, including three-piece wheels, while maintaining the correct offset.

The second problem with big brake kits was every day driveability. Kits have been known for excessive pad wear, heavy brake dust, heavy squealing, and an unbalanced front-to-rear bias. The AP/KVR Brake Kit takes care of this problem by employing the use of a four-piston front caliper and the use of the o.e. rear caliper with 13" rotors front and rear. This results in a very well balanced front-to-rear bias. And with multiple pad compounds available, owners can dial in their brake kit to fit their personal needs: heavy street, street/track, full race.

The last problem with the brake kits on the market was their high price. There are several brake choices on the market today for the NSX and RM Racing has found a solution to the other big brake kits problems with the AP/KVR Brake Kit. RM Racing was not hasty on the decision to support just any kit.

STOPTECH

Offers a line of big brake kits and components. The company's Aerorotor is aerodynamically designed to improve cooling air flow. The ST4000 caliper line is a series of four-piston units with varying piston diameters, matched to each application. The firm's ST200 line is a series of two-piston caliper with varying piston diameters also matched to applications.

RYANE

Supertrack Brakes increase brake efficiency by replacing the original Honda rotors with huge 13" rotors. And as you probably already know, sometimes, size DOES count!! Ryane offers two kits. Both come with aircraft-quality CNC machined billet aluminum caliper mounting brackets and hardware. You don't need any fancy equipment because the kit can be easily installed using simple hand tools.

Stage One Package will save you money because it utilizes your existing stock caliper. Ryane custom-designed a special bracket so that your caliper and the big rotor can work together to give you the kind of brake capacity you need to tame that animal you've got under the hood!

Stage Two Package is the ultimate kit. If you really want to make use of the 13" rotors then you will want this kit. The kit includes: unique CNC machined brackets, race-proven Wilwood billet aluminum 4-piston calipers (almost 4 times the clamping power and one-third the weight!), with high-performance polymatrix brake pads, braided stainless-steel Teflon flex-hoses, all necessary hardware, and detailed, illustrated instructions. Rear brakes available upon request.

ROTORS

NEUSPEED

Improve stopping performance with these high-quality rotors from Neuspeed. Mill balancing and CNC machining assure vibration-free braking. Slotted or cross drilled versions available.

POWER STOP

These drilled brake rotors are now available for a wide variety of Japanese import applications. These rotors are the exact same size as the factory rotors. This allows you to upgrade your rotors without upgrading to very costly brake calipers. Cross-drilled rotors will eliminate brake fade and also enhance braking in wet conditions. After several stops, spirited driving, and under emergency braking, they will perform better than your original brake components.

Each rotor is drawn to scale and engineered with a specific drilled pattern. This data is then programmed onto a CNC machine. All holes are radiused to the correct wear limit. Radiusing, unlike chamfering, provides a smooth transition from rotor surface to the cooling holes. This reduces stress points and allows superior pad performance. All rotors are constantly checked for accurate balancing and are designed with a unidirectional pattern. A pair must consist of a left and a right rotor. All rotors are cadmium plated to military specifications for a high-performance look while also protecting the machined areas from the elements. The Power Stop cross drilled rotors have been designed to be used on high-performance vehicles but they are also extremely effective for practical street.

POWER PERFORMANCE GROUP INC.

Power Slot rotors are high-quality pieces that have a solid reputation and following of informed tuners. New for this year are platinum rotors made from a premium mill balanced, Italian casting with 50% more slots then plated with a nickel over cadmium process. Super bright and effective. They also have red and blue plated rotors in addition to traditional cadmium.

COMPTECH

Cooler brakes promote longer rotor and pad life, no matter what kind of driving you do. Precision machined holes or slots in these rotors allow hot brake pad gasses to escape, acting as a vent to keep your brakes cooler, leading to improved stopping power.

BRAKE PADS

AEM

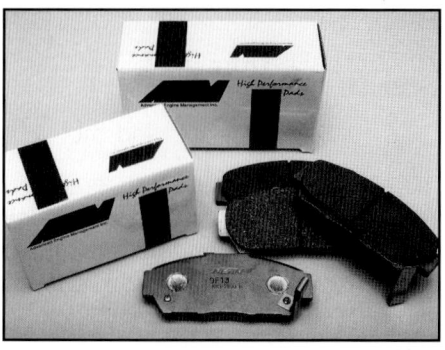

To improve the performance of original equipment calipers, AEM offers its line of high-performance brake pads. Jointly engineered by AEM and Nissin, a major Japanese O.E. brake manufacturer, these pads are made in Japan under strict AEM performance specifications. This added effort yields precise fitment, vast performance improvements, and superb pedal control. These high-performance brake pads reduce stopping distance on wet or dry road surfaces providing an extra measure of security and performance. This is possible because the pads have a higher coefficient of friction. These pads work in harmony with O.E. ABS or non-ABS brake systems. The materials used are superior to those offered as original equipment.

BAER RACING

ALCON PAD UPGRADES, Standard are Textar ST9 units.
Performance Friction 93 Comp
0ALC-13703-93F -- Race/Excellent Combo, Friction & Modulation/CART Spec

PBR PAD UPGRADES, standard are PBR high metallic units.
FRONT
Performance Friction 80 Comp
0PBR-13412-80F — Endurance Racing
Performance Friction 83 Comp
0PBR-13412-83F — Race/Highest Overall Friction
Performance Friction 90 Comp
0PBR-13412-90F — Most Serious Street/Track Events/Very Linear
Performance Friction 93 Comp
0PBR-13412-93F — Race/Best Combination of Friction/Modulation
REAR
Performance Friction 80 Comp
0PBR-13413-80F — Endurance Racing
Performance Friction 83 Comp
0PBR-13413-83F -- Race/Highest Overall Friction

Performance Friction 90 Comp
0PBR-13413-90F -- Race/Track Events/Very Linear
Performance Friction 93 Comp
0PBR-13413-93F -- Race/Best Combination of Friction/Modulation

BRAKEMAN

Hiperformance Pads and more for the following:

Application	Front	Rear
ACURA		
1986-1989 Integra	6-2334	6-2364
1990-1991 Integra	6-2409	6-2374
1992-1994 Integra	6-2409	6-2564
1992-1994 Vigor	6-2503	6-2537
BMW		
1969-1976 2002	6-2085	---
1983-1990 318	6-2493	---
1984-1990 318i, 325, 325i	6-2278	6-2279
1991-1994 318i, 325, 325i	6-2558	6-2396
1977-1979 320i	6-2109	---
1979-1983 320i	6-2174	---
1980-1981 528b	6-2163	6-2164
1989-1994 525i-535i	6-2394	6-2396
1982-1988 528e	6-2395	6-2379
1983-1988 533i-535ie	6-2395	6-2379
1979-1982 633CSi	6-2163	6-2164
1983-1988 633CSi-635CSi	6-2395	6-2379
1978-1986 733i-735i	6-2163	6-2279
1987-1993 735-750	6-2394	6-2396
1991-1995 850i	6-2547	6-2548
1988-1991 M3	6-2395	6-2396
1985-1988 M5	6-2163	6-2279
1991-1993 M5	6-2394	6-2396
1987-1991 M65	6-2163	6-2396
HONDA		
1986-1988 Accord-DX	6-2334	---
1988-1989 Accord-LXI	6-2409	---
1990-1994 Accord	6-2465	---
1980-1994 Civic	6-2465	---
1984-1994 CRX	6-2465	---
1984-1994 Prelude		---
MAZDA		
1979-1985 RX-7	6-2076	---
MITSUBISHI		
1987-1988 Cordia	6-2328	---
1990-1993 Eclipse, exc. 4WD	6-2484	6-2533
1993 Eclipse, 4WD	6-2530	6-2533
1992-1994 Mirage	6-2484	6-2533
1983-1989 Starion	6-2258	6-2144
1990-1994 3000 GT-SL	6-2530	6-2383
1991-1993 3000 GT-VR4	8-2531	6-253283
NISSAN		
1970-1978 240, 260, 280	6-2076	---
1987-1988 200SX, 6 cyl.	6-2266	6-2272
1984-1985 200SX, turbo	6-2422	6-2272
1989-1993 240SX, w/abs	6-2485	6-2272
1979-1981 280ZX	6-2166	6-2167
1982-1983 280ZX	6-2229	6-2230
1984-1989 300ZX	6-2266	6-2272
1987-1988 300ZX, turbo	6-2358	6-2272
1990-1993 300ZX	6-2460	6-2461
1991-1992 NSX 2.0L	6-2509	6-2511

AEM BRAKE PADS

Application	Front Pads	Rear Pads
ACURA		
1997-1998 CL, 4 cyl.	26-130	26-205
1997-1998 CL, V-6	26-120	26-205
1986-1989 Integra	26-105	n/a
1990-1993 Integra	26-200	26-125
1994-1998 Integra, exc. RS	26-140	26-200
1997-1998 Integra, Type R	26-120	26-205
1986-1990 Legend	26-125	26-205
1991-1995 Legend	26-120	26-205
1991-1995 Legend, exc. GS	26-120	26-205
1991-1998 NSX	26-120	n/a
1996-1998 RL	26-120	26-205
1995-1998 TL	26-120	26-205
1992-1994 Vigor	26-120	26-205
HONDA		
1984-1985 Accord	26-135	n/a
1986-1988 Accord DX, LX	26-105	n/a
1988-1989 Accord Coupe DX	26-105	n/a
1989 Accord, coupe Sei	26-125	26-200
1988-1989 Accord LXI, SEi	26-200	26-125
1990-1993 Accord	26-115	26-205
1990-1993 Accord, Akebono Cal	26-130	n/a
1991-1998 Accord, wagon	26-120	26-205
1993-1998 Accord Coupe DX, LX, EX, SE	26-130	26-205
1994-1998 Accord DX, LX, EX	26-205	26-130
1995-1998 Accord, V-6	26-205	26-120
1984-1987 Civic/CRX 1.5/1.6 Si, DX, wagon	26-100	n/a
1988-1989 Civic/CRX, CRX Si	26-135	n/a
1988-1991 Civic/CRX, CRX DX	26-135	n/a
1988-1991 Civic, wagon	26-135	n/a
1988-1996 Civic H.B., 1.5/1.6 CX, DX, VX, Si (w/o ABS)	26-135	26-200
1988-1996 Civic, 1.5/1.6 DX, LX (w/o ABS)	26-135	n/a
1990-1993 Civic EX	26-125	26-200
1993-1995 Civic Coupe DX	26-135	n/a
1993-1995 Civic Coupe EX w/ABS	26-140	n/a
1993-1995 Civic Coupe EX 1.6 w/o ABS	26-150	n/a
1994-1995 Civic EX, LX w/ABS	26-140	26-200
1994-1995 Civic H.B. Si w/ABS	26-140	n/a
1996 Civic DX, HK	26-135	n/a
1996-1998 Civic Coupe, EX	26-160	n/a
1993-1996 del Sol, S, Si w/o ABS	26-135	26-200
1994-1995 del Sol VTEC w/ABS	26-150	n/a
1983-1987 Prelude DX	26-100	n/a
1985-1987 Prelude Si	26-105	n/a
1988-1991 Prelude SE, Si	26-125	26-200
1992-1996 Prelude S, SE, Si (non VTEC)	26-145	26-205
1993-1998 Prelude VTEC	26-120	26-205

Application	Front	Rear	Application	Front	Rear
PORSCHE					
1964-1968 356C, 911	6-2031	6-2021	1978-1990 930, turbo	6-2345	6-2031
1969-1973 911S	6-2084	6-2031	1991-1992 930, turbo	6-2372	6-2031
1969-1973 911T, ES	6-2031	6-2031	1985-1993 944	---	---
1974-1983 911	6-2345	6-2031	1992 968	6-2372	6-2372
1979-1987 911, turbo	6-2345	6-2341	1992 969	6-2372	6-2345
1984-1989 911 Carrera	6-2345	6-2031	**TOYOTA**		
1970-1972 914, 4 cyl.	6-2002	6-2002	1991-1994 MR2	6-2242	6-2528
1970-1972 914, 6 cyl.	6-2002	6-2003	1992-1993 Paseo	6-2242	6-2642
1973-1976 914, 4 cyl.	6-2002	6-2003	1989-1992 Supra	6-2435	6-2337
1981-1987 924 and S	6-2251	6-2252	1986-1990 Tercel	6-2242	---
1981-1985 928	6-2253	6-2252	**VW**		
1986-1991 928	6-2372	6-2345	1990-1993 Corrado	6-2280	---
1973-1976 914, 4 cyl.	6-2002	6-2003	1985-1989 Jetta GLI	6-2280	6-2340
1981-1987 924 and S	6-2251	6-2252	1979-1984 Rabbit	6-2158	---
1981-1985 928	6-2253	6-2252	1984-1985 Scirocco	6-2280	---
1986-1991 928	6-2372	6-2245	1979-1983 Scirocco	6-2158	---
1976-1977 930, turbo	6-2345	6-2031			

BRUTESTOP

Formulated and designed specifically for performance production cars and light trucks, including street rods, muscle cars, and custom cars.

Brutestop gives performance-minded drivers the features they've always wanted in aftermarket disc brake pads. Brutestop's specially formulated friction material gives superior braking power under all conditions — from normal traffic to the most extreme hard-driving situations. And, Brutestop's integrally molded construction is four times stronger than conventional pads using rivets.

AXXIS (FORMERLY REPCO)

METAL MASTER BRAKE PADS

Axxis Brake Pads will give the performance enthusiast superior braking power over the stock friction pads. The metal composition of the pads will give you that extra bite, more effective braking power at higher heat ranges, and reduced brake fading. These pads are great for the street. They don't need to be heated up to a higher temperature range in order to work at peak optimal efficiency. The pads will generate minimal dust build up and have a very minimal wear rate. Works great with your drilled brake rotors!

HAWK PERFORMANCE

High performance Ferro Carbon brake pads that fit most OEM and aftermarket calipers. Developed with partnerships with racing teams in just about every venue.

HT10 S — Very High torque for the most extreme forms of racing. Lightly climbing mu plot. Excellent pad for high decel open wheel formula cars. Developed with Tema Rahal for PPG CART apps.

HT9 G — Very high torque with superior peak feel. Lower wear rate than HT 10 at high temperatures. Designed for stock cars and touring cars over 3000 lbs.

HT8 H — High torque pad with a flat mu plot. Excellent brake modulation characteristics. Designed for a wide temperature range where stock rotors and calipers are used. Good for cross-drilled rotors. Low pad and rotor wear rate. Recommended for showroom stock, rally racing.

Blue MT4 L — High torque pad designed specifically for circle track cars under 2900 lbs. Excellent pad and rotor wear rate. Good brake modulation.

Blue 9012 E — Medium/High torque brake compound. A reliable performer with a wide temperature range. Low pad and rotor wear with good brake modulation. Recommended for road race and rally where low- to medium-temperature performance is required.

DR 97 J — Developed for drag racing. Excellent dynamic and static coefficient of friction. Low pad and rotor wear.

HP Plus N — High performance street material, plus race worthy. Very high torque and rotor friendly for the serious street driver. Can also be used for club racing and driving schools.

HPS F — High performance street material. Extremely low dust, high friction, rotor friendly, silent running brake pad.

COMPTECH

Comptech offers three levels of performance brake pads, for every type of driver and driving condition. Pads sold as matching pairs, front and rear.

Metal Master

Premium asbestos-free semi-metallic brake pad for the aggressive driver who wants a firmer pedal feel and high performance stopping power. For high performance street use.

Hot Street

Very high friction levels even at cold temperatures with no dust or squeal. This is the fastest stopping carbon kevlar road pad available. Great for limited competition and solo events.

Competition

This race-only brake pad utilizes high friction carbon kevlar material designed especially for heavy-duty motorsports. Carbon kevlar pads have a unique ceramic heat shield integrally molded and designed specifically for high-temperature applications to minimize heat transfer.

EBC

GREENSTUFF PADS

These are high-performance sport pads that can be used on the highway without the drawbacks of a full race pad. Brake comes on strong from the first pedal application, delivering an ultra powerful brake effect right up to a blistering 500°C disc temp. Can be used for track days, but monitor wear.

REDSTUFF PADS

A semi-metallic full competition pad for closed circuit use. Although Redstuff has a lower friction level than Greenstuff, brake effect increases steadily with temperature, making this pad ideal for racing. In highway use, this material will "lag" slightly on first application compared to Greenstuff, which is why it is NOT RECOMMENDED for street use.

TURBO GROOVE ROTORS

British-made using quality grey iron castings and precision CNC machined, EBC turbo groove rotors. Available for most import models. Sold in pairs.

BRAKE LINES

BAER RACING

Teflon Braided Stainless-Steel Hose Sets available in the following lengths: 6 - 10", 11 - 16", 17 - 22", 23 - 29", and 29 - 35".

TRD

1985-1989 MR2, 1990-1995 MR2
1986-1992 Supra, 1993-1997 Supra

GOODRIDGE USA
G-STOP BRAKELINE KIT

Goodridge USA has made it easy to improve your vehicle's braking performance. The company's DOT-approved G-Stop Brakeline Kits follow the precise path of your original brake lines, so they're an easy bolt-on swap. Plus, they're the only direct OE-replacement kits that feature stainless-steel braided PTFE hose.

Why make the swap? To get better performance, of course. The G-Stop Brakeline Kits eliminate any spongy feel in the brake pedal and chatter caused by anti-lock brake systems. What's more, the kit's braided hose covering resists line expansion caused by operating system pressures, which means your brake system will respond sooner, reducing your braking distance.

Goodridge offers more than 600 different G-Stop Brakeline Kits for over 850 domestic and import car, truck, and SUV applications, including Mustangs, Corvettes, and Camaros. Plus, the company vows that if you don't see your year, make, and model in its application charts, it will make up a kit just for you. Goodridge also can build custom lines for any application.

The G-Stop Kit's stainless-steel braided lines are available with clear or colored plastic sheathing. The steel hose end fittings feature Goodridge's exclusive platinum finish, and they're permanently attached to the hose via a Goodridge-exclusive crimping method. Each kit is designed to match the look and exact fitment of your vehicle's original lines, so no modifications are necessary. The kits come complete with all bolts, washers, in-line mounting brackets, and locating tabs.

All G-Stop Brakeline Kits are engineered and assembled to exceed federal requirements for use on public roads. In fact, these are the only brake lines in the world that are legal for use on virtually every public road in the U.S., Canada, Mexico, Europe, Japan, Australia, and New Zealand.

Goodridge also is the only company worldwide that guarantees each brake line has passed a stringent series of quality assurance tests, including tensile pull, pressure testing to 3,000 psi, and three separate visual inspections. This meticulous attention to quality before each kit is shipped enables Goodridge to provide the ultimate warranty: G-Stop Brakeline Kits are guaranteed to the original purchaser forever.

NEUSPEED

Specifically engineered, designed, and assembled for your car. An inner Teflon tube covered with high-quality stainless steel provides durability and positive, firm pedal action. Neuspeed's HP series kits feature an additional outer teflon cover to minimize line expansion.

SMC

SMC is a California Tuner that offers attractive high performance stainless braided brake lines. Stainless-steel products are by far the highest quality material available in the market today. The qualities and properties of stainless steel allows these brake lines to resist heat build up, to prevent condensation from occurring, to eliminate possibility of hose cracking or bursting, and to allow maximum flow of pressure to the brake calipers when the brake pedal is depressed.

Utilizing the best lines and fittings available from Goodrich, SMC has matched these stainless braided to the factory lines perfectly. All lines come ready to install and have all the correct mounting brackets to utilize the factory mounts. All lines will come in color-coated synthetic skin to add an attractive and aggressive appeal.

COMPTECH SPORT

Comptech Sport DOT-approved Stainless Brake Lines offer increased braking power by reducing the amount of brake line flex. Each line is precision engineered, utilizing a Teflon inner core wrapped in durable stainless steel. Installs on factory mounting brackets and pressure fittings. No modifications required for installation.

EARL'S

Tests performed by Earl's concluded that vehicles equipped with Earl's HyperFirm™ brake lines, recently approved by the Department of Transportation, stop up to 10% quicker than OE-style rubber brake hoses. The line also includes HyperTemp™ high-temperature brake fluid and HyperGrip™ high-performance brake pads.

ROLL CONTROL

HURST

These adapter fitting kits simplify the installation of a Roll/Control or Line/Loc system into late model Honda vehicles having metric threaded brake line fittings. Designed to be used with the Hurst Roll/Control Installation Kit #567 1510, these kits consist of special conversion fittings needed for a fast, simple installation.

Advanced quality design stainless-steel valve assembly for ultimate corrosion resistance. Fully enclosed epoxy-molded electrical coil for reliability. Attractive finned-aluminum housing helps dissipate heat. Wider lightweight base provides better mounting stability. Field serviceable for cleaning or rebuilding. Threaded port for separate bleeder or brake line pressure gauge. Includes on/off push button switch. 12-volt negative ground systems only.

CAUTION: The Hurst Roll/Control or Line Loc® should not be used as an emergency brake, or any application requiring the solenoid to be activated for a long period of time.

Part #	Application
567 1517	1990-1998 Acura Integra
174 5000	1988-1998 Honda Civic/CRX

ROLL/CONTROL SWITCH

The Roll/Control Switch incorporates a micro switch for an immediate and accurate release. Includes 2 feet of wire for installation hookup to the Roll/Control, nitrous systems, trans brakes, or other 12 volt accessories. 10 amp capacity.

Part #	Description
248 3875	Replacement Switch for Hurst Roll/Control
44050	Anti-Roll Kit

Brake line locks are used in Drag Racing to lock the front wheels and hold the car in the water box for the burnout, or to prevent creeping in the lights. New anti-roll design has better holding power than any other unit currently available. Solenoid valve is totally rebuildable (see Kit No. 44051) and can be disassembled for easy cleaning.

Kit contains a heavy-duty push button switch, switch bracket, coiled wire, rebuildable line-lock valve, fuse holder, and indicator light. Extruded aluminum shifter handle mounting bracket is far superior to any other in use today. Heavy-duty construction and quality components provide reliable operation after repeated use. Universal Momentary Switch (#74122) available separately.

Sport Compact Bolt-On Performance Guide Volume 1 — Suspension

HANDLING KITS

APEX

The Apex Sport Kit consists of four lowering springs plus four special shock absorbers which lower the car by 60 mm at the front and 40 mm at the rear. The short, specially hardened piston rods of these gas shock absorbers provide a more sporty performance than the car's original shock absorbers. Combined with the matching springs, these shock absorbers improve the dynamic driving qualities of your car while maintaining your driving comfort.

Fitting an Apex Sport Kit to your car lowers the car's center of gravity, as a result of which the car's road holding is considerably improved. The result: the car is not only safer, it is also more of a pleasure to drive.

Part #	Application
BMW	
KF 20-1035/45 **	E30 4/6 cyl.
KF 20-1035/51 ***	E30 4/6 cyl.
KF 20-1080	E36 4 cyl.
KF 20-1080/1	E36 4 cyl.
KF 20-5000	E36 Compact
KF 20-6000	Z3 4 cyl. ex.M-susp.
KF 20-6010	Z3 6 cyl. ex.M-susp.
VOLKSWAGEN	
KF 80-1000	Golf I
KF 80-2000	Golf II
KF 80-2000/1	Golf II from 4.89
KF 80-2010	Golf II GTi, 16V
KF 80-2010/1	Golf II GTi, 16V from 4.89
KF 80-3000	Polo I/III
KF 80-3052	Polo 6N
KF 80-6000	Golf III
KF 80-6000/1	Golf III from 9.94
KF 80-6010	Golf III GTi, 16V
KF 80-6010/1	Golf III GTi, 16V from 9.94

** = only for 45 mm housing
*** = only for 51 mm housing

Apex Racing Kit

The engineers at Apex have drawn directly on experience from the world of motor sport in developing the Apex Racing Kit. The extreme demands that racing on circuits puts on the suspension have led to the use of the most advanced and reliable methods of production and only the best materials. Thus the piston rods of the gas shock absorbers are heat treated and hard-chromed and high quality PFTE seals are used. Quality which pays dividends in the form of a long life-span.

The Apex Racing Kit consists of four lowering springs with matching shock absorbers, which, depending on the model and type of car, offers the possibility of lowering the car's center of gravity anywhere up to a maximum of 85 mm. (depending on model/type). Important millimeters, which serve to considerably improve your car's performance! You will notice the difference when driving at speed along winding country roads, but equally if you should have to perform a fast lane-change on the motorway.

The Apex Racing Kit is smoothly adjustable for height. Go for "extremely sporty" with maximum lowering, or for extra comfort with a somewhat higher position. The Apex Racing Kit turns a factory-produced car into a custom-built model.

DINAN

Sport And Performance-Tuned Suspension Systems

While offering your 3 Series an aggressive stance, Dinan Sport and Performance-Tuned Suspension Systems help your 3 Series' tires stick to the pavement, while maintaining a civilized ride. The springs and shocks work together to enable your BMW to hug the road and remain composed, resulting in flatter cornering, better traction, and more predictable handling.

Larger, adjustable front and rear anti-roll bars further reduce body roll and allow you to fine-tune the system to your personal driving style or even for the type of tires you have on your car. The anti-roll bar bushings are manufactured using the same material and process as those that came on your car, so that there is no compromise in quality.

Camber plates deliver a higher level of performance handling by reducing understeer or your car's tendency to push straight ahead instead of turning in. You'll experience steering response that can transform every on-ramp into a racetrack corner.

Three suspension systems, from Sport to Performance, are available to match your driving level. Each offers a stronger dose of cornering capability and sophistication. The Stage 1 Sport System includes matched springs with struts and shocks. The Stage 2 Sport Performance System adds the larger, adjustable anti-roll bars. The Stage 3 Performance System adds camber plates. Most systems are available with your choice of Bilstein or Koni struts and shocks. Koni front struts can be adjusted with a quick turn of a knob, allowing you to fine-tune ride and handling characteristics.

Applications:
3 Series E46
3 Series E36
3 Series E30
328i (E46) 1999
323i (E46) 1999
M3 (E36) 1996-1999
M3 (E36) 1995
328i (E36) 1996-1999
325i, iC (E36) 1992-1995
323i (E36) 1998-1999
318i (E36) 1996-1998
318i (E36) 1992-1995
318ti (E36) 1996-1999
318ti (E36) 1995 M3 (E30) 1987-1991
325i, ix, Convertible (E30) 1987-1991
325, 325e (E30) 1984-1988
318i (E30) 1990-1993
318i (E30) 1983-1985
323i (E30) 1983-1991

ROD MILLAN MOTORSPORTS

Type NR suspension offers a balance of performance, styling, and ride comforts. Type NR damper is engineered and equipped with self adjusting valving mechanism to handle the various road conditions. Each damper offers a 4-step C-ring height adjustment for styling and performance at affordable prices.

Type NR/NA Suspension Kit is based on performance, styling, comfort, and balance. Every aspect about suspension has been reviewed in order to create a new footwork at levels which could not be accomplished with the typical lowering spring or lowering spring with sport shock combination. In a short stroke sports shock absorber, the damping effect must be adjusted in order to absorb the impact from the various road conditions. Most lowering spring and sport shock combinations leads to bumpy and uncomfortable ride quality.

TEIN

Tein's Type NA/NR Suspension Kit expanded the case diameter at the same time it shortened the casing. This allowed for improvement of 130% fluid capacity over normal and maximum stroke. This feature led to stabilizing the damping effect and can bring sporty handling with low-down form with a balanced comfortable ride without needless adjustment of the spring rate and damping effect. In addition, it also allows for changing tires and wheel sizes, an ever popular option.

Type NA suspension kit is designed for high performance driving and autocross / road racing, at an affordable price. With 16 levels of dampening and rebound adjustment, and 4 levels of height adjustments, this gives the Type NA unlimited amount of freedom to fine tune the footwork of your vehicle. The results of this design have greatly reduced the deterioration of performance due to heat expansion, and this design is able to endure longer hard driving without loosing ride quality and dampening consistency.

Tein's upper pillow mount helps integrating the shock absorber and vehicle relation to give drivers a better feel of the road. Depending on the vehicle type, some models offer camber adjustment (sold separately).

Each of Tein's NA/NR suspension kits comes with Tein's own Low-Down S-Tech Springs. Each spring is formed to suit each specific vehicle's spring setting. Three types of springs are available to choose from: hard, medium, and soft.

Type HR provides freedom to raise or lower your vehicle's ride height. Type HR also reduces friction noises and improves damping precision by reducing by half the clearance of the rod guide compared to conventional dampers. All Type HR dampers use a special guide ring at the guide bushing to make the damping control even more precise. With 35mm piston and twin-tube design, this improves durability with the addition of greater damping precision and larger oil capacity. The lower spring seats, seat lock, and upper spring seat are die-cast aluminum for high strength and low weight. Tein's newly formulated oil provides consistence-damping control in both low and high temp. Kit includes: (4) Dampers, (4) Primary Springs, (4) Secondary Springs, (1) Manual, (1) Height Gauge Tool, and (2) Wrench Tools. Available for Toyota, Nissan, Mazda, Honda, Acura, Lexus, Subaru, and Mitsubishi.

RYANE MOTOR SPORTS

Civic Front Drop Spindle

This is a special front spindle designed to lower the front of the vehicle by 2" without changing any of the control arm angles relative to the vehicle chassis. This is the industry-approved method of suspension lowering as it does not alter the manufacturer's geometry design.

WEAPON*R USA

Super Tuner Suspension 2

Part#	Application
ACURA	
STS4	1986-1989 Integra
STS5	1990-1993 Integra
STS6	1994+ Integra
HONDA	
STS7	1986-1989 Accord
STS8	1990-1993 Accord
STS9	1994-1997 Accord
STS10	1998+ Accord
STS1	1988-1991 Civic / CRX
STS2	1992-1995 Civic
STS3	1996+ Civic
STS11	1986-1990 Prelude
STS12	1992-1996 Prelude
STS13	1997+ Prelude

In automotive circles the word spindle is used to describe an assembly which consists of a spindle, an upright member (which separates the upper and lower ball joints), a steering arm, and a variety of brackets for mounting brake components, etc. The actual spindle is the shaft about which the wheel rotates. On a "lowering spindle assembly" the shaft is raised in relation to the upright member, thereby having the effect of lowering the vehicle relative to the wheel. When installing, no other changes are required. Because it does not modify the original factory geometry, no camber kits are necessary, no camber problems result, no induced bump-steer, and no adverse camber gain. When used in conjunction with RMS rear Super Link your car can be lowered a full two inches.

ANTI-SWAY BARS

Addco

Typical understeer problems occur when a car can't negotiate a sharp curve and "mushes out" when cornering. This explains why you see so many tire marks on sharp cloverleafs. Other common problems include tire squeal and rear wheel hop, which lead to a loss of traction.

With the proper anti-sway bars installed in conjunction with the use of quality tires, wide rims, and high quality shocks, the front end of your vehicle will hold a curve just as well as the rear and vice versa, thus giving good balance. Additionally, your vehicle's body will not

ADDCO ANTI-SWAY BARS

Application	Part #	Dia.	Mid-section	Endlink bushings	Endlink Kit
ACURA					
1986-1989 Integra	F:765	3/4"	611	609	013
	R:394	3/4"	611	609	015
1990-1993 Integra	F:561	7/8"	n/a	609	013
	R:456	3/4"	611	609	015
1994-1998 Integra	F:n/a	n/a	n/a	n/a	n/a
	R:641	3/4"	611	609	014
AUDI					
1973-1979 Fox	F:820	1"	613T	n/a	n/a
	R:232	3/4"	611	609	018
1988-1992 90	F:n/a	n/a	n/a	n/a	n/a
	R:477	7/8"	612	609	019
1971-1973 100GL, 1000LS	F:n/a	n/a	n/a	n/a	n/a
	R:232	3/4"	611	609	018
1985-1988 4000, Coupe	F:n/a	n/a	n/a	n/a	n/a
	R:367	3/4"	611	609	015
1980-1984 4000, Coupe	F:791	1"	613B	n/a	n/a
	R:367	3/4"	611	609	015
1977-1983 5000	F:n/a	n/a	n/a	n/a	n/a
	R:328	7/8"	612	609	n/a
BMW					
1984-1990 318, 325i, Convertible to 1992	F:784	1"	613W	n/a	n/a
	R:233	3/4"	611T	n/a	n/a
1977-1983 320i	F:155	3/4"	611	609	013
	R:296	3/4"	611J	609	015
HONDA					
to 1981 Accord	F:191	7/8"	612B	n/a	n/a
	R:282	5/8"	610	609	019
1982-1985 Accord	F:735	7/8"	612B	609	013
	R:366	3/4"	611	609	019
1986-1989 Accord	F:792	7/8"	612B	609	013
	R:379	3/4"	611	609	013
to 1974 Civic, CRX	F:163	3/4"	611B	n/a	n/a
	R:213	5/8"	610	609	013
1975-1979 Civic, CRX	F:163	3/4"	611B	n/a	n/a
	R:241	5/8"	610	609	019
to 1979 Civic, CRX, CVCC	F:187	7/8"	612B	n/a	n/a
	R:241	5/8"	610	609	019
1980-1983 Civic, CRX Sedan	F:177	3/4"	611	609	013
	R:337	3/4"	611	609	013
1980-1983 Civic, CRX SW	F:177	3/4"	611	609	013
	R:339	3/4"	611	609	013
1996-1998 Civic, CRX	F:n/a	n/a	n/a	n/a	n/a
	R:636	3/4"	611	609	014
1988-1991 Civic, CRX	F:561	7/8"	n/a	609	013
	R:456	3/4"	611	609	015
1984-1987 Civic, CRX	F:765	3/4"	611	609	013
	R:394	3/4"	611	609	015
to 1984 Prelude	F:177	3/4"	611	609	013
	R:326	3/4"	611	609	015
1985-1987 Prelude	F:n/a	n/a	n/a	n/a	n/a
	R:404	3/4"	611	609	014
1988-1999 Prelude	F:Inquire				
	R:Inquire				
MAZDA					
1990-1993 Miata	F:574	7/8"	612B	n/a	n/a
	R:475	5/8"	610B	n/a	n/a
1994-1998 Miata	F:557	7/8"	612B	n/a	n/a
	R:486	5/8"	610B	n/a	n/a
1999 Miata	F:172	1"	613W	n/a	n/a
	R:486	5/8"	610B	n/a	n/a
1978-1985 RX7	F:850	1 1/8"	614	609	014
	R:305	3/4"	611B	609	014
1993-1995 RX7	F:501	1 1/8"	614W	n/a	n/a
	R:459	7/8"	612B	n/a	n/a
NISSAN					
1984-1988 200SX IRS, turbo	F:868	1"	613B	609	014
	R:395	1"	613B	609	014
1986-1988 200SX	F:777	1 1/8"	614W	609	014
	R:395	1"	613B	609	014
1989-1993 240SX	F:197	1 1/8"	614W	609	014
	R:489	7/8"	612B	609	013
1984-1988 300ZX	F:766	1"	613B	609	014
	R:395	1"	613B	609	014
1990-1993 300ZX	F:n/a	n/a	n/a	n/a	n/a
	R:417	1"	613B	609	013
1986-1988 Maxima	F:n/a	n/a	n/a	n/a	n/a
	R:448	7/8"	612B	609	013
1989-1994 Maxima	F:n/a	n/a	n/a	n/a	n/a
	R:454	7/8"	612B	609	013
1995-1999 Maxima	F:n/a	n/a	n/a	n/a	n/a
	R:655	7/8"	612W	n/a	n/a
1987-1990 Pulsar, Sentra	F:n/a	n/a	n/a	n/a	n/a
	R:653	3/4"	611	609	014
1991-1994 Pulsar, Sentra	F:n/a	n/a	n/a	n/a	n/a
	R:693	3/4"	611B	609	n/a
TOYOTA					
1985 MR2	F:n/a	n/a	n/a	n/a	n/a
	R:492	3/4"	611B	n/a	n/a
1985-1986 MR2	F:786	3/4"	611B	n/a	n/a
	R:691	3/4"	611B	609	016
1987-1989 MR2	F:786	3/4"	611B	n/a	n/a
	R:231	3/4"	611B	609	015

lean on curves throwing its weight outwards and tilting the front wheels.

While luxury or sport models usually have both front and rear bars, low or mid-range vehicles normally do not; and if the vehicle does, the bar is usually too light to make a noticeable difference. Those who demand superior performance must insist on the most economical and effective means of curing handling problems — an ADDCO Anti-Sway Bar Kit.

Addco kits are available with rubber or urethane bushings. When ordering, please place the letter "U" behind the three digit stock number to indicate urethane bushings. Three digit stock number = kits packed in rubber. Three digit stock number and the letter "U" = kits packed in urethane. Three digit stock number and the letter "S" = kits packed as a competition series. These kits come with a book on handling rubber and urethane bushings and adjustable end-links where applicable.

EIBACH

While the Lakewood Sport by Eibach Pro-Kit Springs represent the major tuning device for your suspension, additional roll stiffness can be achieved by using the Lakewood Sport by Eibach Anti-Roll Kit. Anti-roll bars further reduce body roll and allow fine tuning of your vehicle's suspension. The goal is neutral, predictable handling. Lakewood Sport by Eibach Anti-Roll Bars are cold-formed from high-strength aircraft grade steel and are carefully designed to fit your vehicle without modification.

LIGHTSPEED

Sport Sway Bars Sets

Transmit the power to the ground and reduce excessive body roll. Designed to work with Lightspeed's competition springs. Black powder-coat finish, red urethane bushing and mounting hardware. No drilling or modify needed.

Part #   Application

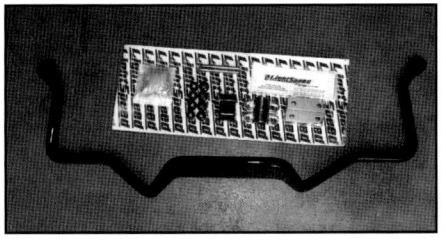

HO3153	1996-1998 Civic EX/HX
HO3217	1996-1998 Civic LX/CX/VX
HO3152	1992-1995 del Sol/ Civic EX/SI
HO3159	1990-1993 Integra
HO3160	1994-1998 Integra

ABD RACING

ABD Racing Sway Bar Kits are the perfect addition for any car to create optimum handling. By installing this package, the body lean in your car will be virtually eliminated. All ABD Racing Sway Bar Kits are manufactured to the highest quality standards and will include all necessary hardware for a complete installation. Polyurethane bushings are used throughout the applications and all parts are covered in a heavy wrap of powdercoating to resist road debris.

Rabbit/Scirocco/Jetta I
 19mm front complete
 19mm front o.e. upgrade
 22mm front complete
 22mm front o.e. upgrade
 25mm rear complete
 25mm rear o.e. upgrade
 25mm front complete, lightweight
 25mm front o.e. upgrade, lightweight
 28mm rear complete
 28mm rear o.e. upgrade
 28mm rear complete, lightweight
 28mm rear o.e. upgrade, lightweight

Golf/Jetta II/Corrado G60
 22mm front complete
 22mm front o.e. upgrade
 25mm rear complete
 25mm front complete, lightweight
 25mm front o.e. upgrade, lightweight
 28mm rear complete
 28mm rear complete, lightweight

Golf/Jetta III/Corrado VR6
 2mm 8v front o.e. upgrade
 25mm 8v front o.e upgrade, lightweight
 25mm VR6 front, lightweight
 25mm rear complete
 28mm rear complete
 28mm rear complete, lightweight

Fox Wagon/Sedan
 22mm front
 25mm rear

Beetle/Golf/Jetta IV
 25mm front
 28mm rear
 Stainless steel adjustable front end links (pair)

ABD Racing offers a set of performance sway bars with a higher bend and larger diameters. Listed below are both choices.

H & R Front sway bar
Beetle/Golf/Jetta IV   22mm

ABD Racing Front sway bar
G/J IV/ Beetle   25mm

ABD Racing Rear sway bar
G/J IV/ Beetle   28mm

SUSPENSION TECHNIQUE

Suspension Technique's Anti-Sway Bars are designed to improve handling and steering response by minimizing body roll. These bars are designed to be the next logical step to complete your S/T Sport or Speed Tech™ Suspension System.

Each bar is specifically designed for each application. Tight bar bends hug the undercarriage providing improved ground clearance and easy installation. The tighter bends, as well as properly engineered mounting hardware and the use of low deflection urethane bushings, allow the bar to work at its maximum potential. Each bar is covered with a high-quality powdercoat finish and limited lifetime warranty.

EIBACH ANTI-ROLL KITS

Part #	Application	Front Dia. (mm)	Rear Dia. (mm)
ACURA			
39372	1990-1993 Integra	21.00	19.00
39384	1994+ Integra (All, Incl. GSR)	25.00	17.00
HONDA			
39373	1990-1993 Accord (exc. wagon)	21.00	18.00
39376	1988-1991 Civic/CRX	21.00	18.00
39379	1992-1995 Civic DX, CX, VX H-BACK, LX, DX 4dr (w/o Factory Front Bar)	25.00	17.50
39380	1992-1995 Civic Si H-Back, EX 4dr (w/ Factory Front Bar)	25.00	17.50
39456	1989-1993 LS400	27.00	21.00
MAZDA			
39405	1990-1993 Miata 1.6L (A)	24.00	15.00
39404	1994+ Miata 1.8L (A)	27.00	15.00
39402	1988-1991 MX6/626	21.00	18.00
39400	1979-1985 RX-7 (A)	28.50	16.00
39407	1986-1992 RX-7 (A)	28.50	17.00
39412	1993+ RX-7	32.00	19.00

All applications, including vehicle make, model, year, and product fitment specifications are included in a separate application guide. If you have additional technical questions, contact Suspension Technique's knowledgeable performance suspension technical department.

TRD
Anti-sway bar

Part #   Application

1990-1995 MR2, front
 1990-1995 MR2, rear
 1985-1987 Corolla, front
 1988-1991 Corolla, front
 1988-1991 Corolla (GTS and SR5), rear
 1985-1987 Corolla SR5, rear

TANABE

Tanabe offers suspension parts that improve the potential and stability of a suspension system. Improved anti-roll performance for maximum traction during cornering. Improve cornering with anything from a subcompact to a big luxury car. Tanabe has also released a popular version for station wagons.

Comes complete with correct billet aluminum brackets and hardware. See installation instructions for information on supplied hardware and installation. Call for more make and model applications.

Swaybar:
22 mm rear (GSR, RS, GS, LS 94-00)
Stabilizer Bar:
22mm (rear)
For Years: 1994+

PROGRESS

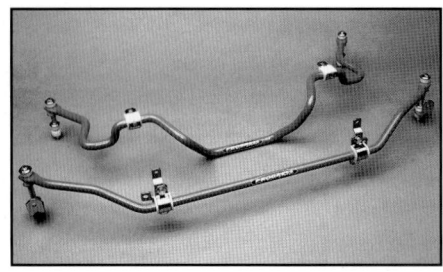

Progress Anti-Roll Bars Systems are aggressive tuning for minimum body roll. New designs for Sport-Compact applications.

PROGRESS ANTI-ROLL BARS SYSTEMS

Part #	Application	Bar Dia.	Part #	Bar Dia.
ACURA				
61.0101	1990-1993 Integra	1.00 (25)	62.0101	.875 (22)
61.1003	1994-1999 Integra	1.00 (25)	62.1003	.875 (22)
HONDA				
61.1015	1998-1999 Accord	1.13 (29)	62.1015	.750 (19)
61.1002	1989-1991 Civic/CRX	1.00 (25)	62.1002	.875 (22)
64.1002	Hardware kit			
61.1003	1992-1995 Civic/del Sol	1.00 (25)	62.1003	.875 (22)
64.1003	Hardware kit			
61.1004	1996-1999 Civic	1.00 (25)	62.1003	.875 (22)
MITSUBISHI				
61.1403	1995-1999 Eclipse, FWD	1.00 (25)	62.1403	.750 (19)
61.1403	1995-1999 Eclipse, AWD	1.00 (25)	62.1404	.813 (21)

SHOCK TOWER BRACES

DINAN

Front and Rear Shock Tower Braces provide crisper handling by reducing the flex that occurs at the shock towers. And they look great. Made from strong, lightweight 6061-T6 polished aluminum with carbon fiber inserts.

AROSPEED

R-SPEC STRUT BAR

Part #	Application
ARO652001	1992+ Civic
ARO652001	1994+ Integra

STRUT BAR

Part #	Application
ACURA	
ARO651000	1990-1993 Integra, front
ARO651034	1994 Integra, front
ARO651010	1990-1993 Integra, rear top
ARO651011	1990-1993 Integra, rear bottom
BMW	
ARO651006	1992+ 3 Series
DODGE	
ARO651028	1995+ Neon, front top
HONDA	
ARO651003	1990-1993 Accord, front top
ARO651004	1990-1993 Accord, rear top
ARO651016	1994+ Accord, front top
ARO651020	1994+ Accord, rear top
ARO651000	1988-1995 Civic, front
ARO651034	1994 Civic, front
ARO651010	1990-1993 Civic, rear top
ARO651011	1992-1996 Civic, rear bottom
ARO651010	1990-1993 del Sol, rear top
ARO651034	1994 del Sol, front
ARO651023	1992-1996 Prelude, front top
ARO651038	1997+ Prelude, front top
MAZDA	
ARO651007	1993+ 626, front top
ARO651014	1993+ MX6, 4 cyl. front top
ARO651031	1995+ Protege, front top
MITSUBISHI	
ARO651012	1990-1994 Eclipse, front top
ARO651026	1995+ Eclipse, front top
ARO651027	1995-1997 Eclipse, rear
ARO651022	1994+ Gallant, front top
ARO651013	1993-1996 Mirage, front top
ARO651043	1993-1996 Mirage, rear top
ARO651040	1997+ Mirage, tower bar
ARO651041	1997-1998 Mirage, rear
NISSAN	
ARO651008	1993-1997 Altima, front
ARO651015	1991-1994 Sentra/200SX, front top
ARO651032	1995+ Sentra/200SX, front top
ARO651033	1995+ 240SX, front top
SATURN	
ARO651045	Saturn, front top
TOYOTA	
ARO651009	1993+ Camry, front top
ARO651005	1990-1993 Corolla, front
ARO651021	1994+ Corolla, front top
ARO651024	1994+ Supra, front
ARO651039	1995-1997 Tercel
VOLKSWAGEN	
ARO651046	Golf/Jetta III

LOWER TIE BARS

NEUSPEED

Lower Tie Bar available for front and rear. The front model eliminates flexing at the lower control arm chassis pickup points. The rear model eliminates flexing in the lower rear sub frame. Both improve stability and handling considerably.

CUSCO

The Cusco Lower Arm Bar provides all the same features as the Cusco Strut Tower Bar by connecting the front control arms or chassis. This reinforces the under body and reduces chassis flexing. By reducing chassis flexing, we are able to divert the cornering force to the springs and shocks, not the chassis. Now the springs and shocks can do their jobs more effectively and efficiently.

OBX

Competition Rear Lower Bottom Brace

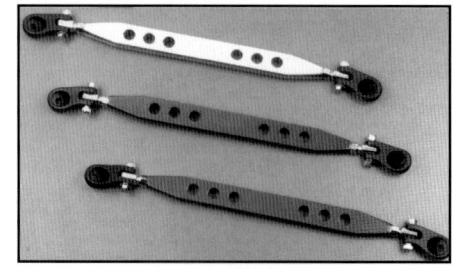

Part #	Application
A1007A	1990-1993 Acura Integra
A1007B	1994-1999 Acura Integra
H1005A	1990-1993 Honda Accord
H1005B	1994-1997 Honda Accord
H1007A	1988-1991 Honda Civic/CRX

H1007C 1992-1995 Honda Civic/del Sol
H1007B 1996-1999 Honda Civic
H1005C 1992-1996 Honda Prelude
H1005D 1997-1999 Honda Prelude
M10053 1995-1999 Mitsubishi Eclipse
M10043 1997-2000 Mitsubishi Mirage

Rear Bottom Type-S (Sport Type)

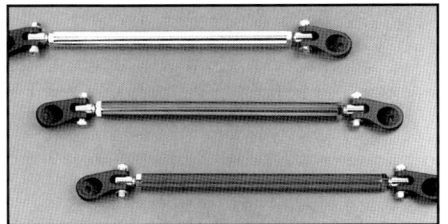

Part #	Application
A1001B	1990-1993 Acura Integra
A1002B	1994-1999 Acura Integra
H1001B	1988-1991 Honda Civic/CRX
H1002B	1992-1995 Honda Civic/del Sol
H1003B	1996-1999 Honda Civic
H1004B	1990-1997 Honda Accord
M1004B	1997-2000 Mitsubishi Mirage
M1005B	1995-1999 Mitsubishi Eclipse

CAMBER & CASTOR ADJUSTMENT COMPONENTS

PROGRESS

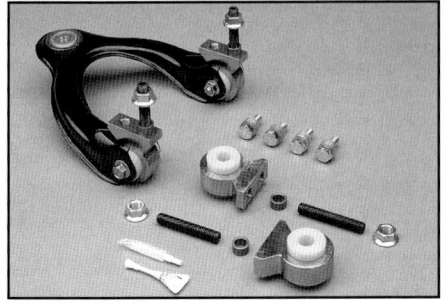

Bolt-on these new camber kits for improved tire wear. Applications include Accord, Civic, Integra, and Eclipse.

COMPTECH

Camber adjuster: front 1.75 degrees
For Years: 1990-2000 Integra
One kit per wheel (2 required per car)

Camber adjuster: front 3 degrees
For Years: 1990-2000 Integra
One kit per wheel (2 required per car)

Camber adjuster: rear 2 degrees
For Years: 1990-2000 Integra
One kit per wheel (2 required per car)

SPECIALTY PRODUCT

Honda EZ arms XR and EZ Arms XR Extreme

Original equipment style arm with camber adjustment from -.5° to +3.5°

PROGRESS CAMBER KITS

Part #	Application	Front	Rear
ACURA			
53.1002	1990-1993 Integra	Pivot Mnt.	Shim
53.1003	1994-1999 Integra	Pivot Mnt.	Shim
53.1011	1996-1998 CL 2.2	Pivot Mnt.	Shim
53.1011	1997-1998 CL 3.0	Pivot Mnt.	Shim
HONDA			
53.1011	1990-1997 Accord	Pivot Mnt.	Shim
51.1004	1998-1999 Accord	Ball Joint	N/A
53.1002	1988-1991 Civic/CRX	Pivot Mnt.	Shim
53.1003	1992-1995 Civic	Pivot Mnt.	Shim
53.1004	1996-1999 Civic	Ball Joint	Shim
53.1022	1992-1996 Prelude	Pivot Mnt.	N/A
51.1004	1997-1999 Prelude	Ball Joint	N/A
MITSUBISHI			
53.1403	1995-1999 Eclipse, FWD	Bushing	Shim
53.1403	1995-1999 Eclipse, AWD	Bushing	Shim

LIGHTSPEED CAMBER KITS

Part #	Description
HO3570	1990-1997 Accord, front -3/4-+1 deg.
HO3572	1990-1997 Accord, front +1.25 -3 deg.
HO3580	1990-1997 Accord, rear 2 deg.
HO3570	1988-1995 Civic, front -3/4-+1 deg.
HO3590	1988-1998 Civic, rear 2 deg.
HO3572	1990-1995 Civic, front +1.25 -3 deg.
HO3570	1990-1997 Integra, front -3/4-+1 deg.
HO3590	1990-1997 Integra, rear 2 deg.
HO3572	1990-1997 Integra, front +1.25 -3 deg.
HO3591	1996-1998 Camber kits, front 1to 3 degrees adjustments

and caster changes from -.5° to +2.5°. Available in a variety of colors. The extreme version has a heavy duty adjustment mechanism and poly bushings with a power-coated tube construction.

GROUND CONTROL RACING SUSPENSION

Introducing a new line of high-performance suspension components for the BMW 3 series chassis. These new bolt-in parts can transform your stock street BMW into a track-ready, weekend racer. New pieces include camber/caster adjustable plates and adjustable ride height spring kits; all bolt-in for easy installation.

Ground Control Racing Adjustable Camber/Caster™ plates are machined of 7075 T-6 billet aluminum and are anodized (type II pewter) for greater durability and appearance. High quality spherical and needle bearings are utilized to eliminate unwanted bushing flex as well as allowing for bind-free suspension movement. The 100% bolt-in design is an advantage if stock components need to be re-installed in the future. Ground Control Suspension Camber/Caster plates can give your BMW up to -3 1/2° of camber. Caster is adjusted separately and independently. Camber/Caster plates are designed to be used with 2-1/2 or 2-1/4 inch I.D. coil-over springs.

HKS

Pillow Ball Upper Mounts

In vehicle suspensions, the upper mounts connect the strut or shock assembly to the body. Most factory mounts are constructed from soft rubber or plastic, and are designed with ride comfort as a priority. Under spirited driving conditions, the factory mounts can flex and distort, hindering the performance of the shock absorber or strut. This may cause the vehicle to lose traction and steering response. The HKS Pillow Ball Upper Mounts are constructed of aluminum and steel for maximum strength and are engineered to enhance the ability of your high-performance suspension. Some applications have adjustable camber plates built into the Pillow Ball Mounts to assist with fine-tuning of the suspension.

CUSCO

Pillow Ball / Camber Adjustable Upper Strut Mounts

Cusco Strut Upper Mount is a connecting device between suspension and chassis. It is made of metal instead of rubber bushing and spherical bearing instead of standard bearing. This replaces your rubber stock upper mount which flexes and causes friction loss during high hard driving. Upper mounts are available in adjustable and non-adjustable types. The adjustable type allows you to adjust your camber without the removal of any suspension components.

TANABE

Pillow-ball UPPER MOUNT

The rubber bushing of the upper mounts are replaced with a pillow ball to eliminate wasted motion of the upper-mount portion. This upper mount is of the vehicle-height-adjusting type, for direct and sharp handling. It also minimizes unnecessary alignment adjustments. The mounts are made of Duralimun 17 plate, and the pillow-ball portion is made of NMB for maximum rigidity and durability.

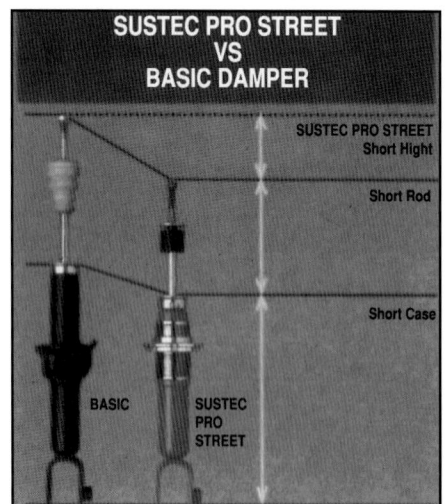

The Tanabe SUSTEC DAMPER and Super H compatible-type improve tire-to-ground contact for direct and sharp handling, using a camber-adjustable strut-type front suspension. The adjustment portion locks at four points. An optional 5-point locking type is also available. Duralumin 17 plate is used for the mount, and the pillow-ball portion is made of NMB. Compatible with SUSTEC DAMPER and Super H combinations.

INGALLS ENGINEERING

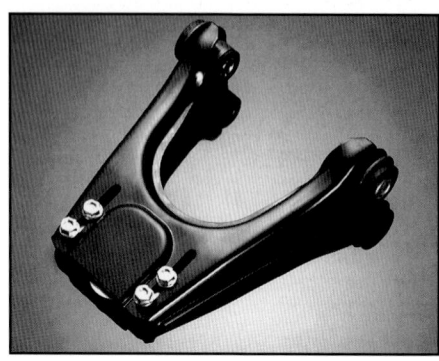

Ingalls Engineering has just released the firm's new CA100 Adjustable Upper Control Arm for the extremely popular 1996-1998 Honda Civics. The CA100 adjust camber from negative 1° to positive 3°. Camber angles on Honda Civics that have been lowered for performance or appearance or remaining at stock ride height can now be adjusted for prolonged tire life and improved handling. The CA100 is engineered for strength, safety, and ease of installation.

Ingalls Engineering is a suspension specialist, designing and manufacturing excellent products for a wide variety of import machines. Here are a few of the company's newest offerings:

3882 R or L, with o.e. Style Rubber bushing

3880 R or L, with polyurethane bushing

Rear Camber Adjuster SmartArm™ Links
1990-1997 Accord
1992-1994 Acura Vigor
1997-1999 Acura CL
1996-1999 Acura RL
This arm comes with the new ball joint. Each part number has a right or left side. Adjusts rear camber -2.00° to +3.00°.

3565
Front & Rear Camber Adjuster
1983-1991 Honda Prelude, front
1988-1991 Honda Prelude, rear
Adjusts camber -1.00° to +3.00°.

3556
Front Camber Adjuster
1997-2000 Honda Prelude
Adjusts front camber -1.00° to +3.00°.

3555
Front Camber Adjuster
1998-2000 Accord
Adjusts front camber -1.00° to +3.00°.

3872
Rear Camber Adjuster, o.e.-style rubber only
SmartArm™ Links
1998-1999 Accord
Adjusts rear camber -1.50° to +3.00°.

3586
Rear Camber Adjuster
1995-1999 Chrysler Sebring (except convertible)
1995-1999 Dodge Avenger
1995-1999 Eagle Talon
1995-1999 Mitsubishi Eclipse
Adjusts rear camber -1.00° to +3.00°.

3842L
3842R
Rear Camber Adjuster
SmartArm™ Link
1990-1994 Eagle Talon AWD
1990-1994 Mitsubishi Eclipse AWD
Adjusts rear camber -2.00° to +3.00°.

3571
Front Camber Adjuster, O.E. Style Rubber
1990-1997 Accord
1988-1996 Civic
1988-1996 CRX
1988-1992 del Sol
1990-1999 Integra
1997 Isuzu Oasis
1991-1996 Legend
1995-1997 Odyssey
1981-1996 Prelude
1991-1996 Vigor
Adjusts front camber -.75° to +1.00°.

CA100
Front Camber Adjuster
1996-1999 Honda Civic
1997-1999 Honda CR-V
Adjusts front camber -1.00° to +3.00°.

SPRINT PERFORMANCE

Suspension Extreme Camber kits available for Acura Integra, Honda Accord and Civic and CRX, and Mitsubishi Eclipse. Allows camber adjustment of front and rear wheels.

K-MAC

Makers of excellent four wheel camber castor adjustment kits. Available for all popular import and domestic sport compacts.

RYANE MOTORSPORTS

Weighing in at 2 lbs. less than the original, Ryane Motorsport's complete replacement lowering trailing arm lowers the vehicle a full 2". You will enjoy the E-Z bolt-on installation and absolutely no unfavorable effects to the original Honda suspension geometry. No link changes or camber corrections are necessary. The original Super Link is superior to all other lowering methods because it merely positions the wheel higher on the trailing arm, thereby lowering the vehicle. No Adverse Camber Gain. No Premature Tire Wear. No Negative Handling Side Effects. No Alignment Difficulties.

Super Link comes complete with urethane bushing and pivot shaft. Entirely powder-coated Electric Blue with a very Wicked Yellow or Radical Red bushing. Includes fully illustrated installation instructions.

BUSHINGS

ENERGY SUSPENSION

Rear Trailing Arm bushing

Honda Civic coil spring front suspension, fitted with performance Hyper-Flex™, replacing the weak and short-lived original rubber. Improves quick off-the-line starts, handling, and stopping.

Hyper-Flex™ is the newest generation of polyurethane that's thoroughly performance tested and race proven. These polyurethane products are available in colors: black, blue, red, and yellow, with additional colors for shock boots.

For those applications where component twisting typically occurs, Energy Suspension's line of black Hyper-Flex™ polyurethane products contain graphite. This graphite impregnation delivers a self-lubricated effect, reducing the need to lubricate components.

Working with Anti-Sway Bar End Link sets, Energy Suspension's Hyper-Flex™ bushings make your vehicle's anti-sway bar system much more effective. In effect, it's almost like buying an upscale/higher performance anti-sway bar system. Dollar-for-dollar, Energy Suspension's anti-sway bar end links and anti-sway bar bushings offer the greatest improvement in performance handling.

These anti-sway bar bushings are available either as standard type or greaseable type. Sets come complete with corrosion resistant zinc and gold irradiate-plated strong 3/8" grade 5 bolts, nylon insert lock nuts, heavy-gauge washers, and mounting brackets. Hyper-Flex™ Greaseable Anti-Sway Bar Bushings feature zerk type fittings, allowing for easy and periodic greasing with a common grease gun. These bushings are designed with unique channels that allow for the lubricating grease to migrate to where it is needed, at the bushing and bar contact area. Greasing also reduces the chance of squeaking as the bar turns during normal operation.

Complete Performance Polyurethane Suspension Bushing Master Sets

Energy Suspension introduces NEW suspension bushing Master Sets -- the Hyper-Flex system™ for many popular car and truck models! Available for both imports and domestics. Now, when purchasing a master set in one convenient box you can replace all of the major suspension rubber bushing components with Hyper-Flex™ performance polyurethane.

Ground Control

Urethane bushings add the final touch to a performance suspension system. Urethane greatly reduces the amount of deflection that rubber bushings allow under performance driving conditions. This reduction in unwanted suspension movement lets the parts that are designed to move (e.g. shocks, springs) work more purely.

Applications:

1984-1987 Civic/CRX
  Front Control Arm Bushings
  Rear Control Arm Bushings
  Transmission Shifter
  Stabilizer Bushings

1988-1991 Civic/CRX
  Strut Rod Bushings
  Front Control Arm Bushings
  Shock Mount Kit

OBX ADJUSTABLE CAMBER KITS

Part #	Application
AC001	1990-1993 Acura Integra, F & R
AC002	1994-1999 Acura Integra, F & R
AC003	1988-1991 Honda Civic/CRX, F & R
AC004	1992-1995 Honda Civic/del Sol, F & R
AC009	1996-1999 Honda Civic/del Sol, F & R
AC005	1990-1993 Honda Accord, F & R
AC006	1994-1997 Honda Accord, F & R
AC007	1982-1996 Honda Prelude, F & R
AC008	1997-1999 Honda Prelude, F & R
AC009	1995-1999 Mitsubishi Eclipse, Front
AC010	1995-1999 Mitsubishi Eclipse, Rear

NEUSPEED

When it comes to Euro Performance the new front-wheel drive Beetle is the perfect project vehicle. Adding larger tires and wheels, upgrading the horsepower, or just want more performance, better handling, and reliability? You'll need the following:

Part #	Description
15-3117	Front Control Arm Bushing Set
15-5105	Front Sway Bar Bushing Set (for 21mm sway bar)
15-1105	Motor Mount (lower torque position only)

For selected water-cooled VW vehicles: front control arm bushing sets, rear control arm bushing sets, front sway bar bushing sets, rear coil spring isolators, and rear strut tower bushing sets. These new sets will really improve handling and control on these vehicles, and they last much longer than rubber components. Available for:

1993-1998 Cabrio
1990-1995 Corrado, 4 cyl.
1985-1998 Golf
1993-1998 GTI
1985-1998 Jetta
1990-1997 Passat
1980-1992 Rabbit
1982-1988 Scirocco

Some components not available for all models listed.

Neuspeed Front Sway Bar Bushing Kit retains the original Honda front sway bar, replacing the soft, rubber bar bushings with Neuspeed's precision injected polyurethane units. Results in tighter, more responsive steering and lightning-quick lane changes.

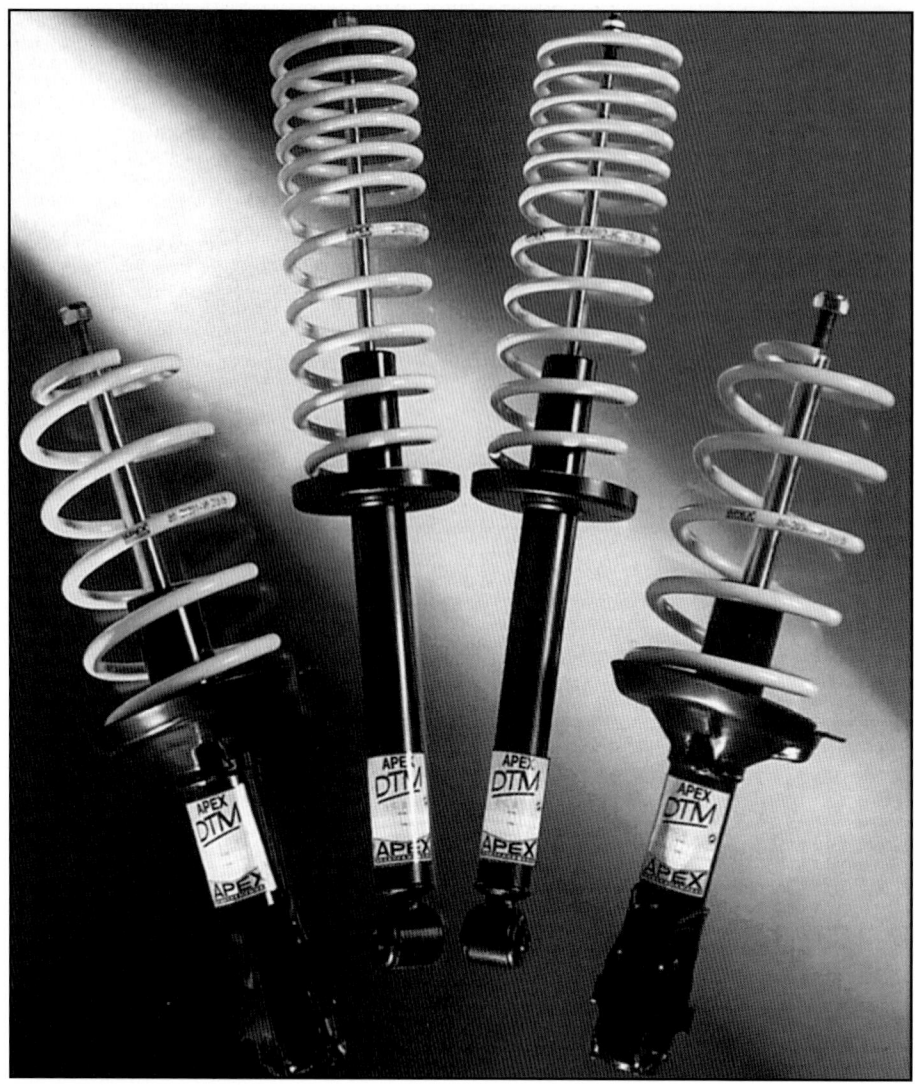

DTM "Sport Kit" Coil-Over Street Shock

SHOCKS

APEX INTEGRATION
DTM "Sport Kit" Coil-Over Street Shock

Features uprated high-performance gas pressurized shocks. Together with the top quality engineered APEX sport springs, the kit will give your car a low and sporty DTM look.

The T-MAX Suspension Series offers one of the most advanced shock absorber designs on the market, incorporating a revolutionary triple-tube design. All struts are short stroke and the suspension system can be upgraded according to specific driving applications. (T-MAX Sports and up only.)

The T-MAX system is the entry-level system designed for the enthusiast. It uses a factory replacement strut that allows the user to have 7-way ride adjustability in the front AND the rear shocks. This shock accepts any OEM factory or factory style after-market spring. The T-MAX also has a 6-way height adjustment by utilizing a C-Clip designed spring perch. (*Some strut type vehicles cannot be lowered through the C-clip perch in front due to space clearance.)

Part #	Application
NISSAN	
237-N007	1995-1998 240 SX
237-N006	1989-1993 240 SX
MAZDA	
237-Z002	1993-1995 RX-7
237-Z001	1986-1991 RX-7
TOYOTA	
237-T011	1991-1995 MR-2
237-T001	1986-1992 Supra

KONI

Many of the Koni Sport dampers are externally adjustable by means of a knob, so they need not be disassembled from the car. The fine-tuning of the damping forces to personal driving style and to different driving conditions is therefore not more than a matter of seconds. The best of fine-tuning technology straight from the world of Formula 1 racing.

The sporting motorist who wants nothing but the very best in road-holding is offered a unique range of Koni complete suspension kits consisting of matching Koni sport shock absorbers and lowering springs. These kits will give the car absolutely superb road-holding qualities and the looks of a real sports car.

With Koni lowering springs, the center of gravity of the car is lowered. Combined with a firmer suspension this will result in even better steering qualities and reduced body movement. The use of lowering springs requires special damping characteristics: the mere application of stiffer springs together with ordinary shock absorbers often has a negative impact on road-holding and comfort, and may even lead to dangerous situations. Therefore, Koni's product range offers you complete suspension kits consisting of matching springs and dampers. Of course, the lowering is limited to such an extent that the car will still remain suitable for normal street use.

KYB

GR-2 gas shock absorbers feature lower pressure for riding comfort, along with improved handling and response only gas shocks can provide, even for smaller cars! KYB GR-2 gas shock absorbers are the economical way to step up from hydraulic shocks to the quality ride and control of gas.

KYB shocks feature: a multi-lip seal to reduce possible oil leakage; patented check valve to control flow of fluid and gas; sintered-iron rod guide to extend life of shock; hard-chromed piston rod to reduce friction; pressurized N2 gas to reduce foaming and aeration and to deliver better performance; seamless cylinder to reduce possibility of splitting; rubber rebound stop for longer life (for most applications); 3-stage rebound valving to give better control; wear-resistant piston ring to reduce friction and leakage; all-weather fluid; 3-stage compression valving to assure fast recovery; and seamless eye ring to reduce possibility of breakage.

AGX

The single damping adjustment on the AGX Shock changes both the rebound and compression strokes. Depending on the model, there are either four or eight stages of adjustment. In addition to the manually adjustable damping settings, AGX features 3-stage, real time, auto-adjustable damping. When driving on smooth surfaces, shock movements are relatively slow and the AGX valving allows the shock to travel freely. As road conditions get rougher, the shock is compressed faster. AGX responds instantly to make response firmer, maintaining tire contact and vehicle control. This 3-stage valve action allows AGX Shocks to adjust to road conditions automatically.

Fast on-car adjustment, built with the advanced engineering and exceptional quality you'd expect from KYB. AGX lets drivers tune their shocks to match driving conditions in seconds. No need to lift vehicle or remove anything to change settings. Damping rate is selected with an external knob on the shock body or a screwdriver slot at the top of the piston rod, depending on model. Sintered iron pistons and guide rods are used for greater strength and durability. Micro-smooth, hardened and chromed piston rods provide long-life reliability from oil seals. Seamless cylinders and eye rings mean no weak points or seam failures. Multi-lip seals and self-sealing packing keep oil in, contaminants out, even under repeated hard use. Patented check valve minimizes foaming to eliminate performance fade.

JAMEX SPORTSLINE

The Jamex Sportsline kit contains lowering springs and sport shock absorbers with shortened piston rods. The installation of a Sportsline kit will ensure a sporty and smooth ride with supreme road stability and an improved, lowered look. In addition to the TÜV approval, the high quality of the Jamex Sportsline is underlined by the 5-year guarantee for the first owner.

Pro-Street is Jamex's most advanced road stability shock absorber range. In order to meet the individual demands of the most demanding motorist, Jamex has developed this range of adjustable gas pressure shock absorbers, especially for road use. Pro-Street kits include specially developed sport springs and the required mounting hardware.

Jamex bumpstops prevent the wheel arch from rubbing the wheel under heavy load conditions. Especially suitable for lowered cars with large tires. Made from high-quality materials. Jamex bumpstops are gas, oil, and frost resistant.

Tokico Advanced Handling Suspension Kit

PROGRESS COMPETITION COIL OVER SUSPENSION SYSTEMS			
Application	Kit Part #	Front Part #	Rear Part #
ACURA			
1990-1993 Integra	75.0101	71.1002	72.0101
1994-1999 Integra	75.1003	71.1003	72.1003
HONDA			
1990-1997 Accord	75.1011	71.1011	72.1011
1989-1991 Civic/CRX	75.1002	71.1002	72.1003
1992-1999 Civic	75.1003	71.1003	72.1003
MITSUBISHI			
1995-1999 Eclipse, FWD	75.1403	71.1403	72.1403
1995-1999 Eclipse, AWD	75.1404	71.1404	72.1404

PROGRESS

ProSport Shock Absorbers

Application	Front Part #	Rear Part #
ACURA		
1990-1993 Integra	70.0318	70.0319
1994-1999 Integra	70.0338	70.0311
1996-1998 CL 2.2 & 3.0	70.0313	70.0314
HONDA		
1990-1997 Accord	70.0313	70.0314
1989-1991 Civic/CRX	70.0312	70.0311
1992-1999 Civic	70.0338	70.0311

TOKICO

Shocks and struts are a direct bolt-in replacement for the thin-oiled stock units that typically last about 40,000 miles. Tokico's twin-tube, low-pressure, gas-charged shock feature tuned valving that has been designed for each specific application and depending on vehicle model, are available in adjustable or non-adjustable versions. A lifetime warranty from Tokico ensures that your investment in quality will provide complete years of trouble-free service.

The adjustable Illumina version is also available for most models. Keep in mind the lower cost shock absorber found in chain stores and most merchandisers do not have the type of sophistication and quality necessary for long life and good performance. The Illumina 5-position adjustable shocks and strut allow the vehicle owner to change the handling balance of the every day driver, to the weekend warriors for autocross and drag.

TRD

Shocks and Struts

1985-1987 Corolla GTS, front shocks
1985-1987 Corolla GTS, rear shocks
1990-1995 MR2, front shocks
1990-1995 MR2, rear struts
1986-1992 Supra, front shocks
1986-1992 Supra, rear shocks
1993-1997 Supra Shock Absorber Set
1993-1997 Supra Shock Absorber Set

PROGRESS GROUP

Progress Competition Coil Over Suspension Systems feature threaded-body aluminum struts that allow ride height adjustment. These are constructed from lightweight alloy for less unsprung weight and are made with large 35mm piston and twin tube cellular gas construction for consistent damping. Exclusive "take-apart" design for easy re-valving. 30mm shorter strut bodies provide lower ride heights and improved ride quality and traction. Polyurethane "Short Stops" allow additional wheel travel. New strut top bushings and spring isolators are also included. Take-apart design strut tops are threaded for easy revalving. Custom valving is simple to install for road and drag racing. "How-to" video available. Complete coil-over system installs without vehicle modifications.

Developed specifically for autocross, road race, and drag race applications. Ride height adjustable 1"-3". Detent locks collar in position every half turn. No lock ring necessary.

APEX INTEGRATION

The Apex Integration suspension provides vehicle lowering as well as vehicle performance. While improving hard cornering handling and improved steering response, the Apex Integration suspension indulges the driver with excellent ride quality. The springs are shot peened and heat wound, powder-coated, and examined for even the most minor flaw. Quality control and development matches and exceeds the specifications of OEM manufacturers.

The N-1 Damper has been derived from the grueling N-1 Endurance Race Series. The N-1 Damper has been designed to endure the constant abuse from long-distance races. Engineered for race tracks, the N-1 Damper uses a 40mm piston with minimal friction to relay precise road surface conditions to the driver. A short stroke/short case design allows for safe lowering of the vehicle. Vehicle stability is excellent through the corners. Shock longevity and high-quality construction make the N-1 Damper a powerful choice for suspension enthusiasts. Available for select models. Type S models feature height adjustment and helper spring. Type R models feature 13-way ride adjustment and height adjustment. Pillow upper mounts optional.

AROSPEED

Arospeed coil-overs give you up to 4 inches of adjustment. You can lower your car from 0 to 4 inches. Arospeed coil-overs come with all the necessary hardware and equipment to get you up and running. Arospeed Coil-Over kits include 4 springs, 4 threaded sleeves, 8 perches, urethane top hats, and tool. Perch and threaded sleeve are made from aluminum and anodized to protect the finish of the sleeves and perches. Springs are powdercoated to protect against rust and help to keep your springs looking good.

Part #	Application
ACURA	
ARO660004	1990-1993 Integra
ARO660004	1994-1999 Integra
HONDA	
ARO660014	1990-1993 Accord
ARO660014	1994-1997 Accord
TBA	1998-1999 Accord
ARO660004	1990-1993 Civic
ARO660004	1992-1995 Civic
ARO660004	1996-1999 Civic
ARO660014	1992-1996 Prelude
TBA	1997-1999 Prelude
MITSUBISHI	
ARO660032	1995-1999 Eclipse

SUSPENSION TECHNIQUES

Nitro Extreme®

The first fully-adjustable performance strut with SPEED SENSOR™ technology comes from Nitro-Extreme®. Patented SPEED SENSOR™ Technology senses and instantly adjusts for changing road conditions. Gas pressure minimizes aeration and fade for consistent performance to match any driving style.

Aggressive rebound and dampening rates improve vehicle control and compliment the progressive rated race springs. A threaded sleeve (permanently bonded to the strut body) and spring seat machined from 6061-T6 hard anodized aluminum, provides four inches of drop adjustment at the wheel. For added safety, the spring seat includes a built in "positive index

APEX INTEGRATION SUSPENSION

Part #	Application	Type MSRP
HONDA		
242-KH003	1990-1997 Accord	No Pillow Mounts, S
241-AH006	1997-1998 Integra	With Pillow Mounts, R
241-AH008	1996-1998 Civic	With Pillow Mounts, R
241-KH008	1996-1998 Civic	No Pillow Mounts, R
255-H001	1992-1998 Civic/Integra	With Upper Pillow Mounts, R
MAZDA		
245-AZ002	1993-1995 RX-7	With Pillow Mounts, Pro
NISSAN		
241-AN007240	1995-1998 SX	With Upper Pillow Mounts, R

lock ring" so that spring settings are maintained even under the most aggressive driving conditions. Special steel-backed DU spring seat bearing rings are specifically designed for high load applications. The rings feature a bronze inner structure for heat dissipation and are coated with a PTFE lead mixture providing a self lubrication low friction bearing surface, enabling easy full load adjustments. Constant taper design race springs feature truly progressive spring rates.

This competition design provides more actual spring travel than conventional lowering coils or economy "bolt-on" coil over kits. Handling characteristics are further enhanced by urethane strut bushings, resulting in decreased deflection for a more positive dampening response. Nitro Extreme's SPEED SENSOR™ strut valving, specific tuned spring rates, and fully adjustable level and height control, make Nitro-Extreme® Adjustable a superb competition balance and control system.

DropFork®

Similar to Suspension Technique's popular dropped spindle technology, DropFork® components are cast of high strength nodular iron and precision machined to exacting tolerances in state-of-the-art CNC machine equipment. Features a 1-1/2" drop without any other modifications and can be used with Suspension Techniques sport springs for additional drop. Powdercoated finish provides increased durability, good looks, and long lasting protection. Covered by Suspension Techniques Limited Lifetime Warranty.

All components are packaged ready to install, complete with all necessary hardware and detailed installation instructions. ProArm® Adjustable Lowering Control Arm components are built from cast high-strength nodular iron and precision machined and manufactured to exacting tolerances. There is no compromise in ride quality or travel and all original suspension travel is maintained. There are no extra costly alignment kits needed; all components are packaged ready to install complete with all necessary hardware and detailed installation instructions.

HKS

The HKS Hiper Damper Kit enables the suspension to be custom tailored to each driver's preference. The Hiper Damper Suspension package offers height and shock dampening adjustments. The shock valving is adjustable externally. All HKS suspension components are constructed from the highest quality steel and aluminum and are designed to stand up to even the most severe road and/or track conditions.

KYB AND EIBACH

KYB has teamed with Eibach, a world leader in performance springs and suspension products, to offer matched spring sets for every AGX gas shock application. AGX Lowering Spring sets by Eibach are designed to safely lower the vehicle and give it a more attractive, sportier stance.

Eibach Spring Systems are the first choice among enthusiasts for upgrading a vehicle's suspension. In addition to improving handling, Eibach Springs substantially enhance overall appearance by eliminating large fender well gaps which create an unfinished look for the vehicle, especially when low profile performance wheels and tires are used.

All AGX Lowering Springs are developed by experienced Eibach chassis dynamics engineers and are tested by seasoned SCCA and other Pro Racing Series drivers for use in a variety of driving applications. Vehicles fitted with the AGX/Eibach combination are exceptionally stable and secure under a wide range of conditions. Eibach designers use proprietary progressive spring rates to properly and safely lower the vehicle's center of gravity, reducing squat under acceleration, body roll, and braking nose dive.

KYB produces a full line of ride control products as original equipment and replacement parts for use in automobiles, motorcycles, light and heavy-duty trucks, buses, rolling stock, and industrial applications. The KYB line includes gas-filled monotube and twin tube shock absorbers, gas cartridges, gas struts, strut mounts, and strut boots.

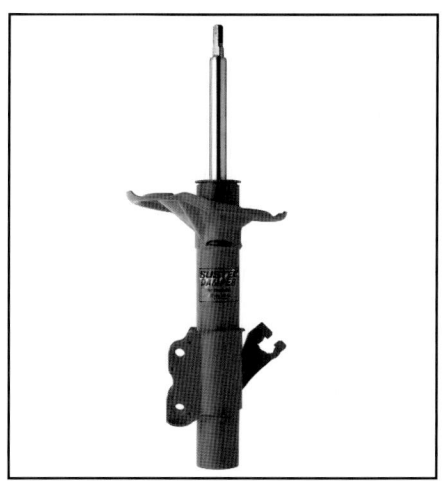

Tanabe Sustec Damper

CUSCO

The Cusco Coil-Over System is the complete system for the street racer that needs to fine tune compression and rebound rates, vehicle height, and degree of camber. This kit includes pressure- and height-adjustable shocks, performance springs, and adjustable strut upper mounts.

H&R

H&R threaded body coil-over suspension systems come directly from engineers who design and develop racing suspensions. Designed from the ground up as coil-overs (not just a modified shock body), the H&R units are handmade in Germany by H&R Spezialfedern, under ISO9001 Quality Assurance Standards. Strict attention to function of the complete suspension system is the number one design priority. Threaded body means that the outside of the strut or shock tubes are threaded like a bolt. This allows the threaded spring perch to be moved up or down to fine tune the ride height, optimizing looks and handling. The specifications of the H&R coil-over is what makes it a true tuner component; shorter shock body, shorter shock rod, custom designed dust boot, and precisely calculated bump-stop height and hardness (shore). The system is completed with a specifically-valved shock matched with high-quality H&R Springs.

TANABE

The Tanabe super sports damper long awaited by car enthusiasts and race-car builders features a short case

AROSPEED LOWERING SPRINGS

Part #	Application	Ride Height/Reduction
ARO604714	1995+ Acura CL 2.2	2.25 Front/2.25 Rear
ARO604713	1995+ Acura CL 2.2	1.50 Front/1.50 Rear
ARO604782	1990-1993 Acura Integra	2.50 Front/2.00 Rear
ARO604723	1994+ Integra	2.50 Front/2.25 Rear
ARO602233	1992+ BMW 325i/328i	1.40 Front/1.40 Rear
ARO602422	1995+ Chevrolet Cavalier	2.00 Front/2.00 Rear
ARO603161	Dodge Neon	1.75 Front/1.75 Rear

CHIKARA LOWERING SPRINGS

Part#	Applications	Ride Height/Reduction
ACURA		
7205	1990-1993 Integra	2.50 Front/2.25 Rear
7201	1994+ Integra	2.50 Front/2.25 Rear
7213	1995+ CL 2.2	2.50 Front/2.25 Rear
BMW		
7227	1992+ 325i/328i E36 (ex. Cabriolet)	1.40 Front/1.40 Rear
7228	1984-1991 325 2/4 Dr.	1.40 Front/1.40 Rear
DODGE		
7226	1994+ Neon	1.75 Front/1.75 Rear
HONDA		
7202	1986-1989 Accord	2.25 Front/2.00 Rear
7203	1990-1993 Accord	2.25 Front/2.00 Rear
7204	1990-1993 Accord	1.50 Front/1.50 Rear
7208	1994-1997 Accord	2.50 Front/2.25 Rear
7209	1994-1997 Accord	1.50 Front/1.50 Rear
7210	1998+ Accord, 4 cyl.	2.25 Front/2.25 Rear
7211	1998+ Accord, 6 cyl.	2.50 Front/2.25 Rear
7200	1988-1991 Civic/CRX	2.50 Front/2.25 Rear
7201	1992-1995 Civic/del Sol	2.50 Front/2.25 Rear
7207	1996+ Civic 2 & 4 dr.	2.50 Front/2.25 Rear
7207	1996+ Civic H.B.	2.25 Front/2.00 Rear
7206	1992-1996 Prelude	2.25 Front/2.25 Rear
7212	1997+ Prelude	2.25 Front/2.25 Rear
MAZDA		
7232	1991-1997 Protege	2.00 Front/2.00 Rear
MITSUBISHI		
7224	1991-1994 Eclipse/Talon	2.00 Front/2.00 Rear
7223	1995+ Eclipse/Talon	2.00 Front/2.00 Rear
7225	1993+ Mirage	1.75 Front/1.75 Rear
NISSAN		
7238	1987-1994 Sentra (exc. SER)	2.00 Front/2.00 Rear
7239	1995+ Sentra/200SX	2.00 Front/2.00 Rear
7240	1989-1994 240 SX	1.80 Front/1.80 Rear
7241	1995+ 240 SX	1.80 Front/1.80 Rear
7242	1993-1998 Altima	2.00 Front/2.00 Rear
7243	1995-1998 Maxima	2.00 Front/2.00 Rear
SATURN		
7237	1990-1997	2.00 Front/2.00 Rear
TOYOTA		
7233	1993-1997 Corolla	2.00 Front/2.00 Rear
7234	1990-1997 Celica	1.50 Front/1.50 Rear
7235	1992-1996 Camry	1.80 Front/1.80 Rear
7236	1991-1994 Tercel/Paseo	2.00 Front/2.00 Rear
VOLKSWAGEN		
7229	1993-1996 1/2 Golf/Jetta III 8V	2.00 Front/2.00 Rear
7230	1996 1/2+ Golf/Jetta/VR6	2.00 Front/2.00 Rear
7231	1998+ Beetle	1.80 Front/1.80 Rear

CHIKARA EXTREME RX SERIES

Part#	Applications	Ride Height/Reduction
ACURA		
7250	1994-1998 Integra	3.25 Front/3.00 Rear
HONDA		
7251	1990-1993 Accord	3.25 Front/3.00 Rear
7253	1994-1997 Accord	3.25 Front/3.00 Rear
7250	1992-1995 Civic	3.25 Front/3.00 Rear
7252	1996+ Civic 2 & 4 dr.	3.25 Front/3.00 Rear
7252	1996+ Civic H.B.	3.25 Front/3.00 Rear

and piston rod that ensures sufficient pump stroke, but is light in weight. Combining these dampers with Super H springs provides optimum control of spring movement at all times. Better traction, outstanding road-holding performance. Optimum matching with Super H springs enables vehicle height to be reduced by roughly 30 mm. The result is cornering as if your car were on rails. The shortened piston rod skillfully suppresses revamp (extension side) stroke resulting from reduced vehicle height. Faithfully reproduces the line you are after while minimizing excessive body changes.

Tanabe Sustec Pro Single and double spring features a 12-step damping-force-adjustor, which optimizes the setting according to the road conditions. Combining this with Tanabe's specially designed springs optimizes traction and handling ability. The rubber bushing of the upper mounts is replaced with a pillow ball to eliminate wasted motion of the upper-mount portion. This upper mount is of the vehicle height adjusting type, for direct and sharp handling. It also minimizes unnecessary alignment adjustments. The mounts are made of Duralimun 17 plate, and the pillow-ball portion is made of NMB for maximum rigidity and durability.

A newly designed helper spring is used above the main spring. Along with eliminating spring play, this also ensures stroke on the extending side. A shorter case solves the problem of inadequate pump stroke resulting from a lower center of gravity. At the same time, the shorter stroke sets the ideal stroke center. The high-density plated casing increases durability.

Racing springs are available in the single-spring type and double-springs type. The single-spring type features Tanabe's original spring-rate specifications. A newly designed square cross-section spring is employed for the double-type, which dynamically ensures stroke on the extending side. The vehicle-height-adjustment system allows vehicle height to be adjusted as desired. Quality PFTE seals are used. Quality which pays dividends in the form of a long life-span.

Tanabe high-quality SUP9/SUP12 is used to minimize setting. Reduces unsprung weight. Tensile strength+ 2000 N/mm. Unbelievable cornering stability with spring rate set according to data obtained from use on the racing circuit. Sufficient stroke is ensured for both the extension and contraction sides. Carefully calculated progressive spring rate.

OBX

OBX Gravitation Control Coil-Over Kit

Product#	Application
HK001	1990-1993 Acura Integra
HK002	1994-1999 Acura Integra
HK006	1990-1993 Honda Accord
HK007	1994-1997 Honda Accord
HK003	1988-1991 Honda Civic
HK004	1992-1995 Honda Civic
HK005	1996-1999 Honda Civic
HK008	1992-1996 Honda Prelude
HK009	1997-1999 Honda Prelude
HK010	1995-1999 Mitsubishi Eclipse
HK011	1997-1999 Mitsubishi Mirage

RYANE MOTORSPORTS

The Ryane Motorsports coil-over kit allows you to convert the existing standard front and rear shocks to the coil-over system. Although originally designed to allow adjustments for transferring weight and balancing the vehicle, coil-overs are frequently used as a lowering system. By making adjustments at the coil-over, you can shift the weight fore or aft and laterally. This makes the suspension very tunable.

A variety of spring rates are available to give the desired firmness: Stage One — Mild, Stage Two — High Performance Street, Stage Three — Race. Small ride-height adjustments can usually be made without adverse effect to the geometry. Large ride-height adjustments can be made but will produce side-effects. Custom springs may be special ordered.

STREET SPRINGS

APEX

Apex Suspension offers a line of highest quality sporting suspension springs. Tested on the track and by

LAKEWOOD BY EIBACH

Part #	Application	Avg. Lowered Inches Front	Rear
ACURA			
39375	1997 RL	1.20	1.00
39174	1996+ 2.2 CL	1.30	1.30
39391	1995+ 2.5 TL, 5 cyl.	1.30	1.30
39392	1995+ 3.2 TL, V-6	1.30	1.30
39366	1986-1989 Integra, rear only, tor.bar		1.00
39371	1990-1993 Integra, incl. GSR	1.40	1.00
39177	1994+ Integra	1.40	1.00
39368	1986-1988 Legend, 4 dr.	1.30	1.30
39370	1987-1990 Legend Coupe, 2 dr.	1.30	1.30
39327	1991-1995 Legend, 2/4 dr.	1.00	1.00
39388	1991+ NSX	1.30	1.30
39377	1991-1994 Vigor	1.30	1.30
39447	1993-1994 Prizm	1.00	1.00
39328	1990-1994 Storm	1.00	1.00
FORD			
39540	1998 Contour	1.30	1.30
39542	1997 Escort ZX2	1.20	1.00
HONDA			
39185	1998 Accord, 4 cyl.	1.20	1.20
39186	1998 Accord, 6 cyl.	1.50	1.50
39386	1982-1985 Accord, 2/4 dr.	1.30	1.30
39367	1986-1989 Accord, 2/4 dr.	1.30	1.00
39174	1990-1996 Accord, 2/4 dr., exc. 6 cyl & wagon	1.30	1.00
39387	1994+ Accord wagon	1.50	1.30
39390	1995+ Accord, 6 cyl., 2/4 dr.	1.50	1.30
39187	1996 Civic	1.30	1.30
39176	1996+ Civic	1.40	1.40
39365	1984-1987 Civic / CRX, rear only, tor.bar		0.80
39173	1988-1991 Civic / CRX, exc. wagon	1.00	1.00
39175	1992-1995 Civic, 2/4 dr.	1.30	1.30
39176	1993+ del Sol	1.30	1.30
39516	1997 Prelude, incl. SH	1.30	1.30
39364	1983-1987 Prelude	1.30	1.30
39369	1988-1991 Prelude, incl. AWS	1.30	1.30
39378	1992+ Prelude, incl. AWS	1.30	1.30
LEXUS			
39462	1992-1996 ES300	1.00	1.00
39467	1993+ GS300	1.30	1.30
39455	1989-1994 LS400, exc. air suspension	1.00	1.00
39470	1995+ LS400	1.30	1.30
39520	1996+ LX450, lift kit	+1.50	+1.50
39466	1992-1994 SC300	1.00	1.00
39469	1995+ SC300	1.00	1.00
39460	1991-1994 SC400	0.80	0.80
MAZDA			
39398	1986-1989 323, 2WD	1.00	1.00
39401	1988-1991 626 / MX6	1.30	1.30
39413	1992+ 626, V-6	1.00	1.00
39142	1995+ Miata/MX5, 1.6L & 1.8L, exc. C&M	1.30	1.30
39409	1992-1995 MX3, 4 cyl.	1.00	1.00
39408	1992-1994 MX3, V-6	1.00	1.00
39410	1993+ MX6, 4 cyl.	1.00	1.00
39410	1993+ MX6, V-6	1.30	1.30
39399	1979-1985 RX7	1.00	0.80
39403	1986-1992 RX7, exc. turbo & GTU	0.80	0.80
39406	1986-1992 RX7, turbo / GTUS	0.80	0.80
39411	1993+ RX7, touring, R1 / R2	1.00	1.00
MITSUBISHI			
39289	1991+ 3000 GT, 2WD, base model, exc. '95+ w/ sunroof	1.00	1.00
39287	1991+ 3000 GT/SL, 2WD, exc. '95+ w/ sunroof (or Spyder)	1.00	1.00
39288	1991+ 3000 GT VR4, exc. '95+ w/ sunroof	1.00	1.00

LAKEWOOD BY EIBACH (CONT.)

Part #	Application		
39530	1997 Diamante ES/LS	1.30	1.30
39418	1989-1994 Eclipse, 2WD, incl. turbo	1.30	1.30
39178	1995+ Eclipse, 2WD, incl. turbo, exc. Spyder	1.30	1.30
39419	1989-1994 Eclipse GSX, AWD	1.00	1.00
39420	1995+ Eclipse GSX, AWD	1.30	1.30
39420	1996+ Eclipse Spyder GS/GST	1.60	1.50
39417	1983-1989 Starion	1.30	1.00
NISSAN			
39438	1995+ 200SX SER	1.40	1.30
39179	1988-1994 240SX, exc. convertible	1.00	1.00
39436	1995+ 240SX	1.30	1.30
39426	1970-1973 240Z	1.00	1.00
39425	1975-1978 280Z	1.00	1.00
39424	1979-1983 280ZX	1.00	1.00
39423	1984-1989 300ZX	0.80	0.80
39431	1990+ 300ZX, incl. convertible & 2+2, exc. turbo	0.80	0.80
39432	1990+ 300ZX Turbo	0.80	0.80
TOYOTA			
39560	1997 Camry, 4/6 cyl.	1.20	1.20
39522	1997+ Camry, 4 cyl.	1.30	1.30
39523	1997+ Camry, 6 cyl.	1.30	1.00
39458	1992-1996 Camry, 4 cyl.	1.00	1.00
39457	1992-1996 Camry, 6 cyl.	1.30	1.00
39452	1982-1985 Celica GT, w/solid rear axle	1.00	1.30
39445	1982-1985 Celica GTS, w/IRS	1.00	1.00
39449	1986-1989 Celica, FWD	1.00	1.30
39446	1990-1995 Celica, exc. all trac	1.00	1.30
39444	1985-1987 Corolla, AE86, RWD	1.30	1.30
39449	1988-1991 Corolla, AE92, FWD	1.30	1.00
39447	1992-1994 Corolla, AE101, FWD	1.00	1.00
39448	1985-1990 MR2, incl. supercharged	1.00	1.00
39451	1991-1995 MR2, incl. turbo	1.00	1.00
39453	1982-1985 Supra, MA50	1.00	1.00
39180	1986-1992 Supra, MA70 incl. turbo	1.30	1.00
39461	1993+ Supra, JZA80 non-turbo	1.30	1.30
39454	1993+ Supra, JZA80 turbo	1.30	1.30
39464	1995+ Tercel	1.30	1.30
VOLKSWAGEN			
39528	1999 Beetle	1.00	1.00

street enthusiasts around the world, Apex's springs are proven performers. Springs lower vehicle for aggressive street stance and lower center of gravity. Most import models available.

AROSPEED

It's a game of who can go the lowest. With Arospeed lowering springs, you will be in front of the competition. Make your car stand out from the crowd while maintaining that comfortable ride. Arospeed Springs offer anywhere from a 1.40" to a 2.50" drop. With applications for most vehicles, you're sure to find the drop that suits your needs.

LIGHTSPEEED

Lightspeeed custom design ultra-high performance springs give you a full 2-1/2 inch drop. Proper spring rates to maintain handling in all conditions. Powdercoated in yellow.

Part #	Application
HO3143	1990-1993 Acura Integra
HO3145	1994-1998 Acura Integra
HO3139	1990-1997 Honda Accord
HO3131	1988-1991 Honda Civic
HO3134	1992-1995 Honda Civic
HO3136	1996-1998 Honda Civic

CHIKARA BY TD PERFORMANCE

Lowering Springs

Progressive rate springs that stiffen your ride the harder you push it. Cold wound and heat tempered spring steel for optimum performance, then powdercoated to protect them from the elements. Standard and Extreme RX lowering kits. A radical 3.25" drop.

Extreme RX Series

These springs give you the lowest possible vehicle profile. When used in conjunction with Chikara EXTREME Series Camber Kits, you will have a slammed import that rides smooth and handles great.

COMPTECH SPORT

Springs (GSR, RS, GS, LS)
Sport Springs (4) 1.4"/1"
For Years: 1994+

Springs (GSR, RS, GS, LS)
Sport Springs (4) 1.4"/1"
For Years: 1990-1993

Springs (Type R)
Sport Springs (4) 7/8" /1/2"
For Years: 1997-1998

LAKEWOOD SPORT BY EIBACH

Lakewood by Eibach

These Pro-Kit Spring sets improve looks and performance by lowering the vehicle's center of gravity, reducing body roll in turns, dive under braking, squat during acceleration, and give the vehicle a more secure feel at all times. Pro-Kit Springs also minimize the ugly fender gap that makes a vehicle look "lifted."

Multi-Pro Spring Kits

Multi-Pro kits include ride-height adjustable shock and spring combinations with Lakewood Sport by Eibach Springs unique double spring system. The tender spring

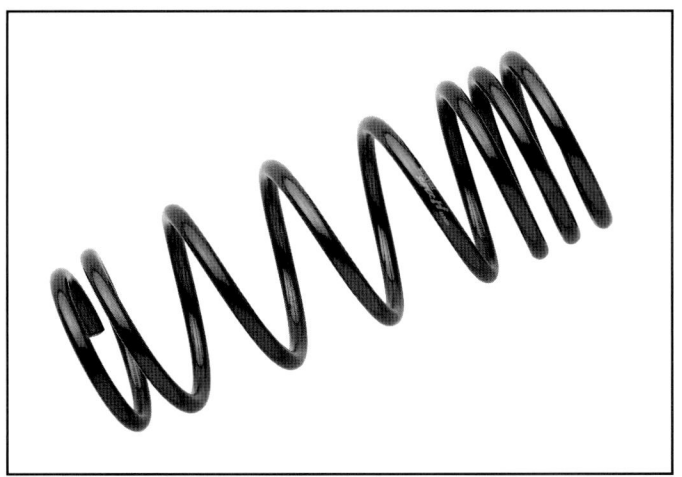
Tanabe Sustec Super H Spring

Jamex Lowered Sports Spring

provides pre-load for the suspension and reduces wheel lift during hard cornering. The main spring supports the weight of the car and provides chassis control during aggressive driving. The Lakewood Sport by Eibach Springs shock absorber features an adjustable lower spring perch which allows the user to easily change the vehicle's ride height to suit the driving conditions. Multi-Pro kits are for high performance street use as well as competition events.

Part #	Application
39385	1994+ Acura Integra
39381	1992-1996 Honda Civic & del Sol
39494	1993+ VW Golf III/Jetta III

H&R

All H&R special springs are produced on specific precision spring coilers. H&R doesn't take any short cuts as this is why H&R is the best quality spring available. All parts are produced in Germany to strict TUV standards to further ensure that only the best materials are used in producing the parts. Pure chrome silicone wire is cold wound and then heat treated and shot peened for stress relief, then tested, washed, and now finished. H&R is proud of its powdercoating process, which will keep these springs looking and performing like new for many years to come.

RSR

Give your car the look it needs with RSR Premium Suspension Springs. Whether you are looking for a set of street or race springs, RSR has what you need! Available for most popular models including: Acura Integra, Legend; Honda Accord, Civic, CRX, del Sol, Prelude, NSX; Mazda Miata, RX-7; Mitsubishi 3000GT, Eclipse; Nissan 240SX, 300Z; Toyota Celica, MR2, Supra.

TRD

Sport Springs available for:

1992-1997 Camry, 4 cyl., w/SXV10 Chassis
1997-1999 Camry, w/MCV20 Chassis
1994-1996 Camry, V-6
Camry, Lowering Spring Set
Camry Solara, Lowering Spring Set
1988-1989 Celica, FWD, turbo only
1990-1993 Celica, 4WD, turbo only
1994-1997 Celica, FWD
1984-1987 Corolla SR5 RWD and GTS RWD
1988-1991 Corolla SR5/GTS
1985-1989 MR2, inc. supercharged
1990-1995 MR2, turbo and non-turbo
1996-1997 RAV4
1993-1998 Supra, non-turbo supercharged only
1986-1992 Supra, turbo and non-turbo
1993-1997 Supra, twin-turbo only

Strut & Spring Assemblies

1997-1999 Camry, V-6 & 4 cyl.
Camry, strut & lowering spring set
Camry Solara, strut & lowering spring set
Camry Solara, strut kit

HKS

Super Sport/Super Form Springs
HKS unique progressive rate lowering springs improve handling characteristics while maintaining comfortable ride quality. Under spirited driving conditions, the HKS springs progressively compress which results in flatter cornering, controlled lane changes, and diminished nose dive induced by hard braking. Available for Acura, Honda, and Nissan.

NUESPEED

Made 100% in Germany by ISO 9002 certified spring-winding specialists. Neuspeed springs are available in a variety of tuning levels to suit your preferences for handling and appearance. Available for most popular sport compacts.

TANABE

Super Down Precedeo
This unequal-pitch spring was developed for those who crave a dynamic, low-riding form with subtle handling. Vehicle height is reduced by 40mm to create a "cool" look. Tanabe's original design eliminates spring play while maintaining suitable stroke. The same optimum materials used in the Sustec System springs are used in the Super Down Precedeo.

JAMEX

A complete range of lowered sports spring kits featuring progressive and linear windings and manufactured from chrome silicon steel. A sportspring kit gives your car not only great road stability but also the close-to-the-road appearance of a sports car. Lowering possible up to -80mm! Available for most popular Asian and European vehicles.

Sport Compact Bolt-On Performance Guide Volume 1
Wheels and Tires

DRAG RACING TIRES

Nitto

The Nitto NT-555R Extreme Drag Radial Tire is an exciting addition to the specialty performance radial tire segment of the Nitto Tire Product Line. Designing a D.O.T. approved, drag racing radial tire was no easy task. Nitto Tires demanded a tire that would outperform all drag racing radial tires, provide impressive control and handling, and still deliver 10,000 to 15,000 miles of tread life of normal street-driving use.

Nitto NT-555R Extreme Drag Radial Tires are manufactured with original tread depth of 6/32nd inch and are constructed with a specially formulated soft racing tread compound to provide maximum traction. However this soft and flexible tread will wear much quicker than tread compounds formulated for regular passenger car tires.

For Street Use: Please observe tread wear frequently. The Nitto NT-555R Extreme Drag Radial Tires are not street legal when the tread depth indicators are reached at the last 2/32nds inch. Please remove the drag tires for street use at this point. The unidirectional tread pattern with slanted grooves and lateral slits allow for water drainage in spite of the very low void ratio. However, Nitto Tires recommends reducing vehicle speeds in all wet driving conditions.

For Drag Strip Use: The Nitto NT-555R Extreme Drag Radial Tires are capable of performing well below the last 2/32nd inch of tread. If used at the track, beyond the 2/32nd inch of tread, discard the tires before the nylon cap-ply becomes visible. Be careful when the tread is below 2/32nd of an inch because the tire will lose its straight line stability as the tread continues to wear down.

Safety Information: Always refer to the vehicle owner's manual recommendations for cold-inflation air pressure. Nitto Tires advise users to check tire air pressure regularly and maintain the recommended cold inflation air pressure. Over- or under-inflation will reduce the life of your tires. Follow the vehicle owner's manual or the tire placard on vehicle for correct inflation.

Various air pressures will affect a vehicle's performance at the track. However, Nitto Tires recommends users to maintain cold-inflation air pressure suggested by the vehicle's owner's manual. In the event that Nitto NT-555R Extreme Drag radials are used at the drag strip at a cold-inflation air pressure less than the vehicle's owner's manual recommendations driver assumes complete responsibility.

HIGH PERFORMANCE STREET TIRES

BFGoodrich

g-Force™ T/A®KD is the new force in performance tires. The result of an entirely new approach to ultra-high performance tire design, g-Force T/AKD is optimized for dry traction on the street. It's the ultimate expression of BFGoodrich brand Traction/ Advantage, designed to deliver near R-compound levels of traction and handling in a more streetable tire. Intended for use on the world's best sports cars, this tire

NITTO DRAG RACING TIRES									
Size	Load Index/ Speed Symbol	Overall Dia. (in.)	Overall Width (in.)	Sidewall Height (in.)	Measuring Rim Width (in.)	Approved Rim Width (in.)	Tread Depth (32nds in.)	UTOG Rating	Max Infl.
/55R14	85V	22.84	8.39	4.42	6.5	5.5 - 7.5	6	100AA	44
/50R15	101V	25.75	11.18	5.38	8.5	75.5 - 9.5	6	100AA	44
/45R15	81V	22.17	8.19	3.59	7.0	6.5 - 7.5	6	100AA	44
/50R16	92V	24.88	9.02	4.44	7.0	6.5 - 8.0	6	100AA	44
/50R16	96V	25.67	9.8	4.84	7.5	7.0 - 8.5	6	100AA	44
/45R16	83V or 87V	23.15	8.19	3.58	7.0	6.5 - 7.5	6	100AA	44
/40ZR17	93V	25.63	10.91	4.32	9.5	9.0 - 11.0	6	100AA	44
245/45R17 -coming soon									

ensures exceptional control and inspires supreme confidence.

The new g-Force™T/A® KDW (Key feature: Dry and Wet traction) is engineered to deliver the maximum levels of dry and wet traction required by the world's hottest coupes and sport sedans. These tires give drivers the confidence to take control of the most demanding roads imaginable.

The Comp T/A®ZR is BFGoodrich® Traction/Advantage at its ultimate: a Z speed-rated ultra-high performance tire engineered to provide the maximum wet and dry handling and control required on the world's finest sports and touring cars while delivering great ride comfort and low noise. Considered by many to be the world's best, this tire inspires envelope-pushing confidence.

The Comp T/A®ZR4 is BFGoodrich® Traction/Advantage at its all-season best. This Z speed-rated ultra-high performance tire is engineered to provide maximum traction and exceptional handling, for greater control and confidence in most weather conditions. These tires have a very high treadwear grade for their class and boast great ride comfort and low noise.

Scorcher™ T/A®

Combining pyrotechnic performance with incendiary appearance, the Scorcher™ T/A® provides an ultra-high level of handling. And full-tread-depth ribs of color that refresh as the tire wears. H- and V-speed rated, and available in the latest 16-, 17-, and 18-inch sizes for the fast-growing performance tire markets, Scorcher™ T/A® is the next big thing in high-performance tires.

DUNLOP

SP Sport 9000

Dunlop has broken new ground on wet road performance with the SP Sport 9000's radical unidirectional tread pattern. The slanted main grooves channel water to the outside of the tire like a turbine wheel. The tread bars at the shoulder edges make less contact with the road so the flow of water to the sides is optimized.

Scorcher™ T/A®

SP Sport 9000

In addition, the linear length of the SP Sport 9000's main grooves are considerably longer than conventional straight grooves. This reduces water build-up in the front of the tread and improves resistance to hydroplaning resulting in more confident wet steering control.

The tread shoulder is extremely important for handling characteristics as tires are supported in these areas during handling and cornering. The SP Sport 9000 features stable shoulder blocks that greatly reduce tread squirm and distortion, offering a high degree of control in hard turns. A triple tread radius provides full, even contact pressure across the face of the tread for improved grip and control in turns.

Dunlop's PSP-B technology optimizes the SP Sport 9000's casing and ply line. This allows the tire to maintain its optimum profile regardless of treadwear for confidence-inspiring durability you can rely on throughout the life of the tire. In addition, the tread depth is computer-optimized for even tire wear.

g-Force™T/A® KD

g-Force™T/A® KDW

The HydroMax traction system features a silica-reinforced tread compound to further enhance wet traction and braking grip. This also greatly reduces rolling resistance. Underneath the tread are Dunlop-pioneered Jointless Nylon Band (JLB) overlays that provide even distribution of contact pressures and significantly reduce growth at high speeds. The result is outstanding high-speed durability and the ultimate in strength and smoothness.

While providing excellent wet traction, silica tread compounds can cause vehicles to develop static charges. The tread of the SP Sport 9000 features a ring made of carbon black compound which is connected to the silica-free base layer of the

D60 A2

SP Sport 8000

tread. This acts as a ground and effectively diverts static charges.

The SP Sport 9000's multi-shift noise reduction system includes longitudinal grooves that are molded at an angle to the direction of travel. These fan-shaped grooves, along with the shoulder bars, form a narrow passage. This prevents the creation of air columns resulting in lower noise levels.

The SP Sport 9000's tread and shoulder grooves are alternated four times. The computer-optimized mix of five different tread lengths in the center area of the tread and three different tread lengths in the shoulder assures that no tread pattern is repeated over the entire tread length. This also helps reduce tire noise by producing sounds of mutually interfering frequencies at the shoulder and center portions of the tread. The resulting sound is, for the most part, not audible to the human ear. Sizes from 195/55ZR15 to 295/40ZR20.

SP Sport 5000

Innovative, asymmetrical tread design provides optimum balance of grip and performance. Large, stable, interconnected outer tread blocks mean exceptional dry cornering grip and stability. Independent inner tread blocks with open-shoulder grooves maximize water dispersion and all-season grip.

Exclusive, high-performance, all-season tread compound (patent pending) optimizes performance in a wide range of driving and weather conditions. Full-width, twin-cut steel belts with jointless nylon band technology boast long-term integrity. Sweeping intermediate tread grooves channel water through contact patch. Four deep, wide, circumferential tread grooves provide excellent water dispersion for improved wet grip and anti-hydroplaning capability. Max flange shield protects expensive alloy wheels from curb scuffing damage. Sophisticated serrated black sidewall design gives you enhanced vehicle appearance. Sizes from P195/65R15 89V to P275/40ZR17 98W.

D60 A2 — "H" Rated All-Weather Performance Radial for World Cars

Advanced high-performance tread compound offers an optimum combination of advanced polymers and small particle high strength (SPHS) carbon black for excellent all-season handling and traction. All-season, high performance tread design for improved grip on wet, dry, and snow-covered roads. Two wide, low angle steel belts provide base of a wide, stable footprint for high-performance handling and long wear. Hard rubber bead apex/high ply turn-up for precise, predictable steering response.

Exclusive twin shift technology noise reduction system with a variable five-pitch tread design provides superb quiet ride comfort expected by today's discriminating performance car drivers. Jointless nylon band construction greatly improves ride comfort by eliminating sources of vibration delivering optimum contact patch shape for handling, traction, and treadwear. 45,000 mile limited treadwear warranty.

SP Sport W-10

Large-sized tread blocks for optimum dry handling performance. Stylish directional tread pattern with waving circumferential grooves for anti-hydroplaning performance. Jointless nylon band belt (JLB) overlay for excellent ride uniformity and contact patch shape. Sizes from P195/55VR1 to 235/40ZR18.

SP Sport 8000 — "Z" Rated Ultra-High Performance Radial

Directional tread pattern offers enhanced anti-hydroplaning performance and maximizes dry grip and handling for high-performance cars. Triple tread radius provides increased contact patch area during cornering for greater traction and control. Twin shift noise reduction for quiet performance sophistication. Jointless nylon band (JLB) overlay for excellent ride uniformity and contact patch shape. Steel or aramid lower sidewall stabilizer for responsive handling and road comfort. Max flange shield rim flange protection feature on 17", 18", 19", and 20" sizes, and selected 16" sizes helps protect alloy wheels from curb damage. Sizes from 195/55ZR14 to 265/35ZR20 MFS.

FIRESTONE

Firehawk SVX

Directional block tread design. All-season traction to help resist hydroplaning. Tread compound that combines all-season traction and V-speed rating. Ultra-high performance handling and high speed capability. Continuous wrapped nylon cap ply and belt edge layers. High-speed capability and handling, lightweight, and even ride. Hard rubber sidewall stiffeners and high body ply turn up.

Firehawk SZ50

C.O.C.S.™ (Computer-Optimized Casing System) calculates the ideal combination of tread design, materials, and tire shape to achieve the desired balance of performance characteristics.

O-Bead™ changes the way the tire

holds the rim creating a tire that is more precisely round and offers superb steering response. L.L.Carbon™, a long-link form of carbon black, reinforces and stabilizes tread rubber. Longer tread life, consistently impressive grip, and handling.

Potenza RE71

World class ultra-high performance V- and Z-speed rated tire for today's ultra-high performance enthusiast vehicles. Race bred tread compound and unidirectional design provide exceptional high-speed handling characteristics in wet and dry conditions. Advanced radial construction for instantaneous steering response and predictable cornering.

Potenza RE910

Features UNI-T®, Ultimate Network of Intelligent Tire Technology. T-Speed rated performance tire. Outstanding wet and dry performance. Tread pattern is derived from Formula One Potenza Racing Rain Tire technology.

Potenza S-02 Pole Position

Features UNI-T AQ™, Ultimate Network of Intelligent Tire Technology. Z-Speed rated ultra-high performance radial. Excellent response and superior grip in wet or dry conditions. Designed for excellent performance as the tire wears.

GOODYEAR

Eagle HP Ultra Plus

Eagle HP Ultra Plus replaces the popular Eagle GS-C ultra performance radial, which made its debut on the 1992 Chevrolet Corvette. The two tires deliver nearly identical performance capabilities, but the longer-wearing tire carries a manufacturer recommended price that is 15 percent lower. Initially Eagle HP Ultra Plus, which is produced in Goodyear's plant in Union City, Tennessee, is available in the following sizes: 205/55ZR16, 225/50ZR16, 225/55ZR, 245/45ZR16, 245/45ZR17, P245/50ZR16, P255/45ZR17, P255/50ZR16, P275/40ZR17, and P285/40SR17.

EAGLE HP ULTRA

A unique directional tread pattern and aggressive tread elements combine to provide excellent wet traction and grip during braking in wet conditions. Dual nylon overlays deliver responsive handling and a smooth ride. Low profile sidewall for the lean, aggressive look ideal for tuner cars.

Directional tread pattern gives excellent wet surface traction. Durable all-season tread compound for all-season traction and long wear. H-speed rated up to 130 mph/210 kph to inspire driving confidence at highway speeds.

EAGLE F1 GSD 2

This Eagle features a striking directional tread design for optimized handling and traction in wet conditions. Sized to fit European sports cars, sport sedans, and plus-size wheel upgrades.

Unidirectional tread design and natural flow tread grooves sweep away water, improve wet braking. High-tensile steel belts and high-ply turn up gives responsive handling, impact durability.

Spirally wound Aramid overlay for smooth ride and high speed durability. Shoulder decoupling groove improves cornering traction.

EAGLE F1S

An ultra-tensile steel ply and aquachannel technology combine to make the Eagle F1 Steel Goodyear's most advanced ultra-performance tire. Patented ultra-tensile steel ply gives precise handling, improved treadwear, and durability. Exclusive Goodyear AATRAX™ tread compound for outstanding treadwear without sacrificing traction or noise reduction. Dual aquachannels for excellent wet traction. Spirally wound flexten overlays give smooth, disturbance-free operation, even at high speeds. Z-speed rated above 149 mph/240 kmh is the highest speed rating available.

MICHELIN

Pilot Sport

Michelin North America has launched its new Pilot Sport ultra-high performance tire. As the most recent addition to Michelin's Pilot performance line, the Sport extends the capabilities of exotic and ultra-

Firehawk SZ50

Potenza RE910

Potenza S-02 Pole Position

GOODYEAR EAGLE HP ULTRA TIRES

Sizes & Specifications

Tire Size	Approved Rim Width	Meas. rim	Section Width	O.D.	Tread width	Max. Load
235/45ZR17	6.0-9.0	7.0	9.1	25.7	8.2	1,477
205/50ZR16	7.0-8.5	7.5	8.8	23.9		1,279
205/45ZR16	6.5-7.5	7.0	8.1	23.2	6.9	1,074
225/45ZR16	7.0-8.5	7.5	8.8	23.9		1,279
215/40ZR16	7.0-8.5	7.5	8.5	22.7	7.1	1,047
215/45ZR17	7.0-8.0	7.0	8.3	24.6	7.2	1,201
225/45ZR17	7.0-8.5	7.5	8.8	24.9	7.6	1,323
215/40ZR17	7.0/t8.5	7.5	8.5	23.7	7.6	1,074
235/40ZR17	8.0-9.5	8.5	9.4	24.4		1,323
255/40ZR17	8.0-10.0	9.0	10.2	25.0		1,477
225/40ZR18	7.5-9.0	8.0	9.0	25.0	7.7	1,236
255/35ZR18	8.5-10.0	9.0	10.2	25.0	9.2	1,323
255/40ZR19	8.5-10.0	9.0	10.2	27.0		1,565

GOODYEAR EAGLE F1 GSD 2 TIRES

Tire Size	Approved Rim Width	Meas. rim	Section Width	O.D.	Tread width	Max. Load
235/45ZR17	6.0-9.0	7.0	9.1	25.7	8.2	1,477
205/50ZR16	7.0-8.5	7.5	8.8	23.9	6.9	1,279
205/45ZR16	6.5-7.5	7.0	8.1	23.2	6.9	1,074
225/45ZR16	7.0-8.5	7.5	8.8	23.9	7.5	1,279
215/40ZR16	7.0-8.5	7.5	8.5	22.7	7.1	1,047
215/45ZR17	7.0-8.0	7.0	8.3	24.6	7.2	1,201
225/45ZR17	7.0-8.5	7.5	8.8	24.9	7.6	1,323
215/40ZR17	7.0-8.5	7.5	8.5	23.7	7.6	1,074
235/40ZR17	8.0-9.5	8.5	9.4	24.4	8.0	1,323
255/40ZR17	8.0-10.0	9.0	10.2	25.0	8.8	1,477
225/40ZR18	7.5-9.0	8.0	9.0	25.0	7.7	1,236
255/35ZR18	8.5-10.0	9.0	10.2	25.0	9.2	1,323
255/40ZR19	8.5-10.0	9.0	10.2	27.0	10.0	1,565

GOODYEAR EAGLE F1S TIRES

Tire Size	Approved Rim Width	Meas. rim	Section Width	O.D.	Tread width	Max. Load
205/55ZR15	5.5-7.5	6.5	8.43	23.90	7.7	1,201
205/55ZR16	5.5-7.5	6.5	8.43	24.88	7.7	1,279
225/55ZR16	6.0-8.0	7.0	9.17	25.75	8.6	1,521
245/45ZR16	7.5-9.0	8.0	9.57	24.65	8.9	1,477
245/45ZR17	7.5-9.0	8.0	9.57	25.67	8.6	1,521
P245/50ZR16	6.5-9.5	7.5	9.96	25.67	9.1	1,576
P255/45ZR17	8.0-9.5	8.5	10.04	26.06	9.1	1,389
P255/50ZR16	6.5-10.0	8.0	10.43	26.06	9.6	1,687
P275/40ZR17	8.5-11.0	9.5	10.94	25.67	9.7	1,433
P285/40ZR17	9.5-11.0	10.0	11.42	25.98	9.9	1,521
P275/40ZR18	9.5-11.0	9.5	10.90	26.60	10.3	1,477
P275/45ZR18	9.5-11.0	9.5	11.60	28.40	10.4	1,819

Michelin Pilot Sport

Michelin Pilot XGT H4

Michelin Pilot XGT Z4 ZP

high performance sports cars, ensuring maximum handling and control in wet and dry conditions.

The Pilot Sport provides outstanding drive handling thanks to its exceptionally progressive grip and uncompromising cornering power. "The Pilot Sport offers performance driven tire customers something they have been looking for -- uncompromised performance and exceptional comfort in a Z-speed performance rated tire," said Holly Waddell, marketing manager for Michelin North America. "The advanced technology of the tread compounds combine powerful wet traction, handling and braking with driver-friendly dry handling."

The Pilot Sport was designed utilizing Michelin's BAZ Technology™ — optimizing high-speed handling and durability. The tire's rayon casing combined with ultra-reinforced sidewalls and lightweight rim protectors promote powerful, predictable cornering while helping to fend off road-hazard damage and protect costly alloy wheels. In addition, the radically swept-back lateral grooves efficiently evacuate water from underneath the contact patch for outstanding wet traction and reduction of tire noise on dry roads.

Pilot XGT H4

Michelin's Pilot XGT H4 all-season,

high performance tire, is the best H-rated high-performance tire Michelin has ever made. Designed for sports coupes, sedans, and roadsters, the XGT H4 brings a powerful and capable all-season option to the already exceptional Michelin Pilot line. The tire's advanced technology, all-season tread compound promotes powerful wet traction, progressive handling and excellent snow traction for a high-performance tire.

"The Pilot XGT H4 truly provides the ultimate in H-rated performance tires with all-season capability," said Ron Wood, Michelin marketing manager for performance tires. "The tire's excellent handling and crisp steering response in wet and dry conditions provide drivers with the most effective product for maximizing the performance capabilities of their cars."

The advanced tread features lateral and circumferential grooves designed to efficiently drain water from the contact patch to maximize wet traction, and sipes designed for positive snow traction and the ability to handle high-torque, high-grip applications.

Massive shoulders stabilized by a high-strength belt package provide powerful, progressive driver-friendly cornering, making the tire easy to lean on and easy to drive hard. In addition, the tire's dynamically stress-balanced casing equalizes loads throughout the rolling footprint to help the XGT H4 deliver exceptional treadwear for its category.

The XGT H4 utilizes Michelin's exclusive FAZ Technology — individual Filaments At Zero degrees to tire rotation — which enables Michelin engineers to place reinforcing filaments precisely where needed, in the amounts needed, for each specific tire design and size. This facilitates fine-tuning to minimize tradeoffs and optimize performance.

Pilot XGT Z4 ZP

All other tires that can hope to run with this one, run for cover when the weather gets sloppy. The Michelin® Pilot® XGT® Z4 radial keeps you going. But this is no milk-toast, all-season tire. It's a stormer, a revolution in performance tire technology with breakthroughs in every area from compounding to tread design.

The Pilot XGT Z4 not only delivers extraordinary dry grip, handling precision, and control in the wet; the attributes that help it handle wide-ranging conditions also make it exceptionally comfortable, durable, and quiet for a Z-speed rated ultra-high performance tire. Too good to be true? No. Too good not to drive. For combining ultra-high performance with practicality, the Pilot XGT Z4 radial knows no rivals.

Tire Size	Load Index
P205/55ZR16	89
P225/50ZR16	91
P225/55ZR16	94
P225/60ZR16	97
P245/50ZR16	96
P255/50ZR16	99
P235/45ZR17	87
P245/45ZR17	89
P255/45ZR17	92
P275/40ZR17	93
P285/40ZR17	95
P245/40ZR18	88
P255/40ZR18	90
P285/35ZR18	89
P255/40ZR19	91
P245/40ZR20	90
P275/35ZR20	89

UTQG Rating:

Treadwear	Traction	Temperature
300	A	A

NITTO

NT-505 Radials

These specialty ultra-high performance radials feature a wide unidirectional tread design for superior traction on dry surfaces and improved braking response. Jointless tread cap plies and single strand jointless wound bead wires improve tire uniformity and provide a smoother ride. NT-505 radials are V speed-rated, up to 149 mph.

NT-450 Radials

Extreme unidirectional tread design provides NT-450 radials with excellent wet weather performance and superior traction performance, while delivering a smooth and quiet ride. A double-V tread design comprised of a combination of slanted grooves and lateral slits provide efficient water drainage to ensure superior wet-road handling. The use of the double center rib and double groove makes it an aggressive and sexy high performance A/S (all season) concept pattern worthy of the title "Extreme Performance." NT-450 radials are V speed-rated, up to 149 mph.

NT-555

This ultra-high performance radial tire accentuates all aspects of pleasure in driving your street machine. The NT-555 is designed to transfer power efficiently to the road, provide superior and reliable traction, even on wet surfaces, resist tread wear, provide high-speed driving stability, and yield a quiet and comfortable ride. ZR-W speed-rated, up to 168 mph.

YOKOHAMA

Parada

Designed with the street tuner in mind, the Parada is a product of extreme thinking, a product whose outstanding performance matches its unique look – massive diagonal tread blocks, low void shoulders, helical long grooves, and one mean solitary circumferential groove. The tread block is designed to maximize grip by laying more rubber on the road. The low shoulder void of the Parada increases the "rubber-to-road" contact during hard cornering and lateral acceleration. This increase should block stability and counteract that "twitchy" feeling that comes with the application of larger, low profile tires on the small sedans prominent in the street tuner market.

Using advanced computer design technology, Yokohama incorporated helical long grooves into the Parada. The angle at which these wide-channel grooves cut into the tread face optimizes wet handling. The elongated, wide-channel, S-shaped groove evacuates water away from the contact patch. In addition, the tread depth decreases at the end of each groove increasing tread block stability and reducing tread squirm during hard cornering. An ultra deep, ultra wide solitary circumferential groove channels water away from the tread area providing outstanding wet handling.

The Parada features a new "flat modulus" compound that remains pliable at low temperatures without sacrificing dry performance when heated. In addition, Yokohama has also used a new base compound in the Parada, allowing the Parada to grip the road and deliver excellent steering response.

Yokohama Parada

Yokohama AVS dB

Yokohama AVID H4

Yokohama AVS Sport

JAMEX WHEEL BOLTS

Part #	Description
230004	M12 1.5 with 29mm thread-length, ball shaped
230005	M12 1.5 with 28mm thread-length, cone shaped
230001	M12 1.25 with 35mm thread-length, cone shaped
230006	M12 1.5 with 39mm thread-length, cone shaped
230007	M12 1.5 with 39mm thread-length, ball shaped
230008	M12 1.5 with 40mm thread-length, cone shaped
230002	M12 1.25 with 42mm thread-length, cone shaped
230009	M12 1.5 with 43mm thread-length, ball shaped
230010	M12 1.5 with 42mm thread-length, cone shaped
230011	M12 1.5 with 45mm thread-length, ball shaped
230012	M12 1.5 with 45mm thread-length, cone shaped
230003	M12 1.25 with 48mm thread-length, cone shaped
230013	M12 1.5 with 55mm thread-length, ball shaped
230017	M14 1.5 with 32mm thread-length, cone shaped
230018	M14 1.5 with 45mm thread-length, ball shaped
230019	M14 1.5 with 47mm thread-length, cone shaped
230020	M14 1.5 with 60mm thread-length, ball shaped
230015	M12 1.5 with 40mm thread-length, Ford
230016	M12 1.5 with 50mm thread-length, Ford

Parada incorporated a functional Rim Protector Bar (RPB) that helps protect expensive wheel packages from potholes and curbs. The Parada sidewall has been specially designed to optimize the RPB placement and function.

The Parada features a Z-speed rating (149 mph+) and is available in 16-inch, 17-inch, and 18-inch sizes: 205/45ZR16, 205/40ZR17, 205/45ZR17, 215/40ZR17, 215/35ZR18, 215/40ZR18, 225/35ZR18, and 225/40ZR18.

AVS dB

Yokohama's new AVS dB is making noise in the marketplace because it is so quiet on the street. The AVS dB (decibel) is the ultimate ultra-high performance tire, combining low noise, ride comfort, and all-season traction into one tire.

The treadblock pattern is designed to cancel noise while channeling water. The tread features tusk grooves that become narrow at their open end to reduce noise caused by trapped air. These same tusk grooves are placed at a 20° angle which is optimum for breaking up noise patterns and effectively channeling water from under the center portion of the tread. A subtle wave pattern in the tuck groove walls prevents distortion of the groove during road contact and minimizes noise caused by escaping, compressed air. Narrow grooves in the shoulder restrict the space required for airflow noise. Finally the tread blocks vary in size and position, which creates a self-cancelling effect on the footstep nose that is common among ultra-high performance tires.

The AVS dB shares compound and construction technology with the recently introduced AVS Sport and is offered in 15-inch, 16-inch, 17-inch, and 18-inch sizes.

AVS Sport

AVS Sport is Yokohama's street version of its winning Formula Atlantic race rain tire. Its Y-shaped tread pattern featuring a continuous center block reduces the amount of groove area, provides a larger contact patch, greater stability on wet surfaces and monster grip in the dry. You'll experience a sense of control that's like riding on rails.

The even groove distribution of the AVS Sport's Y-shaped tread pattern improves drainage as much as 10% over comparable tires because water travels less distance to the groove. Sub-grooves on the shoulder's edge divide the large blocks and reduce the amount of outside tire noise. The Super Performance Silica (SPS) ultra-high performance tread compound resists wear, maximizes dry grip, and optimizes wet traction. Yokohama's innovative SofTech belt technology design enhances the AVS Sport's lateral grip to improve handling and riding comfort. Yokohama's jointless cap and layer construction, strengthened by a steel sidewall insert, effortlessly earns a Y-speed rating up to 186 mph. A rim protector bar is included on all sizes.

AVS SPORT SIZES

205/55ZR1693W
225/55ZR1695W
205/50ZR1791W
225/50ZR1692W
245/45ZR1694W
215/45ZR1787W
225/45ZR1790W
235/45ZR1793W
245/45ZR1795W
P255/45ZR1792W
235/40ZR1790W
245/40ZR1791W
255/40ZR1794W
275/40ZR1798W
P285/40ZR1795W
315/35ZR17102W
235/50ZR1897Y
255/45ZR1899Y
225/40ZR1888Y
235/40ZR1891Y
245/40ZR1893Y
225/35ZR1883W
265/35ZR1893Y
275/35ZR1895Y
285/30ZR1893Y
285/35ZR18
295/35ZR1899Y
255/40ZR1996Y
235/35ZR1991Y
245/35ZR1993Y
295/35ZR19100Y
265/30ZR1989Y
275/30ZR1996Y
P245/40ZR2090Y
255/35ZR2093Y
265/35ZR2095Y
P275/35ZR2089Y
285/30ZR2095Y

AVID H4/V4

If you love driving, you'll love the AVID H4/V4. Created with an insatiable appetite for the rigors of high-performance driving, AVID H4/V4 combines decades of race-proven technology with an uncanny ability to deliver superior ride comfort, low noise, and long treadwear through all kinds of weather. Extra strong honeycomb carbon technology. 20° V-Groove for maximum water drainage. Unidirectional tread design for optimal wet handling ability. Solid center rib for increased high-speed handling and stability. 45,000-mile limited treadwear warranty.

A008RS/RS II

The A008RS is Yokohama's dedicated road-racing DOT-approved, ultra-high performance club racing tire. It offers lateral stability under high-speed conditions with gradual load shifting. The A008RS II is Yokohama's dedicated ultra-high

Mr. Gasket Angle Chrome Tire Valve Stems

Mr. Gasket Tire Screw Kit

Mr. Gasket Flush Mount Tire Valves

performance autocross tire. Engineered for excellent performance in the solo racing environment, this tire handles superbly under low speeds and harsh transitions. Both are engineered to excel in a competitive environment.

A032R
Yokohama's ultimate DOT-approved racing tire. The A032R is a proven winner in Europe and the U.S. It brings racing tire design to the street with new casing, sidewall, and tread compounding directly descended from Professional SportsCar Racing slicks. Road racing has never been the same.

WHEEL AND TIRE ACCESSORIES

MR. GASKET PARTS

Tire Screw Kit
This handy kit was designed to help prevent the tire from spinning on the rim with low tire pressure. Each kit contains 35 grade 8 #14 hex head screws, 5/32" x 5/8" and the proper drill bit to complete two wheels. It's a must for the serious competitor.

Part # 4318   Tire Screw Kit

Flush Mount Tire Valves
This advanced design tire valve will give any custom wheel a clean, smooth appearance by eliminating unsightly valve stems. Manufactured from the highest quality brass and beautifully chrome-plated, these flush mount tire valves are engineered to fit all tubeless applications on most chrome, steel, or aluminum wheels. Packaged 4 per set with special inflator adapter included. Fits .453" valve stem hole.

Part # 5102   Flush Mount Tire Valves

Straight Chrome Tire Valve Stems
Heavy chrome-plating and quality finish add the classic touch to your mag or chrome rims. Fits .453" valve stem hole.

Part # Description

1955 Short Chrome, 2 per set
1957 Flush Mount, 4 per set

Angle Chrome Tire Valve Stems
This unique, angle design was created for use on mag wheels where standard valve stems, such as with the wire-mag wheel, create a clearance problem. Beautiful chrome finish enhances appearance. Four per set. Replaces standard valve stem application. Fits .453" valve stem hole.

1958 Angle Chrome Tire Valve Stems

MCGARD

SplineDrive lug Nuts
A no-compromise design engineered to fit small diameter recesses in new tuner wheels. SplineDrive lug nuts offer a closed-end design, maximum gripping power, more stud engagement, and a greater seating surface than socket-style lug nuts. In addition they're 30% lighter in weight.

SplineDrive lug nuts take safety, dependability, and good looks to the next level. Also fits almost any cone seat wheel styles. The exclusive patent-pending design eliminates

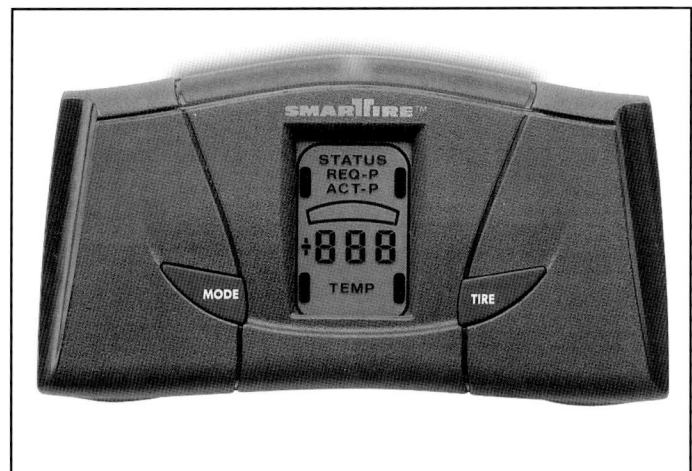

SmarTire Display Module

SmarTire Passenger Sensors

SmarTire Passenger Sensors

GORILLA

Small Diameter Tuner Lug Nuts

The small diameter design fits all tuner wheels. Its closed-end design prevents rusting problems. In addition, the small diameter design produces better torque and prevents breakage. The lugs are heat treated and chrome plated for strength and beauty. The bulge design provides more seating surface than traditional tuner lug nuts.

SMARTIRE

The SmarTire Tire Monitoring System (TMS) is designed for tuners who need the status of the most important piece of equipment — their tires. The system works on both conventional and run-flat tires. With a SmarTire monitor you can keep your tires running at optimal pressure, increasing their efficiency, reliability, performance, and your overall driving safety. The system, which uses wireless technology to monitor the air pressure and temperature in your tires, consists of wireless wheel-mounted sensors and a display receiver mounted within sight and reach of the driver. Each sensor contains: pressure transducer, temperature transducer, centrifugal switch, radio transmitter, unique ID code, and lithium battery.

One sensor is mounted on each wheel, and the tire is then mounted over the sensor enclosing the unit for protection from the elements. The interactive display module shows required pressure, actual pressure, pressure status, and temperature. Using two simple buttons, drivers can check the status of each tire.

The sensors are activated with a centrifugal switch and transmit only when the vehicle is in motion. When the vehicle stops, the sensors return to sleep mode but the driver is still able to see the last signals sent while the vehicle was moving. Sleep mode extends the life of the lithium battery and makes SmarTire virtually maintenance-free.

H&R

Special Springs, LP- Trak+ Wheel spacers

DR for 10-40mm Track Widening

The spacer is fitted between the wheel and hub, using longer wheel bolts. (Wheel bolts are ordered separately. Please check type of bolt head — taper or round and diameter and shaft length.)

DRS for 10 to 40mm Track Widening

This spacer exchanges the existing wheel studs for longer ones. The wheels are then fitted to the hub/spacer with the existing wheel nuts.

DRA for 40+mm Track Widening

This is fitted to the hub with special wheel bolts and has new threaded holes for existing wheel bolts.

DRM for 40+ mm Track Widening

The spacer is fitted to the hub with special nuts and it carries new wheel studs for the existing wheel nuts.

the rust problems associated with open-end socket-style lug nuts. SplineDrive lug nuts completely cover the stud and will not let rust weep out and stain the wheel finish. Never worry about difficult lug nut removal again.

Tuner Wheel Locks

For use on Tuner wheels or wheels with very small lug nut holes.

Part #	Description	Hex Size
25230	1/2 nut	13/16
25254	12 x 1.25 nut	13/16
25257	12 x 1.5 nut	13/16
25330	1/2 nut, black	13/16
25354	12 x 1.25 nut, black	13/16
25357	12 x 1.5 nut, black	13/16

A.1 TURBO Industry Inc.
Turbo Cars, Parts, & Accessories
2621 Pico Boulevard, Unit G
Santa Monica, California 90405
Call 24 hours:
In the USA: 800-535-8872
Fax 310-828-2070
Outside US: 310-827-4800
e-mail: a1turbo@hotmail.com

ABD Racing
Autobahn Designs
2900 Adams Street Suite B-27
Riverside, CA 92504
909-351-9566
Fax: 909-351-9575

Accel
Mr. Gasket Co.
10601 Memphis Ave., #12
Cleveland, OH 44144

Active Autowerke
9940 Southwest 168th Terrace
Miami, Florida 33157
Orders: 800-830-3596
305-233-9300
305-253-8921

A D Accessories
3738 Albury Ave.
Long Beach, CA 90808-2101
562-429-3984
Fax: 562-429-4690

Addco Manufacturing
Company, Inc.
1596 Linville Falls Hwy.
Linville, NC 28646
Sales: 800-338-7015, FL
Sales: 800-621-8916, NC
e-mail: sales@addco.net

Advanced Clutch Technology
P.O. BOX 93425
Palmdale, CA 93590-3425
Shipping Address:
1747 East Ave Q E-7
Palmdale, CA 93550
661-947-7791
Fax: 661-947-5998
e-mail: sales@advancedclutch.com

Advanced Motorsport Solutions
850 West 18th Street, Unit A
Costa Mesa, CA 92627
949-515-1672
Fax: 949-515-1676

Aerocharger Turbo Systems
Division of Aerodyne Corporation
8 Apollo Drive
Batavia, NY 14020
716-345-0055
Fax: 716-344-5623
e-mail: bikesales@aerocharger.com

Aerodyne Dallas
Division of Aerodyne Corporation
151 Regal Row Suite 120
Dallas, TX 75247
214-688-1100
Fax: 214-638-4322
www.aerocharger.com

Aeroquip Industrial Group
Americas Industrial Division
1695 Indian Wood Circle,
P.O. Box 700
Maumee, OH 43537-0700
419-891-5100
Fax: 419-891-5159
www.aeroquip.com

Aerosport
238 Commission St., Unit D
Salinas, CA 93901
831-758-0348
Fax: 831-758-5463
e-mail: info@aerosport.net

American Honda Motor Co. Inc.
1919 Torrance Blvd.
Mail Stop 100-3C-2A
Torrance, CA 90501
310-783-3170
Fax: 310-783-3622

American Products Company
1461 Railroad Street
Corona, CA 91720
800-594-4APC
909-898-9840
Fax: 909-898-9820
www.4apc.net

Apex Integration, Inc.
17091 Daimler St.
Irvine, CA 92614
949-224-1680
Fax: 949-224-1681
www.apexi.usa.com

APEX North America
508 McCormick Dr. Suite I
Glen Burnie, MD 21061
410-451-5921
www.apexsuspension.com

Applied Technologies
& Research, Inc.
17040 S. Hwy. 11
Fair Play, SC 29643
864-972-3800

APR Performance, Inc.
2980 First Street, #M
LaVerne, CA 91750
909-392-0095
Fax: 909-392-3695

Aquamist Dealer
424 Bluff Road
Fort Lee, New Jersey 07024
201-886-9609
e-mail: bka@bellatlantic.net

Arospeed
10776 S.W. 190 St., Unit B
Miami, FL 33157
877-4AROSPEED
877-427-6773
305-969-9973
Fax: 305-254-0151
e-mail: arospeed@mindspring.com

**ARP Automotive
Racing Products**
531 Spectrum Circle
Oxnard, CA 93030
805-278-7223
www.arp-bolts.com
Contact: Bob Florine

ATK Engines
3210 S Croddy Way
Santa Ana, CA 92704
Sales Information:
sales@atkengines.com
Customer Service:
custserv@atkengines.com
Warranty Depart:
warranty@atkengines.com
Export Quotations:
export@atkengines.com
Webmaster:
webmaster@atkengines.com

Autolook
See: KHL Trading Company

Autopower Industries
3424 Pickett St.
San Diego, CA 92110
619-297-3300
619-297-9765
ATTN: Rick White

**Autotech Accessories
and Systems**
13659 Victory Blvd., #120
Van Nuys, CA 91401
818-504-6088
Fax: 818-504-6021

Autotech Sport Tuning
32240 Paseo Adelanto Unit E
San Juan Capistrano, CA 92675
949-240-4000
Fax: 949-240-0450

Azect
5-30, Mikami
Yoro-Cho, Yoro Gun
Gifu, Japan
011-81-58-432-0187
Fax: 011-81-58-432-0709

Baer Racing
3108 W. Thomas Rd.
Suite 1201-Q
Phoenix, AZ 85017
602-233-1411
Fax: 602-352-8445
e-mail: brakes@baer.com
www.baeracing.com

Bilstein
Western Sales:
8845 Rehco Road,
San Diego, CA 92121
800-537-1085

Eastern Sales:
78 Rebeschi Drive,
North Haven, CT 06473
800-745-4636

Blitz Performance Products
4879 E. La Palma Ave. Suite 206
Anaheim, CA 92807
714-777-9766
714-777-9763

**B&M Racing and
Performance Products**
9142 Independence Avenue
Chatsworth, CA 91311
818-882-6422
Fax: 818-882-6694

Bomex
3457 W. El Egundo Blvd., Unit C
Hawthorne, CA 90250
310-355-0181
Fax: 310-355-0182
General Information:
sales@bomexaero.com
Sales: sales@bomexaero.com
Customer Support:
sales@bomexaero.com

Borla
5901 Edison Dr.
Oxnard, CA 93033
877-Go-Borla
www.borla.com

Bosal USA, Inc.
14 Troy Hills Road
Whippany, NJ 07981
800-631-7271
Fax: 973-428-8856
www.bosalusa.com

Brakeman
2455 Blanchard Road
Camarillo, CA 92012
805-491-2185
e-mail: brakeman@hotmail.com

Brembo North America
1585 Sunflower Avenue
Costa Mesa, CA 92626
714-641-0104
Fax: 714-641-5827

Buschur Racing
24 W. Main St.
Wakeman, OH 44889
440-839-1900
Fax: 440-839-5088

Carrera Shocks
5412 New Peachtree Road
Atlanta, GA 30341
Tech: 770-451-8811
Orders only, 24.hr recorder:
1-800-RACE-4-IT
Fax: 770-451-8086

Cerullo
828 Towne Center Dr.
Pomona, CA 91767
909-625-3611
Fax: 909-625-3610
e-mail: cerullo@primenet.com

**Chikara
The Home Town Dealer™ Hotline**
Call toll free to contact the Chikara/TD Performance Products nearest to you! Just call the toll-free 800 number below, enter the access code, and get the Name, phone number, and address of the dealer closest to you. You can even choose to connect to that dealer, without redialing and free of charge.

1-800-500-7414 Access code #0450

**Clutch Masters
High Performance Center**
West Coast:
1330 Glassell Unit N
Orange, CA 92867
714-288-8811
714-288-9093

East Coast:
217-85 98th Ave.
Queens Village
New York, NY 11428
718-217-0139
718-217-0894

ClutchNet
626-448-7432
Fax: 626-448-5737

Comptech USA
4717 Golden Foothill Pkwy.
El Dorado Hills, CA 95762
916-939-9118
Fax: 916-939-9196

Cone Engineering
10883 Portal Drive,
Los Alamitos, CA 90720
714-828-8728
Fax: 714-828-6942
e-mail: info@banzaisports.com

Corbeau USA LLC
9503 South 560 West
Sandy, UT 84070
801-255-3737
Fax: 801-255-3222

Crane Cams, Inc.
530 Fentress Blvd.
Daytona Beach, FL 32114
904-252-1151
Tech Line: 904-258-6174
Fax: 904-258-6167

**Crower Cams
& Equipment Co., Inc.**
3333 Main Street
Chula Vista, CA 91911-5899
619-422-1191
Fax: 619-422-9067

Cunningham Rods
550 W. 172nd Street
Gardena, CA 90248
310-538-0605
Fax: 310-538-0695
e-mail:
staff@cunninghamrods.com

Cusco
See: Greddy

Custom Interiors
815 Central Ave.
Jefferson, LA 70121-1304
504-837-2971
Fax: 504-837-5440

DC Sports
286 Winfield Cir.
Corona, CA 91720
909-734-2030
Fax: 909-734-2792

Dinan
150 South Whisman
Mountain View, CA 94041
650-962-9401
www.dinanbmw.com

Disklok
410 S. San Gabriel Blvd.
Suite 3
San Gabriel, CA 91776
888-4-disklok
626-614-9294
Fax: 626-614-9295
e-mail: info@disklok.com

Drag Performance Products
323-721-9689

Dunlop Tires
See: Goodyear

Dunrite Converters
4509 Shirley Ave, Unit B
El Monte, CA 91731
626-442-1404

Dyson Oil Inc.
P.O. Box 266
Durant, OK 74702
800-456-7665
580-924-8834
Fax: 580-920-0935

Earle's
189 West Victoria Street
Long Beach, CA. 90805
310-609-1602

EBC Brakes USA Ltd.
806 Buchanan Blvd. Unit 115-256
Boulder City, NV 89005
702-293-3332
702-293-1830

EFI Systems, Inc.
3790 Highway 92, Suite 210
Acworth, GA 30102
770-529-3202
Fax: 770-529-3203

EGR Inc.
North American HQ
1932 Lynx Place
Ontario, CA 91761
909-923-7075
909-923-0945

Electromotive, Inc.
9131 Centreville Rd.
Manassas, Virginia 20110
703-331-0100
Fax: 703-331-0161

Elf Race Fuel
Competition Fuels Inc.
304 Gasoline Alley, Suite D
Indianapolis, IN 46222
800-ELF-FUEL

ELP Motorsport
6185 Magnolia Ave, Suite 411
Riverside, CA 92506
909-776-9191
Fax: 909-781-9952

Energy Suspension
1131 Via Callejon
San Clemente, CA 92673
949-361-3935
Fax: 949-361-3940
e-mail: hyperfx@ibm.net
www.energysuspension.com

**The Engine &
Transmission Exchange**
3532 Smith Ave
Everett, WA 98201
800-633-3308
e-mail: zsport@zsport.com
www.zsport.com

EuroLights
e-mail:
info@eurolights.com

Evans Cooling Systems
P.O. Box 434
Parkerford, PA 19457-0434
Tech Support Line:
610-323-3114
Sales: 888-990-2665
610-970-0286
e-mail:
ecs@evanscooling.com

Evans Engineering Center
253 Route 41 North
Sharon, CT 06069
Fax: 860-364-0888
e-mail:
webmaster@evanscooling.com

**Excentrix Auto
Innovations Inc.**
9827 N. Cave Creek Rd.
Phoenix, AZ 85020-1723
602-944-4886
Fax: 602-944-7783

Extrudehone Corporation
1 Industry Blvd.
P.O. Box 1000
Irwin, PA 15642
800-367-1109
724-863-5900
Fax: 724-863-8759
e-mail: exhone@extrudehone.com

EZ Up International
International E.Z Up, Inc.
1601 Iowa Avenue
Riverside, CA 92507
800-45-SHADE
909-781-0843
Fax: 909-781-0586
e-mail: info@ezup.com

FET, Inc.
926 Freeway Drive North BLDG. # 9
Columbus, OH 43229
800-267-1157
614-431-6370
Fax: 614-431-6374
e-mail: webmaster@fet.usa.com

Fidanza Flywheels
4285 Main Street
Perry, OH 44081
440-259-5656
Fax: 440-259-5588

F&L Co., Inc.
1537 E. Del Amo Blvd.
Carson, CA 90746
310-603-2200
Fax: 310-603-2257

Flex.a.lite
P.O. Box 580
Milton, WA 98354
800-851-1510
253-922-2700
Fax: 253-922-0226
www.flex-a-lite.com

Flowtech
AIRMASS Extreme
Exhaust Systems
2605 West First Street
Tempe, AZ 85281
480-966-1511
Fax: 480-966-1197
e-mail:
info@airmassexhaust.com

Fluke Corporation
6920 Seaway Blvd.
Everett, WA 98203
425-347-6100
425-356-5116

Fmax Fabriction
1110 Industrial Avenue
Escondido, CA 92029
760-746-6638
760-746-6682
e-mail: forcemax@flash.net
www.f.max.com

Folia Tec
Hintere Str. 88, D-90786
Furth, Germany
0049-911-97544-0
0049-911-97544-333
www.foliatec.com

USA contact:
ITM.Internat'l
Trade Marketing, LLC.
29 W. Cimarron St.
Colorado Springs, CO 80903
719-448-0613
719-448-0715
e-mail: carstyling@aol.com

Fuel Safe Systems
C/O Aircraft Rubber
Manufacturing, Inc.
63257 Nels Anderson Rd.
Bend, OR 97701
541-388-0203
541-388-0307
www.fuelsafe.com

G.Force Engineering
2311 West 205th Street, Suite 102
Torrance, CA 90501
800-262-6267
323-585-2852
323-587-0119

Goodridge USA Inc.
20309 Gramercy Pl.
Torrance, CA 90501
800-662-2466
310-618-0909
www.goodridge.uk.com

Goodyear
Tire & Rubber Corp. HQ
1144 East Market St.
Akron, OH 44316
www.goodyear.com

Gorilla Automotive Products
2141 East 51st Street
Los Angeles, CA 90058
800-262-6267
323-585-2852
323-587-0119
www.gorilla.auto.com

Gourmet Garage HID lighting by
Generation X Company
El Monte, CA
626-454-1368
www.GenXco.com

Greddy Performance Products
9 Vanderbilt
Irvine, CA 92718
949-588-8300
949-588-6318
www.Greddy.com

Ground Control Suspension
530-677-8600

Gude Performance
28780 Vacation Drive
Canyon Lake, CA 92587
909-244-3533
e-mail: sales@gude.com

Hahn RaceCraft
1981 D Weisbrook Dr.
Oswego, IL 60543
630-801-1417
Fax: 253-830-7558
e-mail: sales@turbosystem.com

HASport Performance/
Honda Auto Salvage
4039 E Winslow
Phoenix, AZ 85040
HASport Performance: 602-470-0065
Honda Auto Salvage: 602-470-0789
Fax: 602-437-4432

Hawk Performance
920 Lake Rd.
Medina, OH 44256
800-542-0972   330-722-4295
330-722-5500
www.hawkperformance.com

Hella, Inc.
201 Kelly Dr.
Peachtree City, GA 30269
e-mail: hella.faq@hellausa.com
www.hellausa.com

HKS USA Inc.
2801 East 208th Ave
Carson, CA 90810-1102

Holley Tech Service,
P.O. Box 10360,
Bowling Green, KY 42102-7360
270-781-9741
e-mail: help@support.holley.com
www.holley.com
For nearest dealer:
1-800-2HOLLEY

Honda Access Sales Corp.
8-18-4 Mobidome
Niiza-shi
Saitama-ken, 352
Japan
011-81-484-778109
Fax: 011-81-484-778800

**Honda/Acura Service
& Installations**
7281 Westminster Avenue
Westminster, CA 92683
714-891-1113
Fax: 714-895-6873

Hose Techniques
Outside California
Orders: 888-999-2817
Orders: 310-320-2660
Tech Line: 310-328-2800
Fax: 310-533-7077
e-mail: hosetech@pacbell.net

United States
HoseTechniques
1603 Border Avenue
Torrance, CA 90501

Japan
HPS HoseTechniques Japan
39-9 Izumi, 1 Chome
Suginami-ku
Tokyo, Japan 168-0062
 03-3322-8888
Fax: 03-3324-7566

HotShot
626-579-9960
Fax: 626-579-9964

HPC Tech
Tech: 800-456-4721
e-mail: hpctech@hpcoatings.com

HPC West
550 W. 3615 S.
Salt Lake City, UT 84115
801-262-6807
Fax: 801-262-6307

HPC Central
400 N. Glade Ave.
Oklahoma City, OK 73127
405-789-2888
Fax: 405-789-2885

HPC Southwest
6313 W. Commonwealth Place
Chandler, AZ 85226
480-753-1320
Fax: 480-753-1329

HPC Queensland
Lot 45 Strathwyn
Brendale 4500, Queensland
Australia
61-7-3881-0885
Fax: 61-7-3881-0887

HPC Victoria
6 Watson Road Industrial Park
Leongatha, 3953 Victoria
Australia
61-0356-624-719
Fax: 61-0356-624-719

HPC New Zealand
Shipping Address:
Unit O
62 Mahia Road
Manurewa
New Zealand
64-9-267-1007
Fax: 64-9-266-3388

Mailing Address:
P.O. Box 181
Manurewa
New Zealand

H&R Special Springs, LP
3815 Bakerview Spur #7
Bellingham, WA 98226
360-738-8881
360-738-8889
www.hrsprings.com

Hypertech, Inc.
3215 Appling Rd.
Bartlett, TN 38133
901-382-8888
e-mail:
techsupport@hypertech.inc.com
e-mail: sales@hypertech.inc.com

**Iceman Cool Air Intakes
Knight Engineering**
45322 North Trevor Ave.
Lancaster, CA 93534
661-940-1215
Fax: 661-940-1217

Ingalls Engineering Co.
34 Boston Ct.
Longmont, CO 80501
800-641-9795
303-651-1297
Fax: 303-651-1298
Sales info: davej@ingallseng.com
Tech Questions:
techinfo@IngallsEng.com

Intrax Suspension
949-252-0800

Jackson Racing
7281 Westminster Ave.
Westminster, CA 92683
714-891-1113
Fax: 714-895-6873

**Jackson Racing Superchargers
Sales & Technical Services**
440 Rutherford Street
Goleta, CA 93117
888-888-4079
805-681-3410
Fax: 805-692-2523

Jacobs Electronics
500 North Baird Street
Midland, TX 79701
800-627-8800
Customer Service:
800-825-3345

JE Pistons
15312 Connector Lane
Huntington Beach, CA 92649
714-898-9763
Fax: 714-893-8297

JET.HOT
Orders: 800-432-3379
Tech Info: 610-277-5646

WEST
1840 West Drake Drive
Tempe, AZ 85283

NORTHEAST
55 East Front Street
Bridgeport, PA 19405

SOUTH
5602 Orchard Road
Pascagoula, MS 39581

JET Performance Products
17491 Apex Circle
Huntington Beach, CA 92647
714-848-5515
Fax: 714-847-6290
e-mail:
Sales@JetChip.com

JG Engine Dynamics
431 S. Raymond Ave.
Alhambra, CA 91803
626-281-5326

Johnny Mac Motor Sports Inc.
4220 E. River Rd.
Dayton, OH 45439-1459
937-298-2856
Fax: 937-298-2876

JSP America Inc.
255 Cooper Ave. Suite 100
Tonawanda, NY 14150
716-871-0262
716-871-0239
www.jspamerica.com

Kaaz Limited Slip Differentials
Newport Exotic Cars
935-A Sunset Drive
Costa Mesa, California 92627
949-631-0990
Fax: 949-631-0909
e-mail:
 newportcars@kaazusa.com
www.kaazusa.com

Katzkin
6868 Acco Street
Montebello, CA 90640
800-842-0590
323-725-1243
Fax: 323-725-1259

KD Kanopy, Inc.
3755 W. 69th Place
Westminster, CO 80030
800-432-4435
303-650-1310
Fax: 303-650-5093
e-mail:
askme@kdkanopy.com

KHL Trading Company
10505 Valley Blvd. #386
El Monte, CA 91731
626-279-1500
Fax: 626-279-1577
e-mail:
info@khltrading.com

Kidde
The Fire Extinguisher Company
1394 South Third St.
Mebane, NC 27302
800-654-9611
919-563-5911
Fax: 919-563-3954

Kirk Racing Products
1433 Montgomery Hwy.
Birmingham, AL 35216
205-823-6025
Fax: 205-823-6550
e-mail: info@kirkracing.com

K.MAC Alignment Kits
204 W. Carleton, Unit C
Orange, CA 92867
714-628-9555
Fax: 714-628-8855

K&N Engineering Inc.
561 Iowa Ave.
P.O. Box 1329
Riverside, CA 92502-1329
800-858-3333
909-684-9762
Fax: 909-684-9060
www.knfilters.com

Knight Engineering
45322 North Trevor Ave.
Lancaster, CA 93534
661-940-1215
Fax: 661-940-1217

König Motoring Accessories
487 West John Street
Hicksville, NY 11801
800-645-3878
516-822-5700
Fax: 516-822-5703
e-mail: cyberkonig@aol.com

KYB America LLC
901 Oak Creek Drive
Lombard, IL 60148
630-620-5555
Fax: 630-620-8133
e-mail: Webmaster@kyb.com
www.kyb.com

LC ENGINEERING, Inc.
1880.B Commander Drive.
Lake Havasu City, AZ 86403
520-505-2501
Fax: 520-505-2503
e-mail: dave@lcengineering.com

Levoc
See: Napolex America, Inc.

Lightspeed Racing
6644 San Fernando Rd.
Glendale CA 91201
800-624-7223
Fax: 818-956-5160
e-mail: Info@LightspeedRacing.com

Lonza
See: KHL Trading company

Mackin Industries
9921 Jordan Circle
Santa Fe Springs, CA 90670
562-946-6820
Fax: 562-944-7719

Made For You Products
P.O. Box 720700
Pinon Hills, CA 92372
760-868-6962
Fax: 760-868-2131

Magnecor
2550 Oakley Park Rd. 200
Walled Lake, MI 48390
248-669-6688
248-669-2994
www.magnecor.com

Majestic TurboChargers, Inc.
Waco, Texas
800-231-5566

Marren Motor Sports, Inc.
49 Burtville Ave., Unit 3A
Derby, CT 06418
203-732-4565

Malvern Racing
271 Malvern Farm Dr.
Charlottesville, VA 22903
804-971-9668
Fax: 804-971-5652

MazdaTrix
2730 Gundry Ave.
Signal Hill, CA 90806
562-426-7960 For Catalog,
Parts Ordering, and Tech info
562-426-4460 For Local
Service and Parts
Fax: 562-426-9646

McGard, Inc.
United States
3875 California Road
Orchard Park, NY 14127-4198
716-662-8980
Fax: 716-662-8985

In Europe
McGard Deutschland
GmbH
Fischeräcker 4
D-74223 Flein
Telefon +49 0-7131 25 99-0
TeleFax +49 0-7131 25 99 32
mc.gard@bvv.de

Mechanixwear
24950 Anza Dr.
Valencia, CA 91355
800-222-4296
661-257-0474
Fax: 661-257-9428

Modern Speed Inc.
9822 Alpaca
South El Monte, CA 91733
626-458-3258
Fax: 626-458-3781

Momo Automotive Accessories
25471 Arctic Ocean Dr.
Lake Forest, CA 92630
949-380-7556
949-380-0132
www.momo.it

MonocoUSA
order: 888-769-SEAT
email: info@MonacoUSA.com

Moroso
80 Carter Drive
P.O. Box 1470
Guilford, CT 06437-0570
203-453-6571
Tech Line: 203-458-0542

Mugen Co., Ltd.
2-15-11 Hizaori-cho, Asaka-shi
Saitama 351-8586, Japan
0-48-462-3111
Fax: 0-48-462-3100
www.mugen.honda.co.jp

North American distributor:
King Motorsports Unlimited
105 E. Main St.
Sullivan, WI 53178
414-593-2800
414-593-2627

Murray Corporation
260 Schilling
Circle Hunt Valley, MD 21031
410-771-0380
410-771-5576

Napolex America, Inc.
2421 W. 205th Street, Suite D101
Torrance, CA 90501
310-782-7171
Fax: 310-782-1771
e-mail: info@napolex.com

Neuspeed/Neumann Distributing
3300 Corte Malpaso
Camarillo, CA 93012
805-388-8111
Fax: 805-388-0030

Nitrous Express
4623 Lake Park Drive
Wichita Falls, TX 76302
888-463-2781
Fax: 940-767-7697

Nitrous Works
1450 McDonald Rd.
Dahlonega, GA 30533
706-864-8544
Fax: 706-864-2206

Nitto Tire Corporation
800-581-2984
www.nittotire.com

NOS
2970 Airway Ave.
Costa Mesa, CA 92626
714-545-0580
Fax: 714-545-8319
Tech Line: 714-546-0592
e-mail: nosinc@earthlink.net

OPTIMA Batteries Inc.
17500 East 22nd Avenue
Aurora, CO 80011
888-8OPTIMA
888-867-8462
303-340-7440
Fax: 303-340-7474

Pacesetter Performance Products
2841 W. Clarendon Ave.
Phoenix, AZ 85017
800-472-7337
602-266-1964
Fax: 602-650-1136
e-mail:
tech@pacesetterexhaust.com

Paxton Automotive Corp.
1250 Calle Suerte
Camarillo, CA 93012
805-987-8660
www.paxtonautomotive.com

Performance Research
1539 Dolgner Place
Port of Sanford, FL 32771
Tech Line: 407-321-6036
Fax: 904-672-0114
e-mail:
prinet@perfresearch.com

Perma.Cool
671 East Edna Pl.
Covina, CA 91723
626-967-2777

Place Racing
1611.A San Bernardino Road
Covina, CA 91722
626-966-4888
626-967-4846
www.placeracing.com

Power Performance Group Inc.
Power Slot Rotors and PBR pads
9001 Oso Avenue Unit "A"
Chatsworth, California 91311
818-709-4800
818-709-4880

Procar by Scat
1400Kingsdale Ave.
Redondo Beach, CA 90278
310-370-5501
310-214-2285

Proformance Engines
2123 S. Jasmine St.
Denver, CO 80222
303-758-4245
e-mail:
PROENGS@AOL.COM

The Progress Group
1390 N. Hundley St.
Anaheim, CA 92806-1301
800-905-6687
714-575-1193
Fax: 714-575-1198

Racepak Data Systems
26806 Vista Terrace
Lake Forest, CA 92630
949-580-6898
Contact: Spencer Eisenbarth

The Racer's Group
29181 Arnold Dr.
Sonoma, CA 95476
707-935-3999
707-935-5889

Racing Sports Akimbo
18239 S. Figural St.
Gardena, CA 90248
310-532-4588
Fax: 310-532-4588
e-mail:
Info@avanche.com

Random Technologies
1313 Temple Johnson Rd.
Loganville, GA 30052
707-978-0264

Raybestos Brakes
4400 Prime Parkway
McHenry, IL 60050
815-363-9000

RAZO
See: KHL Trading Company

RC Engineering
1728 Border Ave
Torrance, CA 90501
310-320-2277
Fax: 310-782-1346
e-mail :
RC@RCEng.Com

Recaro North America
905 W. Maple Rd.
Clawson, MI 48017
248-288-6800
248-288-0811

Red Line Synthetic Oil Corporation
6100 Egret Court
Benicia, CA 94510
800-624-7958
707-745-6100
Fax: 707-745-3214
e-mail: redline@redlineoil.com

Redline Weber
6300 Gateway Drive
Cypress, CA 90630
800-733-2277 Select Option 3
Fax: 714-995-5899 or 815-425-6387
e-mail:
redline@redlineweber.com

Rev Hard Mfg.
7407 1/2 Fulton Ave.
N.Hollywood, CA 91606
818-764-4312
Fax: 818-764-6519

Rod Millen Motosports
17471 Apex Circle
Huntington Beach, CA 92647
714-847-2158
Fax: 714-848-6821

Royal Purple
3648 FM 1960 West, Suite 110
Houston, TX 77068
281-880-7788
Fax: 281-880-7584
www.synerlec.com

RSR
4789 Wesely St.
Anaheim, CA 92807
714-779-8677
www.racingbeat.com

R.T. Quaife Engineering Ltd.
Vestry Road,
Otford, Sevenoaks, Kent
TN14 5EL
England
+44 0-1732 741144
Fax: +44 0-1732 741555
e-mail: info@quaife.co.uk

Ryane Motorsports
3185 East Main Street
Ashland, OR 97520
541-482-4822
541-482-4834

Schroth
See: Autotech Sport Tuning

SI Industries
2175.A Agate Court
Simi Valley, CA 93605
805-582-0085

Specialty Products
P.O. Box 923
Longmont, CO 80502
303-772-2103
303-772-1918
e-mail: info@specprod.com
www.specprod.com

Speed Image
2325 De La Cruz Blvd.
Santa Clara, CA
408-988-6901
www.speedimage.com

Speed Image II
4320 Westminster
Santa Ana, CA 92703
714-534-1113
www.speedimage.com

Split Second
2824 S. Willis St.
Santa Ana, CA 92705
949-863-1359
Fax: 949-863-1363
e-mail: splits@pacbell.net
www.splitsec.com

Sprint Performance Suspension
9450 7th St. #A
Rancho Cucamonga, CA 91730
909-484-1799
909-484-1797
www.sprintspring.com

Stage 8 Fasteners
15 Chestnut Avenue
San Rafael, CA 94901
800-843-7836
415-485-5340
Fax: 415-485-0552
e-mail:
stage8@well.com

Stillen
3176 Airway
Costa Mesa, CA 92626
714-755-6688 ext. 257
Fax: 714-540-1826
e-mail:
info@stillen.com

Stoptech
3015 Kashiwa St.
Torrance, CA 90505
310-325-3799
310-325-6697
www.stoptech.com

STR Performance Products
2355 Foothill Blvd. Suite 501
LaVerne, CA 91750
909-394-4719
Fax: 909-394-2339

Superchips Inc.
134 Baywood Ave
Longwood, FL 32750
407-260-0838
Fax: 407-260-9106

Supersprint North America
3208 Park Center Dr.
Tyler, TX 75701
903-581-1855
Fax: 903-581-8206

Suspension Techniques
559-266-9173

Synergyn®
See: Dyson Oil

TDSA Sports Ignited
213 Roywood Dr.
North York, Ontario
Canada M3A.2E7

TESLA Electronics
1728 Wellesley Avenue
West Los Angeles, CA 90025
800-GTECHPRO
877-887-2681
Fax: 301-665-1831
http://www.gtechpro.com

Thermal R&D Mufflers
7624 Winnetka Ave.
Canoga Park, CA 91306
818-998-4865
Fax: 818-998-3161

Thermotec
P.O. Box 96
Greenwich, OH 44837
Techline: 800-274-8437
419-962-4556

Toru Wing, Inc.
3969 Guasti Rd. Unit C
Ontario, CA 91761
800-999-8678
909-605-9586
909-605-9596

Toyota Racing Development
1382 Valencia Ave.
Tustin, CA 92780
714-918-7526
714-259-1140
www.trdusa.com

Tri-Flo Performance Exhaust
23045 N 15th Ave.
Phoenix, AZ 85027
888-228-7435
e-mail: info@bbtriflo.com

Turbo Clutch
RPS Performance Products
9820 Owensmouth Ave. Suite # 14
Chatsworth, CA 91311
818-993-9174
Fax: 818-993-9177

Turbonetics Inc.
5400 Atlantis Ct.
Moorepark, CA 93021
805-529-8995
805-529-9499
www.turbonetics.com

TurboXS
623 Dual Highway PMB 120
Hagerstown, MD 2174
Technical Support:
tech@turboxs.com
sales@turboxs.com

TWM Induction
325D Rutherford St.
Goleta, CA 93117
805-967-9478
Fax: 805-683-6640
e-mail: twmindsb@aol.com
www.tmwinductions.com

Unorthodox Racing, Inc.
45 D Nancy Street
West Babylon, NY 11704
631-253-4909
Fax: 631-253-4907
e-mail:
 info@unorthodoxracing.com

Urethane Supply Company
1128 Kirk Rd.
Rainsville, AL 35986
800-633-3047
256-638-4103
Fax: 800-824-0087
256-638-8490
e-mail:
info@urethanesupply.com

VDO North America LLC
188 Brooke Road
Winchester, VA 22603
e-mail: performance@vdo.com
Repair & Service for Aftermarket Gauges and Accessories
Connie Heflin
Phone: 540-678-2034
Fax: 540-662-2515
e-mail: cheflin@vdo.com

Velocity Sport Tuning Inc.
24418 Main St., Suite 404
Carson, CA 90745-6368
310-952-0003
Fax: 310-952-0004

VENOM™
8625 Central Ave.
Stanton, CA 90680
800-959-2865
714-828-1406
714-828-0964

VP Racing Fuels, Inc.
16 Brookhill Dr.
P.O. Box 9999
Newark, DE 19714
302-368-1500
302-368-1869

Weapon*R USA
480 Collins Avenue Unit #C
Colma, CA 94015
650-992-9669
Fax: 650-757-9669

Weld Racing
933 Mulberry Street
Kansas City, MO 64101
800-488-9353
Fax: 816-283-3430

Wings West
847 W. 16th St.
Newport Beach, CA 92663
949-722-9995
Fax: 800-493-4105
e-mail: info@wingswest.com

Wiseco Piston, Inc.
7201 Industrial Park Blvd.
Mentor, OH 44060-5396
Fax: 800-321-3703

Jim Wolf Technology
212 Millar Ave.
El Cajon, CA 92020
619-442-0680
Fax: 619-579-8160
e-mail:websales@jimwolftechnology.com

XRP
5630 Imperial Hwy.
South Gate, CA 90280.
562-861-4765

X.TEC
Order: 800-961-XTEC
Technical Support: 519-659-3853

Yokohama Tire Corporation
601 S. Acacia Avenue
Fullerton, CA 92831
800-722-9888

Zen Motorsports
4025 Spencer St. Suite 304
Torrance, CA 90503
310-542-3821
e-mail: info@zen.motorsports.com

Zex Innovation
3406 Democrat Rd.
Memphis, TN 38118
888-817-1008
e-mail: ZEX@COMPCAMS.COM

Z.Speed/Group.A Autosports
25710 Industrial Blvd., #2
Hayward, CA 94545
510-781-0538
Fax: 510-781-0539